RECLAIMING FAITH

Wm. B. Eerdmans Publishing Company
Grand Rapids, Michigan

RECLAIMING FAITH

*Essays on Orthodoxy in the Episcopal Church
and the Baltimore Declaration*

Edited by

Ephraim Radner and George R. Sumner

WILLIAM B. EERDMANS PUBLISHING COMPANY
GRAND RAPIDS, MICHIGAN

Library of Congress Cataloging-in-Publication Data

Reclaiming faith: essays on orthodoxy in the Episcopal Church and the
  Baltimore Declaration / edited by Ephraim Radner and George R. Sumner.
    p.   cm.
  Includes text of the Baltimore declaration of 1991.
  Contents: The place of doctrine in the Episcopal Church / Robert W. Pritchard —
  Doctrine, destiny, and the figure of history / Ephraim Radner — Repugnance and
  the three-legged stool / Christopher R. Seitz — At the crossroads of dogma /
  Russell Reno — Light and twilight, the church and the nations in the drama of
  salvation / George R. Sumner — Two millennia later, evangelizing Jews? / Ellen T.
  Charry — Holy preaching / Ellen F. Davis — Is Christianity good for us? / Ellen T.
  Charry — Memory and communion / David S. Yeago — A confessing faith /
  Alvin F. Kimel, Jr.
  ISBN 0-8028-0677-5 (paper)
  1. Episcopal Church — Doctrines.　2. Baltimore Declaration.　3. Dogma.
  I. Radner, Ephraim, 1956-　　.　II. Sumner, George R., 1955-　　.
III. Baltimore Declaration.
BX5930.2.R43　　1993
230'.373 — dc20   93-1219
                                                                                                    CIP

Contents

III. Practicing Orthodoxy

Foreword

GEORGE A. LINDBECK

THIS book of essays and the Baltimore Declaration which occasioned it remind me of the two similar events in which I participated in the mid-1970s. Their similarities to the Hartford Appeal (1975) and *Against the World for the World*, the collective work that followed it,[1] are striking, but so are the differences. Comparing these two sets of happenings is as good a way as I can think of to put *Reclaiming Faith* in perspective.

One major resemblance is that the Hartford Appeal, like the Baltimore Declaration, was viewed by its authors as a plea for the historic faith, for what Robert Prichard in this volume speaks of as "mere Christianity." Everyone from Orthodox and Roman Catholic theologians to Baptists could, and at Hartford did, join in affirming this. Second, the Appeal repudiated what it took to be the especially pernicious and pervasive errors of its day. Third, while treated in the media as anti-liberal, it tried to escape simplistic categorization by castigating the right as well as the left. Fourth, it failed in this endeavor. *Christianity Today* was too enthusiastic for comfort, and *The Christian Century* was in effect contemptuous.[2] In its different context, the Declaration has evoked similar reactions. Given these parallels, writing this foreword has at times, not surprisingly, been a *déjà vu* experience.

It is the contrasts, however, that are most instructive for our purposes. They tell us much about the changes in the religious situation in this country in the last two decades. The Hartford Appeal, to start with, defended what it took to be biblical themes in the nonbiblical

---

1. *Against the World for the World* (New York: Seabury, 1976).
2. See, e.g., *The Christian Century*, 19 Feb. 1975, p. 183.

language of general principles. It called for religion with "transcendent" reference in opposition to the convictions that, for example, "modern thought . . . is superior to all past forms of understanding reality" (Theme 1),[3] or that "religion refers to human experience and nothing else" and is only "human projections" (Theme 3), or "that Jesus must be interpreted in accordance with contemporary models of humanity" (Theme 4), or that differences between religions are unimportant and "not a matter of conviction about truth but only of personal preference or lifestyle" (Theme 5), or "that the world must set the agenda for the church" (Theme 10), or that "the question of hope beyond death is irrelevant or at best marginal to the Christian understanding of human fulfillment" (Theme 13), or that "the sole purpose of worship is to promote individual self-realization and human community" (Theme 8). This appeal to general principles rather than Christian specifics was appropriate, so it was believed, for a document addressed to the general public with the aim of making clear that the revitalization of the social engagement of the churches (which in the mid-seventies was seen as being in drastic decline from the sixties) required rootage in transcendent faith.[4] "We worship God because God is to be worshipped" (Theme 8).

In contrast to these high generalities, the Baltimore Declaration and the present book are marked by specificity. Their attention focuses on such matters as the triune name, the saving significance of Jesus Christ for all human beings, the church's relation to Israel, and the relation of Christians to Jews. It is on this last point, it should be noted, that the essays in this volume most often express a desire to modify and amplify what the Declaration has to say, though greater sensitivity to feminist issues — none of the original Baltimore six was a woman — is another area where change is called for. In any case, none of these topics was a theme at Hartford (though the relative absence of women — only two were involved in the Appeal — did play a part in later discussions). It is not only the themes, furthermore, but the language that has changed: the language of the Declaration is much more scriptural than that of the Appeal.

Not that these differences imply substantive disagreement. The Declaration and the present book do not deny that "religion" may

3. The full text of the Hartford Appeal is to be found in the book mentioned above, *Against the World for the World*, and also in *Worldview* 18, 4 (April 1975): 39-41.

4. That this is the aim is made clear in the introduction of the Appeal, but the words I have used to describe that aim are suggested by Richard John Neuhaus's comment in *Worldview* 19, 3 (March 1976): 29.

contribute to the welfare of the earthly city, and they agree that making it instrumental to human betterment destroys its efficacy in that or any other area. Revitalization of the church's social engagement, however, is not their focus. The danger they see is different from that of the seventies, and therefore the antidote is different as well.

"Inclusivity" is one name for what they find most threatening.[5] Scientific rationalism and its fideistic counterparts are not the menace they were for the Hartford group (Theme 2). Instead of these, new kinds of religiosity, often of a transcendental bent, have multiplied and found ready entrance in the churches. Anything that claims to be high and holy (and much else besides) tends to be admitted. Such comprehensiveness perhaps made sense when society was culturally homogeneous and professedly Christian, but to the degree to which dechristianization and relativistic pluralism gain ground, it is destructive of church and community. Distinctive beliefs and practices are diluted and held together, if at all, by bureaucratic management rather than communal loyalties. Denominational labels such as Episcopal, Presbyterian, Methodist, or even Roman Catholic increasingly become the names of organizations purveying a variety of religious wares rather than of distinctively Christian communities. They designate collections of special interest groups rather than churches.[6]

Those who gathered eighteen years ago at Hartford, however, were concerned with a different problem. It was not the survival but the mission of the mainline denominations that concerned them. They assumed as self-evident that these churches would continue to socialize sizable numbers of members into at least a modicum of biblical, credal, and practical knowledge of the heritage and imbue them with a sense of communal belonging. It was their social action, not their existence, that was in question.

This shift of concern from failures to act to the loss of communal identity — that is, the precondition of action — explains the stress, which we have already noted, of the Declaration and the present essays on doctrinal specificity and biblical language. This same shift helps also to account for their authorship. Six young and relatively unknown priests from a single diocese of a single denomination produced the Declaration. This suggests that concern about communal identity and "mere Christianity" is particularly vivid at the parish level (or, perhaps,

5. See the Baltimore Declaration, p. 276 in this volume.
6. This is my description of the situation that the contributors to this volume are addressing, and they should not be held responsible for my formulation.

that the fear of being cast as ungenteel heresy-hunters is a bit less). Similarly, the academics who have responded to the Declaration's challenge in the present book are young and not newsworthy (though what they may be in years to come is another matter). By ordinary standards, given this marginality, the book is as unlikely as the Declaration to have much public impact.

The contrast to the Hartford Appeal and the volume that followed it could not be greater. Their initiators were nationally known: the sociologist of religion Peter Berger, and the (at that time) civil rights and anti–Vietnam War activist Richard John Neuhaus. They gathered eighteen established academics, bureaucrats, and church leaders from nine denominations, ranging from Yale Chaplain William Coffin to the conservative evangelical Richard Mouw (now Dean of Fuller Seminary) as well as the Jesuit theologian Avery Dulles and the Notre Dame philosopher and novelist Ralph McInerny. Even the *Christian Century*, despite its lack of enthusiasm for the Appeal, rated it one of the top ten religious news stories of the year. It was intended to attract national attention, and it did.

Attention, however, is sometimes inversely proportional to impact. In trying to speak trans-confessionally to everyone from right to left, the Appeal addressed no one in particular; and as a result, once it ceased to be trumpeted by media such as *Time* magazine, neither church nor academy paid it much heed.

In this respect, the Baltimore Declaration is superior. It has its defects, as the following essays make clear, but it and they both recognize that the problem for the churches once called "mainline" is not properly described as the general loss from the right to the left of religiousness that emphasizes transcendence; rather, it is the threat to their survival as communities in meaningful continuity with historic Christianity. This explains why the Declaration consciously models itself after the Barmen protest against Nazism. Not that the current crisis is comparable in intensity to the one in the 1930s, but it is structurally analogous. To the degree to which the once major communions cease to transmit the historic faith, they leave "mere Christianity" to the sects. No doubt God will in the long run look after the church catholic, so believers will say, but in the short term she will suffer gravely. The kind of communities in which specifically Christian ecumenicity and publicly responsible and generous orthodoxy can flourish are in danger of disappearing.

In conclusion, the authors of the present essays, as I have noted, are young, unknown, and untested in comparison to those like myself who helped to produce the Hartford Appeal and the volume that followed. Yet what they have written in *Reclaiming Faith* strikes me, for reasons that I have partly explained, as fresher, more interesting, and potentially much more influential than the earlier book, *Against the World,* has proven to be.[7] I am grateful that they were sensitized (or not desensitized) to the nature of the present crisis by their studies at Yale, but their way of perceiving the current situation is fortunately not confined to a single university or diocese. It is, if I may trust my own experience, increasingly widespread in the younger generation in many different ecclesial and academic settings. Similarly, although these essayists are with one exception Episcopalian, what they are saying to Anglicans parallels what needs to be said to other mainliners. Perhaps the problems are more vivid in Anglicanism, but they are not different. In its very particularity, this volume achieves a wider relevance than was possible for those who, like myself and others at Hartford, mouthed generalities about the problems of American religion or Christianity as a whole. What is here attempted can and perhaps will be carried further by others in ways peculiar to their specific situations. God-willing, *Reclaiming Faith* will release an avalanche of advocates of "mere Christianity."

7. This comment, it should be observed, is by itself only modest praise. *Against the World,* unlike the Appeal, which it was intended to explain and expand, attracted little attention. One difficulty is that its authors were also involved in the Appeal and thus lacked the critical distance and detachment that the writers of the present essays fortunately have in relation to the Baltimore Declaration.

Introduction: Reclaiming Faith in Gratitude and Submission

EPHRAIM RADNER and GEORGE R. SUMNER

THE Christian church of the West needs to see itself through the eyes of Christians from the younger churches of the world, from Africa and Asia. So Bishop Lesslie Newbigin writes in his popular book *Foolishness to the Greeks*. The reason Newbigin gives for this turning of the lens, however, is not based solely on moral-political or economic considerations, as is so often the case in such calls for intercultural dialogue. Newbigin points to a more fundamental religious concern: the dilution of "Christian tradition" in Western churches by a pervading pagan ideology. Speaking of the relationship between Western and non-Western churches, he writes, "We need their witness to correct ours, as indeed they need ours to correct theirs. At this moment our need is greater, for they have been far more aware of the dangers of syncretism."[1]

If churches in the West have become "paganized" — a judgment Newbigin does not shy away from — they are so, not in the vulgar sense of the word, as it might apply to unbaptized idolaters. Rather, they are "paganized" in that they are filled with modern instances of what Christians of late antiquity called the *pagani*. This Latin word traditionally applied to rustic country dwellers, isolated from the centers of Christian teaching and formed by a mixture of atavistic and innovating non-Christian beliefs. However peculiar the paganism of the modern West, the "pagan church" was not invented only in our age of civil religion and secularism. When Christianity became an

---

1. Lesslie Newbigin, *Foolishness to the Greeks: The Gospel and Western Culture* (Grand Rapids: William B. Eerdmans, 1986), pp. 133, 147; cf. p. 20.

1

imperial religion in the fourth century and rural estates came under the control of episcopal sees and newly converted landowners, the rural *pagani* too were officially brought into the church, though frequently in name only. Untaught by priests and bishops more often than not, this vast population of nominal Christians became the fallow field of Christ's vineyard, through whose thickets of jumbled beliefs the church has continued to stumble and lose its way in Europe and America even to this day. To be sure, there have been changes: modern Christian *pagani* now comprise elite and urban classes, unlike the past. Yet like their ancient counterparts, they continue to subsist within the church, uninstructed in the basic scriptural teachings that have historically given form to the shape of our faith.

"Reformation" in the church's life has generally been seen as a response to this reality, with particular "reforms" designed to penetrate this region of the *pagani* with more theologically educated priests, catechizing missionaries, and bishops who have taken the quality of their charges' faith to heart. At least from the time of St. Gregory the Great in the sixth century, through the Protestant and Catholic reformations and beyond, the renewal of the Christian church has been embodied in the singular vocation of these *pastores docentes* or "teaching pastors" to work among the dispersed *pagani*. Through their efforts alone, the integrity of the gospel has continued to be heard, with varying degrees of clarity, among the expansive body of members that Christ calls his own.

To compare the situation of a church like the Episcopal Church in the United States to that of the early church, made up largely of barely christianized *pagani,* is to state an irony of Christian history: the most "educated" membership of any Christian denomination in the world now carries the mark of an isolated rural population, abandoned to its own confused devices of belief by leaders whose motivation for basic catechetical instruction has suffered a failure of nerve. This is probably a recurrent phenomenon for the church as a whole, and for this church in particular. And while the Constantinian paradigm of a socially sanctioned church perforce made up of nominal members is perhaps cracking in our day, its final ruin must await an epoch we ourselves will not live to witness. What distinguishes the present age of transition from earlier periods is not some unprecedented sociological transformation of the church but simply a novel twist to historical irony: in its very calls for reform, the church unwittingly encourages the uninstructed to increase.

Most of the church has properly recognized that we have a

primary mission to equip the laity to understand, articulate, and act upon their Christian faith. At issue, however, is the nature of such growth in self-understanding. We believe that whatever Christian "self" there is to be understood can only exist as it is grounded in a personal appropriation of a scripturally common Christian language, forming a common set of concepts and attitudes. Instead, attempts at encouraging lay leadership by actively discouraging the role of the teaching pastor in favor of a model of "grassroots" experientialism have actually increased the people's isolation from an understanding of the traditional core of the Christian gospel.

Many adult education programs have happily sought to provide church people with a greater exposure to Scripture. Some of these programs unfortunately assume a level of theological and critical sophistication beyond most participants' grasp. More generally, however, many of these laudable efforts have not been grounded in the regular scriptural preaching and teaching that can explicitly communicate the church's rule of faith to quotidian existence. As a result, the programs themselves often bear limited fruit for the life of the Christian community. Curiously, then, the widespread biblical and credal illiteracy that most parish priests encounter and bemoan owes its intractability, if not its origins, to the modern metamorphosis of *pastores docentes* into the passive agents of contemporary paganization. Where pastors abdicate their teaching office, even in the name of their flocks' empowerment, there the laity is denied the very tools of their own liberation: a clear knowledge of Scripture and of the historic commitments of the Christian church.

There are doubtless teaching pastors in our church. But theirs is a discouraged lot in a church with many priests who have been profoundly and inescapably formed by the worldview of a completely secularized society and educational system. Too many of these ministers are either intimidated by the claims of modernity or sufficiently confused by them that they cannot pedagogically appropriate the Christian Scriptures, doctrinally interpreted by the traditions of the church. A few, in fact, actively repudiate the possibility of such teaching altogether on the basis of arguments they have learned from theological mentors. In his illuminating contribution to this volume, Robert Prichard traces how the core of such traditional teaching, which he calls "mere Christianity," slid from a position of consensus in the Episcopal Church into one of veiled and not-so-veiled disrepute, not least because those charged with encouraging and regulating the vocation of the *pastores docentes* had themselves become prey to the confusions of those modern *pagani* whom they were called to catechize.

We must be careful, in all of this, to avoid the rhetorical temptation to lapse into sweeping and generalized jeremiads. If our church is confused about its teaching, it is in part because the world itself is a more confusing place in which to articulate the gospel than perhaps it once was. Is it fair to decry the demise of the traditional core of Christian catechesis and the motivation to promote it without at least indicating how its retrieval could make sense in a social context like our own? For we live in a time, for better or for worse, when all claims to normative belief and practice are contestable, especially if they are described in terms founded in the historical past. Bishop Newbigin's suggestion that we allow non-Western Christians to judge the nature of our own inherent paganism offers one promising way in which we might begin to understand the positive nature of such a retrieval. As liberation theologians have taught us, though from a constricted religious perspective, Christians from the younger churches outside the West can show us something undeniably authentic, both of what it means to become a believer in Christ and a member of his body and of what it means to maintain that position in the face of the rival cultural forces of paganism.

Both of the editors of this volume worked for several years in different Anglican churches in East Africa. Whatever romantic illusions might have first motivated our work, such illusions were soon dispelled by the realities faced by churches formed and governed by culturally new converts amid difficult material circumstances. The mix of the venal, the distracted, and the apathetic that is characteristic of churches in the West is hardly absent from these African Christian communities, and it asserts itself perhaps more obviously given their lack of that socially acceptable veneer of material decorum with which Western churches have managed to cover their sins for so long. Not all churches in Africa are growing by leaps and bounds, their people do not all quote Scripture from the heart, and few members take much interest in the political implications of the gospel. Africa, no less than America, offers few instances of apostolic purity and innocence within the church of Christ.

Yet, for all that, the two editors in different ways beheld and experienced something that is almost wholly lacking in our own American churches, something profound and literally moving: that is, an actual *struggle* to allow the gospel of Christ to shape, on its own terms, the church and its members. Areas of daily life such as the use of money, drinking, open forgiveness, and the confession of faith within home and work have a Christian priority in parts of Africa whose compulsion derives from the unavoidable experience that the gospel interrupts the life of the world as it is culturally arranged. At its best, the African church still understands the "newness" of Christ, the contrasts between his gifts and the world's, and even the cultural costs involved in receiving him. They see, with greater clarity than we, how the gospel comes to us from somewhere and from something that cannot be identified as of our own making in any respect.

The scriptural literalism, moral rigorism, and evangelical bluntness that inform this peculiarly African struggle are certainly foreign to our own accommodating attitude to the beliefs and behaviors to which we are socially born. But more essentially, we discovered in this struggle by African Christians a set of cognitive attitudes that on reflection appear to be necessary to any sustained movement from paganism to Christianity: gratitude toward that which "comes" to us from without and submission to its form. This is not an original discovery, of course. Western theology has itself traditionally recognized that gratitude and submission are attitudes essentially characteristic of any Christian posture in a world affirmed as subject *ad verbum externum,* to the "external" Word of God. This Word, as Christ in Scripture handed down to us by other Christians, addresses us "from outside" our prejudices and habits. We receive it from those hands of the past with joy, even as we give ourselves up to its particular formative demands.

Gratitude and submission are perhaps no longer seen in the West as necessary buttresses to any rational theological framework capable of embracing the realities of modern contestability. But an encounter with African Christianity, at least, encourages us to consider such a necessity as being real. With this appreciation of gratitude and submission as a guiding theological compass, we and our fellow contributors have approached an important document, the Baltimore Declaration. In its light we have attempted to describe some of the ways in which our church might understand its historic doctrinal claims, governed by attitudes of receptivity that can still make sense in our modern world. We believe that the Declaration marks a significant call to the church's leadership to renew its own teaching vocation in the forming, sending, and encouraging of those *pastores docentes* who have traditionally raised a bulwark against paganizing forces inimical to the gospel of Christ Jesus. Whatever the merits of its particular affirmations, the Declaration should be seized as an occasion for our church's teachers to offer a constructive theological vision that can comprehend intelligently the concrete claims made on our hearts and minds by the gospel entrusted to us from the past. Taking hold of this opportunity, we offer this volume for the "edification" — that is, the upbuilding — of the church.

All of the authors in this volume except one are Episcopalians, and all are called to ministries of teaching. All of us have experience in pastoral work or are deeply involved in the life of the local church. All of us are, we believe, part of a younger generation of scholars for whom the former generation's watchword, "the world setting the agenda for the church," seems closely connected with the present structural disarray all about the household of God. To be sure, the present collection is not intended as a defense of the Baltimore Declaration. The reader will soon discover that contributors sometimes disagree with the Declaration on a variety of matters, and that they sometimes disagree with one another as well on issues of significant weight.[2] But we *do* concur with the Declaration in its call to the task of renewal and reappropriation of the doctrinal heart of our faith: the triune God, revealed for our salvation in Jesus Christ, whose authoritative witness for the life of the church is located in Scripture. Each of us has taken the Declaration not as an object for commentary so much as a springboard for positive reflection on some aspect of traditional Christian doctrine and practice. In so doing, we have sought to banish the tone of bitterness that too often corrupts debate within our church and to demonstrate how a common commitment to the doctrinal core of our faith need not stifle diversity but may instead positively establish diversity's responsible flowering.

With this in mind, we caution those who may be tempted to reject out of hand the Baltimore Declaration and the present volume as two instances of an anachronistic "fundamentalism." In a recent editorial in *Books and Religion*, for example, Gardiner Shattuck, an Episcopal priest and church historian, characterized the authors of the Declaration in just these terms.[3] He explained that, appearances notwithstanding, such a document represents a form of outdated Enlightenment rationalism. He called on liberals not simply to reject but rather to

2. The text of the Declaration is printed in an appendix to this volume. Alvin Kimel, one of the original writers and signers of the Declaration, has provided a brief description of the motivation and purpose of its authors. Readers can compare these original intentions with the sometimes different interpretations given to the Declaration's significance by the contributors to this volume. But in every case, one of the Declaration's main stated objectives will be fulfilled: initiating a serious discussion on the place of doctrinal authority in our church's teaching mission.

3. Gardiner H. Shattuck, Jr., "The Fundamental Things Apply," *Books and Religion* 19, 1 (Spring 1992): 45-47.

understand historically the need for epistemological "certainty" that people like the Declaration's authors seem to feel. But Shattuck's typical diagnosis is itself a symptom of that polarization which excludes the possibility of a serious theological "center." Too often the familiar charge of "fundamentalism" has had the effect of preemptorily shaming liberalism's critics into silence. If we accomplish nothing else, we hope to show the need and the possibility of just such serious discussion by scholars who, though loyal to the normative doctrinal tradition of the church, cannot be dismissed as insensitive to the intellectual demands consequent to modernity.

In our day, a broad range of philosophers and theologians (including Newbigin himself) have in fact made considered attempts to move beyond the rigid rationalistic categories bequeathed us by elements of our Enlightenment past. These efforts have questioned the basic universalizing principles shared by both Enlightenment rationalism *and* contemporary liberalism, whether moored in notions of fundamental reason, experience, or scepticism. Thinkers such as Alasdair MacIntyre have argued instead for the necessary and exclusive *particularity* of traditions — especially religious traditions — as that which alone can provide any lived social framework within which coherent human knowledge, experience, and the appreciation of limits is possible. From this perspective, to uphold and defend the exclusive particularities of the Christian tradition — with its specific stories, historical claims, practical imperatives, and carefully defined corporate and individual life — is not an act of intellectual anachronism or regression. Rather it is, more than anything else, an epistemological and ethical demand for any Christian who would also affirm the reasonable and coherent character of his or her life as a purely *human* being. Having identified oneself as a Christian, virtues such as submission to such a tradition and lived conformance to its particular shape are hardly "fundamentalistic" attitudes drawn from a stream of eighteenth-century positivism. Such virtues are coincident with human rationality itself, understood in Christian terms.

All of the contributors to this volume have studied a theological discipline at Yale University. This represents more than geographical coincidence. While we would disclaim being an intellectual "party," we all have been influenced by the general approach to theological concerns commonly called the "Yale School" and associated with such biblical scholars as Brevard Childs, such historical theologians as George Lindbeck, and such systematicians as the late Hans Frei. These teachers, though gathered at one institution, are but instances in certain respects of the general attempt mentioned above to understand Christian faith particularistically on the "far side" of the Enlightenment. A tacit premise of our volume is that the outlook of this "Yale School," understood broadly, provides a congenial framework in which to take up a challenge like the Baltimore Declaration. (We could add that the converse is also true: the doctrinal crisis of the Episcopal Church is itself an illuminating test for the applicability of these scholars' pioneering work.) Certainly this theological "framework" makes no pretense of being a philosophical or theological system; indeed, the "Yale" approach is antithetical to such systematizing. It functions more as a series of adaptive strategies to remove contemporary intellectual hindrances that prevent Christians in our age from seeing the Scripture-formed tradition of the church in its own distinctiveness and power.

The scholars we have mentioned have, of course, labored in different vineyards.[4] Hans Frei focused on Scripture, particularly the New Testament, as a narrative whose meaning could not be detached from its form and located somewhere "behind" the story itself. His analyses helped to launch interest in narrative theology, which remains a work-in-progress. George Lindbeck has examined the way in which doctrines act as rules in the Christian community. By showing how doctrines function as a "grammar" that regulates our more reflective speech about Christian belief and practice, he has demonstrated how doctrines can be normative and enduring without being reduced to rigid propositions of timeless truths. Finally, Brevard Childs has pioneered a "canonical" approach to scriptural exegesis that takes the final form of the Old and New Testament texts as the primary context for theological reflection. In locating the authoritative norm for the church's life in the canon as a whole, Childs seeks to avoid the dismembering effect on Scripture (and biblical theology) of historical

---

4. Readers can find Frei's central concerns explained in his *Eclipse of Biblical Narrative: A Study in Eighteenth and Nineteenth Century Hermeneutics* (New Haven: Yale University Press, 1974). In addition, his *The Identity of Jesus* (Philadelphia: Fortress Press, 1975) offers an example of a constructive theological project. A provocative testimony to Frei's influence can be found in the collection *Scriptural Authority and Narrative Interpretation*, ed. Garrett Green (Philadelphia: Fortress Press, 1987). For George Lindbeck, see his *The Nature of Doctrine: Religion and Theology in a Postliberal Age* (Philadelphia: Westminster Press, 1984). Brevard Childs's canonical method is most clearly explained in his two surveys *Introduction to the Old Testament as Scripture* (Philadelphia: Fortress Press, 1979) and *The New Testament as Canon: An Introduction* (Philadelphia: Fortress Press, 1984). Mention should also be made of David Kelsey's *The Uses of Scripture in Recent Theology* (Philadelphia: Fortress Press, 1975).

criticism, without thereby ignoring the textual diversity such criticism has highlighted. The frequent echoes of these teachers, among others, that the attentive reader will find in these essays should be understood as the highest form of respect for their work that we can offer.

Most important for the purposes of this book are some of the features common to these three scholars (and to other influential theologians at Yale such as David Kelsey). All of them affirm that human reason, including that employed in the discipline of theology, is specific to historical traditions of discourse. There follows a (sometimes implicit) affirmation of the providential shape of the scriptural canon, which the church community understands as the bearer of this tradition of Christian "reason." On this basis, they believe, Christians are justified in having confidence in the trustworthiness of the tradition's typological-christological interpretation of Scripture as a whole. Finally, this interpretation provides a framework within which the world in its fullness is experienced and understood. These affirmations, taken together, are planks in an intellectual "plausibility structure" (to borrow sociologist Peter Berger's phrase) that can support intelligent and faithful theological discourse in our age. They are not, however, offered as the substance of the church's teaching. Rather, they act as propaedeutic to sound catechesis by constituting a complex of arguments under whose shelter the contemporary church may hear the Word, practice the Christian life, and witness to its truth.

To this extent at least, the scholars of the "Yale School" craft their reasonings for the use of the *pastores docentes,* those charged to teach. Their ultimate intent is to protect and maintain the power and precision of actual Christian speaking and testimony. And they do so through the employment of an unabashed "hermeneutic of gratitude" with respect to the ecclesial community's historic witness of faith, a cognitive attitude analogous, *mutatis mutandis,* to that spirit we had discovered in the altogether different cultural world of East African Christianity. To this degree, there is nothing at work in their approach peculiar to Yale at all. The invitation they offer to both the Christian scholar and teacher is to search the tradition and to ask it questions with joy, receptivity, and expectation. No longer spooked by modernity, pastors are invited back into that attitude of reflection so transparently present in a Thomas Aquinas or a Karl Barth.

The contributors to this volume seek to bring together aspects of this approach and the question of doctrine and theological practice in the Episcopal Church, though from a variety of angles. While we cannot claim that our efforts solve the problems of the Episcopal

Church's current confusion over teaching and doctrine, we do believe that the directions we pursue are appropriate to the challenge. As editors, we discern some common concerns and overlapping themes among these essays. Several authors stress the salvific necessity of *particularity*. Reno emphasizes this with respect to the triune Name and the cross, and Sumner highlights salvation's exclusive narrative location. Other contributions dwell on the concept of *submission*. Davis emphasizes the "otherness" of Scripture, to which we must give our obedient attention in an act of imaginative surrender. Charry underlines the (sometimes surprising) moral consequences of such submission. The theme of *conformance* may be seen both in the way Yeago roots the ecumenical appeal to communion in remembrance and in the way Radner understands the cruciform nature of the church's historical experience in figural terms. Finally, the ecclesial assumption of a close coherence between text and Holy Spirit, present in Seitz's contribution, may undergird all the essays.

In an era in which theological practice designed to serve the Christian church has nearly dissolved, these essays, like the Baltimore Declaration that has motivated them, may appear arbitrary in their focus and whimsical in their purpose. Jeremiah 32 tells us of a time of desolation and discouragement for Israel, when she was overrun by an alien power. Even small constructive acts — the buying and seeding of a tiny field — must have seemed evident folly at such a moment. But nonetheless, at God's command, Jeremiah went out and purchased the ancestral field at Anathoth: "For thus says the LORD: . . . Fields shall be bought in this land of which you are saying, It is a desolation, without man or beast" (vv. 42-43). This volume seeks to reclaim aspects of the faith handed down to us. We realize how inadequate are our efforts to both the task and the times. Still, we must commend these gifts of faith in however small a way, for we believe that they are pledges of God's future for his people.

I. Approaching Orthodoxy

The Place of Doctrine
in the Episcopal Church

ROBERT W. PRICHARD

IN May of 1991, a group of six Episcopal clergy from the Diocese of Maryland issued a statement, which they called the Baltimore Declaration. Patterned after the Barmen Declaration issued by members of the Confessing Church in Germany in May 1934, it was a stinging indictment of the lack of orthodoxy in the Episcopal Church. The Declaration was divided into seven articles, each of which, following the pattern of the Barmen Declaration, contained a biblical quotation, a positive statement of belief, and a repudiation of error.

The Baltimore Declaration was distributed widely within the Episcopal Church. Mailings invited clergy to sign and circulate it. The reactions to the document, which were positive, negative, and indifferent, raised a broader question: What role does doctrine play in the Episcopal Church?

Sacra Doctrina

Thomas Aquinas began the *Summa Theologiae* with a series of questions on the nature of *sacra doctrina,* a logical place at which to begin a major doctrinal work. As commentators on Thomas have noted over the years, however, even this basic starting point involved a certain ambiguity, for Thomas never precisely defined the term. At times he seemed to have used it to refer to a saving faith in Jesus Christ. At other times the term seemed to refer to a discipline of academic theology. Both approaches involved a certain logic, and as a result

13

Thomists have been debating the meaning of the term since the seventeenth century.[1]

One attempting to trace the role of doctrine in the Episcopal Church will encounter a similar phenomenon. While Episcopalians do use the word *doctrine* and various synonyms such as *principles* with some regularity, it is by no means clear that they mean precisely the same thing at all times. Rather, it would seem that they use the term *doctrine* to apply to three interrelated but distinguishable things, which are identified in this essay as "mere Christianity," "Protestant theology," and "Anglican doctrine." Each of the three does involve a certain ambiguity of its own and is subject to change over the course of time. Yet each has a commonsense referent that is easily grasped.

The initial portion of this essay will amplify the meaning of these three terms. The second portion will then make use of them to suggest a general pattern to Episcopalian attitudes toward doctrine. Occasional references will be made to the Anglican Church in England and to the colonial period in America; this essay will, however, make no claims about colonial Anglicanism or the Anglican Church worldwide. The essay will only attempt to show that a pattern applies to the Episcopal Church in the United States: namely, that a nineteenth-century acceptance of divergence of opinion on Anglican doctrine was followed in the 1920s by a working agreement about diversity of opinion on the content of mere Christianity, which has with successive modifications remained in effect.

Doctrine as Mere Christianity

The first and most basic meaning that Episcopalians have assigned to the term *doctrine* is what C. S. Lewis called "'mere' Christianity." He defined it as "the belief that has been common to nearly all Christians at all times."[2] Lewis distinguished this mere Christianity from denominational idiosyncrasies. "I offer no help," he said in his book titled *Mere Christianity*, "to anyone who is hesitating between two Christian 'denominations.' You will not learn from me whether you ought to become an Anglican, a Methodist, a Presbyterian, or a Roman Catholic."[3]

---

1. For a brief discussion of the debate over the meaning of *sacra doctrina*, see James A. Weisheipl, "The Meaning of *Sacra Doctrina* in *Summa Theologiae* I, q. 1.," *The Thomist* 38 (Jan. 1974): 62.

2. C. S. Lewis, *Mere Christianity* (New York: Macmillan, 1960), p. vi.

3. Lewis, *Mere Christianity*, p. vi.

While no document identifies the content of this mere Christianity with precision, Anglicans have, over time, attempted to express its content in a variety of ways. The English Act of Toleration of 1689, for example, distinguished Christians from non-Christians by requiring the following profession:

> I, [N.N.], profess faith in God the Father, and in Jesus Christ his Eternal Son, the true God, and in the Holy Spirit, one God blessed for evermore, and do acknowledge the Holy Scriptures of the Old and New Testament to be given by divine inspiration.[4]

The rites of initiation in the *Book of Common Prayer* pointed in a similar direction. A rubric at the end of the baptismal office in the *Book of Common Prayer* from 1549 to 1789, and within the baptismal services of the 1892 and 1928 prayer books, identified the Apostles' Creed, the Lord's Prayer, and the Ten Commandments as the basic content of a mature Christian faith.[5]

Prior to the mid-nineteenth century, the concept of mere Christianity was most useful to Anglicans in distinguishing orthodox Christian faith from nontrinitarian Christian heresies. When Bishop William White (1748-1836) of Pennsylvania prepared the course of ecclesiastical studies (1804), the mandatory reading list for candidates for ordination, he was particularly concerned, for example, with meeting the

4. Andrew Browning, ed., *English Historical Documents*, 12 vols., vol. 8: *1660-1714* (London: Eyre & Spottiswoode, 1953), p. 402.

5. William McGarvey, *Liturgiae Americanae or the Book of Common Prayer as used in the United States of America Compared with the Proposed Book of 1786 and with the Prayer Book of the Church of England* (Philadelphia, 1895), p. 306.

There have been some slight changes in this wording over time. The 1662 edition was the first to refer to the Apostles' Creed; the 1549 and 1552 editions referred simply to "the articles of the faith." Prayer books prior to 1928 also referred to the church catechism, which was largely an exposition of the contents of the Apostles' Creed and the Ten Commandments.

In 1892 Americans added the closing rubric to the text of the final exhortation of the baptismal office. The 1928 American prayer book moved the material to the examination of the candidates and sponsors that preceded the baptism. It also replaced the reference to the catechism with a reference to "all other things which a Christian ought to know and believe to his soul's health."

The 1979 American prayer book's baptismal office employed a question and answer form of the Apostles' Creed and a rubric specifying the use of the Lord's Prayer. A rubric before the service dictated that "parents and godparents are to be instructed in the meaning of Baptism, in their duties to help the new Christians grow in the knowledge and love of God, and in their responsibilities as members of his Church." It no longer, however, explicitly identified the trio of creed, Lord's Prayer, and Ten Commandments as central to the content of faith.

Deistic rejection of the Trinity. He chose, therefore, Charles Leslie's *A Short and Easy Method with the Deists* (1698) and William Jones's *The Scholar Armed against the Errors of the Time* (1792) for inclusion in the list.[6]

From the eighteenth to the mid-nineteenth century Episcopalians saw the Deist and Unitarian rejection of the Trinity as the major challenge to mere Christianity. By the early twentieth century, some Anglicans sensed an attack from another direction — from the modernist scholars and clergy within the church.

Protestant Theology

At the time at which they first brought their faith to North America, members of the Church of England were acutely aware of the differences between their faith and the Christian faith as understood by the Church of Rome. To the English, who remembered the Spanish Armada and the Gun Powder Plot, Roman Catholics were dangerous religiously, politically, and militarily. Until the nineteenth century, they were prevented by law from holding public office in England. The professions to Rome of Charles II and James II led the Parliament to specify that only those who held "the Protestant faith" could occupy the English throne, a provision that still remains in force.

In order to paint the contrast between Roman Catholicism and the Protestant faith, it was necessary for Anglican authors to minimize the differences among the various Protestant groups. Anglican authors, particularly those writing prior to the English Civil War, took this united approach, although they often excluded Anabaptists from the Protestant consensus. Lutherans, Anglicans, and Reformed Christians shared a basic understanding of the faith, they argued. John Jewel's *An Apology of the Church of England,* a book that English law required every English parish to own, stated the argument in this way:

> As for those persons whom [the Roman Catholics] upon spite call Zwinglians and Lutherans, in very deed they of both sides be Christians, good friends, and brethren. They vary not betwixt themselves upon the principles and foundations of our religion, nor as touching God, nor Christ, nor the Holy Ghost, nor the means of justification, nor yet everlasting life, but upon one only question which is neither

---

6. For a discussion of this reading list, see George Blackman, *Faith and Freedom: A Study of Theological Education and the Episcopal Church* (New York: Seabury Press, 1967), pp. 7-17.

weighty nor great; neither mistrust we, or make doubt at all, but that they will shortly be agreed.[7]

Most of the formative documents of the sixteenth century were shaped with this understanding. Quotations from Luther and from Lutheran creeds were incorporated within the Articles of Religion of the Church of England, and Thomas Cranmer submitted copies of the *Book of Common Prayer* (1549) to Reformed theologian Martin Bucer for review.

As a result of British emigration policies during the colonial period, the Roman Catholic population of British North America was minuscule. Colonial Americans expended little energy upon exposition of the differences between Protestantism and Roman Catholicism, though vestiges of that difference, such as the commemoration of Guy Fawkes's Gunpowder Plot in the prayer book in use in colonial North America, remained.

The unrestricted immigration to the United States during the nineteenth century, however, changed the situation radically. The Roman Catholic Church, once a small minority, rapidly became the largest single American denomination. From about 1840 Episcopalians became increasingly preoccupied with this large Roman Catholic presence. Pastoral letters from the House of Bishops, debates at General Convention, and a variety of written works began to contrast Protestant theology and what Episcopal authors referred to as "Romanism."

Those who painted the contrast generally chose one of two strategies. One approach, followed by Bishop John Henry Hopkins (1792-1868) in his *The Church of Rome Contrasted* (1837), was to compare the Roman Catholic Church with a primitive faith. The Episcopal Church, Hopkins argued, represented a primitive faith from which the Roman Catholic Church had departed. Hopkins and others occasionally distinguished this argument from that about the antiquity of mere Christianity by noting that the Roman Catholic Church was not, strictly speaking, heretical. Hopkins arrived at this position in *A Candid Examination of the Question of Whether the Pope of Rome is the Great AntiChrist*, which was published posthumously in 1868.

The second approach was to distinguish the Roman Catholic understanding of the Christian faith from that of the Reformation. Bishop Charles Petit McIlvaine (1799-1873) of Ohio took this approach in his works, contrasting the justification by faith of Protestants and what he labeled the sacramental justification of Roman Catholics.

7. John Jewel, *An Apology of the Church of England*, ed. J. E. Booty (Ithaca, NY: Cornell University Press, 1963), p. 48. The point of disagreement to which Jewel referred was the nature of Christ's presence in the eucharist.

By the second half of the nineteenth century, however, some Episcopalians rejected both approaches, suggesting that Protestant theology was no longer a useful category. From that time forward the status of Protestant theology was subject to debate. The debate, however, usually centered on specific details of theology rather than the larger systems in which they were cast. Twentieth-century Episcopalians might, for example, question the compatibility of Episcopal ideas about the nature of the church with those of other Protestants, but they accepted the general outlines of modernism and neo-orthodoxy, which were shared across Protestant denominational lines.

Anglican Doctrine

Anglicans, particularly after the British Civil War, have also used the word *doctrine* to refer to those distinctive elements that distinguished the Anglican Church from Reformed Protestants. Anglicans and Reformed Christians agreed on the broad outlines of justification by faith, but they disagreed on three Catholic elements that Anglicans had retained and Reformed Christians had discarded at the Reformation: ordination by bishops, liturgical worship, and a doctrine of the intermediate state. Anglicans had revised those elements along lines that they believed corresponded to the practice of the church of the first five centuries. They had rejected Roman claims that papal consent was needed for a valid ordination to the episcopate and had pared down the seven medieval ordained offices to three (bishop, priest, and deacon). They had eliminated prayers for the dead and references to re-sacrifice from the liturgy and emphasized the once-and-for-all nature of Christ's death on the cross. While retaining the belief that the souls of the dead awaited the return of Christ before entering heaven, they dismissed the Roman Catholic idea of indulgences and purgatory.

Reformed Christians, however, had rejected all three of these elements outright, replacing them with what they argued were more biblical patterns: elimination of the episcopate, immediate rewards and punishments at death, and outlines rather than fixed forms for worship. During the English Revolution the Puritan party attempted to impose Reformed patterns on the Church of England. With the failure of the Puritan program and the restoration of Charles II, Anglican divines such as Bishop John Pearson (1616-1686) constructed a spirited defense of the doctrines that had been under attack.

Thomas Bray (1656-1730), the founder of the Society for the Propagation of the Gospel (SPG), wrote in this vein. The society's missionaries carried a strong sense of the distinctiveness of Anglican doctrine to the areas in which they served. Those in New England, for example, often entered into public controversy over the respective merits of episcopal and presbyterial ordination.

When the Episcopal Church was organized following the American Revolution, bishops and deputies at the General Convention included a reference to doctrine in this sense in the church's constitution and in the ordination offices. The ordination offices contained the following exchange:

> *The Bishop says to the ordinand*
> Will you be loyal to the doctrine, discipline, and worship of Christ as this Church has received them? And will you, in accordance with the canons of this Church, obey your bishop and other ministers who may have authority over you and your work?
>
> *Answer*
> I am willing and ready to do so; and I do solemnly declare that *I do believe the Holy Scripture of the Old and New Testaments to be the Word of God, and to contain all things necessary to salvation; and I do solemnly engage to conform to the doctrine, discipline, and worship of the* [Protestant] *Episcopal Church* [in the United States of America].[8]

The italicized words appeared in Article VIII of the church's constitution.[9] Some dioceses also required a related affirmation of those who served on vestries.

While Episcopalians and other Anglicans all acknowledged the existence of doctrines and disciplines that distinguished the Anglican Church from other Protestant bodies, they did not always agree on how much importance should be attached to distinctive elements. This difference lay at the heart of a disagreement that has marked the Anglican communion since the end of the seventeenth century. One group — consisting of the Tory Churchmen of Queen Anne's reign, the High Church Party of the eighteenth and early nineteenth centuries, Tractarians of the mid-nineteenth century, and Anglo Catholics of the late nineteenth and twentieth centuries — emphasized the importance of the distinctive doctrine, even implying at times that Anglican doctrine was to be equated with mere Christianity. An opposing

8. *Book of Common Prayer* (1979), p. 538; italics added.
9. *Constitution and Canons for the Government of the Protestant Episcopal Church in the United States of America Otherwise Known as the Episcopal Church, Adopted in General Conventions, 1789-1988* (n.p.: printed for the Convention, 1988), p. 7.

block in the church — the Latitudinarians of the late seventeenth century, the evangelicals of the eighteenth and nineteenth centuries, the Broad Church party of the late nineteenth century, and the advocates of ecumenism in the twentieth century — clearly distinguished the doctrines of the Episcopal Church from the content of mere Christianity. At times, moreover, they showed a willingness to compromise some of those doctrines with others in the cause of Christian unity.

All Episcopalians would agree, however, that some elements of Anglican doctrine, such as the form of vestments or the manual acts of the priest in the eucharist, are not fixed truths but are open to change. Curiously, it was precisely the secondary nature of such elements that has made them of such interest to Anglicans. Classical interpreters of the Anglican faith, such as Richard Hooker (c. 1554-1600), argued that the basics of the Christian faith — what Hooker called divine law and what this essay has referred to as mere Christianity — were unchangeable. The only area in which church government could exercise real discretion was in matters that the Lutherans called *adiaphora*, indifferent to salvation. In such areas the church government could appropriately make choices. As a result Episcopalians regularly devoted long hours debating minor issues of ritual and church order, while devoting correspondingly less time to arguing about the content of mere Christianity, which, at least until late in the nineteenth century, they, like Hooker, believed to be unchangeable.

One needs to be aware of these three different referents of the word *doctrine* in order to make any sense of Episcopal claims. The Episcopalian who claims, as late twentieth-century Episcopalians often do, that the Episcopal Church has no doctrine of its own is referring to mere Christianity. The Episcopalian who argues that late twentieth-century discussions with the Lutheran Church violate the doctrine of the Episcopal Church is referring to Anglican doctrine, and most particularly to the Episcopal Church's understanding of the ordained ministry. The Episcopalian who refuses to use the word *Protestant* and the one who is anxious to do so disagree about the status of Protestant theology in the Episcopal Church. The discussions all make some logical sense, but only if one keeps the different points of reference in focus.

Doctrine in the Church

There has been no period since the creation of a separate American Episcopal Church in 1789 in which Episcopalians did not have a keen interest in doctrine. That interest, however, took a variety of forms and often involved the interplay of the three senses with which Episcopalians used the term *doctrine*.

Principles of the Church of England

William White and the generation of Episcopalians who followed the American Revolution, though willing and anxious to overcome differences in order to secure unity, were clear about certain limits to mere Christianity. When Charles Miller, the rector of the oldest Anglican Church in Massachusetts, suggested dropping references to the Trinity from the *Book of Common Prayer*, White was in no mood for compromise. Miller and his congregation went their separate way, becoming the first explicitly Unitarian church in America.

But while the preserving and teaching of mere Christianity was and remained an important concern to Episcopalians, it often took second place in discussions at General Convention and in published works by Episcopalians to the question of what constituted Anglican doctrine. Episcopalians in the late eighteenth and early nineteenth centuries had no qualms about identifying such doctrine. For them it was a matter of practical necessity. Robbed of an institutional tie to the Church of England by the American Revolution, they were left with a serious problem of identity. Connections with the Bishop of London, the Anglican Commissaries, the Society for the Propagation of the Gospel, the inevitably Anglican royal governors, and the English king had been the most visible element that marked them as a denomination. Left without such ties, they emphasized the doctrine that they shared with the Church of England.

Such an approach was implicit from the first page of William White's *The Case of the Episcopal Churches in the United States Considered* (1782). White penned the book in an effort to rally the largely demoralized American members of the Church of England to create a national organization. He identified members of the denomination as Episcopalians, rather than as members of the Church of England. A footnote explained:

> The general term "Episcopal" is usually applied, among us, to the churches professing the religious principles of the Church of England.[10]

10. William White, *The Case of the Episcopal Churches in the United States Considered,* in *Readings from the History of the Episcopal Church,* ed. Robert W. Prichard (Wilton, CT: Morehouse-Barlow, 1986), p. 62.

Over the forty years that followed, White almost single-handedly provided a basic exposition of the principles of the Episcopal Church, one that would serve as a point of reference for Anglican doctrine for the generations that followed. White guided a revision of the Thirty-nine Articles through the General Convention (1801), prepared a reading list for theological candidates (1804), penned the first history of the Episcopal Church (1828), published ordination sermons, and even tried his hand on the Calvinist-Arminian debate.

White's own attitude was remarkably like that of the Latitudinarians of the Glorious Revolution, authors who were well represented on White's reading list. White combined clarity about Anglican doctrine with modesty about the importance of such claims. The generation that followed him pushed his attitude in two differing directions. A high-church party led by such figures as John Henry Hobart (1775-1830) repeated White's version of Anglican doctrine, but dropped the modesty of his claims. The evangelical party, led by such figures as John P. K. Henshaw (1792-1852), kept his modesty about the status of Anglican doctrine, but used formulae open to Anglican readings, though not specially requiring them.

The specific Anglican doctrines that White and his contemporaries espoused included the three issues that had been important in the seventeenth century — episcopal ordination, the intermediate state of the dead, and a fixed liturgy. They also included an Anglican response to the evangelical revivals of the eighteenth century. Eighteenth-century preachers of the Reformed tradition had stressed the necessity for salvation of an adult faith experience, which they called regeneration, rebirth, or renewal. Anglican authors such as Bishop Samuel Bradford (1652-1731) had argued that this was true only in a partial sense. Traditional liturgies, like the *Book of Common Prayer*, reserved the word *regeneration* to describe what happened in infant baptism, an entrance into a relationship with God in which salvation was promised to those who met certain conditions. This regeneration was necessary. A separate adult experience, in which one accepted the conditions of the relationship into which one had entered in baptism, was needed as well. It was, Episcopalians argued, appropriately called *renewal*.[11]

One area in which the differing approaches of White, Hobart, and Henshaw toward the distinctive Anglican doctrines can be easily

---

11. Samuel Bradford, *Discourse Concerning Baptismal and Spiritual Regeneration* (1708). Bradford cited Titus 3, which speaks of both "the washing of regeneration and renewal in the Holy Spirit" (v. 5), in defense of his approach.

illustrated was on the question of the intermediate state. Anglicans found some merit in the idea of a period of waiting between death and resurrection. In his *Lectures on the Catechism,* Bishop White introduced the Anglican position with almost an apology:

> It gives me pain to introduce into these lectures, any matter in which eminent men, equally correct in general theory, have disagreed.[12]

White laid out the Anglican doctrine on the intermediate state, but retained a modesty about the degree to which truth claims could be pressed.

Hobart, in contrast, had no such reserve. As he explained in *The State of the Departed,* a book he penned on the subject, the doctrine of the intermediate state was "expressly revealed in Scripture" and "should be an object of faith."[13] Bishop Henry Onderdonk of Pennsylvania and theologian G. T. Chapman of Kentucky were but two of many to echo Hobart's approach.

John P. K. Henshaw and other evangelicals took a very different position. Instead of pointing to the Anglican position in detail, they moved quickly to a proposition of Protestant theology. The Anglican view, while different from that of other Protestants, shared the same basic conviction that indulgences and the prayers of the living could not change the condition of the dead.

> "Where does the soul go at its departure from this body?" Most persons will answer to heaven, or to hell; and this is true in a certain sense. The state of the soul is then *fixed* — according to its moral character, and the deeds done in the body, either in happiness or misery throughout eternity.[14]

Henshaw did include a line or two to indicate his knowledge of the Anglican doctrine on the subject. A reader could have easily missed the lines, however, perched as they were in the midst of a longer discussion of the basic unity of Protestants on the subject.

12. William White, *Lectures on the Catechism* (Philadelphia: Bradford & Inskeep, 1813), p. 31.

13. John Henry Hobart, *The State of the Departed,* 4th ed. (New York: Standford & Swords, 1846), p. 127.

14. John P. K. Henshaw, *Theology for the People: In a Series of Discourses on the Catechism of the Protestant Episcopal Church* (Baltimore: Daniel Brunner, 1840), pp. 139-40.

The Oxford Movement and the Plurality of Doctrine

Episcopal understandings of the place of doctrine in the life of the church remained largely unchanged until the 1840s. By that decade, news of the Oxford movement reached the United States. The equilibrium of the church parties, which agreed on Anglican doctrine but disagreed on the emphasis attached to it, may have already begun to teeter. The Oxford theologians, however, upset the balance entirely.

They questioned one of the basic assumptions of Episcopal theologians: that adult renewal was necessary. On the contrary, they suggested that adult renewal was a misguided Protestant concept. Oxford theologian Edward Bouverie Pusey (1800-1882) voiced the Oxford objection to adult renewal rather bluntly in *Tract 67*. Those who believed in the necessity of adult renewal only "imagined that they hold Baptismal Regeneration." In fact, they were guilty of "using it as a screen to hide from themselves the necessity of the complete change of mind and disposition necessary to them."[15] They believed "that Justification is not the gift of God through his sacraments, but the result of a certain frame of mind, of a going forth of themselves and resting upon their Saviour."[16]

The Oxford theologians believed, perhaps correctly, that the doctrine of adult renewal was not to be found in the Reformation or in the early church; rather, it was grounded in the evangelical revivals of the eighteenth century. Indeed, as they noted, it did involve a certain confidence in the human ability to respond to God's grace.

In place of this identification of Anglican doctrine with evangelical Protestant theology, the Oxford divines suggested another equation. Such theologians as William Palmer (1803-1885) propounded a "branch theology" that identified the Anglican, Roman Catholic, and Orthodox Churches as three branches of a single tree. These three branches shared a basic catholic theology but differed in geographical location and some unessential details. From the Reformation to the early nineteenth century most Episcopalians had understood Anglican doctrine, although distinctive in some ways, as a subcategory of Protestant theology. For Oxford theologians this was entirely wrong. Anglican doctrine was catholic.

15. Members of the University of Oxford, *Tracts for the Time*, 6 vols. (London, 1840-42; repr. New York: AMS Press, 1969), vol. 2, tract 67, p. 8.

16. Edward Bouverie Pusey, quoted by Charles Pettit McIlvaine in *Righteousness by Faith*, a new and revised edition of *Oxford Divinity* (Philadelphia: Protestant Episcopal Book Society, 1986), p. 54.

John Henry Newman's *Tract 90* was an attempt to defend this proposition in detail. In it he argued that the teaching of the Thirty-nine Articles and the *Homilies* of the Church of England on justification, the intermediate state of the dead, the invocation of the saints, the number of the sacraments, eucharistic presence, eucharistic sacrifice, and celibacy was compatible with that of the Council of Trent. Newman explained in his introduction:

> It is often urged, and sometimes felt and granted, that there are in the Articles propositions or terms inconsistent with the Catholic faith. . . . The following Tract is drawn up with the view of showing how groundless the objection is. . . . That there are real difficulties to a Catholic Christian in the Ecclesiastical position of our Church at this day, no one can deny; but the statements of the Articles are not in the number; and it may be right at the present moment to insist upon this.[17]

Oxford theologians wished to replace the category of Protestant theology with the new category of catholic theology.

Episcopalians spent the next thirty years locked in a serious debate about precisely what it was that they believed on the subject. Evangelicals tried simultaneously to defend Protestant theology and their vision of Anglican doctrine: Oxford movement theologians were wrong because they were simply attempting to introduce Roman Catholic errors into the Episcopal Church. This was the approach taken in McIlvaine's *Oxford Divinity*. High-church Episcopalians, by contrast, did try to distinguish the threat posed by a growing Roman Catholic Church from the attitudes of the Oxford theologians, with which they had some sympathy. Repeated efforts to find mediating positions were unsuccessful. An exasperated Charles Wesley Andrews may have summed up the situation most accurately when he complained that Episcopalians seemed to hold seven different understandings of the word *regeneration*.[18]

In the end, American Episcopalians met the challenge of the Oxford movement in the same way as their British coreligionists. Oxford advocates were never successful in the United States — or in

---

17. Members of the University of Oxford, *Tracts for the Time*, vol. 6, tract 90, p. 2.

18. C. W. Andrews, *Review of the Baptismal Controversy with a Statement of the Argument for Revision of the Office for Infant Baptism*, 2d ed. (Philadelphia: The Episcopalian, 1869).

England — in convincing all Episcopalians that Anglican doctrine was catholic rather than Protestant. Their attempt to do so, however, redefined the theological landscape. Earlier in the nineteenth century Episcopalians had agreed upon the content but not the status of Anglican doctrine. By the end of the century, the competition between those who saw Anglican doctrine as catholic and those who regarded it as Protestant meant that even the content was in question. There was, to be sure, clarity within the individual church parties, but denomination-wide discussions were marked by the acceptance of alternative views. The 1938 report of a Committee of the Archbishop of Canterbury on Doctrine would reflect this change in attitude. When members of the committee dealt with such staples of Anglican doctrine as the intermediate state of the dead, they were forced to conclude that Anglicans held either of two possible opinions.

The few statements of Anglican doctrine that Episcopalians did adopt after 1870 focused on lowest common denominators, elements on which both Anglo Catholics and evangelicals could agree. In 1873, for example, when older high-church bishops joined with evangelical colleagues in the House of Bishops to discuss renewal, they could only agree on the negative proposition that the moral change that evangelicals still regarded as taking place in adult renewal did not take place in baptism. Unable to agree as to whether adult renewal actually existed, they adopted a proposition that did not rule it out.[19]

The Quadrilateral, the well-known ecumenical statement adopted by the General Convention in 1886 as a result of the efforts of William Reed Huntington (1838-1909), was similar in character. The Quadrilateral declared the Episcopal Church's willingness to discuss reunion with any denomination that acknowledged four "principles of unity exemplified by the undivided Catholic Church during the first ages of its existence." The four principles were:

1. The Holy Scriptures of the Old and New Testament as the revealed Word of God.
2. The Nicene Creed as the sufficient statement of the Christian Faith.
3. The two Sacraments, — Baptism and the Supper of the Lord, — ministered with unfailing use of Christ's words of institution and of the elements ordained by Him.
4. The Historic Episcopate, locally adapted in the methods of its

19. For further discussion of the subject, see Robert W. Prichard, "Theological Consensus in the Episcopal Church" (Ph.D. diss., Emory University, 1983).

administration to the varying needs of the nations and people called of God into the unity of His Church.[20]

The statement, which was adopted by the Lambeth Conference of 1888 in a slightly revised form, was a significant departure from earlier statements. As a statement of mere Christianity, it lacked the overt declaration of the Trinity contained in earlier anti-Deistic statements, though the Nicene Creed clearly outlined the doctrine of the Trinity. It also omitted any of the specific language about eucharistic presence, justification, regeneration, or renewal that had occasioned debate in the middle of the century.

As a statement of Anglican doctrine, it omitted any reference to the intermediate state of the dead.[21] It said nothing of baptismal regeneration and limited the necessary scope of a fixed liturgy to the dominical words in the eucharist and baptism. The familiar emphasis on apostolic succession was there, but with a new modifier — "locally adapted in the methods of its administration to the varying needs of the nations and people called of God into the unity of His Church" — that distinguished the national character of the Anglican Communion from the international uniformity of the Roman Catholic Church.

Huntington's statement was a stroke of genius, one not easily repeated. He had avoided the points of greatest conflict between evangelicals and Anglo Catholics, pleased evangelicals by making what most regarded to be an ecumenical overture to other Protestants, and yet made the appeal to catholic theology favored by Anglo Catholics. Perhaps because of the difficulty of drafting any more suitable statement, Huntington's Quadrilateral became a fixed element in the Episcopal understanding of Anglican doctrine. It was repeatedly reaffirmed by General Conventions and Lambeth Conferences. It has played a role in the ecumenical dialogues into which the Episcopal Church entered in the twentieth century. The 1979 *Book of Common Prayer*

20. *Book of Common Prayer* (1979), p. 877.
21. The substitution of the Nicene for the Apostles' Creed was not accidental. The reference in the Apostles' Creed to Christ's descent into hell was the text on which Episcopal speculation about the intermediate state of the dead had been based. The hell to which Christ went could not have been, Episcopalians argued, the place of damnation. It must have been the place of waiting to which the souls of Christians went prior to the return of Christ on the Last Day. By choosing the Nicene Creed, Huntington avoided the debate over the intermediate state.

The bishops who met at Lambeth in 1888 were not in entire agreement with Huntington's proposal; they added the Apostles' Creed to the second point of the Quadrilateral.

added the text of the statement to its historical documents section and
added Huntington's name to the church calendar.

The Quadrilateral was not so much a finished statement with
which Episcopalians could enter into firm agreements with other denominations as a compromise among Episcopalians. Only with that
recognition can one make sense of the checkered history of attempts
to follow up on the Quadrilateral's declared intention to move toward
unity: the departure from the Episcopal Church in 1907 of Anglo
Catholics opposed to opening Episcopal pulpits to Protestant guest
preachers; the failed attempt in the 1930s to merge with the Presbyterian Church; and the scattered opposition to the proposed concordat
with the Evangelical Lutheran Church of 1991. As a compromise, the
Quadrilateral may have obscured rather than resolved differences in
understanding Anglican doctrine.

Episcopalians had accepted pluralism in Anglican doctrine by the
1870s. This pluralism would, in turn, influence the way in which they
met the theological challenge of modernism.

The Broad Church

By the end of the nineteenth century, modern biblical studies, geology,
astronomy, and psychology questioned many of the assumptions that
had been commonplace among Christians earlier in the century.
Scholars both within and outside of the church doubted the verbal
inspiration of Scripture. They no longer accepted the historical accuracy of the creation account in Genesis 1, the crossing of the Red
Sea in Exodus, and many of the miracles recorded in the Gospels.
They questioned the possibility of virgin conception, of resurrection
of the body, of a literal hell, and of an end to the world for other than
natural causes. They argued that many of these traditional elements
— not all agreed on precisely which — were remainders of Jewish and
Greek mythical thought and could be omitted from a new reconfigu-
ration of mere Christianity, one that took into account the findings of
modern science and that would be acceptable to intelligent, modern
persons.

There were advocates of this modernist version of mere Christianity in most Protestant denominations in America and Europe and
to a lesser degree in the Roman Catholic Church. Modernist sentiments, while only slowly reaching the rank and file of the laity, were
well represented in universities and theological seminaries. In England, for example, faculty at Oxford University contributed to two

important collections of essays. *Essays and Reviews* (1860), an early statement of modernistic sentiments, questioned both the verbal inspiration of Scripture and the eternity of damnation.[22] Later in the century, *Lux Mundi* (1889) suggested that the first twelve chapters of Genesis were "conveyed . . . in that form of myth or allegorical picture, which is the earliest mode in which the mind of man apprehended truth."[23] In America during the same period, William Lawrence (1850-1941), dean of the Episcopal Theological School of Cambridge, Massachusetts, assured students that they need not believe in six literal days of creation.[24]

Within the Anglican Communion, interest in a modernist reading of mere Christianity was not confined to one church party; those attracted to it came from both evangelical and Anglo-Catholic backgrounds. Late nineteenth-century Episcopalians used the term "broad church" to refer to the coalition of church members who advocated this modernist approach. Charles Gore (1853-1932) and other contributors to *Lux Mundi* were Anglo Catholics. The Episcopal Theological School at which William Lawrence taught had been founded at mid-century to represent an evangelical point of view. The primary institutional manifestation of this coalition was the Church Congress (1874-1934), a series of gatherings at which Episcopal speakers — Anglo Catholics, evangelicals, and those who identified themselves only by the broad church label — delivered speeches on biblical interpretation, social action, and other issues of common concern.

The configuration of mere Christianity advocated by broad church Episcopalians and other modernists was frequently justified by appeals to a "deeper" or "more spiritual" reading of Scripture, one that was based more upon a relationship of trust and commitment than upon any specific propositional content. German theologian Albert Schweitzer's *Quest of the Historical Jesus* (1906) was typical of this modernist approach. Schweitzer explained that modern Christians need not accept much of Jesus' teaching since his thought was based on outmoded Jewish eschatology. Nonetheless, Schweitzer ended his book with an appeal for personal relationship:

22. F. L. Cross and E. A. Livingstone, *The Oxford Dictionary of the Christian Church*, 2d ed. (New York: Oxford University Press, 1983), s.v. "Essays and Reviews."

23. Charles Gore, "The Holy Spirit and Inspiration," in *Lux Mundi: A Series of Studies on the Religion of the Incarnation,* ed. Charles Gore, 13th ed. (New York: Thomas Whittaker, 1890), p. 298.

24. William Lawrence, *Fifty Years* (Boston: Houghton Mifflin, 1923), pp. 42-43.

[Jesus] comes to us as One unknown, without a name, as of old, by the lake-side, He came to those men who knew Him not. He speaks to us the same word: "Follow thou me!" and sets us to the tasks which He has to fulfil for our time. He commands. And to those who obey Him, whether they be wise or simple, He will reveal Himself in the toils, the conflicts, the sufferings which they shall pass through in His fellowship, and, as an ineffable mystery, they shall learn in their own experience Who He is.[25]

Jesus, the unknown, called men and women into relationship with him.

Bishop A. C. A. Hall of Vermont used a related argument in his *The Doctrine of the Church* (1909). The volume was the first of a projected "Sewanee Theological Library," which was designed to provide "a statement, in convenient form, of [the] Doctrine, Discipline and Worship" of the Episcopal Church for clergy, laity, and theological students. Hall explained the difference between intellectual assent and mere Christianity:

Belief primarily means intellectual assent, the acceptance of a statement as true on the authority of the speakers. In this sense belief may have varying degrees of certainty, corresponding with the authority of the speaker (his knowledge and his veracity). The acceptance of God's word will be absolute; our faith is unhesitating when once we are assured that a statement is from Him. Religious faith is a knowledge of spiritual facts, which could not be discovered with certainty by man's unaided reason, but which are revealed by God.

But Christian faith means more than mere intellectual assent. It stands for the acceptance by the whole man, in mind and heart and will, of the divine word, so that the man shall be moulded by the truth revealed. Further still, faith is specially used of a relation and attitude towards *a person*. In this sense it means not only belief that such an one exists, and belief that what he states is true, but also the trustful surrender of ourselves to the person in whom we believe. . . . It is to faith of this kind directed toward God and our Lord Jesus Christ that the great promises in the New Testament are made.[26]

25. Albert Schweitzer, *The Quest of the Historical Jesus: A Critical Study of Its Progress from Reimarus to Wrede,* second English ed. (London: Adam and Charles Black, 1948), p. 401.

26. A. C. A. Hall, *Doctrine of the Church,* Sewanee Theological Library (Sewanee: The University Press, 1909), pp. 19-20.

For Hall, mere Christianity involved a surrender to the truth revealed by God.

Hall's distinction between assent and surrender involved a certain ambiguity about the nature of truth, one that he shared with the broad church leaders. Truth was both a relative commodity discovered by intellectual endeavor and an absolute given by God. But how was one to be "assured that a statement is from" God? Were not those university and seminary professors who saw themselves as being on the forefront of intellectual discovery suggesting that absolute truth was in fact unattainable?

Broad church leader Phillips Brooks (1835-1893) hinted at that possibility in the new definition he suggested for heresy. Brooks argued that rejection of the truth that God declared could not be equated with either disagreement with church authorities (what he called "the ecclesiastical idea" of heresy) or departure from some fixed standard ("the dogmatic idea"). Heresy for Brooks was a moral failure, a willful holding of ideas that one knew to be untested:

> Unless we hold to the authority of the Infallible Church, the ecclesiastical conception of the sin of heresy is impossible. Unless we hold that all truth has been so perfectly revealed that no honest mind can mistake it (and who can believe that?), the dogmatic conception of heresy fails. But if we can believe in the conscience, and God's willingness to enlighten it, and man's duty to obey its judgments, the moral conception of heresy set definitely before us a goodness after which we may aspire, and a sin which we may struggle against and avoid. . . . There is a sin which this word describes, which it described to Paul and Augustine and Taylor — a sin as rampant in our day as theirs. It is the self-will of the intellect. It is the belief of creeds, whether they be true or false, because we choose them, and not because God declares them. It is saying, "I want this to be true," of any doctrine, so vehemently that we forget to ask, "Is it true?" When we do this, we depart from the Christian Church, which is the kingdom of God, and the discipleship of Christ. With the danger of that sin before our eyes, remembering how often we have committed it, feeling its temptation ever present with us, we may still pray with all our hearts, "From heresy, good Lord, deliver us."[27]

27. Phillips Brooks, *Essays and Addresses: Religious, Literary and Social* (New York: E. P. Dutton and Company, 1894), p. 19.

Brooks's configuration made it virtually impossible to identify any fixed content to the mere Christianity to which individuals were asked to surrender.

The broad church leaders of the 1880s had been educated in the Episcopal tradition of earlier in the century that identified the content of mere Christianity with the Apostles' Creed, the Lord's Prayer, and the Ten Commandments. While they were willing to question such credal propositions as the virgin conception of Jesus, they generally did so indirectly, so as not to openly challenge the earlier standard. Phillips Brooks was himself a master of this approach. In his extremely popular sermons and essays, he practiced a kind of revision by silence. He simply said nothing about the historical truth of virgin conception, biblical miracles, or other elements of biblical history contested by modernist scholars, but he did not challenge any traditional position directly.

So long as broad church leaders took this approach, the Episcopal Church was spared any great controversy about modernism. One parish priest — Algernon Crapsey (1847-1927) of western New York — was defrocked in 1906 for his outspoken modernist views. Nonetheless, Episcopalians had none of the investigations into the orthodoxy of seminary faculties of the sort that convinced Union (New York) biblical languages professor Charles Augustus Briggs (1841-1913) to leave the Presbyterian ministry for that of the Episcopal Church in 1898. Episcopal General Conventions issued no sweeping anti-modernist statements like that which Pius X issued in 1907.

What would happen, however, when broad church modernists moved from indirect to more direct assaults on traditional doctrines of mere Christianity? What would happen when what they were omitting from their alternative view of mere Christianity became more readily apparent to the church membership at large? This was precisely what began to happen by the end of World War I. John Wallace Suter (1859-1942), a broad church leader who would later become the custodian of the *Book of Common Prayer*, sounded a modernist challenge to traditional thought in an address to the 1919 Church Congress. He declared that there was "readiness on the part of the whole church, in all its parties or schools of thought, for modernist revisions in doctrine." It was time, for example, to reject the doctrine of original sin.[28]

---

28. John Wallace Suter, "Essentials," in *Church and Its American Opportunity: Papers by Various Writers Read at the Church Congress in 1919* (New York: Macmillan, 1919), p. 106.

Matters came to a head in 1923. In that year Percy Stickney Grant (1860-1927), a New York rector known for his political activism, preached a widely publicized sermon in which he appeared to deny the divinity of Christ. Bishop William Lawrence's autobiography also appeared in that year, a work in which Lawrence spoke of the general disbelief by seminary students in the virgin conception of Jesus. A book by retired bishop William Montgomery Brown (1855-1937) entitled *Communism and Christianity* (1920), an eccentric work in which Brown declared that it was his goal to "banish the Gods from the skies," was receiving increasing publicity as well.[29] Influential laypersons began to circulate petitions and call for ecclesiastical trials. Anglo Catholics, suspicious of the direction in which the Church Congress was moving, created a separate Anglo-Catholic Congress.

Members of the House of Bishops responded by searching for some alternative to Phillips Brooks's view of heresy. Bishop William Manning of New York (1866-1949), an Anglo Catholic who had always had some reservations about the broad church movement, played a leading role in this effort. He used the intellectual assent/personal surrender distinction common to many modernists, but developed it in a different way. Commitment did not only mean, as some modernists suggested, commitment to the person of Jesus; it also meant commitment to the articles of the church's creeds.

Manning took Percy Stickney Grant to task in the pages of *The New York Times* and pressured him into resigning from his parish. Manning also drafted a pastoral letter for the 1923 special meeting of the House of Bishops. The letter distinguished *belief in* doctrine from a belief that was "deeper and higher, and more personal." Manning then went on to say, however, that

a clergyman, whether Deacon, Priest, or Bishop, is required as a condition of receiving his ministerial commission to promise conformity to the doctrine, discipline and worship of this Church. Among the offenses for which he is liable to be presented for trial is the holding and teaching publicly or privately, and advisedly, doctrine contrary to that of this church. . . . [Further,] to explain away the statement "conceived by the Holy Ghost and born of the Virgin Mary," as if it referred to a birth in the ordinary way, of two human

29. William Montgomery Brown, *Communism and Christianity* (Gallion, OH: Bradford-Brown Educational Company, 1922), p. 3.

parents, under perhaps exceptionally holy conditions, is plainly an abuse of language.[30]

For Manning, and for the House of Bishops that signed the letter with him, intellectual inquiry was not to mean departing from the core of mere Christianity, which they believed to be found in the creeds of the church.

Despite rumors of ecclesiastical trials, only one person was defrocked following the 1923 meeting, and he was a bishop. William Montgomery Brown was brought to trial in 1924. Many members of the House of Bishops believed that Brown was mentally unstable and should have been treated with leniency. However, when asked at his trial whether he could affirm the creeds of the church, Brown said that "there [is] no one in [the Episcopal] church or in any among the churches who believe all the articles of the creed literally."[31] The bishops, faced with such a direct challenge to their credal standard of orthodoxy, found Brown guilty and deposed him from the ministry.

As a working agreement, the credal test was more a placing of limits upon modernism than a repudiation of it. The bishops of the Episcopal Church seemed to accept a position so long as one could argue that it was in keeping with a serious attempt to interpret an article of the creed, rather than a direct denial of it. The seriousness of the attempt was generally demonstrated by references to discussions at theological seminaries and universities. Percy Grant, though pressured into resigning, avoided actual trial with this approach. He defended himself in the pages of *The New York Times* and in his book *Religion of Main Street* (1923) by noting that the opinions that he voiced were similar to those stated by prominent faculty members in Anglican institutions in England. Lee W. Heaton (1889-1973), a Texas priest charged with but never tried for heretical opinions on the virgin birth, followed a similar strategy. He lined up support from the faculty of three Episcopal seminaries to demonstrate the appropriateness of his theological statements.

The credal test of the 1920s played a role in regard to mere Christianity similar to that which the Quadrilateral had played for Anglican doctrine in the 1880s. It did not resolve differences so much as sketch the boundaries between which differences of opinion were

---

30. *Journal of the General Convention of the Protestant Episcopal Church in the United States . . . 1925* (printed for the convention, 1925), pp. 470-71.

31. Hugh Martin Jansen, Jr., "Heresy Trials in the Protestant Episcopal Church, 1890-1930" (Ph.D. diss., Columbia University, 1965), pp. 294-301.

allowed to exist. Some Episcopalians believed in the virgin conception of Jesus, the resurrection of the body, and the return of Christ on the Last Day. Others did not. So long, however, as both modernist and more traditional Christians were willing to justify their opinions as interpretations of the creeds of the church, they could coexist.

The acceptance of plurality in mere Christianity, undoubtedly eased by the previous acceptance of plurality in Anglican doctrine, helped the Episcopal Church to weather the theologically turbulent 1920s. The Depression and the Second World War then distracted attention from the theological innovation. The Church Congress stopped meeting in 1934, and the organizations that sought to provide leadership in its place — the Liberal Evangelical Church Congress (1933), led by figures such as Walter Russell Bowie (1882-1969), and the Liberal Catholic movement, advocated by Frank Gavin of General Seminary — lacked the hard edge of modernism of the early 1920s. The debate over the content of mere Christianity was stilled, but was not resolved.

The Roomiest Church in Christendom

The credal compromise over the content of mere Christianity that had been forged in the 1920s helped to maintain the peace in the Episcopal Church until approximately 1965. It was particularly well suited to the period between the end of the Second World War and 1965, for it accorded well with the version of Protestant theology shared by most mainline denominations during that period. By 1965, however, a familiar scenario began to repeat itself; as in the 1920s, some members of the Episcopal Church began to challenge statements in the creeds directly.

Neo-orthodoxy was the version of Protestant theology shared by most mainline denominations in post–World War II America. It was the American adaptation of the "crisis theology" of Europe. Union Seminary, no longer under the direct auspices of the Presbyterian Church, was the seedbed for neo-orthodoxy. Reinhold Niebuhr (1892-1971) and Paul Tillich (1886-1965) were the anchors of the faculty. Beginning in the 1930s, a whole generation of future Episcopal seminary professors studied with them. By 1960 those who had spent some time at Union taught theology or apologetics at five Episcopal seminaries — Bexley, General, the Episcopal Theological School, Sewanee, and Virginia. Their presence was not limited to theology, moreover. At Virginia in 1960, for example, three of five full professors had studied at Union.

Although Union was interdenominational, there were multiple connections to the Episcopal Church. Niebuhr's wife Ursula was an Anglican. Paul Tillich's first doctoral student was Clifford Stanley, who would teach at Virginia Seminary. Niebuhr and Tillich's colleague Frederick Clifton Grant (1891-1974) was an Episcopalian. Grant came to Union after serving on the faculty of three different Episcopal seminaries — Bexley Hall, Berkeley, and Seabury-Western. He served as coeditor of the *Anglican Theological Review* from 1924 to 1931 and as sole editor from 1932 to 1955. In 1938 and 1941 Grant played a leading role in organizing two encore sessions of the Church Congress, which served to introduce many Episcopalians to neo-orthodoxy.

Neo-orthodoxy was attractive to Episcopalians precisely because it recognized the tension between acceptance of modern scholarship and adherence to a traditional faith, a tension with which they were already familiar. The scholars whom Americans identified with neo-orthodoxy — Tillich and the Niebuhrs in the United States and Barth, Brunner, and Bonhoeffer in Europe — did not themselves agree on precisely how to strike a balance between modern scholarship and faith. Tillich, for example, favored a method of "correlation" with which human questions were met with divine answers. Barth, in contrast, believed in a paradoxical relationship in which divine revelation spoke to and called into crisis a world that was so bound in sin that even attempts to retain the divine message were soon corrupted. Taken as a whole, however, the theologians that Americans identified as neo-orthodox differed in kind from the modernists of the 1920s. Unlike them, they had learned from world war that the fruits of modern science were not inevitably trustworthy or desirable and that the language of the New Testament about sin and repentance had much to say, even to a modern world.

Modernist clergy, at least initially, had been rather careful about the language they used outside of the seminary and university community. They did so with good reason, for they understood that all that they said would not be received with favorable opinion. The neo-orthodox, in contrast, found their theology a useful vehicle for a popular exposition of mere Christianity. Episcopalians of the post–World War II era produced a Sunday school series (the Seabury Series), the Church's Teaching Series for adults, and countless Sunday sermons based on the approach of neo-orthodoxy.

The shared nature of neo-orthodox theology eased relations with other Protestant denominations, making it possible, for example, for non-Episcopalians to join the teaching faculties of Episcopal seminaries for the first time. The shared interest in neo-orthodoxy also contributed to the ease with which Episcopalians joined in such ecumenical organizations as the World Council of Churches, the National Council of Churches, and the Consultation on Christian Unity.

There were wonderful advantages to this shared sense of theological tradition. Episcopalians had rich resources upon which to draw in their explanation of mere Christianity, and they also had a workable sense of Protestant theology that was based not upon an anti–Roman Catholic polemic but upon a common experience provided by Union Seminary and other neo-orthodox classrooms. Many parishes felt no hesitation in using Sunday school materials designed for other denominations.

There were, however, disadvantages in this situation as well. Identification with a broad theological movement can involve a loss of denominational identity. Episcopal advocates of neo-orthodoxy were hard-pressed to specify anything particularly Episcopal about the way in which they taught theology. Indeed, at times they argued that there was no such thing as Anglican doctrine, at least in the realm of theology. When they did try to point to something distinctively Episcopal, they usually reached for something intangible, a style or character that was particular to their denomination.

This approach was evident in *The Faith of the Church* (1951), the third of the six-volume Church's Teaching Series. The series, which also included volumes on Scripture, church history, ethics, and liturgy, was produced by the Episcopal Church for adults interested in learning more of the Christian faith. James Pike (1913-1969), then dean of the Cathedral of St. John the Divine in New York, collaborated on the third volume with Norman Pittenger (b. 1905), who was on the faculty at General Theological Seminary.

Pike and Pittenger, both of whom had studied at Union, identified their denomination as "the roomiest Church in Christendom."[32] The authors went on to explain what they meant by the term:

> It is roomy, not because it does not care about what people believe, but because it knows that the truth of the Christian Gospel is so wonderfully rich and so infinitely great that no single human expression can exhaust all its truth and splendor. . . . It welcomes new

32. James A. Pike and W. Norman Pittenger, *The Faith of the Church*, vol. 3 of the Church's Teaching Series (Greenwich, CT: Seabury Press, 1956), p. 3.

truth, new insight, the contributions of scientific and secular thought, with the certain confidence that all truth is God's truth.[33]

Six years later Pittenger expanded on this explanation in a book entitled *The Episcopalian Way of Life:*

> One might say that a special characteristic of Episcopalians is willingness to differ in interpretation, even a positive delight in this difference, providing that there are basic agreements about the basic things.
>
> This special quality has often been described by saying that the Episcopal Church is the most comprehensive of Christian communions, or (in the words of a recent writer) that it is "the roomiest church in Christendom." Whether or not this be true of the Episcopal Church in contrast with other Christian bodies, it is certainly the case that the quality of "comprehension" or "roominess" is an obvious fact about the Episcopal Church. How otherwise could one explain the "highs" and the "lows" and the "broads" within our fellowship? Or the plain difference in church services, despite the fact that the Prayer Book is used in them all? Or the variety of explanations of the credal formulae, as one goes from parish to parish? Those of us who are of the Episcopal Church think that this is all to the good. We do not regret the differences; we rejoice in them. Our ideal, however badly it may be realized, is that on essential matters there should be a basic unity; on unessential matters, and on interpretations of basic matters, a willingness to differ; in all things, a spirit of generosity and mutual understanding.[34]

Pittenger's statement was a skillful and concise summary of the Episcopal acceptance of pluralism in Anglican doctrine of the 1870s and the acceptance of pluralism in mere Christianity of the 1920s. Episcopalians accepted "high" and "low" parties. They agreed on the basic credal formulae, but they gave one another permission to disagree on their interpretation of those formulae.

Interestingly, Episcopalians of the 1950s did not attribute this attitude to their predecessors of the 1870s and the 1920s. Rather, they used a historical argument of a sort that may have been as typically Episcopalian as anything else they did: they attributed this expansive attitude of recent creation to the English Reformation. Pittenger and Pike had, for example, explained in *The Faith of the Church* that

33. Pike and Pittenger, *The Faith of the Church*, pp. 3-4.
34. W. Norman Pittenger, *The Episcopalian Way of Life* (Englewood Cliffs, NJ: Prentice-Hall, 1957), p. 13.

this special quality or genius of the Anglican Communion, in matters of faith, may be discovered right here. The English Reformers were very clear about the appeal to history. They insisted that the basis for the Christian faith is in the saving acts of God, recorded in Holy Scripture. . . . But they were equally concerned to emphasize that the ancient Fathers of the Church provided an invaluable clue to the kind of interpretation of the Scriptures which is sound and accurate; a norm by which later interpretation of the Scriptures could be judged. And this insistence of the English Reformers involved them, of necessity, in a recognition of two other factors: the place of religious experience and the value of reason.[35]

Episcopal advocates of neo-orthodoxy argued that they had learned from the English Reformation to live with the diverse claims of Scripture, history, religious experience, and reason.[36]

While there was some merit to this claim — sixteenth- and seventeenth-century Anglicans did accord a somewhat higher place to primitive authors as guides to reading Scripture than did many other Protestants — it also involved important problems. It cut Episcopalians off from their own recent past and from the lessons about the delicacy of the balance between modern innovation and traditional faith.

There was a second problem as well. The Scripture-history-religious experience-and-reason claim soon took on a life of its own, particularly by the 1960s, at which point the leading figures identified with neo-orthodoxy had ceased their active work. Pittenger and Pike had suggested a certain hierarchy to the sources of authority that they identified. Richard Hooker (c. 1554-1600), the Anglican divine usually credited for this configuration, had done the same.[37] By the 1960s and 1970s, however,

---

35. Pike and Pittenger, *The Faith of the Church*, p. 17.

36. The claim to these four sources of authority was not original to Pike and Pittenger. It was made frequently by those exposed to neo-orthodoxy. See, for example, Randolph Crump Miller, *What We Can Believe* (New York: Charles Scribner's Sons, 1941), pp. 202-8. Miller did not suggest, as Pittenger and Pike later would, either that the appeal to these authorities was particular to the Episcopal Church or that it was based in the Anglican Reformation. Miller received his doctorate at Yale, at which Reinhold Niebuhr's brother H. Richard Niebuhr taught. In 1936 he joined the faculty of the Church Divinity School of the Pacific. He later returned to the faculty of Yale Divinity School.

37. In his *Of the Laws of Ecclesiastical Polity* Hooker had given primary importance to "whatsoever Scripture doth plainly deliver." This was followed by "whatsoever any man can necessarily conclude by force of reason" (convictions and ideas that had the force of common consent) and by "the voice of the Church" (the official pronouncements of the bishops of the church). "Inferior judgments" — the

many Episcopalians had begun to treat the authorities — often identified with a three-legged stool (made up of Scripture, tradition, and reason) or with a four-legged stool (comprising Scripture, tradition, reason, and experience) — as being of equal value. In a theology textbook widely used in Episcopal seminaries, for example, British theologian John Macquarrie listed six authorities for theology — experience, revelation, Scripture, tradition, culture, and reason — and defined heresy as "the distorted kind of theology that arises from the exaggeration of one element at the expense of the others."[38] At least on a popular level, this new view of the equality of authorities was quickly read back into the historical record, designated a central Anglican characteristic, and attributed to Richard Hooker and other sixteenth-century divines.

This historical reconstruction gave Episcopalians of the 1960s a false confidence. Episcopalians had, they believed, juggled multiple authorities of equal value for four hundred years with no apparent difficulties. They were unmindful of the doctrinal crisis of the 1920s and so soon repeated it.

English bishop John A. T. Robinson set the tone in his book *Honest to God* (1963). The work itself was in many ways a simple retracing of some of the major themes of neo-orthodoxy; references to Tillich and Bonhoeffer abounded. The introduction, however, promised something far more sweeping:

> I believe we are being called, over the years ahead, to far more than a restating of traditional orthodoxy in modern terms. Indeed, if our defence of the Faith is limited to this, we shall find in all likelihood that we have lost out to all but a tiny religious remnant. A much more radical recasting, I would judge, is demanded, in the process of which the most fundamental categories of our theology — of God, of the supernatural, and of religion itself — must go into the melting. Indeed, though we shall not of course be able to do it, I can at least understand what those mean who urged that we should do well to give up using the word 'God' for a generation, so impregnated has it become with a way of thinking we may have to discard if the Gospel is to signify anything.[39]

---

private opinions that twentieth-century Americans understand today to be the results of reason — finished a distant fourth. See Richard Hooker, *Of the Laws of Ecclesiastical Polity*, 5.7.2.

38. John Macquarrie, *Principles of Christian Theology* (London: SCM Press, 1966), p. 17.

39. John A. T. Robinson, *Honest to God* (Philadelphia: Westminster Press, 1963), pp. 7-8.

It was a repetition of Suter's 1919 call for a reformulation of mere Christianity.

Two Americans soon joined their voices with Robinson's. Paul M. van Buren (b. 1924) of the Episcopal Theological Seminary of the Southwest asked in his *Secular Meaning of the Gospel* (1965) whether the traditional idea of God was not dead. James Pike, by then bishop of California, referred to the Trinity as "excess baggage" in his *Time for Christian Candor* (1964).

Such statements were clearly breaking the credal agreement of the 1920s. Authors were no longer couching their work in the vocabulary of interpretation; they were directly challenging important elements of mere Christianity. As in the 1920s, the House of Bishops responded to this challenge. Bishop Henry Louttit (1903-1984) of South Florida and eleven others in "the Committee of Bishops to Defend the Faith" were unsuccessful in bringing Bishop Pike to trial; they did succeed, however, in gaining a resolution of censure in the House of Bishops (1966).

The censure did little to quiet Bishop Pike, who went on further to challenge orthodoxy with his book *If This Be Heresy* in 1967. With his death, however, two years later, Episcopalians began to inch forward toward a new formulation of the 1920s credal standard.

Richard Norris's *Understanding the Faith of the Church* (1979), a volume in a second Church's Teaching Series, was indicative of this reformulation. Norris's work contained some familiar elements from the credal standard of the 1920s. "Such texts as those of the Apostles' or Nicene Creed" were not, Norris wrote, "infallible" and did need to be "interpreted or explained." They were, nonetheless, "reliable" and really did "provide access to that relationship with God which is Christian faith." They were consequently "guides and norms for the theologian who tries to give a public account of the sense of Christian existence."[40]

This sounded like the language of the 1920s, but the setting in which the words were written was in fact quite different. In 1920 the idea of a plurality of interpretations of mere Christianity was relatively new. Those modernists who wished to interpret the virgin conception or resurrection of Jesus in nonliteral ways shared at least a background and vocabulary with those who took those words to be literally true. By the 1970s, however, that was no longer the case; fifty years of

---

40. Richard Norris, *Understanding the Faith of the Church* (New York: Seabury Press, 1979), pp. 8-9.

doctrinal pluralism and an increasing acceptance of pluralism in society at large meant that Episcopalians had difficulty in identifying any single version of mere Christianity as normative for the denomination. The Church's Teaching Series might uphold the central role of the creeds, but for many Episcopalians creeds simply represented one among an almost infinite number of opinions held in a diverse church. This diversity extended, moreover, beyond the relatively small group of modernists of the 1920s, most of whom were clergy educated on the East Coast. It now reached the laity and all geographical corners of the church.

Urban T. Holmes argued that the 1979 prayer book reflected this new pluralism:

> The spirit of the prayer book is inclusive, not exclusive. This means that it both expects theological differences among those who participate in its rites and provokes those who find it necessary to be sectarian to reject its theological implications. There is no way to insist upon uniformity of belief. In this period of explication of the book we must expect to live with the uncertainties and frustrations begotten of pluralism.[41]

The church had become, to use a term employed by John Booty in *The Episcopal Church in Crisis* (1988), a "pragmatic church," distinguishable from a "confessional church" that "demands of its members that they accept certain doctrines" and an "experiential church [that] demands of its members that they have some form of religious experience." The pragmatic church, in contrast, "requires that its members participate in what the church does as the church."[42] Such a church, Booty noted, "is the inclusive church."[43] Edmond Lee Browning (b. 1929), elected as presiding bishop of the Episcopal Church in 1985, agreed. At the time of his election he indicated that inclusion would be a major theme of his episcopate. The Episcopal Church should be a church in which there were no outcasts.

Booty noted a characteristic of a pragmatic church. It was a body

---

41. Urban T. Holmes, "Education for Liturgy," in *Worship Points the Way: A Celebration of the Life and Work of Massey Hamilton Shepherd, Jr.*, ed. Malcolm C. Burson (New York: Seabury Press, 1981), pp. 139-40.

42. John Booty, *The Episcopal Church in Crisis* (Cambridge, MA: Cowley Publications, 1988), p. 139. Booty, in typically Episcopal fashion, traced the idea that the Episcopal Church was a pragmatic church from the 1950s to the 1980s and then attributed the idea to Richard Hooker and the English Reformation.

43. Booty, *The Episcopal Church in Crisis*, p. 140.

"whose most pressing problem may be that of setting boundaries." Confessional and experiential Christians were welcome only if they shared "a reluctance to identify any human doctrine or experience with the ultimate will or truth of God."[44] To put it in another way, any definition of mere Christianity was welcome, except one that suggested that there was a normative content to mere Christianity.

The credal agreement of the 1920s had, therefore, changed. To the agreement of the 1920s — that the exposition of Christian doctrine be labeled an interpretation of the traditional creeds, rather than a replacement of them — was added a new condition: theological formulations had to contain an advance acknowledgment that they were themselves chronologically and culturally conditioned. Norris, for example, explained in the first page of the preface to *Understanding the Faith of the Church* that there "were no absolutely final answers" about the nature of God or of human life and that it was not his aim "to legislate about the church's faith or make it clear what every Christian is bound to agree with."[45]

Praying Shapes Believing

In this setting, many Episcopalians chose a more indirect method of theological exposition. If being a member of a pragmatic Episcopal Church meant doing what Episcopalians did, and if the action that most united Episcopalians was the use of the *Book of Common Prayer,* a theological exposition of the liturgy — which did of course contain creeds — might be the most effective way of entering into conversation about mere Christianity. This, indeed, was a route taken with increasing frequency in the 1980s and 1990s.

The formula that Episcopalians used to express this idea of the relationship between worship and theology was *lex orandi, lex credendi* — "the law of praying [is] the law of believing." Episcopalians borrowed the idea from twentieth-century Roman Catholics, particularly since Vatican II.[46] Leonel Mitchell in his *Praying Shapes Believing* (1985), for

---

44. Booty, *The Episcopal Church in Crisis*, p. 140.
45. Norris, *Understanding the Faith of the Church*, p. xv.
46. British liturgical scholar Geoffrey Wainwright has traced the current Roman Catholic discussion of *lex orandi, lex credendi* to three sources: (1) an eighteenth-century speculation by E. Renaudot and J. A. Assemani on the theological importance of Eastern liturgies that they collected; (2) an effort by George Tyrrell and other advocates of modernism to appeal to the liturgy as a source of "wise and temperate" theology; and (3) J. A. Jungmann and other leaders of the twentieth-

example, credited Roman Catholics Aidan Kavanagh and Robert J. Taft for introducing the idea to him.[47] In 1989 Episcopalians became so enamored with it that editor Richard Wentz added the words *lex orandi, lex credendi* to the cover of the *Anglican Theological Review*.

This new approach had advantages. By appealing to the whole liturgy and not just to the creeds, it provided a starting point on which most Episcopalians could agree. It did not, however, resolve the theological tension about mere Christianity that had been part of the life of the Episcopal Church since the 1920s. It simply added yet one more qualifier to the equation used for church-wide discussion of mere Christianity. An exposition of mere Christianity was to be seen as an interpretation of the creed or other elements of the liturgy that made no claim to be final or authoritative.

The *lex orandi, lex credendi* approach involved a new tension as well, for some see the principle as an effective theological end run: to change the liturgy is to change the heart of the church. This may be — as some liturgical scholars have suggested — a misunderstanding of the *lex orandi, lex credendi* principle.[48] It is, nonetheless, a strategy used with increasing frequency in the Episcopal Church. The debate on human sexuality, for example, which has occupied the General Convention since the mid-1970s, has been conducted largely on liturgical terms. Episcopalians debated who should be ordained and whether — as the Standing Commission on Human Affairs suggested to the 1991 General Convention — new rites should be drafted for the blessing of same-sex unions. Episcopalians have had far less discussion of the implication of such actions for the understanding of the doctrine of sin.

This lack of serious discussion about the effect of ethical changes on the underlying understanding of sin — and, therefore, of justification and grace — is one manifestation of a general inability or unwillingness to meet doctrinal matters head-on. It is, to be sure, a particularly explosive one. (As a perceptive member of the English General Synod commented, "You can have a pluralism of dogmatic theology as much as you like, but you cannot have a pluralism in sex

---

century liturgical movement. It was the third of these that most influenced Episcopalians. See Geoffrey Wainwright, *Doxology* (New York: Oxford University Press, 1980), pp. 218-22.

47. Leonel L. Mitchell, *Praying Shapes Believing: A Theological Commentary on the Book of Common Prayer* (Wilton, CT: Morehouse, 1985), p. 305.

48. See, for example, Aidan Kavanagh, "Primary Theology and Liturgical Act," *Worship* 57 (July 1983): 321-24.

ethics because in this matter people know what we are talking about.")[49] The emotions that this issue stirs may be stronger, but the inability or unwillingness to enter into a doctrinal debate on the implications of changes in cultural sexual values is in keeping with a century-long attempt by Episcopalians to avoid sharp conflicts on doctrinal matters.

*   *   *

The Baltimore Declaration addressed an increasingly confusing doctrinal situation. It asked an eminently simple question, but one that needed to be asked about the status of that which we Episcopalians "recite by rote in our worship."[50] Have we so qualified the way in which we enter into denomination-wide discussions about the content of mere Christianity that the discussion is no longer meaningful?

If the Baltimore Declaration has a positive, long-term result in the church, it will be this: it will serve, like the lad's question in the story of the emperor with no clothes, as a call to Episcopalians to take the content of their faith with greater seriousness.

49. *General Synods Reports* 10, 1948 (1979), quoted in Robert E. Rodes, Jr., *Law and Modernization in the Church of England: Charles II to the Welfare State* (Notre Dame: University of Notre Dame Press, 1991), p. 369.

50. Ronald S. Fisher, Alvin F. Kimel, R. Gary Mathewes-Green, William N. McKeachie, Frederick J. Ramsay, and Philip Burwell Roulette, cover letter to the Baltimore Declaration, 26 May 1991.

Doctrine, Destiny, and the Figure of History

EPHRAIM RADNER

I. Introduction: Doctrine, History, and Apocalyptic Figure

OUGHT we to take the Baltimore Declaration seriously? The Declaration seems to imply throughout its articles — indeed, it says so explicitly in its preface — that the church should take as its normative rule for doctrine a set of verbal articulations drawn from the distant past, from Scripture and from "historic creeds and ecumenical councils." As a result, there are many who will sense something willfully anachronistic about the Declaration's character as a whole, posturing in its small corner of the church in a way that seems to ape the giant gestures of a Luther or an Athanasius standing bravely "against the world." But the world, and the church with it, has changed in the intervening millennia: no longer do the popular mobs of Constantinople riot over christological doctrines; no longer do the principled objections of a German monk sway an empire. History itself has rendered appeals to an authoritative past and its dramatic players something of an impertinent amusement.

Such an attitude points to more than an abstract criticism of attempts at reappropriating ancient doctrine. I have had seminary students who were convinced, in a manner analogous to the early Quakers, that God was driven into hiding after the time of the apostles. His reappearance, in their eyes, coincided with the nineteenth century's developing struggles for human emancipation — with movements of social revolution among the working poor, with the fight for women's rights and increased sexual freedom, with the assault on colonialist

46

mentalities. On the other side of the table have sat students for whom the visage of God was given eternal form in the councils of Nicea and Chalcedon, the rest of history to the present being but a fluctuating commentary on this revelation.

Tied to the service of describing such diverse divine histories, doctrine scurries to take cover in their narrow shadows. For behind contrasting views like these lies a common conviction: particular human histories — epochs, experiences, struggles — are privileged places where God is recognized. To the degree that Christian speech reflects these areas of historical privilege and to the degree that doctrine describes the God recognized in these moments, such speech and doctrine are acceptable. But only to this degree. The question then arises, whose history shall we privilege? In fact, the notion that such privilege exists at all raises further and more serious questions: questions about the sovereignty of God over history as a whole; questions about the useful meaning of transhistorical realities such as the church as Christ's body; questions about the very possibility of a Christian destiny capable of comprehending the particular actions and souls of historically constrained beings such as we are.

These are unavoidably critical questions for our church today, riven by conflicting theological appeals to historical privilege. We have sidestepped them until now only by asserting — in faith alone? — some continuity between such competing areas of temporal preeminence and their descriptive grasp of God. The past "develops" into the present, we have insisted, and every past has some divine merit, which itself gives rise to a new moment of unfolding recognition, and so on and so on. Are these claims, however, claims that will stand up to the contradictions of historical experience and of the speech about God in which they issue? The unfolding nature of God's recognizability over time seems instead to reveal a host of unrecognizable gods, whose various divine shapes vie over specific forms of Christian life that few would think possibly congenial. How shall we join in lines of mutual recognition the Crusades, the English Civil War, and marching in the South for civil rights? Do we recognize in the inclusive "church without outcasts" the faces that are traced in tenth-century frescoes of the Last Judgment? Are they servants of the same Christ who today proclaims a decade for "evangelism" but in the sixteenth century tore the church to shreds? Only by digging a ditch into which the most repugnant of these forms are variously cast, and then straddling it with a loud declaration that diversity is comprehended, can such a claim to continuity be maintained.

This is a curious posture for any church to adopt. One leg of the Episcopal Church, for instance, rests on liturgical uniformity, of sorts, governed by phrases drawn from vaguely apprehended pasts; the other stands on a host of competing descriptions of God; and underneath lie the debris and carcasses of less welcome selves, marked mysteriously as "Christ's own forever." The whole provides an image of historical incoherence that serves only the practical status quo of the church's social configuration, however much its critics inveigh against it. For nothing can change without a recognizable history, no one can repent without the words drawn from such recognition, and God cannot renew unless he reigns over such times and speech as these.

I take the Baltimore Declaration seriously. But I do so because I believe that the very descriptive speech for God that the Declaration commends — its "doctrines" — affords a framework of recognition that can truly comprehend our church's contorted history within the single grasp of God. Taken together, the trinitarian description of God, the authoritative unity of the scriptural history within this description, and the exclusive christological figure in which this historical unity is embodied all trace the contours of a singular form within which God embraces the conflicted life of the church, and through it, the world. If such a divinely unitary grasp of our varied historical experience does not exist so as to make possible our talk of a recognizable God, then not only is the Christian church's witness incomprehensible to human ears, but the church itself is nothing but a prism through which to view the arbitrary shackles imposed by time upon our social consciousness. We could not be heard in a historical world, for we would have nothing to say about its divinely given shape.

By defining the descriptive language for God in the way it does, the Declaration at least implicitly provides a vision of the relation of historical experience to doctrine that can ground our common identity as a church in a realistic understanding of God's sovereignty over history. I will be calling this relation of Christian doctrine to historical experience "apocalyptic" and "figurative." But this will prove only a technical way of designating a view of divine sovereignty that is already embedded in the way we make use of scriptural language liturgically. Shielded from the inroads made by historical criticism into our more discursive speech, and from the literalizing moralism that follows in its wake, our language of common prayer has instead continued to affirm a view of God's historical rule that mirrors the New Testament's own: that is, a conviction that the whole of history is revealed — apocalyptically — in the shape of Scripture's texts, which individually and

together render the figure of Christ. It is a stark view in its challenge
to all forms of subjective privilege: the Holy Spirit exercises power as
it historically conforms God's gathered people to the images and shapes
of the Bible. This initiative, this relationship, and these forms alone
predominate in history. The consistent praying of the Psalter, for example, in Daily and Pastoral Offices and in the Eucharistic Lectionary,
has determined that, like it or not, we continue to receive the specific
images of the scriptural text rendering the historical person of Christ
(as in Psalm 22 on Good Friday) and through it the Christian church
as well (as in Psalm 48 for the consecration of a church). In doing so,
we uphold, perhaps unconsciously, the subsuming historical power of
the figure given in these texts. We are submitting ourselves, in prayer,
to the overriding reality that God is ordering and will order conclusively our historical existence as a people in a way that conforms to
these figures revealed over time in Scripture, embodied in the single
figure of Christ, and structured in our lives by the self-giving of the
Holy Spirit.

When I argue, then, for the reappropriation of doctrinal norms
within our own particular moment, I will also be arguing for the
continuously and historically assertive reality of this scripturally given
figure of Christ. Because historical experience ultimately "looks like"
or settles around this figure of Christ, the figure itself must be articulated in a continuously recognizable fashion. This is all, in fact, that I
will take "doctrine" to mean: any and every verbal description of God
that the church accepts as rendering God commonly recognizable
within its community. However various and broad descriptions of a
person may be, for example, if they cannot render this common referent recognizable to others who know or seek to know the person,
they are useless at best and erroneous at worst. Thus, if the single
figure of Christ crucified under Pontius Pilate and risen on the third
day informs the contours of our contemporary history, as it has informed the past, this common figure is the warrant and norm for all
subsequent human articulations of its shape in a specifically recognizable manner.

For just this reason, Christian doctrines must themselves form
part of the historical figure to which they are submitted: just as the
figure takes the form of a cross, so too will the doctrines that render
this figure recognizable be contested and abused. This will be the last
point of my argument, and it is an important one in that it indicates
the figural meaning lying behind our present confusions. To embrace
"orthodoxy" or "right doctrine" (that is, doctrines of figural recogniz-

ability) is to embrace a form of life in which God in Christ is properly described — but described in a context that must necessarily conform both those who speak and their common ties to the image of Christ's own figure, which is discerned lying within ditches more often than it is seen straddling them. Any church and any Christian who wish to affirm such orthodoxy must govern their confession by the prospect of this future.

II. Relating Doctrine to Historical Experience: Three Inadequate Types

What is at stake in understanding Christian doctrine in terms of its essential tie to a scripturally apocalyptic figure is the very nature of God's sovereign and, we believe, saving relationship to our historical existence. The Baltimore Declaration's foray into the realm of doctrinal principles contested by historical experience recognizes this implicitly. In repudiating those perspectives that would submit to the chasms of privilege dug between doctrinal epochs — between Nicene trinitarianism and contemporary monism, for instance — it recognizes that anything short of this repudiation would involve visions of historical arbitrariness to which God, too, is subordinated.

To grasp this fact is already to become aware of the need we have to hold on to our "doctrines of recognizability" in an apocalyptic and figural framework. Consider for a moment the general claims of those who would have us let them go. Victor Hugo noted that Napoleon could not have won the battle of Waterloo for one simple reason: such a victory was not "within the law of the nineteenth century," a law he did not hesitate to claim as God's own.[1] And the "laws" of the twenty-first century, we must admit, would seem to stand firmly against appeals to theological formulae penned by a few old men from some distant and constricted culture. The laws of the twenty-first century demand new doctrines, for something new is always happening. They call for the relegation of speech to action, in an era of fatal social inequities. They press us to abandon our theological speech altogether, as we tremble at the edge of planetary destruction, silencing our doctrinal drones in the shadow of an unprecedentedly uncertain future. The laws of the twenty-first century, like those divine laws of the past, are laws of history; they condition and legitimate our speech and action,

---

1. The remark is made in Hugo's *Les Misérables*, "Cosette," 1:9.

manifested now in one guise, now in another. If they are valid, they must have us dismiss out of hand appeals to a recognizable God, from within a recognizable past and future, eliciting speech that grants recognizability its human access.

To press my argument for the figural and apocalyptic location of Christian doctrine, I must explore the character of these competing "laws." These I will divide into a number of types, each depicted in terms of the way in which it views historical experiences — things that "happen" — as divine conditioners of doctrine. Each type demands strongly contrasting readings of the nature of historical experience, of God's relation to it, and of the church's identity within it. The test I apply to these competing types is the simple one of historical coherence in a Christian perspective. Can these competing types offer praise to God, even as they trace the fate of Christ's body, led by his Spirit, through the gauntlet of formative persecution and institutional struggle, through a violent and madly divisive Reformation, through periods of stasis and rigidification, through revolution and social arrogance, through marginalization, shrinkage, and present dissension, all under the aegis of "God with us"? Can they, like Paul, cry out in answer to the question "Is Christ divided?" (1 Cor. 1:13) "God forbid!" yet at the same time acknowledge how even today he is crucified, figuratively, again and again (cf. Heb. 6:6)? Can they compellingly account for the history of our church's long fragmentation and present contortions, and in so doing also offer to us the figure of a saving Lord for our obedient and joyful conformance, a Lord who can and does embrace this history as his own? A view that sees the relationship of historical experience to doctrine in terms of an apocalyptic figure can do this best of all. And this is what I shall now attempt to show.

Type 1: Something Is Always Happening: Social Subjectivism in Its Developmental and Liberationist Versions

That Victor Hugo could speak of a "law of the nineteenth century" at all was due to his immersion in the romantic view of history's constant and progressive mutability. This way of looking at history is perhaps second nature to most of us, despite our worries about whether "progress" is real. We have all been raised on the axioms of biological development and change in cultural forms and intellectual ideas, and the notion that "something is always happening" that conditions our thought and experience in constantly new ways may seem to require little explication.

In general, and with respect to doctrine, the conviction that "something is always happening" elevates the various and sundry events and circumstances of history to positions of influence such that they are seen inescapably to determine the formulation of doctrine in significant, even substantive ways. Historical experience itself — the socially subjective aspect of what "happens to us" — becomes the fundamental arbiter of doctrinal form. Now it may be "inescapable" that this is the case simply because we are irreducibly historical creatures, or it may be because, in addition, God's own being is intrinsically historical. The view that "something is always happening" comes in two versions, versions that are related to these last two understandings of inescapability, which give rise, respectively, to the formulation of the laws of development and of liberation.

The first version, which I will simply call the "developmental" view, takes seriously the one historical event that has happened in the past — the revelation of God in Christ — yet relativizes our understanding of this one thing according to the various exigencies of historical experience. Doctrine "develops," the argument goes, according to all the "other" things that inevitably happen to us and shape our understanding of the world and of God. Since John Henry Newman's *Essay on the Development of Christian Doctrine,* first published in 1845 and revised in 1878, is perhaps the most influential example of the view that doctrine develops substantively under the effects of historical experience, we can turn to his thought briefly.[2]

In converting from Anglicanism to Roman Catholicism, Newman had sought to justify, although not perhaps to prove, the integral continuity of the nineteenth-century Roman Church with the apostolic community of the New Testament and the later early church. To do so, he realized that he needed some way of accounting for the manner in which catholic doctrine had been formulated in the interim, formulations that had led the Reformers and Protestants to charge "corruption" and "innovation." Newman did this by appealing to the reality of doctrine's necessary "development," a reality he based upon the way in which "ideas" in general take hold of public consciousness.

Newman calls Christianity, even the Christian revelation, an "idea" (or better, a set of ideas, of which the incarnation is a principal

---

2. On Newman, and subsequent ideas on the development of doctrine in Roman Catholicism, see Aidan Nichols's recent survey *From Newman to Congar: The Idea of Doctrinal Development from the Victorians to the Second Vatican Council* (Edinburgh: T. & T. Clark, 1990).

one); and by this he means, not some simple and discrete concept, but a complex experiential reality as it is grasped by the human subject. Since he is notoriously vague about this vocabulary, it is enough to recognize here how Newman has shifted the conditioning terms for doctrine. Instead of emphasizing the integrity of the "one thing" that has happened in the past — the revelation of God in Christ — he concentrates on the subjective appropriation of that reality. For Newman, ideas are by nature initially formless, and only over time is their multifaceted reality gradually perceived. Ideas are never learned "whole"; they are only grasped from their aspects, in a historical series, over time. Ideas are not "out there" — in the biblical text, for instance — but are "in" the writers and readers of revelation, moving partially from implicit to explicit apprehension.

Since Christianity is an "idea" for Newman, it is lively only as it is gradually apprehended over time. Knowledge of the idea and the articulation of that knowledge, therefore, are inextricably bound up with the historical circumstances of the knower: lively ideas "take possession" of particular minds and are thereby gropingly uttered, becoming part of a public discourse; once given this more explicit life, ideas become interrogated, criticized, expanded, and finally associated with other ideas; and finally, out of all of these particular historical contexts, they cohere into a system that embodies the original idea in its socially evolved completeness. This whole process, the end-point of which is fixed only by the vigor of the idea in question — and Christianity's is the most vital of all — embraces the reality of "development." Only social and historical engagement with the idea and alteration to the idea can reveal it most purely: the idea's substance is known less at its source than in its "full flowering." This is the basis for Newman's famous remark that "here below to live is to change, and to be perfect is to have changed often."

We need not concern ourselves with the particular elements in Roman Catholic doctrine that engage Newman. What is important for us to note is that Newman can justify the central importance for doctrine of the fact that "something is always happening" because he feels he can identify a certain continuity that somehow binds, if not the events of history themselves, at least their influences together into a whole. This happens because the "idea" of Christianity that develops in time does so as governed by "Spirit" — that is, by the indwelling power of God.

Developmental views of doctrine in Newman's wake really go no further. They stress continuity under divine, usually pneumatic, guidance. They tend to see the conditioning factor of historical events as providentially guided, and therefore as somehow "necessary" to the temporal unfolding of divine truth as it is explicated in the church. And they have also maintained, in large measure, Newman's shift to the knowing (and experiencing) human subject in his or her social relations as the primary determinant of the significance of historical conditioning.

Since the nineteenth century, this continuity of development has tended to be understood as "progressive" in the sense of "more and more" of the truth being unfolded. Metaphors and models used for development have, in turn, reflected such progressivism: for example, "implicit" to "explicit" knowledge, models of "scientific method," and organic images such as the germ to the mature plant. In most cases, to say that "something is always happening" and that therefore doctrine must inescapably change in response has also meant positing an ameliorative view of historical experience — at least as it touches upon the church.

Here we can point to one obvious problem associated with the idea that "something is always happening" that necessarily leads to "more and more" understanding in continuity with the past: the notion that things are "getting better" for the church, particularly with respect to its doctrinal grasp of the truth, is, on the face of it, contradicted by the church's own history of doctrinal dissension, particularly as dissension manifests itself today. One way to frame the problem more precisely is to look at it in terms of the category of "recognizability": in a historical situation of competing doctrinal claims, how shall we recognize the authentic Christian "idea" legitimately developed?

Newman, for instance, claimed that one could recognize the church of the early Christian martyrs in the Roman Catholic Church of nineteenth-century England. As he put the matter, the very appearance of the church that had inspired the hatred of Roman persecutors was similarly articulated by modern opponents of Catholicism: both the early church and the Roman Catholic Church were seen as being superstitious, secretive, fanatical, and antisocial. It was the same church! The problem, however, is that Newman made this claim about the general "feel" of Catholicism at the same time that he tried to justify the development of elements in the church that clearly rendered it *un*recognizable in the eyes of Protestants and Anglicans. Newman's criteria of recognizability were obviously different from those of his Protestant critics.

But even Protestants, who have more recently accepted limited views of doctrinal development (in terms of "pruning" and reform), must face this problem.[3] If there is something "more" or something "else" that can now be known and perhaps formulated doctrinally, even if only in a transient historical fashion as the "occasion demands," one wants to know on what basis we can recognize that the something "more" or something "else" is not completely "other" from the historical precedent. Frequently one falls back on guiding "principles," from some ambiguous rule of "love" to key formulations like the Lutheran version of "justification by grace alone, through faith alone, in Christ alone," or to principles of Scripture's "self-interpretation." But just as Newman's original project demonstrated, the standard of discernment, as of change itself, has shifted to particular understandings of the way in which human subjects know things under various circumstances. And the diversity of our contemporary anthropologies and epistemologies assures the church of continuing and intractable dispute over the question of recognizability.

This is particularly the case, therefore, when the church is formally divided and at odds with itself. Historically developmental views of doctrine rarely have the means to deal with — and usually ignore outright — the historical appearances of utter confusion within the church, appearances that have certainly not dissipated in their offense since the Protestant Reformation.

A version of the "something is always happening" view of doctrine and history that avoids these problems, in part by throwing out *in toto* the constraints of continuity and recognizability in favor of an unlimited subjectivity of knowing, is the attitude generally adopted by so-called liberation theologies. Speaking broadly, most liberation theologies are premised on the conviction that historically situational difference is (and ought to be) altogether definitive of doctrinal formulation. Relying on a variety of forceful theories about the social construction of human experience and knowing, liberation theologians have stressed that the "one Christ" is necessarily mediated by the distinctive historical moments, material conditions, and cultural structures of any given person or people. To deny this fundamental law is, according to this view, itself an act of unfaithfulness.[4]

3. For an exposition of this limited notion of development in recent Protestantism, cf. George A. Lindbeck, "The Problem of Doctrinal Development and Contemporary Protestant Theology," in *Man as Man and Believer*, vol. 21 of *Concilium: Theology in the Age of Renewal* (New York: Paulist Press, 1967).

4. A useful anthology to consult is an older work entitled *Frontiers of Theology in Latin America*, ed. Rosino Gibellini (Maryknoll, NY: Orbis Books, 1979). The

They argue this for theological reasons, however. Believing that the reality of God in Christ is embodied historically in the struggle of the poor to be liberated from oppression, it follows that the primary intellectual task of the church is to analyze those social conditions in which the dynamics of oppression are at work. Neither these conditions and dynamics nor the methods of analysis can be historically uniform, however, so that in fact the church's mission is to explore as fully as possible the *particular* elements of historical conditioning that apply in any given social setting. Precisely because God is primarily apprehended and served in the midst of these particular settings, it is ultimately improper — even "evil" — to grasp at any articulation of the truth that goes beyond such historical particularism.

In this context, in fact, doctrine is often discarded completely, and ad hoc theology takes its place. Even this theology, however, can be no more than a set of self-consciously "ideological" constructs whose limited purpose is to analyze the way in which historical forces structure social oppression. Instead of investigating who Christ might be "in himself," such ideological theology serves to illuminate the political and economic factors that, in a given moment, exclusively disclose Christ as being "in the Christian." With respect to doctrine, historical events are regarded as realities that render the church's teaching ever open-ended, because these realities are themselves wholly diverse except in their capacity to enclose concrete relationships of social injustice. The turn to the priority of ethical practice that this entails, of course, is the substantive side of liberation theology's complete turn to the subject, although now given a completely social construal. This is a turn that the conviction "something is always happening" seems to necessitate.

This ethical turn to the social subject, however, is buttressed by the more general belief that there *is* a God, active in Christ, whose being asserts itself in a particular and uniform fashion on behalf of the poor. These are substantive claims, and they are claims with a reach that extends consistently throughout history. But given the priority that liberation theologians attach to particular and discontinuous historical moments, it is difficult to ground such claims in anything other than a diverse appeal to varying principles — sometimes biblical, sometimes christological, sometimes "apostolic," and sometimes "pneu-

essays by Joseph Comblin, Hugo Assmann, and Enrique Dussell give good overviews of some common attitudes to doctrine's complete subordination to historical determination, and I have their thoughts in mind in what follows.

matic" — by limiting the contexts in which the Holy Spirit speaks decisively to the experience of the oppressed. By providing these authoritative criteria, much of traditional church doctrine can be evaluated and rejected as itself being the oppressive and mistakenly "ahistorical" projections of a perverted community of faith tied, at least in its speech, to blinding social commitments.

There is an obvious self-contradiction involved in these legitimating appeals, for they undermine the very value that liberation theologians place on historical particularity by writing off almost two millennia of church experience — experience historically rooted for a certain period of time, to be sure, in the limited arena of European culture. While liberation theologians often apply an eschatological model to history — liberation is something inaugurated by Christ and partially instantiated in these last times in the open promise and hope of a future fulfillment — it is not one that seeks to explain the reality of centuries of the gospel's "obscurity" and the Spirit's seeming conformity, in the lives of the poor, to the utterances of oppressive ecclesial cultures; these times and cultures and the doctrine they produced are simply judged negatively and cast off.[5] The most that can be done is perhaps to "retrieve" possible instantiations of the authoritative principle from the past, explicating the low profile of these examples in terms of their marginalization by dominant structures of power.[6]

In the end, one cannot escape the impression that there is at work in the consciousness of many liberation reflections a sense that, in addition to "something always happening" in history, there has been some one thing that is "new" and decisive for the present — an epochal coming-to-awareness of the nature of political oppression, for instance. This alone accounts for the fact that the lengthy history in which God

5. In addition to the essays mentioned in n. 4, one can see this self-contradictory repudiation of "Western" doctrine, on the basis of historical particularism no less, in a well-known (in the United States) statement of liberation theology such as the *Kairos* Document, which opposes "centuries" of the "wrong" type of faith and spirituality in the European churches (the origin of what they call the "Church Theology" of English-speaking churches in South Africa) with the proper "principles" of the gospel given voice in the "Prophetic Theology" of liberation. Cf. *The Kairos Covenant: Standing with South African Christians* (New York: Friendship Press, 1988), pp. 23ff.

6. This is the way in which some Roman Catholic liberation theologians are able to embrace certain aspects of the Protestant Reformation (e.g., laicization, anti-feudalism, and evangelical "promise"). Cf. Leonardo Boff, "Luther, the Reformation, and Liberation," in *Faith Born in the Struggle for Life*, ed. Dow Kirkpatrick (Grand Rapids: William B. Eerdmans, 1988), pp. 195-212.

was active on the side of the politically and materially powerless has
rested in obscurity for so long and is only now being unveiled in its
fullness of implication.

The view that "something is always happening" that should shape
the form and even the substance of doctrine trades on a peculiarly
modern fascination with the historically determining character of the
human subject. Developmental theories of doctrine tend to locate
continuity in the intrinsic nature of individual knowing or social transformation; liberationist theologies, disregarding the need for continuity, completely subordinate doctrine's form and content to the exigencies of particularistically defined and subjectively experienced social
conditions. In both cases, however, historical experience is granted
divine coherence only according to human measures. Clearly, when
such measures confront the inchoate and the confused, experiences
that by definition defy human attempts at synthesis, historical experience itself will be denied divine significance. The social subjectivist
construal of doctrine and history begins by elevating human experience; it ends by accepting only those doctrines that conform to a
truncated history of the church and the world.

Type 2: Something Unprecedented Has Just Happened: The Decisive New Moment

One way of dealing with the dilemma faced by social subjectivists is to
emphasize and embrace the value of just this historical truncation. On
the whole, it has been left to (generally) Western theologians of feminist
and so-called postmodern or deconstructionist persuasions to articulate
this particular vision.[7] The vision itself, however, is not simply confined
to small academic circles. Anyone who gives credence to the unprecedented importance for religion of the "secularization" phenomenon is,
at least to a degree, affirming the centrality of this "new thing" that
has happened. One could even argue that, to some extent, it is possible,

7. A short and accessible presentation of all this, from a post-Christian Quaker
perspective, can be found in Daniel Liechty's *Theology in Postliberal Perspective*
(Philadelphia: Trinity Press International, 1990). A volume that demonstrates how
some theologians of professed Christian commitment attempt to work within this
type (to my mind unsuccessfully) is *Varieties of Postmodern Theology*, ed. David Ray
Griffin, William A. Beardslee, and Joe Holland (Albany: State University of New
York Press, 1989). On their account, Liechty's general concerns, which I use for
my sketch, represent only one extreme form of the "decisive new moment" type.
The authors themselves commend other versions of the type that are more receptive
of Christian tradition.

within a rigorously historicist eschatological framework, to see something like the Protestant Reformation as such a unique and privileged event (as some hard-line Protestants continue to do).

But we are here talking about something uniquely novel in a relentlessly contemporary sense. Whatever it is exactly, something has happened *in our own day*, according to this view, such as to condition the possibility of articulating Christian doctrine in a way that is not only novel and "unanticipated" by the tradition but altogether reconstitutive of the very notion of doctrine itself. There is a sense in which one might wish to call this new thing "eschatologically" significant, were it not for the fact that such traditional religious categories themselves are no longer valid in the alleged "new epoch" in which we live.

Proponents of the "decisive new moment" share with a Type 1 understanding of "something is always happening" the view that historical experience is the main conditioner of doctrine:

> We simply cannot know Godself in any way that bypasses historical means. Godself remains closed to us. We are inextricably bound within the nexus of our humanity for expressing and assessing our images, constructs and models of God. Therefore, whatever Godself is or is not, our constructs of God are human constructs, and subject to the varieties of human historical and social existence.[8]

But unlike the "something is always happening" type, here the social subjectivist perspective is underlined to serve as an appeal to a *particular* historical vocation that is unique in time. In Daniel Liechty's view, for instance, this vocation is "species survival" in the face of unprecedented threats to our planet:

> Because we live as a species in radically new circumstances, circumstances in which our survival as a species is at stake if we continue to hold fast to the values of our culture which have brought us to this precipice, so we must be willing to critically examine even our most cherished assumptions.[9]

How have we come to this place in history? The answer is variously stated. Phenomena like the Enlightenment or the flowering of capitalism, colonialism or the Holocaust, the destruction of the environment, and so on have each contributed to this unprecedented

---

8. Liechty, *Theology in Postliberal Perspective,* p. 33.
9. Liechty, *Theology in Postliberal Perspective,* pp. 5-6.

human predicament. But these historical experiences also provide the basis for a new way of construing the nature of "truth," and with it, a new way of construing religious belief that is required by the moment. A cornucopia of theoretical tools drawn from the students of these episodes are now marshalled to demonstrate how the philosophical and religious assumptions deriving from the past are no longer pertinent: cultural linguistics, epistemological pluralism, and literary deconstruction all fulfill roles in challenging the authority of past worldviews that have attempted to synthesize historical experience into a coherent vision.

"Cherished assumptions" that are now properly called into question by such critical scrutiny include traditional theistic discourse and Christian doctrine, which, history has taught us, embody demands of a humanly constructed "absolute" that lead, by some psycho-social logic, to the oppression, destruction, and death that now threaten the future of our race. In place of religious language as a vehicle for expressing historical and experiential coherence, the new era calls for the construction of an "observable common moral and ethical stance toward the world [as] a more adequate basis for assuming a unity of spirit."[10] Such an ethic is described in terms of loving anarchism, iconoclasm, and subversion with respect to any claim to universal truth or absolute divine presence, both of which encourage human overreaching and self-destruction.

The decisively new moment, therefore, requires an explicitly "honest" rejection of the traditional claims of Christianity and of the whole value of continuity in the faith. On this score alone, Christians must wonder whether Type 2 has any relevance for discussions of Christian doctrine at all. Nevertheless, calls for a "new basis" for religious belief have been made, and some of these are happy to make use of historically Christian artifacts, like the person of Christ as presented in Scripture. Since this material is now deliberately read, however, according to subversive critical and literary techniques designed to unmask and then explode its traditional construals, it is best to see these attempts at reusing traditional Christian categories less as genuine options for Christian theology than as examples of what might potentially infiltrate the church's common speech from what is, to all extents and purposes, a new religion altogether.

Proponents of the "decisive new moment" type freely admit this. The principles that they use to evaluate the discourse of this new

---

10. Liechty, *Theology in Postliberal Perspective*, p. 63.

religion or outlook — "mutuality," "freedom," etc., in the case of someone like Liechty — are purely ethical structures derived from the nature of the new historical moment itself, not from the historic constitution of the church's understanding of its language. There is no unease with respect to this past, however, no attempt to argue for reformation or return to some unperverted wholeness, but only a claim that what is happening now is completely on its own, that it is different and unexpected. To say that "something decisively new has just happened," in complete discontinuity with the past, is to adopt a relentlessly consistent perspective according to which history not only relativizes doctrine but swallows it up completely. Doctrine is engorged — but so too is the past, and the claims of the past, and the sense that the past provides divine pressures that reveal the future. "For centuries, we could at least rely on God to save us," writes Liechty wistfully. No longer.

Type 2, then, sees history's relationship to doctrine as its destroyer, and to this extent the type is not really a useful tool by which to analyze specifically Christian experience. It would be impertinent to ask, within this framework, "What of Nicea? of the Reformation? of unity torn? of groping and yearning for a line between our moments?" These are questions that cannot be answered, since the historical experience of the present has been definitively set apart from any coherent, not to say divine, connections over time. "Church" itself, as a recognizable body of a historical figure, is no longer a term that can bear the weight of temporal continuity. It is a delusion to think otherwise.

But there are Christians who flirt with Type 2, in part because of the ease with which it emerges from aspects of Type 1. In many ways the Baltimore Declaration frames its "articles" from within a perspective that is opposed to both. The Declaration's explicit repudiation of the "new" and of "revisionism" in favor of the authority of "historic creeds and ecumenical councils" along with "Holy Scripture" makes this obvious. Because of these repudiations, should we infer, therefore, that the Baltimore Declaration is simply setting itself up, against these positions, as a call for the reauthorization of specific and unchanging ancient doctrines? There are no doubt many who will assume that this is just the case, and an examination of the ahistorical vision of doctrine that they employ is given in the type that now follows.

Type 3: Something Critical Has Happened, but Only Once:
The Unchanging Apostolic Deposit

This is the traditional view of what counts as a significant historical conditioner to doctrine. It comes in both a generalized catholic and more particularized late and post-Reformation version. In the generalized version, which held sway until the Reformation, doctrine is seen as historically informed in a substantive way solely by a single happening: the revelation of God in Christ, in his prophecy, incarnation, death, resurrection, ascension, and Pentecostal giving of the Spirit. To say that "something has happened" to which doctrine responds in this case is to say that doctrine articulates a unitary set of events whose figure is completely given in the past and is commonly accessible in the present to repeated representations, in a discrete fashion. In this way, events after the apostolic age have no intrinsic doctrinal significance.

Early Christians, of course, recognized that doctrines were frequently elucidated in the face of attacks — by heretics, unbelievers, persecutors, and even demons — but these attacks were never seen as conditioning or determining doctrine but only as occasioning doctrinal enunciation. This is a crucial point to realize: to say that "one thing only has happened" of significance is not to deny that many things of all kinds are constantly happening and thus forming the circumstances of individual Christian lives and of the church. Many "small things" also happen, but they carry no weight in shaping the terms of Christian doctrine. They act as "angry wasps buzzing about," as the Council of Ephesus described those whose opinions the formulations of the gathered "Fathers" were designed to rebut.[11] And even though heretics can be called "blasphemers," can be characterized as "mad" and "disgusting," and can be accused of being "pupils of the devil" — someone like Athanasius enjoyed flinging these epithets — their influence is never more than incidental to the actual *way* in which doctrine is expressed, a doctrine whose only real formative burden is the truth of Christ. An Irenaeus, for instance, did not deny the variation of expression that might accompany teaching the faith, but he limited such differences to degrees of individual intelligence and attitude brought to bear on the unitary deposit of that faith, whose basic shape was, in any case, guarded and secure.

How is the faith secured? The "something happened, but only

11. The words are Cyril of Alexandria's, taken from a letter promulgated by the Council. Cf. *Decrees of the Ecumenical Councils*, ed. Norman P. Tanner (Washington, DC: Georgetown University Press, 1990), vol. 1, p. 71.

once" version depends on a strong conviction that the truth of God's revelation in Christ is both clear and continuously available to the church, whatever the circumstances. The early church ordered its expression of faith on what it claimed to be the infallible witness of Scripture (including under this rubric, eventually, the writings of the New Testament) and the proper interpretation of Scripture as attested to by a historical stream of testimony reaching back to the apostles. This ground was both unshakable and uniform. All that doctrine attempted to do and could do was to explicate this ground with more or less clarity, irrespective of that explication's context. Irenaeus wrote:

> The Church, having received this preaching and this faith, although scattered throughout the whole world, yet, as if occupying but one house, carefully preserves it. She also believes these points just as if she had but one soul, and one and the same heart, and she proclaims them, and teaches them, and hands them down, with perfect harmony, as if she possessed only one mouth. For, although the languages of the world are dissimilar, yet the import of the tradition is one and the same. For the Churches which have been planted in Germany do not believe or hand down anything different, nor do those in Spain, nor those in Gaul, nor those in the East, nor those in Egypt, nor those in Libya, nor those which have been established in the central regions of the world.[12]

What else could doctrine be, in such a perspective, except "univocal," in the sense that it speaks of one truth, in one voice, and in a singularly perspicuous way for all people? Since the revelation of Christ, nothing of import changes: something was given, once and for all, and now history, even the history of doctrine, is uniform. There can be no alterations, for example, to the creed of Nicea — in fact, there can be no new creeds at all — and all are to confess the same faith with the same words and with the same intention.[13] This focus on expressive and cognitive unity of doctrine was embodied, finally, in a concern for the corporate unity of the church, whereby Christ would not "be divided up" among factions precisely of doctrinal allegiance.[14]

---

12. Irenaeus, *Against Heresies*, 1.10.2, in *The Ante-Nicene Fathers*, vol. 1 (Grand Rapids: William B. Eerdmans, 1975), p. 331.

13. Cf. the statements made at the Council of Ephesus, in *Decrees of the Ecumenical Councils*, pp. 64ff., and the definition of the faith given at Chalcedon, pp. 83ff.

14. The "Fathers" of the First Council of Constantinople end their conciliar letter on just this note: "In this way, with the account of the faith agreed between

In presenting the views of early catholicism in this way, we must be careful to acknowledge our description's slightly distorting character. For early Christians, there *was* a certain movement to be expected from history, although one whose sequence was fairly well apparent. Further, although in one sense history must seem a rather bland affair from this perspective in that the significance of its particular events is strongly relativized, in practice certain sharply felt experiences like persecution and suffering are given relief just because they form an experiential aspect of the "one thing" that has happened — that is, the life of Jesus, the Christ. The intransigently traditionalist notion that the "apostolic deposit" demands a unitary and static divine-human history is in fact more clearly the product of what a later age desired the early church to affirm than it is necessarily an accurate picture of that affirmation itself. I refer particularly to both the Protestant and Catholic views of history and doctrine that crystallized in the seventeenth century.

Indeed, seventeenth-century theologians of all stripes evidence a peculiar rigidification in their ideas of history, as Owen Chadwick has pointed out.[15] Not only did Catholics such as Bossuet and earlier Saint-Cyran stress the wholly static nature of doctrinal truth and its formulation, in ways that pressed Irenaeus's descriptions to exaggerated limits, but Protestants as well, in their mutual polemic with Rome, claimed similar allegiance to an unchanging deposit. Duvergier de Hauranne, the Abbot of Saint-Cyran and mentor to the community of Port-Royal that so influenced Pascal, had as his epitaph the curt phrase "you shall have no new truth" *(non erit tibi veritas recens)*. William Cave, on the other hand, joined many of his seventeenth-century Anglican friends in defending the English Reformation from the charge of schism by describing Protestantism as the "restoration" to light of the "primitive" apostolic doctrine and practice of the church, after centuries of Roman corruption. In both cases, "true" Christian doctrine was identified with an unchanging doctrine, and the historical experience of the church itself was interpreted, though with different

---

us and with Christian love established among us, we shall cease to declare what was condemned by the apostles, 'I belong to Paul, I to Apollo, I to Cephas'; but we shall all be seen to belong to Christ, who has not been divided up among us; and with God's good favour, we shall keep the body of the church undivided, and shall come before the judgment-seat of the Lord with confidence" (*Decrees of the Ecumenical Councils*, p. 30).

15. Cf. Owen Chadwick, *From Bossuet to Newman*, 2d ed. (Cambridge: Cambridge University Press, 1987), chap. 1.

emphases, in terms strictly governed by this immutable quality of the apostolic tradition.

Historical criticism has perhaps undermined, for many, the claim to continuity and uniformity of doctrinal substance that the "something happened, but only once" version of the law of the apostolic deposit is based upon. Further, modern suspicions about the supposed accidental and irrelevant nature of historical circumstance with respect to doctrinal formulation have led many to read this early church perspective as a form of ideologically charged special pleading.

But we should note more importantly that the main problem with this traditional attitude toward what has "happened" in the face of doctrine is the practical one of not being able to account for seemingly irresolvable disputes. However one managed to explain ongoing schisms, even between East and West, nothing in the "something happened, but only once" scheme could quite come to grips with the reality of something like the Protestant Reformation, where the internal life of one major portion of the church was irreparably sundered in pieces. To anticipate somewhat a point that I will emphasize later, we can note how differently the theologians of seventeenth-century Protestant "scholasticism" explained the Reformation in comparison with the sixteenth-century Reformers themselves. The latter were able to bring to bear an apocalyptic understanding of history on the question of the fate of (corrupted) doctrine in the course of nine hundred years of the church's experience by claiming that this history was demonically informed according to the figure of the cross itself. This at least began to make sense of the convulsions of the age and the sorry wanderings of the past. Later Protestants, however, while continuing to attribute the interlude of the medieval papacy to the Devil, saw the Reformation instead in terms of a simple corrective rather than as a coherent moment of the previous history of the church as a whole. Nine hundred years of the church's history simply stood as a best forgotten (and unimaginably broad) line drawn in the otherwise unchanging sands of religious time.

III. Doctrine and Figurative Apocalyptic

It is critical to underline that, in addition to rejecting Types 1 and 2, the Baltimore Declaration cannot be construed responsibly without also rejecting the type of "apostolic deposit" vision of history and doctrine we have just examined. For to read the Declaration as a document merely calling for the resuscitation of specific ancient doctrines would be to cast it into the grip of yet another instance of historical incoherence. What is the Episcopal Church or what is Anglicanism if it cannot claim its present constitution as well as its present moment of doctrinal confusion as being somehow *recognizably* tied to a past that includes its issuing from a unified church, establishing itself in a posture of division, and then stumbling to its present place at the edge of embattled dissension? If we reject visions of historical mutability that render doctrine unrecognizable or irrelevant, then we must also reject a vision of history that consigns the bulk of its hard edges to a realm altogether devoid of divine sovereignty and significance.

There is another way, another line of connection, another realm, and it is found within the prophetic structure of the New Testament itself. The chasm of historical experience, into which would otherwise fall such doctrine as describes a recognizable God, is properly bridged and filled by the final type, which I will now present.

Type 4: Something Has Happened, and Everything That Still Happens and Will Happen Is Dynamically Conformed to It: Doctrine within the Apocalyptic Figure of Christ

In contrast to the frameworks represented by our previous three types, the New Testament understands the relationship of doctrine to historical experience in a way that is foreign to our manner of envisioning history in either linear or purely discontinuous terms. We are accustomed, by now, to the claim that "biblical" thinking views the course of human experience as purposeful and temporally guided to a divinely appointed "end." But that this implies some kind of serially innovating direction (or even lack of direction) to historical events is more derivative of modern analytic sensibilities than of scriptural attitudes. For the New Testament, divine providence is not a disembodied idea or "plan" to be worked out by God over time. Rather, I hope to show how this originally Christian notion of God's sovereignty over history involves the experience that events even now embody the fullness of an order already given by God in the figure of Christ.

In the context of this discussion, I will continue to take the term *doctrine* to refer generally to those descriptions of God that the Christian community accepted as recognizable, particularly in its public teaching. If we consider how the New Testament approaches the notion of "doctrine" as it takes form in history, we can observe two general directions of relationship, which may appear initially to be in some tension. In the first place, there is the temporally "backward" relationship, in which the church presents articulations of the Christian faith that are located in the events of Jesus the Christ — in his life, words, and resurrected power. These events mark the content and power of the gospel and have been properly identified as forming the basis for the *kerygma* or proclamation of the living person who is Jesus even today. But they are also explicitly identified in the Gospels as "teaching," as something defined in terms of pedagogic content. And this description is itself founded on the self-referring nature of the proclamation and ministry of Jesus the "teacher" ("master" in most English translations).[16]

Because of this unsystematic identification between kerygmatic proclamation and pedagogy, what the Gospels tell us is the actual content of Jesus' explicit "teaching" forms the whole substance of what is also frequently described as the "good news." It includes his initial preaching (e.g., Mark 1:21-22); the vast array of instructions given in the Sermon on the Mount (cf. Matt. 5:2); the kinds of proclamation that include the specific scriptural teachings regarding the fulfillment of prophecy in his person (e.g., Luke 4:15); the detailed explication of his suffering, death, and resurrection (e.g., Mark 8:31), which itself is given detailed elaboration in the passion narratives; and even the more abstract — and what we would perhaps call more "doctrinal" in the modern sense — descriptions of his relationship to the Father and to human salvation (e.g., John 6:56-59; 7:16).

When, as in Acts, the apostles themselves are spoken of as "teaching," the same unity and expanse of reference is underlined (cf. Acts 1:1; 4:2, 18; 5:42). What they say is linked primarily to the person of Jesus the Christ, whose own self then assumes the central and initiating power of their words. Not only does their "teaching" describe Jesus as the Christ in such a way that his words, deeds, and life render the terms of that description; but the apostles insist that the Jesus given in this description is the one who authorizes and effects even now their own continued redescription of his person through time. This is what

16. This is one of the most common titles for Jesus in the Gospels, the Greek original of which *(didaskalos)* has usually been rendered, in all but the most recent English translations, as "Master." The title, however, refers to the rabbinic character of Jesus' role and not to the hierarchical position of authority that Jesus repudiates in Matthew 23, for instance, which is rendered by an altogether different Greek word. In fact, the early church took Jesus' title of *didaskalos* and applied it to its own office of teacher (cf., e.g., 1 Cor. 12:28), clearly fixing the significance in identity of both Jesus' and the church's instructional act.

is meant when they, and the authorities who forbid them to teach, speak of their words as being uttered "in his name."

It is this initial experience of the person of Jesus, who is dynamically present in the gospel teaching itself, that first suggests the need we might have to find a specific term that is able to identify the nature of the apostolic description of Christ. The "backward-looking" character of their doctrine could be construed in terms of a "representation" of the shape of Jesus' life and words. But this would be a representation, not in the sense of verbal reiteration, but, properly speaking, in terms of providing for a continued embodiment of his person, given under the particular pattern of his lived experience. For the apostolic church soon grasped how the authorizing presence of Jesus in its teaching is best understood in terms of its own imitative following of his life as it has been described. (This is the burden of Paul's own appeal to his apostolic authority on the basis of his "weakness" on the model of Jesus.) Whatever events take place in the life of the church, the substance of its teaching clearly maintains this temporal link to a past whose shape continues to assert itself in the church's present.

The term I have chosen by which to identify this particular nature of the New Testament church's description of Jesus is *figure:* the apostolic church's teaching renders, I propose, the "figure of Jesus." The word *figure* was regularly employed in patristic exegesis and derives from New Testament usage of the Greek word *typos*, a nontechnical term for something that has been shaped according to a determined form that is replicable — a statue, image, pattern, or written guideline. For our purposes, "figure" suggests an embodied and imitable shape that, as the referent of the apostolic teaching, is also informed by a scripturally and historically prophetic aspect. For in addition to being "backward-looking," the New Testament also construes history's formative relationship with doctrine in a clearly "forward-looking" direction that is governed by a strong apocalyptic perspective.

The perspective is "apocalyptic" — that is, "unveiling" — not only because it is shaped by the expectation of the imminent end to history, but because that end is scripturally recognizable as having been given "revealed" form in prophetic figures of word, deed, and person.[17] In this perspective, "teaching" (or "doctrine," as it is translated

---

17. Unlike many present-day construals of the eschatological pressures that are placed on doctrine, the New Testament makes little reference to the Holy Spirit in this regard. The Spirit is linked to the teaching of the church as it moves into the future only rarely, and always in the kind of backward-looking way we have

sometimes in the later writings of the canon) is linked quite openly to specific *events* and to their experienced contours as they are taking place in an "expected" — because providential and scripturally prophesied — manner. Far from adopting an increasingly rigid Type 3 view of teaching as a strictly maintained deposit of propositional "dogmas" and "traditions" — a currently popular assessment of the matter — later New Testament writings such as the pastoral Epistles understand doctrine with a *heightened* appreciation of its relationship to the apocalyptically providential shape of history, including past and future together.

In the first place, later New Testament writings share a conviction that dissension and division within the church, tied to contending teachings and doctrines, derive from the peculiar moment of the end times. These are the "last days" in which we are assaulted by Satan, sometimes described in terms of the "antichrist" (cf. 2 Thess. 2; 1 Tim. 4; 2 Tim. 3; 2 Peter 1–2; 1 John 2:18ff.; 2 John; Jude 17ff.; etc.). This consistent vision is usually disregarded today, both in its linkage of doctrinal diversity to satanically prompted disunity and in its linkage of such division to a particularly culminating and figurally prophesied moment of history that shapes the church integrally.

Second, and more positively, the church's doctrine is given form within this historical dimension as the embodiment of faithful "readiness" for the return of Christ and for the judgment that this will bring. To take but two examples: both of the "confessions" of faith, found in 1 Timothy 3:16 and 2 Timothy 2:11-13, confessions that scholars have identified as formalized traditions of teaching — articulated doctrines, if you will — are brought into play in these letters precisely in the eschatological context of satanic conflict we have mentioned. They are articulations of "remembrance," of "God's firm foundation," of truth's "pillars," each designed to stand as a positive element of formation for the salvation that is drawing near.

This function for teaching is particularized even further, however. Not only do the "doctrines" expressed in these contexts deal specifically with the figure of Christ — with his incarnation, resurrection, death, ascension, apostolic teaching, imitation, and judgment — as in the two

---

just described, as a "reminder" and a "witness" and a "protector" of something already given in the past. The pneumatological questions touching on the relationship of doctrine and history are complex, but they are extremely important to contemporary debates, particularly when they are framed by Type 1 and Type 2 perspectives. It is enough to note here, however, that the New Testament does not concern itself with these questions.

examples from Timothy just mentioned or in the Johannine Epistles (e.g., 1 John 2:18ff.; 2 John 4-11). But the *manner* in which their articulation is to be worked out in the course of events is itself what we can call a "figuration" of Christ's person. This is explicitly stated in 2 Timothy 2, where sharing in the suffering of Christ is what it means to be a witness to the doctrinal tradition of the church (cf. v. 3). It is given expression more generally in texts on teaching like 1 Peter 4, where the preaching of the gospel seems to merge with the church's practical embodiment of Christ's own passional experience. More substantively, the formative influence of right teaching in this time of conflict lays the foundation for the kind of eschatological change by which Christians take on the very image of Christ, in likeness to him (cf. Col. 2:20–3:4; 1 John 2:27ff.).

A critical elision of theological vocabulary is at work in all of this: Christ as the very *eikon* or "form" of God (cf. Col. 1:19) stands in historical continuity with the prophetic figures of his incarnation, life, death, resurrection, and judgment that are given in Scripture; these historical shapes themselves are fulfilled in the person of Jesus and stand as a dynamic pattern, a pattern that the church describes in giving its teaching and in which the church's own life is given historical contour. The overall picture of doctrine given in these later New Testament writings, then, is that of a *conformative* framework through which the Christian in the church is appropriated into the figure of Christ, a figure that itself structures historical events. That is, the historical events in which the church participates, most especially as it teaches, are themselves given in the figure of Christ's own experience as described in the gospel. This can be expressed in the following chain of assertions: the culminating moment of demonic attack at the end of time is characterized by divisions moored in teachings; the articulations of right teachings, properly descriptive of Christ's person and forged in the midst of this demonic time, lead themselves to a peculiar experience of suffering; and this last experience establishes, in part, the framework by which likeness to Christ is fulfilled.

If we put together both "backward-looking" and apocalyptic locations of teaching, we can define the New Testament's understanding of the relationship of doctrine to historical event as follows. First, *something has happened, something that is definitive for all time:* this is the embodied person of Jesus the Christ. One aspect of this single event is the way in which events prior to the incarnation are included within it, as in a figure — that is, those events depicted in the Hebrew Scriptures stand as figures for the Christ who is to come and include within them the experience of his body, the church (cf. 1 Cor. 10:1ff.). Another aspect of this single happening, however, is the historical struggle at the end of the ages between Satan and the victorious and suffering Christ, the shape of which conforms to the figure of Christ fully described in the events of his incarnate life. Second, having stated it this way from the start, we can affirm that many important things are happening now, but all of them are important *only as they are part of the single figure of Christ*, whose life, suffering, and new life structure current history according to his own shape. *Many important things are happening now, but in a unitary way.*

Thus, while contemporary events are elevated in their significance, with respect to doctrine's formulation — they stand as doctrine's abrasively eschatological moment — their significance is grasped only as they are seen to be part of this single, *already given* figure. Their importance does not lie in the challenge posed by some intrinsic novelty that they might possess, but simply in the constrained satanic (yet divinely providential) role they play in molding the church into Christ's image. Right doctrine, in contrast, does not only describe that figure of Christ; its very enunciation within history's pressures and assaults is part of that figure itself. While history has purpose, it is not given in a purely sequential fashion, whether developmental or discontinuous; it is given, rather, in a figure — the figure, it seems, of the embodied, suffering, and victorious Christ — to be grasped whole and experienced whole as that which constitutes the summation of temporal creation. Rolled into one, the exclusive historical determinants of doctrine that inform Types 1, 2, and 3 are here synthesized and subordinated to the dynamic pressures that the single figure of Christ ineluctably exerts on temporal experience.

That this vision can pose some significant challenges to the ways in which we often look at doctrine today, even at our most obdurately conservative, may only be superficially apparent. Apocalyptic consciousness, we know, has faded in traditional churches. An appreciation of the demonic as a force, not only in history, but in the history of doctrine, is surely foreign to most of us. But beyond these seeming anachronisms lies the New Testament's understanding of history itself as figured, as experientially shaped according to an inescapable form that is itself doctrinally described. *This* challenge touches on the entire manner in which today we evaluate the *fact* of doctrinal contentiousness and ecclesial division, an evaluation that might itself properly constrain any doctrinal projects we may entertain.

IV. What Has Happened to Anglicanism?
The Church as Figure

There are those who sympathize with the Baltimore Declaration because they perceive a need to rehabilitate the doctrinal norms of the apostolic deposit, and they believe that this is what the Declaration is about. There are also those who reject the Declaration on the grounds that such a rehabilitation of ancient doctrine is confounded by the constantly changing conditions of social experience throughout history. But both groups should recognize, in light of an apocalyptic and figurative understanding of doctrine, that their respective positions together may derive from a serious misconstrual of the church's place in history. To say that neither of these two groups can agree about what doctrines are "true" today is not enough; we must also grasp how each, in different ways, has been unable to account for the actual historical experience of the church they claim to represent. Since neither group can place its notion of doctrine within a coherent history that includes the violent dismemberment of the church as well as its continued dissension, neither can properly address the need for a consistent criterion of divine recognizability within even our present historical experience as Christians. In effect, while each group can account for their vision of doctrine, they cannot account for the church itself, and for the Anglican Church in particular, as Christ's recognizable body. This is something that the apocalyptically figurative understanding of doctrine does explicitly, as I will now show.[18]

18. The case of the Anglican Newman emphasizes this paradox. In trying to use the historical creeds against *both* Roman Catholic and Protestant-minded Anglicans, he revived the seventeenth century's practice of fixing a historical line of doctrinal normativity after the first four ecumenical councils, in the fashion of the "apostolic deposit" type. But confronted by this point in the mid-nineteenth century with the growth of a denominationally pluralistic society and a stultified Anglican practice, this fixing of the line could be sustained only with difficulty in either of two ways. First, one could insist that nineteenth-century Anglicanism was in univocal continuity with the church of the councils, in such a way that the upheaval and division of the Reformation could be ignored; or second, one could claim that the doctrines of the early church had to be reinterpreted as forming the basis for development, and not as being the whole and explicit substance itself of all subsequent doctrine. Newman finally opted for the latter developmental view and saw that he had to abandon Anglicanism itself, since it seemed to be tied to an unrealistically static view of historical experience. Many Anglicans of his time, however, stubbornly insisted on the former view concerning the apostolic deposit. Both views, however, were a repudiation of the actual experience of Anglicanism as a church born in travail, wrenched into a number of different doctrinal postures over the centuries, yet somehow in all of this still constitutive of the recognizable body of Christ.

For it is not the case that we *must* somehow choose between these two ways of warring over a pervertedly portrayed church. Nor does the Baltimore Declaration's appeal to normative doctrine demand such a choice. The fact is that what became the "Anglican Church" actually derived from an experience of faith that was fundamentally informed by the apocalyptic and figurative views of history and doctrine that I have outlined above. And precisely these views and the realities they embodied continue to provide the most recognizable and compelling description of the historical church as Christ's body that grew up in its wake. It is not so much that the early Anglican Reformers provide us with ecclesiological principles to which we should conform our doctrinal formulations today; rather, their own experience of the church in Christ embodied a prophetic figure already given in Scripture, to which, if we believe them, we will inevitably conform our communal destiny, like it or not.

The first thing to be said about the early English Reformers of the sixteenth century is that they did not adhere to the "apostolic deposit" type of doctrinal construal associated with their Protestant descendants in the next century. This distinction is true for Reformers on the Continent as well. Early reforming Anglicans accepted the authority of the creeds and of the early councils, to be sure. But they did so initially only in an ad hoc and nondogmatic way, within their own highly apocalyptic reading of history and of the Reformation's place in the course of history. In the minds of sixteenth-century theologians such as Cranmer and Jewel, for whom the consent of the "old doctors" and the "old church" was of weighty significance, the early church was in fact a generally and normatively faithful church. But whatever normative force the early theologians of the church carried, they had gained that force for two reasons not intrinsic to the early church's constitution itself: first, the Reformers themselves could show that such primitive doctrine as was promulgated by the councils, for instance, had been based on Scripture;[19] and second, the early church was temporally located within a prophetically figured stream of history in which a period of faithfulness was to precede the long apostasy of Rome, culminating in the eschatologically final restoration of the (reformed) church in the sixteenth century.

19. Thus the sixteenth-century texts of the Articles of Religion tell us that, not only may ecumenical councils "err, and sometimes have erred, even in things pertaining unto God," but that the creeds themselves are authoritative only in that "they may be proved by most certain warrants of Holy Scripture."

This last is the second point to be made about the English Reformers. It is hard to overemphasize — today, anyway — its central importance, which, while it may count little in our evaluation of the abstract truth of Protestant doctrine, is the essential ground of its formulation. Most of the great English Reformers — Cranmer, Latimer, Tyndale, Foxe, Hooper, and others — were strictly wedded to an apocalyptic understanding of the nature of their reforming mission, and in this they were at one with many prominent Continental Reformers (e.g., Luther and Bullinger) and in continuity with medieval traditions, both orthodox and dissenting (e.g., the Lollards).[20] They had no doubt, of course, that theirs was a faith articulated in accordance with the apostles. But their goal was not so much to make that apostolic faith live again as it was to be faithfully conformed to the apostolic figure at the now culminating moment of God's historical design.

Common to all of their thinking was a rather extreme "historicist" tendency in their understanding of prophecy — that is, they carefully sifted and proposed specific correlations between historical events and the images described in scriptural representations of history's course. In general, this did not result in a simplistic one-to-one identification of text and event; rather, they followed a more subtle (and perhaps diffuse) method of figural exegesis by which universal history was seen as being figured in its entirety according to a given text, even while discrete events mirrored this larger figure in more particularistically figured derivatives. (Thus, for instance, Reformers understood that the experience of the church in England was not itself the complete fulfillment of scriptural prophecy but participated in the figured experience of the church universal.) Commenting, for example, on Luke 21:25, regarding Jesus' description of the "signs in sun and moon and stars," Archbishop Sandys explained the image as a figure of the church, whose "darkening" by persecution and apostasy was represented both in the early days of the Roman Empire and more emphatically in the present: "She was never, I think, in greater distress, the enemy never more cruelly bent, Christ in his members never more bloodily crucified, than even in these our days."[21] The single figure imposes, not its sole impression, but its historically clearest impression in the present — the last days — embodied in England only particularistically.

20. See especially Richard Bauckham's *Tudor Apocalypse* (Oxford: The Sutton Countenay Press, 1978).
21. *The Sermons of Edwin Sandys, D.D.* (Cambridge: The University Press [for the Parker Society], 1841), p. 356.

Within this historicizing figural framework, the Reformers uniformly identified the promised antichrist, let loose before the final consummation of the ages, with the succession of popes who had emerged after the sixth century. Roman doctrine on various key matters — the eucharist, purgatory, indulgences, Mary, and so on — represented the "delusions" and "deceptions" of Satan, deviously propagated through the church. Those who sought reform, however, who suffered in consequence and who finally were driven out or left "Babylon," awaited, as the faithful remnant, the imminent end of all things.

The compelling interest of the English Reformers in adopting this vision of history did not lie in its abstract theological attraction. Rather, the Reformers were captivated by the apocalyptic perspective's practical response to their historically specific moment, a moment that they presupposed to be providentially orchestrated by God. In the first place, this perspective gave a coherent answer to the experience of both (Protestant) suffering and (Roman) apostasy. The latter was predicted, to be sure, in 2 Thessalonians 2, for example; but its vigor and destructive force, personally encountered, was properly explained only by the appeal to the historically structuring figure of Jesus' cross: "the godly number [reigneth] most of all, whan they seme to the wicked least of all to reigne, as whan they suffre persecucion and death for Christ. For after none other sorte reigneth his churche here, than he reigned afore them whose tryumphe was greatest upon the crosse."[22] As Bullinger had stressed, the eschatological hiddenness of the true church was intrinsic to its form after the figure of the triumphant and glorious Lamb of Revelation 5:6, a Lamb "standing, as though it had been slain."

This figural reality also provided the Reformers with an apologetic handle for answering the Catholic charge that Rome had been in continuity with the church of the past, while Protestants had been "nowhere" for the alleged long centuries of obscurity and increasing faithlessness. Obscurity, the Reformers countered, had been prophesied and figured in the cross, and it was therefore properly speaking a *mark* of the true church, not its denial. Bishop Jewel, therefore, could easily distinguish the forces of antichrist from those of the true faith. As for the former, "what armour shall they have, and with what weapon shall they fight? Anti-christ shall furnish his men with spear,

22. John Bale, *The Image of Bothe Churches* (1548), cited in Bauckham, *Tudor Apocalypse*, p. 117.

and sword, and fire. Christ shall send his men into the field naked, and armed with patience."[23] What marks the church? Nakedness, in waiting.

This vision, for all of its valorizing of doctrines critical to the integrity of the church — doctrines like those of *sola gratia, sola fide, and solus Christus* — was remarkably open, risking, and accepting of contestability. This was in large measure because it understood these doctrines to be measures of figural recognizability whose own fate was to bring their proponents into conformance with the figure of Christ's self-giving. As with the reforming movements of early monasticism, of the eleventh-century orders of secular clergy, and of early Franciscanism, the sixteenth-century apocalypticism of the English Reformers had the odd appearance of a doctrinally conservative spirit wedded to the radical risk of attempting the ecclesially untried. For, as in all these cases, its historical openness was predicated on a common dynamic of conformance to the recognizable features of Christ's scriptural figure.

In addition, we must emphasize how the whole tenor of the apocalyptic and figurative construal of doctrine held by the Reformers contained within it a prophetic note: as the church stands naked and in waiting, the material aspect of its own future is figured in advance. We are led to expect, to embrace, and only ultimately to emerge from a history in which the true descriptions of God, figured in Christ, are contested, assaulted, and repressed. This is the future that is opened up — or better, that is laid open continually by Christ from the moment that the darkness of his own tomb was given over to the light.

The Reformers claimed that the apocalyptic figure of Christ, now given to the church, reveals itself in history — for a time, as God has chosen — through the very veiling of its own inclusive power. And when we observe the subsequent history of their church (and ours) we see that, to the degree that the early reforming vision faded, there arose just those alternative views of "apostolic deposit" and "social subjectivism," the juxtaposition of which issues in the paradox under which we now live. It is worth sketching this history because it marks the very assertion of that figure recognized by the Reformers.

With the passing of Mary Stuart's persecution of Protestants, with the stabilizing of reforming policy under Elizabeth I, and particularly with the English defeat of the Catholic Armada of Spain in 1588, the

23. John Jewel, *Exposition of the Second Epistle of St. Paul to the Thessalonians* (on vv. 11-12), in his *Works* (Cambridge: The University Press [for the Parker Society], 1847), vol. 2, p. 929.

apocalyptic and figural framework in which the Reformation had been understood began to disintegrate. This disintegration moved first into a form of postmillennial optimism — Christ would return after a long period of prosperity. But as the seventeenth century wore on, with its various travails among Protestants, Anglicans attempted to limit the normative reach of reforming upheaval by viewing the Reformation as only a corrective moment in an otherwise unperturbed experience of reconstructed order. This marks the complete transformation in Anglican consciousness of the Reformation as an apocalyptic event into a simple "restoration" of order. "The design of the Reformation was to restore Christianity to what it was at first, and to purge it of those corruptions with which it was overrun in the later and darker ages," as Bishop Gilbert Burnet wrote in 1678.[24] These "darker" ages, of course, soon became identified with "superstition," and the restoration with a kind of rational and ordered religion of stasis. Increasingly, the tendency was to ignore history altogether as a conditioner of doctrine in favor of some faith in the vague emergence of self-evident religion. The inherent "fallibility" of the church continued to be upheld, but its figural weight was heavily veiled.

Some standard for religious truth was offered, to be sure. The myth of Reformation as "restoration" — the repristinating for reuse of something that had been obscured — entailed some fixing of early tradition as unperverted and "original" norm. Here we see, then, in the later seventeenth century, that certain theologians, such as Bull and Pearson, began asserting the intrinsic normative status of the early church "Fathers" and the ecumenical councils in matters of faith, while defending (as Elizabethan Anglicans did) the right of particular commonwealths to regulate matters of ecclesial order not essential to salvation. But this definition of an orthodox standard was just as suited for the primitivist impulses of non-Jurors like William Law and early Methodists like Wesley — who could simply ignore centuries of the church's life as irrelevant in their attempt to grasp some lost purity — as it was for defenders of some morally self-evident rational religion, like Joseph Butler in the eighteenth century. History, for both groups of Anglicans, was drained both of its particular and of its universalizing figures, and any real historical basis for the acceptance and rejection of normative standards of doctrine became obscured and forgotten.

Today we find Anglican theology, even among its more liberal

---

24. Burnet, in his "Preface to the King," in vol. 1 of his *History of the Reformation of the Church of England* (London: W. S. Orr and Co., 1850).

evangelical proponents, as consistently vague about the relation of history to doctrine as was the eighteenth century. The Reformation as a unique or at least a paradigmatically figural moment in the church's history — whether in a negative or a positive sense — is a perspective largely ignored. Many theologians have opted instead for a mild version of doctrinal development, usually tied to the value of moderated cultural "diversity," which is seen to be enshrined in the Elizabethan Settlement and given flesh in the practice of prayerbook revision by national churches. Through the 1960s, these tendencies produced little of novel interest theologically. But as they became joined to the kind of evolutionary thinking that began to infiltrate theology in the late nineteenth century (in Maurice, Gore, Temple, and Charles Raven, above all), they became, even unconsciously, primed for a union with the extreme forms of Type 1 and Type 2 construals of doctrine and history: something is always happening, so we change, and must change, and must reflect our historical and cultural milieu ever more narrowly; and something marvellously new has just happened, so we may and must rethink and reformulate everything from the ground up.

Many people in the Episcopal Church may not realize this, priests included. We recite the creeds regularly, we hear Scripture read according to the lectionary, and to this degree we seem to be participating in some historic stream of tradition. But these recitations and recitals are frequently joined to vague interior reinterpretations of their significance, in which events such as the incarnation, the resurrection of the body, or the return of Christ are granted perhaps a metaphorical resonance for ethical practice and imaginative consolation, but no more. They are reinterpretations that if made explicit, as they sometimes are, would not be very different from many of the more radical proposals for reconstruing or even dispensing with traditional doctrines that professional theologians have advanced.

All of this, then, may well represent the long filling-in of a figure laid out for our expectation within the very pages of the gospel. But to this degree it is only an apocalyptic expression, the particular fulfillment in these last days of a generalized prophecy concerning the de facto character of the church. What I have called the Type 4 construal of the relation of doctrine to history is only a construal in the light of this figural reality. It is not itself some instrument of grace, conferring salvation on those who acknowledge its adequacy. Nor does an affirmation of Type 4 such as the English Reformers held — and such as eighteenth-century (and most twentieth-century) Anglicans ignored — automatically disclose the normative legitimacy of other doctrines that each group may hold. It merely tells us what will in fact become of the church that holds particular doctrines and how the fate of doctrines will ultimately be given in terms of their figural recognizability as they are shaped in the dangerous arenas of contestability.

This being the case, we can see how the Baltimore Declaration must take its confessional stand only in the shadows of the larger figure of the church's inevitably painful conformance to Christ's figure. It does this, therefore, not as the presumptive claimant to the mantle of the faithful remnant, but, much less grandly, as a momentary participant in the inevitable molding of its church's figure in the hands of the One who subjects his own body to the conflictual contest of descriptive recognizability. In accepting this role, quite apart from the particular doctrines it commends, the Declaration can avoid the historically irrational contradiction marked by views of doctrine like those of Type 1's frenetic vision of something always happening and Type 3's blinkered insistence that one thing only can happen to engage our lives. This is not to say that the normative authority of particular doctrines is not inevitably uncovered in the conscious acceptance of this participatory role. But the very standards by which the norm could possibly be demonstrated are necessarily buried in the agonal destiny of the figurated church itself. "And they all said, 'Are you the Son of God, then?' " On the basis of what universal reason could an answer to such a question ever be determined? None whatsoever, beyond the eventual consequences of bald assertion. "And he said to them, 'You say that I am' " (Luke 22:70). Assertions such as these, in this world, must necessarily suffer difficult dispute.

V. Embracing the Figure of All Happenings: Orthodoxy in the Episcopal Church

Episcopalians ought properly to wonder what it might mean to follow the example of the Declaration, within the framework of this vision of doctrine's relation to history.

We must first appreciate how the apocalyptic and figurative framework sets a particular scene for our church. At the least, it necessarily includes the English Reformation and its ecclesial ramifications as part of the figure of an eschatological (because demonic) dissension, still at work in and of one piece with the current disintegration of doctrine altogether. The dissension, of which the demise of dogma in the church is but a representation, is "necessary," not in terms of its virtue, but in terms of its place in the figured design of God's historical self-display in the crucified and resurrected Christ. According to this vision, the only basis on which we might faithfully hold on to a historic standard of faith — backward-looking, as it were — is to submit, in a forward-looking way, even to what might be the dissolution of Anglican particularity; even, that is, to the death of a denomination in an as yet unimagined fashion. Doctrinal assertion will itself be part of this process of submission. Further, within the prophetic expectations born of this scene, some particular normative constraints emerge with respect to Scripture, to doctrine in particular, and to our attitudes toward the church of which we are a part.

First of all, in entering this landscape of confessional expectation, Episcopalians will discover again how to treat Scripture as their exclusive norm for figural recognizability — that is, for both recognizing and describing in a recognizable way who God is within the humanly accessible limits of historical experience. This norm must apply both to their common speech and to their forms of common life.

This ought to be possible without falling into the sterile debates about the dangers of "fundamentalism" that have so irrationally plagued contemporary Episcopalian discussion on the Bible's authority. Scripture is significant primarily as it constitutes, in a unique fashion, the verbal description of Christ's figure, which traces the "image of God." As I have indicated, this figure of Christ comprehends the details and specifics of his life, undetermined by any principle of coherence other than their proper connection to his divine form. Further, this figure is traced by the whole of Scripture, both Old and New Testaments, and as such is the proper basis of traditionally recognized forms of scriptural discourse and interpretation like prophecy, typology, and allegory. But as a description of a *figure,* Scripture is fundamentally distinguished from the categories of "history" or even "narrative," the theoretical explication of which so bedevils modern biblical interpretation.

As the figure of Christ, and as a set of figures, Scripture is properly read "literally," but only in the sense that the shapes into which its particulars fall are taken as revelatory of God in themselves, quite apart from any theory about *how* things "take place" (a theoretical interest both fundamentalists and their opponents share). Rather, the primacy given to Scripture's figure, and the conviction that the temporal experience of the church conforms to these shapes, is founded on the belief that God "shapes" both Scripture and historical experience together in a figure that describes his own life. The critical religious issue is not first "did this or that happen?" but "has God, in time, so given himself in these shapes?" The historical past *is* divinely figured, as much *through* Scripture as prior to it.

Because the exclusive normativity of Scripture lies in its figural character, however, Episcopalians will have to acknowledge the way in which Scripture's figures must determine not only patterns of speech — doctrine — but also the historical shapes in which the church's life is actually rendered. With regard to realities such as the economic control that the maintenance of church property exerts on mission, or the bureaucratic stranglehold our ecclesiastical institutions have on decision making and leadership, or the academic sequestering of theological discourse — to realities like these and many others Scripture's figural norms provide not only a moral judgment but predictive clarity: they reveal to us that the church will inevitably come to God stripped of her goods, that she will be led by the fire of holiness, and that all her daughters and sons will be prophets. The difference between immersing oneself in these normative scriptural patterns or not is the difference between welcoming the inevitability of the church's struggle for figural conformity with joy or with wailing.

With respect to doctrine in particular, Episcopalians who follow the lead of the Declaration must prove willing to embrace the dangerously limiting posture of "confession." By "confession" I mean simply the particular and public utterance of those patterns of scriptural recognizability by which the church's own figure is being formed. These patterns will be limiting to doctrine on two grounds. The first is perhaps obvious: because doctrines are descriptions of a figure that is given original expression in Scripture, they clearly look backward to Scripture's own shapes as authoritative. Since the figure of Christ has already been given, there are no novel figures to be unveiled, only future conformances to be fulfilled.

But the constraining nature of a particular past upon doctrine is made more explicit on another ground: the actual experience of the church's fragmentation and upheaval, in which the Episcopal Church is a significant participant. Since this history of division is itself a proper figure of the final conflict in which the church lives, it provides a particular force to the limits of the past on doctrinal articulation. In theory, the figurated reality of Christ might be clear at any given moment in history, and therefore the recent past might be as good a possible location of Christ's historical refiguration and proper description as any. But *in fact*, our historical experience of the church's division and dissension is a sign of how "far gone" is the night (Rom. 13:12) and to what pitch the "mystery of lawlessness . . . already at work" has risen (2 Thess. 2:7). In this situation, we are forced to more exclusive redescriptions of the original (i.e., scriptural) figures, even as we submit to the present figure's unfolding burden. While we know that they are one and the same, we realize also that the clarity of the present figure is given only in the figure of the past.

For this reason, and for this reason alone, the classical trinitarian and christological doctrines have, within the figural framework, a "presumptive descriptive clarity." But this in no way means that they are above contestability. For one thing, these doctrines themselves regulate, in a basic manner, the whole figurative framework in which they are given authority.[25] As "axioms" for the interpretation of Scripture from a given perspective, they are clearly open to being questioned by those who approach Scripture with some other set of presuppositions. Further, even within a commonly accepted framework of scriptural interpretation, it is possible that the preeminent descriptive capacity of certain classical doctrines could be questioned in relation to other alternative articulations, and that therefore reasoned justifications for the continued authority of these classical doctrines would be required.

Because of this, Episcopalians should realize that the articulate "confession" of faith that is demanded by a recognition of the church's figural role must necessarily expose its speaker to two kinds of risks. First, there will surely arise the violence of being dismissed, ignored, marginalized, or silenced through a broad set of historical circumstances that together form the contours of the necessarily imposed divine figure. But in addition one will also encounter the incessant assaults of questioners, disparagers, and informed opponents whose particular concerns touch upon precise matters of theological propriety. In a church where, like other institutions, it has become increasingly unacceptable to disagree or officially tolerate conflict or engage in fundamental disputes, it is important for Christians of all theological

---

25. Cf. George Lindbeck, "Scripture, Consensus, and Community," in *Biblical Interpretation in Crisis*, ed. Richard John Neuhaus (Grand Rapids: William B. Eerdmans, 1989), p. 77: "Thus a certain way of reading Scripture (viz., as a Christ-centered narrationally and typologically unified whole in conformity to a Trinitarian rule of faith) was constitutive of the Christian canon and has, it would seem, an authority inseparable from that of the Bible itself. To read the Bible otherwise is not to read it as Scripture but as some other book, just as to read Homer's *Odyssey* for philological or historical purposes, for example, is to turn it into something other than an epic poem."

perspectives to entertain the possibility that doctrinal contention might provide the positive scaffolding for holiness. This might be so, not because diversity of doctrine is somehow sacred — if doctrine does not at least tend toward figural "univocity" it is religiously meaningless — but because diversity stands as the eschatologically necessary material out of which a recognizable figure is rendered in our final struggle for communal conformance to Christ.

Finally, let me suggest some attitudes that ought to characterize such confessing candor. In general, these attitudes can be summarized under the aspect of "submission" — in particular, submission to the passional contestability of a confession in the face of whose figural prospect we can only hope to remain joyfully and humbly open. What prospect might this be, and in what attitude must we greet it?

A church that denies its own history must also deny its own positive figural vocation. So I have argued. But such a church can never escape its figural destiny altogether, a destiny that implies the disappearance, through suffering, of all that obscures the figure of its Lord, of division, dissension, and the misdescriptions of God's form in Jesus Christ. To engage in the "patient" proclamation of this historically constrained figure in *this* context is to expect the difficult yet inevitable demise of the context itself, even of the denominational body itself. This will come, not through schism or further division, but through the passional submission — "patience" — to those very forces that appear to assault the church. To ask "into what will this small church disappear?" cannot be a strategic question at this point; it can only be the curious musing permitted to unshakable hope. We are not asked to form a new denomination, as some defenders of the "apostolic deposit" seem to think, or to join with other splinters of the ecclesial vine. We are only called steadfastly to proclaim a gospel and serve its Lord in terms constrained by the past, even as we allow the present and future to strip away particular institutional pretensions to durability. It is a call to a certain kind of sanctity, firm in one's confession, but faithful to one's place in this particular church as it has been given by and received from God.

This conclusion points to the necessary expansion in theological and practical significance of the Declaration's brief observation, in its preamble, that "we are well aware of the possible personal and professional costs of such a confession in the present situation." These costs, given in the figure of Christ and touching the very shape of his ecclesial body, have not yet been measured in this small church. That they will be, however, is certain. In George Lindbeck's words, spoken to a Lutheran church living through these same times:

Jesus and the apostles took as their models the prophets of old who died rather than withdraw from the mixed company which is God's people. They did not even become disaffected or inactive. They tirelessly worshipped and worked in temple and synagogue until they and the gospel message were anathematized or worse.[26]

---

26. George Lindbeck, "Ecumenical Directions and Confessional Construals," *Dialog* 30 (Winter 1991): 123.

Repugnance and the Three-Legged Stool: Modern Use of Scripture and the Baltimore Declaration

CHRISTOPHER R. SEITZ

Introduction: Propositional Arguments from Scripture

THE Baltimore Declaration is not so successful in solving a problem as in pointing one out. The problem involves the Bible. More specifically, it involves confident modern use of the Bible. The problem with confident use of the Bible is one acutely felt in the Anglican tradition in the modern period, but it is by no means our problem alone.

The form of the Declaration exposes the problem. Each article begins with one or more statements from Scripture, highlighted with special italicized print. There then follows a short prose account in defense of some theological confession thought to be under attack by modernity but in reality consistent with Scripture's own plain-sense declaration. A negative repudiation clause in bold print recapitulates the argument and presents a forceful summary.

The implication of the form adopted is that Scripture is authoritative, that its authority can be stated propositionally through the citing of individual verses, and that argumentation involving matters of Christian faith should begin and end with Scripture. In addition to this formally structured assertion, a similar statement is made within the body of the final article (article 7). In language reminiscent of the Thirty-Nine Articles, the Holy Scriptures are said to "contain all things necessary to salvation." Then, in addition, several further statements are made in an effort to describe the nature of the Bible's authority, the character of the inspiration infusing "God's Word written," and the appropriate place of tradition and context in modern interpretation, as well as a cautious endorsement of "responsible biblical criticism." The Declaration's use of terms such as *writers, redactors,* and *editors* similarly reveals an irenic acquaintance with modern biblical criticism. In conclusion, the repudiation clause reasserts that over and above the content of Holy Scripture nothing can rightly be claimed as authoritative. The final sentence states that "Old and New Testaments [do not] stand hermeneutically, materially, and formally independent of each other."

The content of this final article, both because of its detail and because of its effort to square a certain responsible modern use of biblical criticism with more traditional views of inspiration and the role of "tradition" as such, represents a special matter of concern that must be looked at on its own. It is the formal structure of the Declaration, and particularly its propositional use of Scripture verses to introduce and buttress an argument, that points up the chief problem with the document.[1] By "problem" I mean the difficulty with the document as a vehicle of change in the modern Episcopal Church. It could of course be argued that the document does not have this purpose but is self-consciously non-apologetic. But I doubt that. The tone of the final article suggests that an effort is being made to articulate a doctrine of Scripture that the authors both endorse and wish to commend to a wider body of faithful Christians.

The problem, then (if I am entitled to use the term based upon my understanding of at least a partial intention of the document), is that precisely such a propositional use of Scripture as the document adopts is what has come under assault in the modern period. Even more pious and "responsible" forms of biblical criticism would not take a turn toward propositionalism of the sort adopted in the form of the Declaration, even if many of the central theological convictions were of shared concern (e.g., the Trinity, doubts about "inclusive" language, etc.). Even were we to wish it otherwise, this form of "argument from Scripture" will only persuade the insider, the one already disposed to read Scripture in this fashion, the one already doubtful about modernity's legacy and ongoing contribution to the church and the world. (Over and above this, it is another question altogether whether such a person is interested in the nuanced use of biblical criticism hinted at in the final article.) This returns us again to the question of intention

---

1. For a discussion of various models for interpreting the Bible and assessing its authority, see David Kelsey, *The Uses of Scripture in Recent Theology* (Philadelphia: Fortress Press, 1975).

and the degree to which the document truly seeks to bring about change through argument and persuasion. If it does not, then one could conclude by the general lack of interest the document has generated in the Episcopal Church that the authors' purpose was ironically achieved: they felt a need to commend the faith and did so, whether anyone was interested or not. No one felt a need to adopt their view of the character of biblical authority, and so no one did.

But I want to look at the document as proposing a way of reading Scripture that the authors both believe in and wish to commend to the church at large. And under this set of circumstances it is the final article and the form of the argument from Scripture adopted in all of the articles that present the greatest problem for the modern church — and that includes a church that may otherwise share the authors' concerns about the assaults of modernity and inclusivity. Propositional use of Scripture has been rendered problematic by the modern world with its rival descriptions of natural, social, and historical science. For a host of reasons far too numerous to explore here, the Bible has since the eighteenth century been dethroned as a document of propositional authority.[2] The authors themselves seem to be aware of this in the final article, which is not a defense of propositional scriptural warrants but rather a fairly modern-sounding attempt to square biblical criticism with more traditional statements regarding the sufficiency of scriptural authority or the continuity of God's revelation across Old and New Testaments, matters of special concern to early (sixteenth-century) Anglicanism in its struggle for identity over against Puritanism and Roman Catholicism.

Precisely in their wanting to have it both ways, the authors expose a tension particularly acute in the Anglican tradition, with its twin and sometimes paradoxical commitments to traditionalism in worship and prayerful assembly, on the one hand, and optimism about the use of reason and natural law, on the other. Obviously the authors of the Baltimore Declaration would more readily admit an allegiance to the first commitment than to the second. And yet the final article appears to flirt with the same familiar Anglican "trinity" (Scripture, reason, tradition) that, in my view, produced the very climate of biblical and theological reflection that the authors are at pains to expose and repudiate.

2. See Hans Frei, *The Eclipse of Biblical Narrative* (New Haven: Yale University Press, 1974).

Scripture, Reason, Tradition:
The So-Called "Three-Legged Stool"

It is quickly becoming something of a commonplace in modern Anglican thought to justify liberal application of historical criticism to the
Bible on the grounds that this jibes with a "traditional Anglican principle" of Scripture, reason, and tradition, our "three-legged stool" of
authority, our "threefold cord" that will not be quickly broken.[3] Historical criticism is to be fully endorsed because of our (unique) understanding of dispersed authority generally and our more specific commitment to reason as an authoritative "leg" equal in length and
durability to other "legs" on our sturdy stool.

   To be sure, Anglicans are also quick to place riders on this already
rather imprecise conception of authority and the special role of reason.
Is the order correct? Put another way, are all legs of equal length? Instead
of a stool with three legs, should we adopt instead the (not entirely
inappropriate) metaphor of a couch, with four or more legs, including
most often "experience" if not also, as in one recent formulation, "episcopacy" and "vocation"?[4] More complicated, what is the exact relation-

---

3. This sort of notion appears both explicitly and implicitly in two recent
handbooks: *Anglicanism and the Bible*, ed. F. Borsch (Wilton, CT: Morehouse Barlow,
1984); and *The Study of Anglicanism*, ed. S. Sykes and J. Booty (Philadelphia: Fortress
Press, 1988).

4. See T. Wright, "What Is the Anglican Communion?" *Virginia Seminary
Journal* 44 (1992): 31-39. Wright says, "I would like to see a fifth element added,
and placed, if anywhere, before Tradition and Reason: Scripture, *Vocation*, Tradition, Reason, and Episcopacy" (p. 36). John Booty proposes his own modification
in *What Makes Us Episcopalians?* (Wilton, CT: Morehouse Barlow, 1982), p. 32:

> Scripture and the Tradition aligned to it possess priority over reason and
> experience. . . . We must, however, acknowledge another priority, the prior-
> ity of perception. We are first of all reasoning, experiencing people. . . .
> Human development, too, holds a priority. . . . Tradition, understood in
> terms of the Church's authority, comes first, conveying the Scripture to us,
> convincing us of its nature until by experience we affirm its truth.

At another place he recognizes that the Anglican divines "on the whole regard
Scripture interpreted through tradition and reason as authoritative" ("Standard
Divines," in *The Study of Anglicanism*, p. 164). Borsch states: "In the dialogue of our
experience and reason with tradition and Scripture it would be a mistake to grant
one an absolute primacy." But then he seems to back off: "There are, however,
reasons why the Bible may be said to have certain forms of primacy" ("All Things
Necessary to Salvation," in *Anglicanism and the Bible*, p. 219). In David Scott's view,
"scripture, tradition, and reason/experience work together with each other, inform-
ing each other like good marriage partners," becoming as it were a "gyrocompass
for the flight of faith" ("Liberalism and the Episcopal Church," *Good News* [magazine

ship of one pole of authority to another?[5] And more complicated still, when and where do we see an actual application of this "traditional Anglican principle" to help address a real modern issue before the church, like the ordination of women, or abortion, or homosexuality? The general impression left by this (on the face of it) extraordinarily synthetic principle is that it is impossible to use synthetically and only serves a negative or restrictive function in modern discussions — that is, to argue for the inadequacy of one or two legs (usually Scripture and tradition) over against a third leg (usually reason or experience). It may be that as a synthetic principle the triad functions unconsciously in modern discussions, but then what is the point in elevating it to the status of a principle to begin with, as well as claiming that it is somehow our unique "Anglican" way of reading the Bible that avoids the charges of fundamentalism on the one hand (to be avoided as once leprosy was) and yet allows us to be "enlightened traditionalists" on the other?[6]

Problematic for a different set of reasons is the notion that the authority of Scripture, reason, and tradition is a true, uniquely indigenous Anglican "principle" in the first place, and that in addition this "principle" belongs both to the classic period (associated with the thought and writings of Richard Hooker) and to subsequent centuries of Anglicanism, thus establishing a sort of thread of continuity — like apostolic succession? — spanning five centuries of biblical interpretation, if not more. That Hooker mentions authorities alongside Scripture is not to be denied, and surely among them are tradition and reason. But several matters plague easy identification of the "three-legged stool" as a principle of great antiquity, much less as one that

---

of the Diocese of Connecticut], 1986). I find all of this very confusing. How helpful is this triad with all order of slash-marks and further modifications?

5. See (and note the order in this title) *Scripture, Tradition and Reason: A Study in the Criteria of Christian Doctrine*, ed. R. Bauckham and B. Drewery (Edinburgh: T. & T. Clark, 1988), in which "what is at stake throughout the volume is *the one problem of the relationship between the three*" (p. vii).

6. See Reginald Fuller's caricature of John Burgon in "Historical Criticism and the Bible," in *Anglicanism and the Bible*, p. 147; repeated in his essay "Scripture," in *The Study of Anglicanism*, p. 79. More recently P. Cuthbertson has again seized upon Burgon for another lampooning in "The Authority of Scripture in the Episcopal Church," *St. Luke's Journal of Theology* 34 (1991), with his own repeat performance in "Known, Knower, and Knowing: The Authority of Scripture in the Episcopal Church," *Anglican Theological Review* 74 (1992), in both places citing a still earlier essay and critique of Burgon by A. Richardson (1944). Poor Dean Burgon, dusted off from a very different climate of debate to be set up as a straw dog because he regarded the Bible as the Word of God, a very real danger to be avoided!

has also characterized Anglican biblical interpretation through the intervening centuries and that can now be used with equal force and commendation in the modern period.

First, to speak of Scripture, reason, and tradition as a sort of principle or even as a hermeneutical lens in the writings of Hooker is misleading. The very few explicit references to the triad in Hooker's writings merely establish the general rule.[7]

Second, Hooker's understanding of all three is extraordinarily different from ours in the late twentieth century. Hooker defended a use of reason and tradition over against Puritanism in order to make room for the authority of the church in matters where the Scriptures *were silent* (church vestments, architecture, etc.). Then, over against the claims of Roman Catholicism to possess the sole authoritative tradition of biblical interpretation, Hooker sided with the Continental Reformers in elevating Scripture above the church and in making a fairly clean distinction between canon and tradition. The question for those who seek to retrieve the "three-legged stool" of Hooker for our century is whether anything like the same context of argument and church controversy exists now as did in the sixteenth century, thus providing a warrant for using the triad and also for claiming that in so doing we are being true to the mind of historic Anglicanism. Vigorous defenders of historical criticism as applied to the Bible should exercise the same critical faculties with respect to church history, lest a loose "principle" that functioned in one historical context is dragged kicking and screaming into a very different climate of intellectual, ecclesial, and cultural debate.

Third, and related, it is outrageous to think that one could conflate Hooker's sixteenth-century understanding of reason (corporate, Thomist-Aristotelian, tied to natural law before the cleavage between natural and revealed truth) with reason as understood in the seventeenth, eighteenth, and nineteenth centuries (consider Spinoza, Locke, or Schleiermacher),[8] much less reason as understood in our century (individual, experiential, capable of distinctions between revealed and

---

7. "What Scripture doth plainly deliver, to that the first place both of credit and obedience is due; the next whereunto, is what any man can necessarily conclude by force of Reason; after these, the voice of the church succeedeth" (Richard Hooker, *Laws of Ecclesiastical Polity*, vol. 5 [London, 1597], 8.2).

8. Or Kant. As Winfree Smith rightly notes, "Richard Hooker meant by reason what Thomas Aquinas meant. He did not mean what Immanuel Kant meant when he wrote his little book *Religion Within the Limits of Reason Alone*" ("Dominical Authority in Time and the Roles of Scripture, Tradition, Reason," *St. Luke's Journal of Theology* 34 [Special Issue, 1991]: 47).

natural truth), and much less still with the application by "unaided reason" of the historical-critical method of interpreting the Bible.[9] Hooker would have been shocked and confused by the notion that reason is the faculty given to humankind to establish which New Testament Epistles were truly authored by Paul and which were not, which sayings of Jesus can be trusted as "authentic" and which cannot, what really happened at the Reed Sea, the social background of Deutero-Isaiah, and the like. To defend critical approaches in the modern period on the grounds that biblical folk also exercised authority over the divine word[10] would have puzzled Hooker, for whom the distinction between canon and tradition and between prophets/apostles and biblical interpreters was simply assumed.

Fourth, where can it be shown that "Scripture, reason, tradition" functioned as a hermeneutical principle that was especially Anglican in the centuries that separate Hooker's from our own? (More on this in a moment.)

Finally, what does it mean that historical criticism took its initial bearings by severely questioning all corporate, ecclesial interpretations of Scripture prior to the Enlightenment, a move that can be seen in as late and as irenic a figure as Gerhard von Rad, for whom allegory and even some forms of typology were threatening ahistorical tendencies that were to be avoided and eschewed? The point is this: historical criticism established the very ground on which it stood by arguing for a sharp disjunction between "tradition" and "the plain sense of Scrip-

---

9. A view explicitly articulated by A. S. McGrade in "Reason," in *The Study of Anglicanism,* p. 106: "Hooker held that the Church could reasonably prescribe contrary to a biblical precept, if the purpose of the precept *in its historical context* could be understood to be irrelevant in current circumstances" (p. 106; emphasis mine). McGrade then compares Hooker to Locke on this score. But to suggest that Hooker was a proto-historical critic because of his understanding of reason is to confuse a hermeneutical problem with a problem of historical criticism. I do not know what biblical texts McGrade has in mind (none are cited). When in the Thirty-Nine Articles the ceremonial law of Moses ("as touching Ceremonies and Rites") is said not to be binding on Christians, this is not due to an insight from biblical criticism or reason; rather, it is because of an intra-biblical theological discussion about the law. Much in the same way, Paul treats the law as deficient not so much on the basis of historical analysis as on the basis of theological analysis (see Romans and Galatians). To call such a move an exercise of historical-critical reason confuses a hermeneutical and theological problem with a modern historical one.

10. Compare especially Cuthbertson's analyses in the works cited in n. 6. Jack Spong likewise argues in this vein and is completely oblivious to the distinction. See most recently Spong's "Dialogue on Human Sexuality," *Virginia Seminary Journal* 44 (1992): 52-57. We are just like biblical people, though usually better.

ture" interpreted according to the emerging historical and literary-critical canons. How then are we to embrace historical criticism as defensible on the grounds of an alleged Anglican principle of "Scripture, reason, and tradition" when it was exactly this post-Enlightenment reason that insisted on a sharp polarity between Scripture historically interpreted and the tradition of the church, thus by definition ruling out any clean notion of complementarity? And yet, in Hooker's formulation, the complementarity of all three was assumed as indispensable, allowing the church to interpret reasonably where Scripture was silent ("reason"), with one eye trained on past, corporate, catholic interpretations ("tradition"). Historical criticism is not and never was content to pick up its shovel only where Scripture is silent.

But to return to the fourth point, where did the modern notion of a "three-legged stool" of authority, rooted in Hooker and a unique legacy of subsequent Anglicanism, come from? In my view, it is nothing more than a twentieth-century invention,[11] smuggled in in an effort to accommodate an older, traditional understanding of the Bible's authority with a new and sometimes hostile worldview, now fully in place, for which the basic biblical narrative has long since been eclipsed (both by modernity and by the critical method set up to cope with it),[12] forcing us to speak of categories like fundamentalism, literalism, or liberalism, where Hooker and his contemporaries would have contemplated very different lines of division for altogether different cultural and intellectual reasons.

In the modern church "Scripture" remains a historic given, but its authority is difficult to perceive and articulate in anything but a personal sense, given our awareness of the distance of its historical and social context from our own. *No century has felt this distance more acutely than our own.*[13] "Tradition" points to a reality that Hooker would probably have

---

11. It is anticipated in the nineteenth century by the final acceptance of historical criticism by the Anglo Catholic Charles Gore, now a sort of vanguard figure for Anglicans of otherwise different churchmanship and stripe. See Gore, "The Holy Spirit and Inspiration," in *Lux Mundi,* ed. C. Gore (London: John Murray, 1889), pp. 315-62.

12. See Frei, *The Eclipse of Biblical Narrative.*

13. Here I would disagree with the opening sentence of the Declaration: "Throughout the history of the Christian Church, there have been times when the integrity and substance of the Gospel have come under powerful cultural, philosophical, and religious attack." At no point in time has the church faced such a massive encroachment on its texts, its authority, and its ability to speak with a clear voice to itself and to society as it must at the present time as it is faced by a worldview poised to rival both Scripture and tradition without even trying very hard.

considered under the rubric of "reason": namely, our belief in the trustworthiness of natural law in a *corporate*, nonindividualistic sense. And "reason" has come to mean the exercise of *individual* human emotion and rationality as applied to authoritative texts, church decisions, and all manner of ethical discourse and general decision making. The triad "Scripture, reason, tradition" may speak volumes about where we are as a modern church, but in my judgment it says very little about either the century of Hooker or subsequent centuries of so-called classical Anglicanism. And much less still does it offer a possibility for biblical interpretation in the modern period that will move beyond the fundamentalist vs. rationalist impasse, presenting us with a truly corporate reading of Scripture that is prepared to deal with the historical distance, literary complexity, social and ethical sharpness, and sheer theological force of the biblical text within the context and challenge of late twentieth-century Christianity. Before discussing in more detail the possibility of such an option, it is necessary to return to the Baltimore Declaration and reexamine its understanding of Scripture in the light of these remarks concerning the inadequacy of the so-called "three-legged stool" model for modern biblical interpretation.

Article 7 and the "Scripture, Reason, Tradition" Approach

It should be clear from the previous two sections that the propositional argument from Scripture approach used in the Declaration is in effect a throwback to the climate of confessional and scholastic arguments from Scripture popular in the sixteenth and seventeenth centuries. This is in some sense consistent with the self-conscious intention of the Declaration to model itself on precisely such early Reformation and post-Reformation formularies. But the question was raised in the opening section whether or not the same could be said of the content of the final article (article 7), where the most substantive statements are made concerning the character of Scripture and the nature of biblical authority. We must also consider the possibility that by articulating one view of Scripture in some detail in article 7, and by modeling another approach to Scripture in the actual form and structure of the document, the Declaration is in fact at cross-purposes with itself and as such reflects precisely the sorts of tensions regarding use of the Bible in the modern period that were revealed in our discussion of the "Scripture, reason, tradition" model.

As noted above, the opening statement of the Declaration's final article is nothing more than a quotation from Article 6 of the Thirty-Nine Articles, though lacking the stipulation clauses of the latter ("so that whatsoever is not read therein, nor may be proved thereby, is not to be required of any man, that it should be believed as an article of Faith, or thought to be requisite or necessary to salvation"). Both the original article and its abbreviation in the Declaration are concerned to circumscribe the proper realm of the Bible's authority as involving matters of our salvation — not, for example, descriptions of the origin of the universe, inerrant geographical and historical reckonings from antiquity, or a concern with "authentically" or "inauthentically" ascribed authorship and other such matters near to the heart of historical-critical method. The second line (and a similar sentence in the repudiation clause) makes even more explicit that with respect to inspiration there can be no external critical criterion that would render one portion of Scripture more or less inspired than another. Here we see a full recognition of the social, historical, and literary complexity of the biblical text in its final form, and at the same time a steady refusal to use this sort of critical recognition as the means by which to set up a grid of priority, with higher value placed on one critically reconstructed portion of text than on another.

It is in the third sentence that we confront the endorsement, such as it is, of modern biblical criticism. To be sure, biblical criticism is to be used responsibly, it is to be used "under the guidance and lordship of the Spirit," and it is to be used within a specific context: "the tradition and community of the Christian Church." But who is to determine when these various criteria are met? What may well be one person's "responsible" use of biblical criticism is almost certainly another person's irresponsible use. And what eventual heretic did not claim to be working under the "lordship of the Spirit"? Here we have biblical criticism, a highly rationalistic method — according to its own canons ineluctably "objective" — now to be hedged in by these various subjective criteria that the document enjoins ("responsible," "spiritual," "Christian"). As to "tradition," it again strikes me as naive to assume for even the best of reasons any easy rapprochement between "Scripture" and "tradition" in the same breath as one endorses a biblical criticism whose entire originating purpose was to call into question "tradition" as an adequate category of biblical interpretation.

In this third sentence we see a classic Anglican tendency — namely, the attempt to justify a critical endeavor by placing its practitioners under various subjective constraints. But why go down this road to begin with? The real question to be raised is this: What positive value do the authors of the Declaration truly place on biblical criticism? If it is such an unqualified good, why the need to place it under the very constraints it originally sought to be free of? The phrases that follow return to notions of the Bible's authority that are virtually foreign to the climate and ethos of biblical criticism (the Scriptures in their entirety have to do with Jesus Christ; they are the decisive moral and confessional authority; the Holy Scriptures confront us daily, devotionally, with God's Word). And if there is any conviction dear to the heart of biblical criticism, it is that the Old and New Testaments are "hermeneutically, materially, and formally independent" of one another. Yet precisely the opposite is held to be true by the Declaration.

The Word Versus the Word

A somewhat different approach to the question of authority in Anglicanism from that represented by the Baltimore Declaration seeks to establish a distinction between the Word of God as the (incarnate or risen) Lord, second person of the Trinity, as against the Word of God written — that is, the Holy Scriptures of Old and New Testaments. On this logic, the church does not stand under the authority of God's Word written (the Bible) so much as under the authority of the Word of God, Jesus Christ. Theologians otherwise as divergent as Karl Barth and Paul Tillich are argued to be twentieth-century proponents of just such a distinction. Modern Anglicans otherwise as divergent as David Scott, Philip Cuthbertson, Jack Spong, and Fred Borsch — and, for other reasons, James Barr and John Barton — also make reference positively to such a distinction and commend it to their respective audiences.[14] Such a distinction plays

---

14. Cuthbertson commends Tillich (in "The Authority of Scripture in the Episcopal Church," p. 36); Barton commends Barth (in *People of the Book?* [Louisville: Westminster/John Knox Press, 1988], p. 81). Presumably here was a place where the two theological combatants agreed! Scott (and C. Hancock) are the most subtle on this matter: "The unity of the scriptures, likewise, does not reside ultimately in the words on the page as much as in the one in whom 'we live and move and have our being.' . . . Classical Anglicanism believes that God's Word of truth is found in the pages of the Bible, but it is not contained (without remainder) in the pages of the Bible" (unpublished essay read to the Conference of Anglican Theologians, 1992). Cuthbertson and others are far less subtle: "The Bible as the word of God is not to be confused with Christ as the Word of God, for the Christian's fullest revelation is in our loving relationship with the Person of Christ" ("The Authority of Scripture in the Episcopal Church," p. 36; "Known, Knower, and Knowing," p. 173).

Spong contrasts the "literal Bible," "quoting the scripture," and "the Bible I

nicely into one agenda of early biblical criticism — namely, the isolation of eternal ideas and abiding theological truths apart from the dross of historical contingency, with the Bible in its entirety representing historical contingency, and Jesus Christ the eternal Word of God. With respect to the Word of God distinction that is argued for, presumably only those portions of Scripture that truly inculcate Christ, the Word of God, are to be regarded as the Word of God, else a charge of "biblicism" might be lodged. (To be sure, exponents of this view rarely make a distinction in such crude form, Spong being the least subtle).

While this approach bears a superficial resemblance to the *Sachkritik* logic of Martin Luther as applied to the whole of Scripture (truly authoritative is "what inculcates Christ"), it could only with difficulty be attached to the sort of reformed Catholicism of sixteenth-century Anglicanism, which on this score tended to move more instinctually in the direction of Calvin than in the direction of Luther.[15] It is for this reason that Article 7 of the Thirty-Nine Articles refuses to set the Old Testament over against the New ("for in both everlasting life is offered to Mankind by Christ") and similarly resists any easy demotion of portions of Scripture not explicit in manifesting a concern with the Word of God, Jesus Christ ("wherefore they are not to be heard, which feign that the old Fathers did look only for transitory promises"). Similar concern to avoid such simple distinctions can be seen in the commendation of the Old Testament Law, from which "no Christian man whatsoever is free from the obedience of the commandments

---

read," which "justifies slavery," "treats women as male chattel," and "justifies a tribal mentality," with "the grace of God, made known in Jesus Christ," "the call of Christ out of limiting prejudices," and "the inclusive love of God" ("Dialogue on Human Sexuality," pp. 52-53). Further examples could be multiplied. Spong says further that the "clear teaching against homosexuality" comprises "the only two verses in Leviticus that anybody's ever heard of" (p. 53). He should tell that to Henry VIII, whose interpretation of Leviticus (against that of the Roman Church, in support of his remarriage) established the jurisdictional and ecclesial authority of the Church of England, from which Spong's Episcopal baptism, ordination, and consecration ironically derive.

Borsch states, "Indeed, to imagine and worship a God that could somehow be defined by human words would be a form of idolatry" ("All Things Necessary to Salvation," p. 222). I wonder how Wycliffe, Tyndale, Coverdale, Cranmer, Luther, and other Bible translators would have responded to this sort of distinction? See also James Barr (*Holy Scripture: Canon, Authority, Criticism* [Philadelphia: Westminster Press, 1984], esp. chap. 1) and John Barton, who states in *People of the Book?* without further ado: "it is not the Bible that is the Word of God, but Jesus Christ" (p. 81).

15. Note Hooker's appreciative dedication of *Laws of Ecclesiastical Polity* to John Calvin.

which are called moral." And when Cranmer wrote his famous collect regarding the authority of Scripture, there is no whiff whatsoever of concern with a distinction between the Word of God written and the Word made flesh: "Almighty God who hath caused all Holy Scripture to be written for our learning. . . ."

On this score the Baltimore Declaration is a distinct improvement over most modern formulations. It speaks of the Word of God, Jesus Christ, and the Word of God written with no suggestion of an implicit tension between the two, and in fact with a degree of complementarity truly reminiscent of sixteenth-century Anglicanism. In my judgment this has to do with its more positive assessment of the third person of the Trinity, the Holy Spirit, who is both the author of Scripture and the insurer of its proper reception and obedient response. "Through the Holy Scriptures the Church hears anew every day . . . that divine Word who renews and inspires, teaches and corrects, judges and saves." One recent essayist concerned to guard this complementarity in the name of a positive assessment of Scripture's material function in the church was the late Winfree Smith.[16] In a minority-voice article he was likewise concerned to retain a positive role for Scripture and was particularly cautious about the abiding value of most of biblical criticism for the church.

Conclusion: Repugnance, Biblical Criticism, and Modern Use of Scripture

It is time to return to the question posed earlier: What positive value can be placed on biblical criticism? This, it seems to me, is the question raised by the Baltimore Declaration, by "Scripture, reason, tradition" proponents, and by the church and the world in the late twentieth century. For nearly two centuries, diverse forms of biblical criticism have dominated the intellectual life of theological institutions abroad and, to a lesser degree, in this country. For at least the entirety of this century, Episcopal clergy have been trained in biblical studies fully under the domination of historical-critical methodology. While the influence on laity and larger ecclesial decision making may be more "trickle-down" in character, nevertheless there has been no clear rival to the methods, approach, and general ethos of historical-critical interpretation of Scripture.

In my view, historical criticism plays no positive role whatsoever.

16. See Smith, "Dominical Authority in Time."

Its only proper role is negative. It establishes the genre, form, possible setting, and historical and intellectual background of individual biblical texts. It shows how the Bible is not like other books, such as history books, novels, encyclopedias, comic strips, or medieval liturgical tracts. Its force is explanatory. Its entire rationale is to explain the origins, development, and final stabilization of biblical texts. It does this in order to address a modern dilemma, one that has its roots in the Renaissance, that developed its maturer form during the Enlightenment and the centuries that followed, and that now must contend with widespread secularity, postmodern intellectual trends, and a church in confusion and disarray.

This dilemma was brilliantly chronicled by the late (Anglican) Hans Frei in his book *The Eclipse of Biblical Narrative*. Prior to the eighteenth century, the Bible was thought to cohere with the world it described, directly and without "authorial" imagination or interference. The distance from God to world to text to reader was potentially (when available in the vernacular and without clerical overlay) quite narrow. One need only read a sample of the accounts of sixteenth-century Bible translators (Erasmus, Tyndale, Cranmer, Luther) to get a clear sense of this cohesion. This cohesion was splintered with the rise of modern historical, social, literary, and natural sciences.

Now this is an absurdly brief summary of Frei's and others' observation. What historical-critical method was designed to do was to explain the cleavage between the biblical text and the world it described by recourse to theories of authorship, editorial shaping, and historical and social settings. Or, to use the language of the Thirty-Nine Articles, conceived for a very different purpose, the first task of biblical criticism was to spot *repugnance* in the literature — that is, evidence of narrative disjuncture, literary seams, logical breaks, and inconsistencies. Portions of the text so dissected were then assigned to various "human writers, redactors, and editors" (Baltimore Declaration, article 7) and were argued to occupy various points of standing on a reconstructed historical and social map. A distinct chronology, worldview, and intellectual, social, religious, and theological history were then imaginatively reconstructed that very soon overshadowed the world of the biblical text in its own form and literary configuration.

Prior to this "eclipse" of the biblical narrative, the "tradition" of biblical interpretation had been concerned with other matters, but chief among them was the identification of organizing patterns and types that would provide unity and cohesion across a very complex two-Testament story. And of course major concern was devoted to proper hearing and obedient response to these narratives, which were thought to give the church life in this world and access to the divine life. In no small measure (look only at the history of art), it was the biblical world that informed our world, and not the reverse. But the reverse is precisely what the modern world — with its rival descriptions of cosmology, psychology, natural science, anthropology, and now even theology — has bequeathed to us.

In my judgment, the patterns of inclusivity and modernity that the Baltimore Declaration is at pains to repudiate are nothing more than attempts to address a world very far removed from the climate of confessional statements the document imitates and to a certain extent participates in. Much of the inclusivity agenda is carried out with an awareness of and indeed enthusiasm about the conclusions of biblical criticism as a critical discipline, which has the (positive) capacity to render the biblical world interpretable, but which in so doing domesticates the Bible and leaves it impotent truly to change our church, our world, and our life before God. The Baltimore Declaration correctly spots this threat. My only caveat is that even in its mild endorsement of biblical criticism as a positive good it confuses the true role that biblical criticism can and must have if the church is to gain life from its Scriptures again.

What, then, is the proper role of biblical criticism? First, it is to exercise its explanatory function in helping us to appreciate the letter of the biblical text in all its foreignness and complexity. It is to teach us to be close readers, straining to hear something other than our own voices. Second, it is not to confuse its explanatory function with matters of exposition, ethical and theological application, or simple rhetorical persuasion. Explanation is not the same thing as *kerygma,* exposition, synthesis. Third, it is to restrict itself to the task of spotting "repugnance," of showing how it is that the Bible is not a simple, single-authored document, free of seams and tensions — literary, theological, logical.

In all of these ways, then, biblical criticism has only a preparatory function. It is not to be used as an end unto itself. The true goal of biblical interpretation for the church is not to ignore or deny but to move beyond "repugnance." Here the method of biblical interpretation associated with the work of Brevard Childs comes as a welcome complement to prior critical proclivities.[17] Childs is concerned with the

17. See the following works by Childs: *Biblical Theology in Crisis* (Philadelphia: Westminster Press, 1970); *Introduction to the Old Testament as Scripture* (Phila-

biblical text in its final, stabilized form, the form in which it is (generally) presented to the church in liturgical settings, devotional reading, and some forms of biblical study. Canon has implications for the text itself and for the seeking of synthesis and patterns of figuration, but it likewise self-consciously identifies the context in which it works as ecclesial. The Bible expects a certain type of readership: it is not an inert positive, even as it retains this potential eternally, but requires also the assistance of the Holy Spirit.

In making important distinctions about the character of the biblical text and the proper context for interpretation, a canonical approach can positively harness the negative function of biblical criticism in such a way as to bridge the chasm presently separating the biblical text from the modern world. It fully recognizes the "eclipse" identified by Frei, and it stands in the same general tradition as that which gave rise to biblical criticism as a positive tool. But it now seeks to move beyond the limited descriptive role of biblical criticism as historical or social analysis toward a recovery of the abiding theological value of the biblical text in its final form.[18] Here the tension between "Scripture" and "tradition" is not overcome by reducing the Bible to a "tradition process" just like our own (so Cuthbertson), but rather by refusing to set "objective biblical criticism" over against so-called precritical exegesis by the church, identifying the former with "Scripture's plain sense" and the latter with crude, primitive, fanciful exegesis from an unenlightened age.

Article 20 of the Thirty-Nine Articles captures nicely one concern of Childs's canonical approach when it states: "The Church may not expound one place of Scripture, that it be repugnant to another." Critical method is trained to spot "repugnance" as part of its responsibility as a literary science. But the church has a charge to move beyond this spotting of "repugnance" toward an assessment of larger unitary purpose, something that most preachers instinctively understand. It is precisely here that the critical biblical training given to preachers seems most unhelpful. Because the canonical approach works with the negative findings of biblical criticism and then pushes beyond these findings toward a reading that is "non-repugnant," it offers the preacher,

---

delphia: Fortress Press, 1979); *The New Testament as Canon: An Introduction* (Philadelphia: Fortress Press, 1984); *Old Testament Theology in a Canonical Context* (Philadelphia: Fortress Press, 1985); and *Biblical Theology of the Old and New Testaments* (Minneapolis: Fortress Press, 1993).

18. This abiding theological value cannot be reduced to propositional statements.

teacher, pastor, and devotional reader an alternative to either biblical criticism or a fundamentalism concerned with riveting the biblical text to a worldview with which it never should have been expected to cohere.

There is much about the Baltimore Declaration that should give the church hope. It represents a courageous effort to say something of positive theological value to a church in disarray. But it is time for the church to move beyond both propositional arguments from Scripture and a biblical criticism whose chief purpose must now be shifted into a new arena if it is to have any abiding afterlife. Anglicans are notorious seekers of the *via media*. Here is an opportunity to seek what is positive about the concerns of both fundamentalism and biblical criticism (understood as a negative, preparatory discipline), but then to move beyond both toward the recovery of a method for interpreting Scripture that is not antagonistic to "traditional" readings from earlier ages, that is capable of reasonably assessing literary "repugnance," but that is finally concerned to find larger unitary purpose and theological synthesis in a book on whose proper interpretation the life of the church depends.[19]

19. There is not space in an essay such as this for further illustration of the sort of approach to biblical interpretation that I am advocating. For further study, see above all Childs's *Introduction to the Old Testament as Scripture*, where fresh readings of individual biblical books are set forth on the basis of a canonical approach. From the perspective of a systematic theologian, see also George Lindbeck's essay "The Story-Shaped Church: Critical Exegesis and Theological Interpretation," in *Scriptural Authority and Narrative Interpretation*, ed. Garrett Green (Philadelphia: Fortress Press, 1987), pp. 161-78.

I have presented my own exegetical proposals in several essays, including the following: "Isaiah 1–66: Making Sense of the Whole," in *Reading and Preaching the Book of Isaiah* (Philadelphia: Fortress Press, 1988), pp. 105-26; "Job: Full Structure, Movement, and Interpretation," *Interpretation* 43 (1989): 5-15; "The Prophet Moses and the Canonical Shape of Jeremiah," *Zeitschrift für die Alttestamentliche Wissenschaft* 101 (1989): 3-27; "The Divine Council: Temporal Transition and New Prophecy in the Book of Isaiah," *Journal of Biblical Literature* 109 (1990): 226-46. In two recent books I have attempted to move beyond the older historical-critical reading of Isaiah toward a fresh canonical interpretation: *Zion's Final Destiny: The Development of the Book of Isaiah* (Minneapolis: Fortress Press, 1991) and *Isaiah 1–39*, Interpretation Commentary Series (Louisville: Westminster/John Knox Press, forthcoming).

II. Claiming Orthodoxy

At the Crossroads of Dogma

RUSSELL RENO

THE deepest impulse behind confessions of faith is doxological, the desire to speak the truth about God, to give voice to the beauty of holiness in the fullest possible sense. However, the particular forms that historical confessions take are shaped by confrontation. Their purpose is to respond to the spirit of the age by rearticulating in a pointed way the specific content of Christianity so as to face new challenges as well as new forms of old challenges. As a result, formal confessions are characterized by pointed distinction. They are exercises in the drawing of boundaries where the particular force of traditional Christian claims is sharpened to heighten the contrast between orthodoxy and heterodoxy, between true faith and false belief. There is just no way around this. Confessions involve the affirmation of something quite definite with a seriousness and specificity that entails the repudiation of countervailing beliefs. Moreover, and more importantly, these affirmations and concomitant repudiations are more than just scholastic exercises. As they shape our beliefs, confessions structure our identities.

Given their real content and practical importance, formal confession is more than a challenge to those who would diverge from tradi-

---

I would like to thank C. FitzSimmons Allison, Alvin Kimel, Eleanor McLaughlin, Ephraim Radner, Philip Roulette, George Sumner, Kendell Soulen, and David Yeago for reading various drafts of these thoughts on the Baltimore Declaration and providing me with encouragement and substantive guidance in revision. This essay has greatly benefited from their community of theological reflection.

tional claims. Confessions are also and perhaps more often enemies of the fainthearted and apathetic, the complacent and lukewarm. For in their integrity, Christian commitments are far harder than we would like them to be, and the inner purpose of formal and polemical statements of faith is to raise the stakes of commitment by portraying spiritual possibilities in the most contradictory possible terms. The goal is to force choices that are otherwise suppressed in the muddle of everyday belief and practice. As a consequence, in many cases and especially in the case of the Baltimore Declaration, formal confessions are not resented by those who are directly challenged and repudiated — quite often the heterodox relish clarity of opposition since they, too, see the need for clear definitions and commitments — and instead the Erasmian fence sitters are the ones who raise objections to the substantive *form* of confession, even as they genuflect in some vague way to the content. The sharpness of the contrasts, especially as they are cast in the negative form of denial and rejection, invites exactly the sort of criticism that one would expect from those who would like to remain untroubled by theological concerns. Surely, it will be thought, the religious life cannot rest on the spirit of condemnation. For is it not written, "Judge not, that you be not judged" (Matt. 7:1)? Moreover, could such emphasis on doctrinal statements really be healthy? Perhaps there is some truth in the Declaration's formal statement, but should we not seek to unify and include those who are seeking God in good faith rather than dividing according to antiquated doctrinal issues? For did Jesus not say, "He that is not against us is for us" (Mark 9:40)?[1]

---

1. One particularly prevalent criticism of the Baltimore Declaration expresses no disagreement, instead complaining that such confessional statements are not only unnecessary ("redundant catechizing") but also dangerously authoritarian ("an inquisitorial spirit"). This criticism shows very little insight into the conditions necessary for arbitrary exercise of authority and is an illustration of the practical significance of a theologically substantive confession.

The allusion to Erasmus should bring to mind a peculiar juxtaposition in Erasmus's exchange with Luther over the question of free will. In Erasmus's introduction to his treatment of the question, he bemoans the need to dispute doctrinal matters. Can we not be free, he wonders, from these troubling debates? Are they not the very demons of disruption and division? And where does Erasmus find liberation from these demons? He finds his freedom, interestingly, in acquiescence to the authority of the church. And is this acquiescence born of the conviction that the church teaches true doctrine? No, his acceptance is grounded in the belief that it matters not what the church teaches! In this acceptance Erasmus sees a solution to disruption, division, nasty encounters, and heated debates. But at what price is this peace bought? I challenge any critic of substantive theological confession to find a more powerful defense of naked ecclesiastical authority. All

To pose these objections, however, is to ask the Baltimore Declaration to set aside the classical role of confession that brings to bear on every situation the New Testament metaphors of division and differentiation — the wheat from the chaff, the sheep from the goats. The underlying assumption of this essay is that, troubling though such images might be for the modern believer, the need for differentiation, even separation, is inescapable. As the wisdom of the New Testament recognizes, such distinctions sharpen the reality of our spiritual situation. Real alternatives face us, and a clear grasp of the fact that a decision is both necessary and decisive can precipitate difficult commitments and painful moments of personal and institutional self-definition. And if the Christian life is really about difficult personal and social transformations, then the challenging and potentially divisive character of formal confessions cannot be set aside without serious consideration. As a result, whatever our final assessment of the content of the Baltimore Declaration, we cannot hide behind the foolish claim that Anglicanism is "nonconfessional." We must take the Baltimore Declaration's form as a confessional challenge seriously precisely as a potentially difficult occasion for hard choices about the future shape of Christian belief.[2]

---

that is taught must be accepted, all that is commanded must be obeyed, for to fail to accept and obey disrupts, and there are no convictions, no doctrines, and no beliefs that warrant disruption.

Luther was very alive to this extraordinary defense of authority for its own sake masquerading as irenic agnosticism, and the vigor of his defense of the need for theological assertions is motivated by his recognition that the freedom of Christians is grounded in the very real *content* of Christian belief. The perspicuity of the New Testament is crucial. Only in light of its clear content can one gain some critical leverage over the many sedimented layers of authoritative traditions and institutions that constitute the church in which we live. For Luther, given the liberating effect of theological content, preaching what cannot be known, as Erasmus does, only binds us to those given structures and beliefs of the present. It is the word of hopeless dependence. In contrast, preaching what *can* be known frees, for it gives the believer a place to stand strong against the various "authorities" of this world. In this respect, any confession that accurately states the true content of faith is the very opposite of authoritarian, for such a confession is the crucial foundation of Christian liberty.

For texts relevant to Luther's debate with Erasmus, see the prefaces of "On the Freedom of the Will" and "On the Bondage of the Will," in *Luther and Erasmus: Free Will and Salvation*, ed. E. Gordon Rupp and Phillip S. Watson (Philadelphia: Westminster Press, 1964). For an extraordinarily lucid account of the basic issues at stake in Erasmus's rejection of confessional conviction, see Terence Penelhum's *God and Skepticism: A Study in Skepticism and Fideism* (Dordrecht: D. Reidel, 1983), esp. pp. 18-39.

2. Writing in the early 1930s, when the need for difficult choices was so immediate, Dietrich Bonhoeffer recognized the need for the "No!" as well as the

Not only are these choices real; they are also doctrinal and dogmatic. The Baltimore Declaration willingly adopts the devices and terminology of doctrine. Many believe that such concerns are secondary, if not alien to Christianity. For them, the heart of the matter is the experience of God, spiritual development, moral action, the sense and taste for the infinite. Compared to these supposedly more significant realities, the (very old) theological disputes found in the Baltimore Declaration are seen as nothing but the dead letter. This essay will try to disabuse the reader of this false dichotomy. By analyzing the specific content of the Declaration I shall attempt to show the personal and spiritual significance of the theological commitments expressed. I hope to convince the reader that the content of the Baltimore Declaration is a very alive letter that has decisive significance for the ways in which we understand our relation to God. Just as the reader cannot escape behind the canard that Anglicanism is "nonconfessional," so also the reader cannot try to sidestep the challenges of the Baltimore Declaration by dismissing it as "mere" doctrine. In both respects, then, as formal confession and as doctrinal statement, I refuse to allow the Erasmian fence sitter to dismiss the Declaration without engaging its *content*.

And what of the content? There is little question but that the choices posed by the Declaration will cut deeply into our future as a Christian people. Only the faith of an ostrich with its head firmly planted in the sand can ignore the whirlwind of theological reinterpretations of traditional Christianity.[3] From moral questions to Scrip-

---

"Yes!" of Christian proclamation. He observed, "There can be no credal confession without saying 'In the light of Christ, this is true and that is false!' The concept of heresy belongs necessarily and irrevocably with the concept of credal confession." We need to recognize that, for Bonhoeffer, the need for Christian judgment does *not* serve political or institutional purposes. It is *not* a mechanism of suppression or a technique for consolidating institutional power. For Bonhoeffer, the "No!" of repudiation serves the broader, singular "Yes!" of gracious affirmation, which he insisted was the center of the Christian vision. As he wrote, "The concept of heresy emerges from the fellowship of the Church and not from an absence of love. Only when man does not withhold the truth from his brother, does he deal with him in a brotherly way. If I do not tell him the truth, then I treat him like a heathen. When I speak the truth to one who is of a different opinion from mine, then I offer him the love I owe him" (*Christ the Center* [New York: Harper & Row, 1978], pp. 75-76). For Bonhoeffer, to fail to confess clearly and forcefully is to fail to love sincerely and fully, and as he grew to realize, the disastrous consequences of this double failure know no limit other than the mercy of God.

3. Remarkably, a certain sensibility prevails that seems to agree with the affirmations of the Baltimore Declaration but finds it "unnecessary." Certainly, this

ture, from liturgy to the language of the creeds, proposals abound for new directions and new formulations. Throughout this consideration of the Declaration, I will do more than try to convince the reader that the choices posed by doctrinal confession are real. I will also argue the case for orthodoxy, and I will argue in two ways.

First, I will press the case for religious honesty and integrity. The hope that *all* of the new religious possibilities of the present are consistent with the tradition such that they may be affirmed as legitimate developments of major themes or helpful recoveries of forgotten or suppressed dimensions of the Christian witness is wishful thinking. Incompatible alternatives are already upon us, and they need to be recognized as such.[4] An interest in or affection for Christian symbols,

---

thinking goes, God does not "need" the Episcopal Church to "defend" his revelation! However, this is naivete that begs the question. The Baltimore Declaration is not "defending" anything. It is addressing the real issue: Does the Episcopal Church need to defend the integrity of *its* character as a witness to God's revelation? Does the Episcopal Church need to rearticulate its identity with a forcefulness appropriate to the contemporary context?

Assessing the contemporary context is difficult. However, for those who harbor the illusion that radical revision (e.g., repudiations of the Trinity, rejections of Jesus as the Son of God, affirmations of the unity of Creator and creature) is not at least a *major* current in modern Christianity, I suggest sampling some of the following, all of which are written by professors of theology at "mainline" seminaries: Tom Driver, *Christ in a Changing World: Toward an Ethical Christology* (New York: Crossroad, 1981); Carter Heyward, *Touching Our Strength: The Erotic as Power and the Love of God* (San Francisco: Harper & Row, 1989); Gordon Kaufman, *The Theological Imagination: Constructing the Concept of God* (Philadelphia: Westminster Press, 1981); Sallie McFague, *Models of God: Theology for an Ecological, Nuclear Age* (London: SCM, 1987); Rosemary Radford Ruether, *Sexism and God-Talk: Toward a Feminist Theology* (Boston: Beacon Press, 1983); and a useful collection of recent work, *Lift Every Voice: Constructing Christian Theologies from the Underside*, ed. Susan Brooks Thistlethwaite and Mary Potter Engel (New York: Harper & Row, 1990). In every case, though with varying degrees of sophistication, clarity, and moral passion, these representative theologies set aside (if they do not bitterly repudiate) basic Christian doctrines.

4. One of the crucial developments in recent theological work is the clearmindedness of leading revisionists. They have no illusions about the choices that their new visions impose upon the church. For example, religious pluralist Paul Knitter speaks forcefully about the "theological rubicon" that separates traditional Christian claims about the centrality of Christ from his own vision of the centrality of the Ultimate. See Knitter, "Hans Küng's Theological Rubicon," in *Toward a Universal Theology of Religion* (Maryknoll, NY: Orbis Books, 1987), pp. 224-30, as well as his extensive treatment of the need for and implications of pluralism in *No Other Name?* (Maryknoll, NY: Orbis Books, 1985). Knitter, like fellow pluralist John Hick, has no illusions about what it means to cross the Rubicon. As Hick observes, "The older theological tradition of Christianity does not readily permit religious

finding Christian liturgy uplifting and ennobling, needing the pscho-
logical continuity of Christian self-identification — this is *not* the same
as believing in Christ. And at a certain point we need to be honest with
ourselves and with others when our choices simply remove us from
anything recognizably consistent with the Christian tradition.

But our confessional choices are governed by more than con-
sistency. Being in continuity with the tradition also means living in the
light of God's redemptive love. As such, a second way of arguing
naturally follows upon the first. Throughout I also try to show that
orthodoxy saves, that a consistent confession of the very "old" way of
talking about God is bound up with the possibility of a very new way
of life. Here I pose the choices facing contemporary Christians in a
manner that is unabashedly apologetic. In this way I try to return to
the doxological root of all confession. For at the heart of this essay on
the Baltimore Declaration, an essay that like the Declaration is properly
described as polemical, is the desire to convince the Erasmian fence
sitters who populate the Episcopal Church in such great numbers that
we are offered the real possibility of living in the beauty of holiness, a
beauty formed by the jagged clarity of the cross.

*   *   *

Broadly speaking, the Baltimore Declaration is directed against a pervasive predisposition that acknowledges the need for, if it does not
openly advocate, what the preface to the Declaration describes as "a

---

pluralism. For at its center is the conviction that Jesus of Nazareth was God — the
second Person of the divine Trinity living a human life" (*God Has Many Names*
[Philadelphia: Westminster Press, 1980], p. 26). Thus, such a conviction must be
set aside. Though Hick might tolerate the *myth* of God incarnate, *faith* in a triune
God is repudiated as incompatible with a commitment to religious pluralism. The
Son of God cannot be carried across the theological Rubicon.

We ought not to thank Knitter and Hick simply for a clear account of the
deepest choices facing us with respect to interreligious dialogue. The fact that they
swim so easily through the water of modern liberal theologies of experience as they
build their cases for radical revision is a powerful witness to the fatal weakness of
much of what has passed for "mainstream" theology in this century. This weakness
is evident as well in the criticism of liberative theologies. The focus of this criticism
is not methodological. Both theological liberalism and the theologies of liberative
praxis agree on the priority of human experience in theological inquiry. But, as
Susan Brooks Thistlethwaite and Mary Potter Engel observe, "The question of *whose*
experience serves as the basis of theological reflection is the critical question for
understanding the difference between theologies of liberation and Protestant liberalism" (*Lift Every Voice*, p. 79).

thoroughgoing revision of the faith." How should we characterize this supposedly powerful and widespread sensibility that is driving the agenda of revision? A comprehensive answer to this question would involve an extensive survey of contemporary theological literature. I shall, however, forego that opportunity and instead shall give a far more general characterization, focusing on three flashpoints of controversy, which I call the three dogmas of modernity: inclusivity, relevance, and ambiguity. These are not "secular" dogmas.[5] All three grow out of powerful religious intuitions, and as such they have a strong theological appeal as well as a general cultural currency. I shall attempt to give voice to this appeal in order to indicate the power of these dogmas over the contemporary Christian scene. Over and against these modern dogmas I shall pose the basic theological reasons that the Baltimore Declaration articulates for rejecting inclusivity, relevance, and ambiguity as the trinity shaping the Christian future. In this way I hope to bring clarity to both the real significance of doctrinal commitments that, though posed in a fresh way by the Baltimore Declaration, have always been central to Christian belief, and the frightfully clear choices that such doctrinal commitments pose for the future of the Episcopal Church.

Ambiguity or Clarity

The dominant dogma of modernity is ambiguity. This dogma has the most established pedigree in modern culture, and it underwrites the dogmas of inclusion and relevance. The dogma is multifaceted, but the gist of the matter is as follows: Because of the diverse historical character of Christian witness, the partiality of human perception and understanding, and finally, the ultimate mystery of the divine, all the propositions that constitute the core of traditional Christian belief are strictly partial, relative, and uncertain. In short, the relation of Chris-

---

5. No understanding of the present situation is possible if we insist on analyzing it as "secular." In spite of Harvey Cox's now twenty-five-year-old prophecies, the secular city has not come to pass. Instead of secularism, the many voices of modernity (or shall we say postmodernity?) seek to reconstruct our spiritual identities. The imperative is not worldliness; rather, the quest is for ever new forms of transcendence. As a result, the three dogmas constitute a *religious* challenge to Christianity. The question is what *kind* of spiritual identities we will have, not whether we will be "religious." For an account of the religious shape of modern Western culture, see Lesslie Newbigin, *Foolishness to the Greeks: The Gospel and Western Culture* (Grand Rapids: William B. Eerdmans, 1986).

tian claims to divine reality is highly ambiguous. In light of this ambiguity, any attitude of conviction or certainty is foolish at best, arrogant and "imperialistic" at worst.

This commitment to ambiguity needs to be unfolded. Consider the diversity of Christian witness. There is no single Gospel. There are, rather, four Gospels. Moreover, as our understanding of early Christianity increases we can see that the New Testament itself is but a limited part of the very diverse set of ancient responses to Jesus of Nazareth, many of which have traditionally been suppressed as heretical. Further, the New Testament is a document written in the language, metaphors, and thought-forms of ancient Mediterranean society. Not only is the New Testament the narrowly "orthodox" view; it is also only the view of one historical moment. To these insights about the historicity and diversity of the New Testament we might also add the general observation that the writers of the Gospel stories, like other finite human beings, were limited in their insight and understanding. We should no more expect the author of John's Gospel to possess a finality of understanding than any other devout believer. Finally, the proponents of ambiguity seek to certify these insights by appealing to the traditional claim that God is, finally, a mystery, and as such, no merely human statement can articulate divine identity.

The central role of the dogma of ambiguity is evident. To the extent that Christians remain unsure of the true nature of God, there can be no clear standards by which to judge other religions. All possibilities are included in the ambiguity of faith. Moreover, to the extent that choices are, in fact, made, these choices cannot be determined in light of the ambiguity of faith. How, after all, can we gain the certainty necessary for action from a fundamentally ambiguous source? Instead, we sift through that unclear and chaotic collection of claims, images, and symbols that we call Christianity according to our own self-identified experiences of transcendence.[6]

---

6. In "Interreligious and Interideological Dialogue: The Matrix for All Systematic Reflection Today" (in *Toward a Universal Theology of Religion* [Maryknoll, NY: Orbis Books, 1987]), Leonard Swidler utilizes the logic of ambiguity to justify an appeal to experience. He begins by evoking the philosophical authority of the dogma of ambiguity. For Swidler, the historicization of truth, the sociology of knowledge, the limits of language, and the omnipresence of interpretation "de-absolutize truth." In light of these "insights" into the relative nature of truth, Swidler joins Paul Knitter in proposing a "new model" for understanding Christian claims. "The new model reflects what our pluralistic world is discovering: no truth can stand alone; no truth can be totally unchangeable. Truth, by its very nature, needs other truth. If it cannot relate, its quality as truth must be open to question" (p. 12,

In light of the underlying importance of this dogma, a response is crucial for those who intend to defend traditional Christian self-understanding from the revisionary spirit of the age. The insight of the opponents of the dogmas of ambiguity is simple: the very saving quality of the divine initiative on our behalf is its clarity. If we cannot be sure about the most basic elements of the Christian proclamation, then we can be sure of nothing in our relation to God. And if we are sure of nothing in our relation to God, then we are, finally, left to our own devices. But this is, of course, precisely the *problem.* To be left to our own devices is to be left in bondage to our own self-affirmation, a self-affirmation that blinds us to God and our neighbor. Jesus' role, so the story goes, is to redeem us from this bondage. And this redemption, comments Paul, is through faith. That is to say, we are redeemed from the ambiguity and the false clarity of our own self-affirmation by a clear faith that Jesus of Nazareth really is the Christ, the Messiah. For Paul, all else follows from this basic faith. This is so because the natural upshot of seeing clearly that Jesus is the Messiah is the imperative uttered by John the Baptist: "He must increase, but I must decrease" (John 3:30). Only when one has taken seriously this imperative can one respond to the needs of someone other than oneself.

The Baltimore Declaration begins and ends with unequivocal affirmations of the clarity of God's revelation. The first article attempts to give expression to the real presence of God in Christian life and worship. We are not dealing with spectral symbols or soluble images; our liturgical practice is not grounded in the shifting sands of merely human projections; our confessional identities are not formed by the vain graspings of the human imagination. No, as the first article emphatically affirms, Christianity is characterized by the fact that it is centered upon the "proper name" of God, a name that can be used with the certainty (and fear) that it really places us within the presence of God. The final article of the Declaration reframes this confidence in light of God's proper story. Just as the proper name is the real name of God, so also the Scriptures constitute the real story of God's dealings with his creatures. Given the centrality of the dogma of ambiguity, we need to listen carefully to the affirmations and repudiations of these two articles, which frame the Declaration as a whole.

---

quoted by Swidler from Paul Knitter, *No Other Name?*). And what of the truth of the man Jesus, who could not "relate" to Pilate's questions? Woe unto the man of sorrows, whose travails forced him to stand, and die, alone. Swidler is untroubled. As is nearly always the case for patrons of ambiguity, the "openness of truth" defaults to human self-projection. In the end, for Swidler, "we must build our 'theological' language, terms, categories, and images on our common humanity" (p. 20).

In the first article, the affirmation is simple: the triune name, Father, Son, and Holy Spirit, is "proper." That is to say, it "faithfully identifies the Savior and Lord of the Holy Scriptures." At stake here is the question of God's clear identity as the One who is for us — Emmanuel. As such this appeal to the concept of "proper name" serves the deepest possible purpose: in the trinitarian name, especially in its use in worship and prayer, we are dealing with the one and true God. However unfathomable that name might be, however impenetrable we might find the promises made in baptism and in eucharistic fellowship, we can be confident in (and feel constrained by) the fact that this name "locates" us at the center of the divine drama. The appeal to "proper name" is useful in explicating this claim. Just as a contract signed by a person using his own unique and proper name binds him to performance of the conditions of the contract regardless of the "mystery" of his personality and the ambiguity of his motivations, so also the revelation of God's proper name binds God to the terms and conditions of that revelation. In this way, the definitive "properness" of the trinitarian name is a guarantee of the basic reliability of the apostolic tradition in creed, polity, and liturgy that has developed "under" the triune name.

Of course, theologians have chosen a number of devices for affirming the reliability of the apostolic tradition that do not use the device of "proper name." Roman Catholics have emphasized the magisterial authority of the see of St. Peter. Eastern Orthodox theologians have made much of the historical integrity of the "divine liturgy." Anglicans have often appealed to apostolic succession. Protestant groups have emphasized scriptural authority. The advantage of the Declaration's approach is that it does not seek to secure the reliability of faith through the medium of transmission — through apostolic succession or liturgical continuity, for example — nor does it rely on theologically contested notions of ecclesiastical or scriptural authority. Instead, the Declaration begins with the trinitarian affirmation that is an expression of the content of faith. As such, the triune name is a clear expression that includes within itself all other aspects of the "apostolic experience of Christ." In this sense, and unlike other strategies for expressing the reliability of the Christian tradition as a genuine and decisive revelation of God, the affirmation of the threefold name has a very broad ecumenical reach. Here, *the* identifying feature of genuine Christian faith and practice is the use of the triune name. We do *not* fully and reliably identify true and faithful responses to God by appeals to polity, the use of peculiar vestments, doctrinal subtleties, or certain forms of scriptural interpretation. Thus, an appeal to a quite clear criterion for reliable witness — we can easily recognize when an individual or a community is or is not using the triune name — can liberate us to be as ecumenical as is possible within the constraints of that clear criterion.

Any evaluation of this appeal to God's "proper name" must take seriously the fact that *some* articulation of the identifiability of God is indispensable to Christian faith.[7] As noted above, to the extent that we admit that the challenge of the Christian life is perseverance in the midst of temptation and hardship, an assurance that we are dealing with God in the Christian context would seem to be an absolute necessity. The most minimal degree of assurance would be that, at the very least, Christianity has the right vocabulary with which to grapple with the divine mystery. Christians might fail to use the triune name rightly, might fail to make the meaning of that name real internally, or might misunderstand the import of all that the triune name stands for in the wider context of the tradition and contemporary experience. However, the name itself remains "proper," and in spite of all the inevitable failures, it keeps the individual believer and the community of worshipers from wandering into the many wildernesses of complete falsehood and self-deception. To deny that the name of God invoked at every turn in traditional Christian worship is reliable, true to its subject, binding God in some important sense to "be there," is to suggest that doubt rather than faith would be the appropriate virtue in a life spent seeking God. And we have every reason to believe that doubt, that condition of uncertainty and ambiguity, only leaves us vulnerable to the unspoken "necessities" of contemporary life.[8]

---

7. Karl Rahner writes, "What is fundamental to the idea of Christian truth, anterior even to any definite content of its message, is that here and now, in God's name, God's word went forth unambiguously demanding obedience, and continues to go forth perpetually, ever new. The reference back precisely to this event and to the authority that makes itself known in it belongs, therefore, to the essence of Christian truth" (*On Heresy* [New York: Herder & Herder, 1964], p. 8). For Rahner, the reality of Christianity as a religion of salvation is bound up with the clear, unambiguous status of its core content.

8. A victim of the distinctively new and modern form of ancient "necessities," Dietrich Bonhoeffer suggests that the ethical failures of German Christians may have grown out of a theological tendency to keep God safely shrouded in the "beyond" of unknowable ambiguity. Too often, he notes, "religious people speak of god when human knowledge (perhaps simply because they are too lazy to think) has come to an end, or when human resources fail — in fact it is always the *deus ex machina* that they bring on to the scene." Bonhoeffer rejects this god beyond the boundaries of knowledge. He observes, "The transcendence of epistemological

In the repudiation that follows this affirmation in the Declaration's first article, the authors of the Declaration try to foreclose this possibility. The Declaration affirms the triune name as definitive and unsurpassable. As a consequence, any attempt to modify or replace this reliable center of gravity is rejected. A popular example of this is an inclusive language modification of the triune name to Creator, Redeemer, and Sanctifier. Here we find an attempt to provide synonyms for a proper name. Difficulties emerge immediately. Who are we worshiping under this description? Do these three "concepts" require us to identify a fully *personal* God whose innermost identity is defined by the love of parent and child? Does the second term, *Redeemer*, force us to acknowledge that the life of a person in first-century Palestine, an individual "crucified under Pontius Pilate," is internal to the life of the one Eternal God? Does this new name do anything but direct our attention away from the drama of the Son, who endured the travails of a far country, by allowing us to refocus ourselves upon generic "religious" ideas such as creation and redemption? But what kind of creation? What kind of redemption? To a large extent, those who use this modified trinitarian formulation presuppose explicitly Christian content for these concepts. We should be clear, however, that such a modified trinitarian formulation does *not* name that content. The traditional name of Father, Son, and Holy Spirit does, and thus, to the extent that we confess that the particular Christian content of creation and redemption is decisive, we must persevere in the use of the name that does in fact do the basic work of naming — that is, identification of the true

---

theory has nothing to do with the transcendence of God," and he insists that "God is beyond in the midst of our life. The church stands, not at the boundaries where human powers give out, but in the middle of the village" (*Letters and Papers from Prison* [New York: Macmillan, 1972], p. 282). Only in the middle, as a real, identifiable presence, unequivocal, "not in weakness but in strength," can God meet and triumph over the all too real, all too ordinary and identifiable evils that cling to human life. The presence of God, real in the sense of being identifiable like all other things — indeed, perhaps more real because ultimately identifiable — is the key to Bonhoeffer's ethic of worldly responsibility. Warning against misunderstanding, Bonhoeffer writes, "I don't mean the shallow and banal this-worldliness of the enlightened, the busy, the comfortable, or the lascivious, but the profound this-worldliness, characterized by discipline and the constant knowledge of death and resurrection" (p. 369). A very specific God brings us to life, birth, and rebirth. Only by seeing this God in the clear light of day, only by awakening to the fact that Christianity is a "religionless" life that welcomes the foolishness of Emmanuel, God with us — with us in the perfectly ordinary way of having a *name* — can we enter into the dark night of discipleship. And "in so doing we throw ourselves completely into the arms of God, taking seriously, not our own sufferings, but those of God in the world — watching with Christ in Gethsemane" (p. 370).

subject. This feature of the triune name — that it points clearly and unequivocally to the story of the relation of the Father to the Son, which gives new and concrete meaning to salvation — cannot be gainsaid.[9]

In this attempt to drive home the clarity of God's revelation, a difficulty emerges. The issue turns on the uniqueness of the triune name. The Declaration states that God has "definitively and uniquely named himself in Jesus Christ." In this formulation, the Declaration seems to suggest that the trinitarian formulation is the *only* genuine and useful name of God. This suggestion turns on how we read the word *unique*. There are two possible meanings: (1) unique as "sole" or "singular," or (2) unique as "decisive" or "definitive." In this context, the first meaning is false to the Christian witness. One instance will suffice to show that the triune name is not the sole name of God: God has also revealed the name "I AM WHO I AM" (Exod. 3:14). Though this name might not be "proper" in the sense that the triune name is proper, it is certainly not a false name of God.[10] This should lead us to recognize that the only possible reading of the claim that the triune

9. The inescapable concreteness and truly present human and worldly shape of the Christian vision is absolutely basic to the life of faith. Unreformed by the triune name, a straightfoward religious sense of *mysterium tremendum* leads away from rather than toward the cross. As Karl Barth observes, we subsist in a perennial desire for the safety of a purely transcendent God: "O man; how you try to flee and save yourself and secure your own safety, inventing a God in himself who is only an object, who in his peaceful unity will not beset us on all sides [Ps. 139:5], who will not scan us behind, before, and from above with his eyes, but who on the far side of his subjectivity will be enthroned by us at a safe distance" (*The Göttingen Dogmatics*, vol. 1 [Grand Rapids: William B. Eerdmans, 1991], p. 101). Throughout Barth's vast corpus the theme is ever present. The triune name constantly redirects our religious passion back toward the very present and immediate drama of the man Jesus who was called the Christ. Only by this redirection can the diversity of human experience come under the *kyrios Iesous* (cf. pp. 102-3).

10. Though the revealed name "I AM WHO I AM" is not false, Emil Brunner suggests that this name has, in fact, been misleading within the Christian tradition. For Brunner, the speculative urge to link the God of Christian revelation to the concept of Being finds all too useful material in the "I AM" of the Old Testament formulation. As a result, emphasis shifts away from the particular Person whose identity is disclosed in the proper name and comes to rest in a generic metaphysics of the divine nature. This speculative danger suggests the need to guide our responses to the many names of God by the definitive witness of the proper name. Brunner is aware of this need, although his own meditations on the name of God circle rather awkwardly around the triune name. This indirection is perplexing, especially since the triune name identifies so decisively the particular relations of divine identity and action, rather than the speculative universality of a Supreme Being or the ultimate "I AM." Cf. Brunner, *The Christian Doctrine of God: Dogmatics*, vol. 1 (Philadelphia: Westminster Press, 1949), pp. 117-37.

name is definitive and unique is that this uniqueness is a reinforcement of the basic meaning of definitive: unsurpassable and decisive, final and "proper," but not necessarily sole or exclusive.

In light of the possibility of other names of God, in our faith and practice we might well call upon God in a number of different ways. Here we *could* experiment "with names and images created by our fallen imaginations or supplied by secular culture," or more pertinent still, those names and images suggested by the diversity of the very apostolic witness that the triune name summarizes. An affirmation of Father, Son, and Holy Spirit as the "proper" name of God in no way proscribes nicknames, honorific titles, or functional descriptions. God is not misdescribed as Wisdom or Love, nor is God mistakenly spoken of as Creator or Lord. To follow the basic line of thinking suggested by the Declaration we need to affirm the triune name as proper or definitive, but we need not presume that this affirmation closes off avenues of exploration. In fact, the clarity of the triune name provides the very light with which to explore the fullness of human experience. As a consequence, to confront the dogma of ambiguity, the basic faith that needs to be affirmed is that the triune name is *definitive* in the sense that it really and reliably names God.

Having set aside singular uniqueness as an overzealous specification of the definitive quality of the divine name, we can attend to the consequences of the first statement of the Declaration. Two practical conclusions follow. First, names repugnant to the triune name are proscribed. It is one thing to acknowledge that, although a person has a proper name, that same person might be known under other descriptions. It is quite another to claim that a person might have contradictory names or self-descriptions. A simple instance of contradiction is the description of God as hate. This clearly violates the relations among the Persons implied in the triune name. More narrowly and more relevant to the contemporary context, names that mimic the threefold formulation in modified terms are deeply problematic. For example, though one might entertain images of divine motherhood, one could not insist that God can be named, even proximately, as Mother, Daughter, and Holy Spirit. Similarly, though one is certainly drawn to an understanding of the different modes of divine activity — creative, redemptive, and sanctifying — one should not use the modalistic formulation Creator, Redeemer, and Sanctifier, even as a supplement to rather than as a replacement of the traditional name. In both cases, the formulations cannot help but give the impression of replacing the traditional name, and as replacements they drive a wedge between God's inner self as named in the Trinity and God's actions as described in the Old and New Testaments. The female trinity does so by virtue of the brute contradiction between the names used and the specific content of the Christian story, and the modalistic trinity drives a wedge insofar as it reduces the specific content of that story to vague generalities. As a consequence, neither name can serve as the touchstone of God's promise to "be there" in Christian faith and practice.

The second practical upshot of an affirmation of the triune name as definitive has a broader application. The trinitarian formulation *names* God, but it does not in and of itself make God real for the individual. A great deal of consideration needs to be given to the texture of the tradition that the triune name includes, as well as to the distinctive personal and communal potential for understanding. In this way, the question of the many other names of God might be a question of great relevance, and experimentation with various alternatives might be quite helpful. The key question involves the role of approaches that, though not directly contradictory to the triune name, are not explicitly trinitarian. Here the logic of the Declaration's position is direct. This experimentation is affirmed if and only if it takes place within the context of an appropriate and unequivocal use of the definitive triune name. The search for new insights, or the renewal of old insights, is reliable, helpful, and nurturing only if it is a search that is centered around an unqualified affirmation of God's proper name. Specifically, if God is definitively named in the trinitarian formulation, then the decisive invocations of divine presence in baptism and eucharist must be done in that name. This invocation serves as a reliable ground for other dimensions of Christian life and worship where alternative names of God might be entertained — indeed, must be entertained. Under this definitive name, experimentation may be vindicated as an effort to plumb the depths of the mystery of the Trinity. Experimentation must, however, be repudiated if it is a search for an alternative.

Article 7 transposes the same issues regarding the definitive identifiability of God to the question of scriptural authority. Here, the Declaration wants to say nothing more than that the Holy Scriptures constitute a perspicuous and reliable witness to God's true identity. Just as Father, Son, and Holy Spirit is God's proper name, the Bible tells God's "proper" story. As a consequence, similar repudiations follow. The "plain testimony" of the scriptural witness may not be gainsaid by appeals to extrinsic criteria. Of course, this does not foreclose some serious questioning grounded in the peculiar twists and turns of the very same "plain" testimony, not to mention suggestive poetical and allegorical moments. Moreover, some serious doubts based on the integrity of the text itself might be raised about received interpretations of key passages. However, like our images of God, the exploration of the abundant possibilities of Scripture must take place *within* an affirmation of these canonical writings as decisive and definitive. The Bible is, in a word, authoritative — it tells it like it is. This does not mean that no other resources provide insight into the divine; definitive and unique are not the same as sole and exclusive. Rather, the affirmation of biblical authority means that what we read in Scripture really describes the divine reality; it is a reliable and trustworthy witness by which other sources must be tested.[11]

In both statements the authors of the Declaration give clear expression to a crucial choice facing contemporary Christianity. Either we will affirm the reliability or "properness" of the credal and scriptural traditions, or we will adopt the dogma of ambiguity. This is a very real "either/or," not one created by the artifice of theological abstraction. The first choice is a commitment to a life spent discovering the difficulties, pleasures, and challenges of a certain identifiable truth. It is a choice to live as a *specific* kind of person. The second choice is to build

11. Here we need to set aside the "fundamentalist" *reductio*, which is too often used as a bludgeon to beat away any appeal to the authority of Scripture. At issue in article 7 is *not* some peculiarly modern commitment to either the literal, propositional inerrancy of every jot and tittle of the Bible or a magical, oracular doctrine of direct scribal inspiration. Literalism as a theory of the form or transmission of scriptural authority is not the upshot of the classical doctrine of inspiration. In this respect, the Baltimore Declaration echoes Calvin's broad affirmation that "all right knowledge of God is born of obedience" (*Institutes* 1.6.2). For Calvin, the material content of a disciplined and obedient waiting upon the witness of the Holy Spirit is found in the canonical texts of the church (cf. *Institutes* 1.7.4). No ornate literalistic theories need be promoted to insure, as Calvin does, that the proper object of this obedience is Holy Scripture. Thus, an obedient waiting in the textured world of Scripture is not to be confused with an apotheosis of the literary artifact called the Bible. The text is not to be treated as a compendium of divinely spoken truths to be directly applied in every situation and circumstance. Instead, as the Declaration makes clear, we can leave open the exact form of the text's power to reveal God's identity and purpose (propositional? literary? allegorical? poetical?). We need only affirm that the text is the decisive *center* of the Christian community's attempt to respond faithfully to God's revelation in Christ, and that our acceptance of the authority of this text gives reliable focus to our own attempts at faithful response. As a result, all developments within the formation of Christian identity, both personal and communal, must find their justification and purpose within this reliable center, even though justification and purpose may not, and in some cases cannot, take on direct propositional form. The doctrine of inspiration requires nothing more than the acceptance of this decisive authority, but it also requires nothing less.

one's life around spiritual possibilities rather than actualities. It is the project of being a generically spiritual person or (and this is almost always the same) a fragmented person torn in different directions by forces within the self and society that offer a multitude of options in the haze of ambiguity. If Christianity is, in fact, a religion of salvation, then being found in the first choice is far more consonant with the deepest purposes of the Christian message than remaining lost in the second.

Further, the choice between clarity and ambiguity has everything to do with our relation to our neighbor. In the seemingly "responsible" refusal — who could be so presumptuous? — to affirm a definitive or proper name for God hide troubling consequences.[12] For ambiguity can be quite a comfort when we are challenged with the possibility that the pure otherness of God might be present in the familiarly alien faces of the sick and the poor, the widow and the orphan, the hungry and the naked. Far better would it be for us if we could look into the eyes of the stranger and release ourselves with the "humble" acceptance of the "fact" that our ideas and words for God are always too small, too narrow, and too grossly inadequate to warrant anything really *difficult* from us. Yet, if in the "arrogance" of faith we choose the revealed God, Father, Son, and Holy Spirit, we may well find that this clarity penetrates very deeply into our lives, and that the direction of travel — away from self and toward others — becomes as proper as the name

---

12. In his *Commentary on Prayer Book Studies 30* (New York: The Church Hymnal Corporation, 1989), Leonel L. Mitchell engages in this ritual of epistemic humility. He observes, "Whether in prayer or in academic theology, the language in which we speak of God is necessarily metaphorical, or analogical. We cannot use human words to speak of God in the same sense in which we use them to speak of human beings." Forgetting, perhaps, that speaking of God in the same way that we speak of human beings is exactly what the Gospel stories do, Mitchell continues with a classic statement of the dogma of ambiguity: "Any image of God or theological construct we may have is too small, too narrow, and grossly inadequate." Moreover, to support this dogma, he adduces the authority of the Cappadocians, the scholastics of the Middle Ages, the Reformers, the Caroline divines, and contemporary theologians! At work here is a crucial shift in the notion of divine mystery. Leaving off contemporary theologians, for the authorities marshaled by Mitchell, the mystery of God is *within* the revealed certainties of faith. The mystery is that we *can* speak of God with the familiar words we use in everyday life. Echoing the assumptions of modernity, for Mitchell the mystery has shifted. Instead of the mystery of the God who has overcome the barrier between the divine and the human, we now have the barrier of mystery, a generic state of human rational and linguistic inadequacy that God seems powerless to overcome. In the end, we need to wonder wherein the presumption lies: in the credulity of faith or in the smug assurance that we cannot speak of God?

that serves as the origin and destination of the Christian life. As a consequence, if the Christian life really is about salvation and service, *some* affirmation of a specific clarity in the Christian witness, *some* confession of God's specific identifiability, is an indispensable part of Christian proclamation, and the triune name would seem to be an indispensable foundation for that affirmation.

Our Relevance or God's Relevance

The dogma of ambiguity leads directly to the dogma of relevance.[13] If the life of faith has no clear center of gravity, then there is every reason to try to discern new faiths that satisfy contemporary demands and needs. Taking for granted the corrosive assumptions of the dogma of ambiguity, the turn to relevance trades on the assumption that traditional beliefs, scriptures, and liturgies cannot be the essence of religion. What matters is one's "spirituality." To this end, any amount of tinkering is permitted as long as it is vindicated by gains in "spiritual" or moral or political "growth." After all, if the objective form of Christian identity is marked primarily by ambiguity and uncertainty to the degree that no statement, story, or conviction has definitive status, then surely we are permitted to construct beliefs and practices to suit con-

---

13. Erasmus's approach to doctrinal questions in his dispute with Luther over free will illustrates this connection clearly. For Erasmus, the doctrinal "subtleties" of Christianity are marked by an obscurity that is best set aside in the interest of promoting the practical benefits of Christianity. He writes, "There are some things which God has willed that we should contemplate, as we venerate him, in mystic silence; and, moreover, there are many passages in the sacred volumes about which many commentators have made guesses, but no one has finally cleared up their obscurity" (*Luther and Erasmus*, p. 39). In one respect this is surely true. Many portions of the Bible are difficult to fathom. The Reformers were well aware of this difficulty. For example, Calvin refrained from writing a commentary on the Book of Revelation. He found himself unable to say anything clear or certain about the text. However, when Erasmus turns to identify the obscurity of Christianity, he does not point toward the apocalyptic dreams of John of Patmos. Instead, he singles out the Trinity, the incarnation, and original sin! *These* are the obscure matters that Erasmus thinks Christians should pass over in silence. The key move to relevance is evident when Erasmus turns to that which Christians may, in fact, know with certainty. Doctrinal and scriptural ambiguity is resolved by appeal to morality. As Erasmus writes, "There are other things about which God has willed to be most plainly evident, and such are the precepts of the good life" (p. 39). The puzzling uncertainty of belief may be set aside in the interests of the clear dictates of the practical life. With this move from ambiguity to relevance Erasmus proves himself to be a true *pater* of modernity.

temporary circumstances. Indeed, given the gray inconclusiveness of doctrinal ambiguity, are we not positively obligated to turn to the clear dictates of *our* needs, desires, and religious sensibilities? This approach is evident in many areas: environmental, liberation, black, gay, and feminist theologies, to name but a few. The Declaration does not address all of these approaches. Instead, it focuses its attention mainly on feminist theologies of relevance.

Here the argument is that male images of the divine undermine women's spirituality. The notion is that male figures (most specifically, Father and Son) perpetuate (if they are not in fact the causes of) patterns of social domination. In fact, for some feminist "historians" the origin of Christian notions of divine fatherhood and sonship is the male urge for domination. The obvious consequence is that women can never lead healthy, life-affirming spiritual lives unless they are able to center their spiritual identities around female images of the divine. Thus, female images of God are affirmed as decisive and relevant to women's spiritual journeys, and these images are substituted for the unhelpful and sometimes destructive male images that have predominated in the past.

Responding to the triumph of this limited, "my experience" relevance is the focus of article 6. From the outset, homage is paid to the universality of divine love. The emphasis upon universality is crucial to the task of defeating the spurious modern dogma of relevance. Nurturing, protecting, and caring, God's love knows no invidious distinctions between black and white, Jew and Gentile, male and female. As Christ died for the sin of the whole world, so also the gospel of that act is preached to the whole world. In other words, the definitive clarity that we find affirmed in articles 1 and 7, the specificity of Father, Son, and Holy Spirit, as well as the specificity of ancient Israel and Jesus of Nazareth, is not and cannot be an impediment to a universally efficacious expression of divine love.

In the repudiation, this line of thinking takes on clear contemporary meaning. False inferences from the specificity of God's revelation to contemporary life are set aside. It does not follow that because God chooses to express divine love in the form of words or deeds of a man named Jesus of Nazareth that the words and deeds of men are somehow exalted by virtue of a shared "maleness." Nor could one infer that traditional notions of fatherhood are happily affirmed by the fact that the word Father is integral to the triune name. In both cases a simpleminded isolation of a single dimension of the Christian witness leads to the false assumption that this single dimension can be mapped directly onto single features of everyday life. For example, this train of thought supposes that if Jesus is male, then God's purposes in Christ are relevant only to a corresponding maleness in present experience.

Strangely, this kind of thinking seems to have wide currency in the contemporary context.[14] Yet, as a pattern of inference, it leads directly to absurdities that, if true, are devastating to Christianity. For example, such assumptions lead to the claim that if Jesus lived in Palestine, then Jesus' life only has relevance for those living in present-day Palestine. Or, more refined still, if Jesus lived in ancient Palestine, then his life was relevant only to those living in ancient Palestine. The highest expression of the one-to-one mapping of similar features to similar circumstances is a reduction of Jesus' death to the narrowest kind of relevance, for if the decisive message of Christianity is found on the cross, then that message is only relevant to others who die on crosses. This may seem like a silly claim that no one would make, but it is certainly implicit in the pattern of thought that would restrict the relevance of Jesus to a corresponding male circumstance in the believer. In each instance, the assumption prevails that a particular feature of the Christian witness applies only to the very same particular feature in current life.

The troubling consequences of this narrow approach, which assumes that particular kinds of things (e.g., Jesus' maleness) only have relevance to other things that share that particularity, are explicitly set aside in the doctrine of the incarnation. There, the central claim is that the man Jesus of Nazareth — the full and concrete particularity of a fully and completely human person — has universal significance, the univer-

---

14. For example, Episcopal Divinity School professor of theology Carter Heyward writes, "Christology is actually an exercise in patriarchal logic" ("Jesus of Nazareth/Christ of Faith: Foundation of a Reactive Christology," in *Lift Every Voice*, p. 195). With this equation, Heyward is insisting that the ecumenical creeds of the church are irrelevant to any except "ruling class fathers and sons" (p. 198). But further, Heyward seems to reject more than the Chalcedonian formulation. She also has less than approving things to say about the New Testament terms and images associated with Jesus of Nazareth. She writes, "In worshipping Jesus as *the* Christ, *the* Son, *the* Savior, we close our eyes to the possibility of seeing that the sacred liberating Spirit is *as* incarnate here and now among us as She is in Jesus of Nazareth" (p. 197). Thus, for women to use traditional christological language "is much like trying to draw fresh milk from a very sick, tired, dry, sacred, and, as it turns out, very male goat" (p. 198). To overcome the old and sick stories of the New Testament, Heyward determines that feminist theologians "must set new terms for our faith"; otherwise the "christic meanings" of the New Testament will not become real for women (p. 199). For women, new life is not possible in the man Jesus of Nazareth; "christic meanings" must await the development of "new terms."

sal significance of a fully and completely divine being. This universal relevance contradicts all the common contemporary claims that the Christ of the New Testament does not "speak to" this or that experience. Since Jesus was white, the Gospel stories cannot fully address black experience. Because Jesus was male, the New Testament cannot adequately enrich women's experience. These kinds of claims are incompatible with the claim that God expresses divine love fully and definitively in Jesus Christ. If the life rendered in the Gospels really is the full and definite story of God's love — and such would seem to be the root insight guiding the use of the phrase "Son of God" — then it must, perforce, have comprehensive and not limited relevance.

The tradition's rejection of limited relevance is not accidental, for such thinking is invidious. What pastor has not heard a prominent parishioner bemoan the irrelevance of the itinerant religious leader, Jesus of Nazareth? He had no family, no job, no social role. In other words, he had no responsibilities. As a result, how could he recognize, much less speak to, the ambiguities of economic necessity? Political responsibility? Familial obligations? As a result, how can this man Jesus say anything relevant to the moral and spiritual troubles of the hard-working doctor, the company president, or the political representative? More chillingly, who can forget the endless train of scholars and theologians in this century and the last who gnashed their teeth over Jesus' Jewishness? Surely, they thought, *that* could not be relevant, and acting as forefathers of the many contemporary patrons of relevance, they simply expunged that which offended them and reshaped the particularity of Jesus to suit their own "special needs" — a "Nordic religious need" that differs only in particulars from the many special "needs" of the present: "women's experience," "black experience," "gay experience." In every case, the patrons of limited relevance turn the incarnation on its head. Instead of seeking the universal and truly relevant love of God in the particular man Jesus of Nazareth — a love that judges, redeems, and transforms us as we are, whomever and wherever we are — these high priests and priestesses of the moment universalize their particularized identities and judge the man Jesus accordingly.[15]

15. We would be entirely mistaken if we assumed that all concern for the present ethical and especially political reality of Christian faith implicates us in the dogma of relevance. Not all concerns for liberation reverse the implications of the incarnation. Indeed, striking differences emerge in a consideration of politically oriented theologies. Consider this key statement by Gustavo Gutiérrez: "To know God is to do justice" (*A Theology of Liberation* [Maryknoll, NY: Orbis Books, 1973],

The refusal to accept the universal relevance of the particular witness of Jesus Christ is closely linked with the second suggestive line of thought found in article 6. The dynamic seems to be as follows: where the universal significance of Christ is denied, emphasis turns to the task of creating that significance. In other words, where the incarnational claim that God became human in Jesus of Nazareth is resisted, energy is shifted to finding God in one's own experience. Yet again, where the traditional affirmation that God's love is definitely expressed in the unfamiliar world of the gospel is rejected, the inevitable consequence is that we seek to find God's love in the familiar world of our own self-images as "spiritual" or "ethical" or "liberative" beings. In each instance the Declaration recognizes that the emphasis has shifted from salvation by God's love to salvation by our own efforts. Against this shift in emphasis the Declaration reiterates the traditional claim that God's grace is the sole and exclusive cause of salvation: we are justified by God's decisive action; we are not justified by our religious, psychological, political, or moral works.

And this is not "merely" a traditional claim. The incarnational affirmation of the universal relevance of Jesus Christ and the repudiation of perennial projects of constructing localized, particularized saviors according to self-identified localized and particularized needs ring true. How can the New Testament be a gospel, a word of good news, if it is but another spiritual catalogue of images and possibilities available for the project of self-salvation? How can *Christ* really be a word of grace and freedom if it is not a liberation from our limited range of experience and our self-determined needs? How can we have hope if, forsaking God's promise (singular!) in Christ, we must rely on the many spiritual alchemists masquerading as disciples who make so many promises to turn the leaden self-images of our age into gold? How can Christianity be a calling to love if it is not a challenge to the narrow scope of our self-involvement and self-understanding? How

p. 194). Remarkably, when Thistlethwaite and Engel comment on this classical insight in their liberation primer, *Lift Every Voice*, they reverse the arrow of implication: to do justice is to know God. Now we have a concern for justice that dictates the terms of faith rather than a faith that dictates the terms of justice. Thus Thistlethwaite and Engel feel no compunction in urging the "old" liberation theologians forward. They write, "One of the greatest tasks still facing [theologians such as Gutiérrez] is the acknowledgement that God is known *in* the struggle to make the connections between different struggles for justice around the world" (p. 80). In this "acknowledgement" we lose Gutiérrez's strenuous effort to explicate the way in which God frees us to be human, an effort that any responsible theology for the present day must take seriously, and we inherit the comical notion that *we* free God to reveal himself in our self-identified struggles for "justice."

can we ever see our neighbor if we are not confronted with a Christ who demands that we take him with the utmost seriousness precisely because he is universally relevant, whether we want him to be or not?[16]

When grace is costly, when God's love makes its very hard demands, an affirmation of universal relevance leaves nowhere to hide. When the call comes that tests us, a clear recognition that God does the saving cuts off the obvious excuse that we are not yet ready, that we must do something more to "prepare" ourselves, that we have to postpone the hard stuff until we have "worked things out," until we have "strengthened our spirituality," until we have found something that "speaks to" our experience. For it may well be that when we meet Christ in the neighbor, he "speaks against" us rather than "speaks to" us! In each of these instances, the search for relevance is the most profound modern manifestation of the perennial human inclination to escape the responsibilities of a relation to God in which divine love is the sole authority, and to turn inward to construct a much "freer" and more "personally satisfying" relation to a god of our own making.[17]

16. The banality engendered by the dogma of relevance is evident in the inability of patrons of relevance to respond to these questions. Tom Driver serves as a typical illustration. With regard to Jesus Christ, Driver proposes a paradigmatic subordination of Christ to present "needs." He writes, "The primary question we ask is not who Jesus was, nor who the disciples thought he was, nor what his early followers had in mind when they called him Christ. The decisive question is who Jesus is today, what *we* have in mind if we call him Christ" (*Christ in a Changing World* [New York: Crossroad, 1981], p. 15). With this approach, Driver suggests the comforting thought that God is who *we* have in mind — how *very* exciting! No wonder, then, that Driver describes himself as "angry" at the "Christofascism" of the "traditional" belief that God is in Christ rather than in our minds. For such an "authoritarian" conviction does not allow us to transform, as Driver does, God's self-revelation into our own self-discovery. After all, an Easter faith requires us to believe that a man who has suffered death now lives at the center of our lives. The implications of Easter elicit a testy response from Driver: "[The affirmation that Jesus is the Son of God] does not express *my* relation to Jesus nor that of Christians who appear to me most ethically sensitive" (p. 16). In light of this rejection of all that might challenge *me* and *my* circle of self-selected friends, what exactly is "radical" about Driver's theological approach?

17. For a suggestive account of the issues at stake in the perennial urge to reconstruct Christianity to suit the needs of a specific race, a specific culture, or a specific gender, see Jon D. Levenson, "The God of Abraham and the Enemies of 'Eurocentrism,'" *First Things* 16 (Oct. 1991): 15-21. While Levenson may outrun himself in his ambitious attempt to link diverse moments in the triumph of relevance, a common theme emerges: the scandal of the particular form of Jewish and Christian revelation. At every turn, the patrons of relevance explain away such "restrictions" in the interest of some "deeper," more "liberating," more "nurturing," more "natural," or more "universal" reality.

The Declaration's affirmation of the universal saving scope of God's love in Christ sounds a resounding "No!" to each of these escapes into the illusions of relevance.

Peter's Denial or Paul's Affirmation

The motto of the dogma of inclusivity is broadly this: One God, many paths. The proponents of inclusivity think along the following lines. If God is truly a God of love, then his love must extend to all his creatures. Moreover, if his love is an affirmation (and if love is anything, then surely it is an affirmation of the beloved), then God's pervasive love must be an affirmation of us all. Finally, if who we are is diverse (Jewish, Christian, Buddhist, or Hindu), then God's universal love must be an affirmation of us all in our diversity. Ergo, God's love affirms the integrity of our Christianness, Jewishness, Muslimness, etc. In other words, God's love is inclusive; it vindicates and makes efficacious the many paths that humans have historically taken to the divine. As a consequence, Christians ought to recognize as valid and legitimate the insights and traditions of other religions.

In order to follow through with this conclusion, the proponents of inclusivity must reinterpret the specific content of traditional Christianity. In interfaith dialogue, the difficulties of inclusion center on the fact that traditional Christian belief takes certain specific details about the tribes of Israel and, more problematically still, the person called Jesus of Nazareth to be absolutely decisive. This is evident in the part of the creed that reads, "[Jesus Christ] was crucified also for us under Pontius Pilate. He suffered and was buried." The creed proclaims that the death in first-century Palestine, under the authority of an identified Roman authority, of the person named Jesus who was called the Christ has ultimate significance for all of humanity. The dogma of inclusivity challenges this convergence of specificity and ultimate significance. The dogma asserts that other religions, other constellations of specificity, offer equally legitimate paths to God. As a result, there is nothing *necessary* about specific Christian claims.

Articles 3, 4, and 5, concerning knowledge of God, salvation, and the special role of Judaism, address the issue of the necessity of the Christian constellation of specific claims. At each turn the Declaration gives voice to the scandalous claim that the universal and eternal God is bound up with the particular nation of Israel and the man Jesus of Nazareth. This affirmation does not turn its back on inclusivity. Indeed, more than the other two dogmas of modernity, the dogma of inclusivity rests on a sensibility that is profoundly orthodox. The problem, however, is that the sensibility comes unhinged from its true source within the Christian frame of reference. There is no question but that inclusivity must be affirmed, but this affirmation must always be under the sign of the cross, a sign that directly contradicts the spirit of the modern dogma of inclusivity. Thus, whatever inclusivity might mean, it is an inclusion *into* Christianity, *into* the specificity of "crucified . . . under Pontius Pilate"; it is not an inclusion *in addition to* Christianity.

In article 3, the Declaration handles the question of authentic knowledge of God. Here the affirmation of the Trinity as the proper name of God is developed more fully. The triune name identifies the Son as the historical person whose life is "proper" to the inner life of God. As a result, knowledge of the life of that person, known to us as Jesus of Nazareth — as well as knowledge of God's covenant with the people of Israel, into which Jesus was born, lived, preached, and died — is genuine and authentic knowledge of God. There may be a great deal of intratextual as well as historical-critical questioning about the specific details of this history and life. However, just as the inner mystery of the Trinity does not undermine its role as the definitive center of gravity for Christian faith and practice, neither does the welter of questions about the historical person Jesus of Nazareth prevent him from playing the definitive role in our quest for knowledge of God.

But why *should* Christ play a definitive role? After all, is not the purpose of religion knowledge of God, and is not the story of Christ but a means to that end? Why should we tie God so closely to this rude story? Are we not confusing the messenger with the message? Here the Declaration gives voice to an uncompromising trinitarian Christianity. Yes, answers the Declaration, the purpose of religion is knowledge of God, but as Christians we know that God is Father, Son, and Holy Spirit. Moreover, the Son is no distant abstraction. Rather, he is that person Jesus of Nazareth who lived in a particular time and place and whose fate is told to us in the New Testament. As such, the one and eternal God is fully and completely identified with a discrete set of events and a particular set of stories. Consequently, "saving and authentic knowledge" of God — that is to say, the kind of knowledge born of the intimacy of genuine relation between God and the human person — will always be knowledge of *that* God who "was crucified also for us under Pontius Pilate."

The Declaration recognizes that to say anything else involves the fundamentally anti-Christian presupposition that Christ's life and death are not integral to God's eternal identity. And this would seem to be implied in the banal inclusivity that insists that any number of different religious beliefs and practices are equally "valid." Such a conviction entails the assumption that Christ is inessential, that we might somehow know and love some God who is above the events in first-century Palestine. The consequences of this unfortunate assumption are disastrous. The motivation that lies behind the Declaration's repudiation of "Christ vacant" approaches to God is the recognition that to deny that true knowledge of God is bound up with knowledge of the crucified and risen Lord is to say that Christ's life and, most poignantly, his death are somehow dispensable. To put the matter somewhat differently, to claim that God is knowable independent of Christ, as proponents of modernity's superficial inclusivity of acquiescence insist, is to say that Christ's words on the cross, "My God, my God, why hast thou forsaken me?" (Matt. 27:46), are not transfigured in the divine presence, which is total, but rather are final, deadly, and hopeless.[18] To avoid such a conclusion, the Declaration firmly repudiates the notion that God can be anything other than God in Christ.

Given the importance of this repudiation, we must also understand its limits. The Declaration acknowledges that God is free to reveal himself outside the historical Christian proclamation of Jesus of Nazareth as the Christ. As such, it might well be the case that individuals beyond the sphere of explicitly Christian belief could attain some degree of "authentic" knowledge of God, even though such seekers have no knowledge of the events that are reported in the New Testament. As we saw in the discussion of the Trinity as the proper name of God, the definitive and ultimate status of God's identity in Christ is

---

18. In a very telling conversation transcribed in *Lift Every Voice,* Mary D. Pellauer gives expression to the hopelessness of the dogma of inclusion. She observes that women who struggle to overcome the experiences of violence articulate new spiritual insights. However, these new voices are constrained by the fear of perpetuating the domination that is the root of their own suffering. Regardless of the vocabulary of theology, the anxiety of inclusion is at work. Pellauer questions, "If we start talking this language [or any language about God], will we offend people whose beliefs are different from ours? Will we be caught in the same imperialistic trap that's trying to turn everybody into my theology?" (p. 182). And this anxiety builds as one's sensitivity to inclusion increases. The only hope is that we might be destroyed so that our identities can be dispersed into the four winds of spiritual possibility, threatening nobody's self-image. This, then, would seem to be the upshot: we must pray that we should be fully and finally lost so that we will not be found in the imperialistic trap of a faith that knows its own identity.

not exclusive in the sense of being the sole or unique existential possibility for knowledge of God. As a result, individuals who participate in other religions may be dealing with the triune God in their philosophies and theologies, and dialogue with such individuals and serious study of such philosophies and theologies may be very enriching as Christians continually seek to live in the fullness of Christ.

At first glance, the repudiation found in article 3 gives the impression of closing off this dialogue since it denies that we may look to this sort of dialogue as integral to gaining knowledge of God. This is not the case. The warning issued by the Declaration does not concern the fruitfulness of conversation. Instead, as the article tries to make clear, at issue is our interpretation of the final destination and significance of such dialogue. The free offer of God to those outside the historical proclamation of Christian Scriptures cannot be understood as independent of God's triune identity. That free offer is only "saving and authentic" if it leads towards God's true identity in Christ. The crucial affirmation remains. Christ is the unequivocal center of any noetically significant relationship to God, however hidden that center might remain. Thus, as Christians, we may not forsake that center in the interests of humility: we must always be humble in assessing our grasp of God's revelation, but the deeds done on our behalf are not ours to negotiate away. Nor may we entertain the false hope that somehow we can sidestep the hard message of the cross by discovering some "higher" unity in interreligious dialogue.

In article 4 the question of truth is transposed to the question of salvation. Where Christ is the proper revealer of the divine nature, he is also the proper agent of divine salvation. In Christ the definitive act of reconciliation and redemption is effected. At this point, the definitive act of salvation is persuasively linked to the language of exclusivity. Salvation, in contrast to revelation, lends itself to exclusive status. We might have degrees of knowledge, but salvation is an all-or-nothing affair. Either our sins are forgiven and we are made right before God, or we are not. Partial salvation makes little sense. As a result, the definitive act of salvation is decisive, unique, and all-inclusive. Thus, although there can be proximate forms of knowledge subordinate to the definitive knowledge of God revealed in Christ, there cannot be partial salvations unified in the definitive salvation in Christ. Salvation simply *is* the act of atonement and redemption offered in Christ. In this sense, then, the Declaration is quite justified in moving from an emphasis on the definitive to the unique.

For the patrons of inclusivity, this isolation of the specific life and death of Jesus of Nazareth as the unique and indispensable point through which all God's saving love reaches out to the world and through which the world must respond is anathema. "Christian imperialism in its purest form!" they cry. But what is the alternative? What would it mean to say that Jesus Christ is not the unique act and offer of God's saving love? What would it mean to say that other acts and offers might serve as paths to God's eternal affirmation of love? To say such a thing would have direct consequences for our reading of the New Testament. If other acts and offers are possible, then the events that befell the man Jesus of Nazareth have no final and inescapable significance. Concretely, if the man Jesus is not the unique and indispensable center of all that gives life in our relation to God (the "Son of God," in traditional credal terms), then the person about whom we read in the Gospels should be venerated, perhaps, as a valid spiritual possibility, but should never be worshiped as divine actuality.[19] More directly, the death of this "optional man" is, strictly speaking, unnecessary. Given other possible saving moments, there is no ultimate need for *that* death. The cross is but one possibility among many, one of the many offers, one of the many paths. Such a conclusion raises pointed questions. Why all the suffering in the Christian story? Why the ugliness of its central symbol, the cross? Why death if there are other ways to salvation? Would any but a perverse God allow those horrible events recounted in the passion narratives if there were *other* possibilities open for the expression of divine love?

These issues may seem to be mere theological abstractions —

19. A patron of inclusivity, John Hick is well aware of the triumphalist logic of the central Christian conviction that Jesus is the Son of God. As a result, he identifies revision of this belief as the necessary starting point for any sensible, responsible approach to Christianity. Setting aside this trinitarian claim would make Christianity a more suitably "open" member of the community of "world religions" (cf. *God Has Many Names,* p. 26). The Baltimore Declaration agrees completely with Hick's assessment of the central, "triumphalist" logic of the claim that Jesus of Nazareth is (in the words of the Nicene Creed) "the only-begotten Son of God, begotten of the Father before all worlds, God of God, Light of Light, Very God of Very God, begotten, not made, being of one substance with the Father, by whom all things were made." The difference turns on the kind of "liberation" we need in the late twentieth century. For Hick, we need to be liberated from the constraints of "mythological" thinking to become generic religious seekers with a full spectrum of symbolic options at our disposal in our quest for the One. For the writers of the Baltimore Declaration, we need to be liberated from the spectral realm of religious possibilities in order to be found as a very specific and concrete biblical world, as children of God in Christ. We cannot underestimate how much turns on the real spiritual differences that this choice entails.

hypothetical questions about events that occurred in the first century — but the threat of inclusivity cuts more deeply. The Declaration identifies a loss of the church's mission of evangelism. This is more than a concern for what is often thought of in the limited sense of "missionary activity." It is not only those outside of the church but also those within it who need to be "evangelized," for being a disciple of Christ is a task without end. And in that task, without a forceful affirmation of the indispensable centrality of Christ, how can *I* keep my eyes on the cross? When my reading of the New Testament confronts *me* with the demand for suffering or sacrifice, why should *I* view that suffering or sacrifice as in any sense necessary? If God's offer in Christ is not unique, then why not select some more attractive, less frightful offer? The dogma of inclusivity has consequences for the pulpit as well. How can Christian leadership preach a cruciform discipleship when other paths are available? Indeed, given the obvious truism that *unnecessary* suffering is evil, is the preacher not obligated to direct others *away* from the cross whenever possible? In both cases, the dogma of inclusivity challenges far more than the "missionary mentality." An inclusion that sells the inheritance of faith cuts to the quick of Christian identity and raises the possibility that in both pew and pulpit we might talk *ourselves* out of being followers of Christ.

The threat to Christian identity posed by the dogma of inclusivity takes on pointed significance in article 5. There the Declaration considers the special case of Judaism. The concern is straightforward: how does Christianity square a definitive witness to Christ with the special role assigned by God to the people of Israel? Here the Declaration is clear that no amount of moral anxiety about anti-Semitism or remorse about the many failings of so-called Christian culture can compromise the affirmation of Christ as the sole and universal savior. Thus, all discussion of Judaism must take place under the sign of the cross.

In spite of the inexorable triumphalist logic of God's salvation in Christ, the difficult question of *how* Christ's salvation is made real for those who live according to the promises made to Abraham and Moses is central for an understanding of Jewish-Christian dialogue. How are Jews saved "in Christ"? Here I think the Declaration needs to introduce an important subtlety to prevent misinterpretation. The Declaration needs to give stronger scriptural content to its affirmation that Jews are "a reverend and blessed people" and to revise its repudiation more precisely to indicate the special status of Judaism, while still firmly setting aside the spirit of Esau that characterizes so much of contemporary Jewish-Christian relations. Specifically, with respect to the special status of the Jews, Christians must maintain the universal Lordship of Christ and at the same time argue that by virtue of God's covenant with Israel, a covenant that is already Christ-formed, the gospel of Jesus the Messiah has a unique impact when proclaimed to the Jews.

In its insistence that Jesus be preached to Jews, it would seem that the Declaration overreaches. To be sure, this overreaching is likely motivated by the fact that the patrons of inclusivity dictate that Christians may not or should not preach to Jews. Clearly this must be rejected, for it entails either a patronizing withholding of the truth or a denial that Christ *is* the truth. In his meditations in Romans on the peculiar response of the people of Israel to the full revelation of their identity, Paul neither overreaches nor patronizes nor denies. For him, all that is real and true and saving in the Mosaic covenant is included in God's definitive revelation in Christ. As a consequence, Paul feels free to speculate that the ultimate meaning of Judaism is to serve the saving purpose of God in Christ — triumphalism without a doubt. However, the specific form of Israel's service in Christ is "disobedience." That is to say, precisely by being Jews rather than Christians, Jews continue to participate in the divine plan of salvation. Paul affirms Judaism as, paradoxically, "in Christ" by rejecting the gospel so as to continue in the Mosaic covenant. Jews are "saved" by failing to see what Paul recognizes as the evident meaning and purpose of the history of Israel.

The question of Judaism is a specific instance of the general case of the "mediation" of God's love. All that is true and saving is so to the degree that it is "in Christ." This in no way prejudges the particular ways in which others come to speak the truth or to attain salvation — there may be as many ways as there are nicknames of God. By virtue of the unique relationship of the Old and New Testaments, Christians can know that the Mosaic covenant stands as a peculiar instance in which the center remains efficacious even as it is hidden, and the gospel saves even as it is rejected. Jews are the chosen people, and as such, the trajectory of Jewish history after the death of Christ is woven into the fabric of God's purposes in Christ. They need not be evangelized because, in the peculiar and conflictual ways that Paul sought to understand, Jews already live within the logic of God's saving love.

We need to recognize that other religions are not necessarily bound to God's revelation in Christ and that there can be no confidence that they are, in fact, paths that follow Christ even in their disobedience. We may hope and guess as to the ways in which other world religions participate in the revelation of God in Christ. However, there is no promise, no certainty, that the many religious forms that Christians encounter throughout the world serve God's purposes, hidden or revealed. Hence, the Christian relationship to, for example, Islam needs to be quite different from the Christian relationship to Judaism. Where Christians *may* preach to Jews without the urgency of conversion, they *must* evangelize members of other world religions. In spite of this difference, however, in both cases the Declaration is justified in insisting on an affirmation of the decisive, definitive, and culminating role of Christ in the drama of divine love.

The "may" — and certainly the "must" — conflicts with the dogma of inclusivity. The irrevocability of the Mosaic covenant is sealed "in Christ"; the truth of secular philosophies is found "in Christ"; the saving power of the religious identities of Muslims and Hindus is given "in Christ." In each case the dogma of inclusivity is scandalized by the religious "imperialism" of insisting that all affirmations must be affirmations "in Christ." Yet, the compelling logic of the Declaration's identification of the definitive or "proper" status of God's revelation makes such an approach unavoidable. If Christianity really is about faith in Christ as the Son of God, and if the Son really is one with the Father, then everything that is in the Father is in the Son. That is to say, if Christianity really does ground itself in the triune name, then it is committed to saying that Jesus Christ fully participates in the ultimacy of God and that, as such, he is God, the Alpha and the Omega. As a consequence, to be a Christian is to say that, just as all things come from God, all things are also "in Christ."

A refusal to express inclusion "in Christ" might stem from the conviction that the logic of Christianity is not clear enough to draw such conclusions. The refusal might also flow from a rather unappealing view that Christians must refrain from speaking their hearts because it might offend those who disagree — hiding the lamp under the bushel so as to avoid hurting the feelings of others. Finally, such a refusal may be the result of an uncertainty about whether Jesus of Nazareth ought really to be called "the Christ." None of these possibilities constitutes a promising way of moving forward into the fullness of God's love; each in its own way serves to keep the very peculiar texture of God's love in Christ at an arm's distance. For if we cannot speak to others with the full force of the phrase "in Christ," then we can hardly speak to ourselves the far harsher and far more scandalous and unwelcome word "in Christ."

Confession for the Future

The Baltimore Declaration is no blueprint for the future. It solves no perplexing moral questions. It dictates no canonical or liturgical action. It commands no particular pastoral approach. It sets no methodological agenda and writes no sermons. The Baltimore Declaration does, however, guide us through a historically decisive crossroads of dogma, a crossroads that has everything to do with the kind of people we will become. While the Declaration does not prejudge the evident mystery of where we are headed — both personally and as the corporate body called the Episcopal Church — it unequivocally affirms that the future is to be grasped only insofar as we are willing to stoop, as did Mary Magdalene, and look into the empty tomb. Renewal, revival, and rebirth are to be found only to the degree that the church is willing to live in the clear light of the triune God. Genuine leadership is possible only if the way forward is grounded in the ever New Testament. The truly revolutionary can be preached only to the extent that clergy are able to recognize that the Son on the cross is the Alpha and the Omega who can really challenge and transform a modern world that believes that it has seen it all. The living word of grace can be spoken only when we accept the fact that we live, not in the small world of our own experience, but in the firstborn of all creation. In each and every case, the Baltimore Declaration confesses that, for all the ambiguity of faithfulness in our *fin de siècle*, our hope can only be grounded in the faith that the Spirit leads into the clarity of the triune God revealed in Christ, into the inclusivity of the risen Lord, and into the universal relevance of him who was crucified for us under Pontius Pilate.

That the Baltimore Declaration poses these possibilities with confessional clarity is an important contribution to a church struggling, often unknowingly, with the dogmas of modernity. To say, as the Declaration does, that Christ's story is the proper story of God's purposes with his creatures is a direct and unequivocal challenge to the faith that succumbs to the sirens of relevance and sells its inheritance to purchase the cheap satisfactions of passing fashion. Such an affirmation is also a challenge to a faith that is ashamed of its own overarching significance and that sets aside the inclusion "in Christ" in order to affirm others with passionless civility rather than risk the discoveries of genuine interreligious confrontation. To say, as the Declaration does, that Christ reveals the proper name of God derails a faith that is grounded in the gray-on-gray of ambiguity and that, in the world of uncertainty, can find no point at which to withstand the forces of social and political "necessity." The choices are upon us.

When we choose our dogmas, we need to recognize that the Christian dogmas are both easier and more difficult than the dogmas of modernity. The clarity of revelation breaks through the ambiguity of our muddled thinking. The relevance of Christ overcomes our limited sense of who we are and what we need. The universal inclusivity of Christ is real enough to overcome our differences and make us one in him. Yet, though the offer is easy, the demand is hard. God's love is powerful enough to save us in spite of our disinclination; however, that love is also pure enough to demand our transformation. The clarity of truth creates the imperative to do the truth. The inclusivity of Christ reaches down into the deepest and most secret chambers of our hearts with a relevance that is cruciform. At the crossroads of dogma, the question we face both personally and as a church is whether we will do the easiest of things — *Credo!* — that leads us down the hardest of paths.

Light and Twilight: The Church and the Nations in the Drama of Salvation

GEORGE R. SUMNER

I. Overture: Setting the Stage

> *I charge you in the presence of God and of Christ Jesus who is to judge the living and the dead, and by his appearing and his kingdom: preach the word, be urgent in season and out of season, convince, rebuke, and exhort. . . . For the time is coming when people will not endure sound teaching.*
>
> 2 Timothy 4:1-3

IN its section on salvation (article 4), the Baltimore Declaration "repudiate[s] the false teaching that Jesus is merely one savior among many — the savior of Christians but not of humankind." The opponent here is the pluralist position, expounded most prominently by John Hick and Paul Knitter,[1] for this position denigrates specific religious claims in favor of an unknowable transcendence hidden equally behind all religious communities. Pluralism has abdicated the very task of understanding the Christian doctrines of revelation and salvation and so is appropriately rejected. But the pluralists themselves do not represent the real problem; their recent popularity points more disturbingly to a failure of nerve on the part of the church at large to commend the claims to universality and finality at the heart of the gospel.

---

1. The most important works of these authors are John Hick's *An Interpretation of Religion: Human Responses to the Transcendent* (New Haven: Yale University Press, 1988), and Paul Knitter's *No Other Name?* (Maryknoll, NY: Orbis Books, 1985).

To be sure, there are valid theological questions that theology must address with respect to the gospel's universal claim. Pluralism benefits from this tangle of problems, which worries many contemporary Christians. If theology could make sense of these legitimate issues, it would cut off pluralism's food supply. Believers may be uneasy about jettisoning the church's universal claim to salvation, but they worry, as have fellow Christians in earlier ages, about the salvific status of unbelievers. Today one wonders about the proverbial inhabitant of an isolated Chinese village, while theologians of the Middle Ages worried about the unevangelized child "raised in the woods" (a case they wrongly supposed to be largely hypothetical). Only a short step leads to the question about the status of the indeterminable number who have heard the gospel in some deficient or distorted way. What might be called a "hard" Augustinian view of this question, wherein the elect are only to be found among the baptized, violates more than just the sensibilities of modern people; it also calls into question for us the very theological principle Augustine himself meant to affirm, the universal sovereignty of God.

Likewise, many of today's Christians, while uneasy about an outright rejection of the church's claim to a unique, final revelation in Christ, are troubled by the diversity and seeming relativity of religions and cultures, an impression reinforced by modern social sciences. Within the confines of the church, the interest in and debate over indigenization is evidence of this concern. How is the church to make universal claims in a myriad of cultural settings, and how is it to overcome the charge of cultural myopia?

A general's most important decision is his first, the ground on which to engage the enemy. The Baltimore Declaration (understandably, given its genre as a confessional document) fixes its attention on the points of greatest polemical interest: a strong affirmation of the exclusivity of Christ as the agent of human salvation and the missionary zeal that is pinned tightly to this affirmation. The Declaration is correct in what it defends and in what it attacks. Yet it might leave an unfortunate impression. The reader might suppose that, if he or she imagines the possibility of the salvation of unbelievers, the urgency of Christian mission will proportionately decline. But the real problem is that the battle has been joined on alien territory.

Pluralism assumes a "flat" landscape stripped of temporal, historical differences. It would compare religious systems as so many dispensers of a generic product called "salvation," all of which line a single shelf, though with differing trademarks. Its account has a static, distant, abstract quality, as a result of which Christianity's claim cannot help but seem excessive. These opponents have excluded the factor of historical dynamism, the three-dimensionality or "depth" in the picture of Christianity that renders the Christian account coherent and credible.

The biblical narrative, on the other hand, conveys to the Christian a distinctive sense of history, that progression of times and seasons through which the church is in pilgrimage. As a result, other communities and claims cannot be accurately assessed by the Christian theologian independent of the "new thing" God has done in Jesus Christ. History cannot appear monochromatic. "Three-dimensionality" and historical perspective require the theologian to differentiate between the times "then" and "now" for the Gentiles; a belief or practice that might have been appropriate in the former times is superseded once the time for mission to the Gentiles has dawned. (This understanding of our present age will be explicated in detail in the section that follows.) So our thinking about the religions and cultures of the peoples of the world can never omit this added variable, the discernment of the times, the foreground and background determined by the ongoing history of salvation.

By contrast with pluralism's caricature, the normative Christian theological tradition did not understand itself first of all as a system of abstract concepts. Rather, it placed the scriptural narrative at the center and sought to convey the meaning of that narrative as it employed a variety of conceptual redescriptions. But the redescriptions always depended upon the narrative for their meaning, lest in each age the faith degenerate into some new sort of philosophical school or mystery cult. In spite of intense theological disputes, the consensus of the tradition understood the primary agent of the narrative of both the Old and New Testaments to be the triune God who has decisively worked the salvation of the whole world in Jesus Christ. This did not preclude but rather warranted theologians to reflect further on the various times and dispensations and so the various modes by which God worked the one salvation in Christ. To be sure, traditional theologians made sense in different ways of this "three-dimensionality," the dispensations of salvation, but they were unanimous in attributing salvation in all ages and for all human beings to Christ.[2]

---

2. Perhaps the clearest example in the history of theology of the orthodox insistence on "three-dimensionality" is Irenaeus, who sets out, in his response to gnostic systems that understood themselves as alternative dispensers of salvation,

The theological movement identified loosely as "narrative theology" seeks to restore the story to its central place and so to subordinate the diverse conceptual redescriptions theology must offer to explain that story. Such an approach promises to be a way of maintaining that "three-dimensionality" required to put the vexing contemporary questions I have mentioned in their proper context. Proponents of a narrative theology seek to read the Christian canon as a typologically united story with the crucified and risen Lord Jesus Christ at its heart. Hans Frei has traced how the Gospels, and in particular the passion accounts, themselves render for the believer the identity of Jesus Christ as the risen One. While Frei seeks precisely to focus on the meaning found in the narrative and to avoid the entangling questions of historical reference, he affirms that the believer can only think of the risen Christ so rendered as supremely real and necessarily present.[3]

Understanding what the New Testament means by the "risen" Christ requires attention to the meaning and associations of "resurrection" as found in the Old Testament (and especially in Daniel 12). The "resurrection of the dead" is first of all an eschatological expectation; to say that Christ is risen is to make an eschatological claim.[4] If Jesus Christ, risen even as the world still journeys toward its end, is the narrative center, then *this* peculiar narrative is distinguished by its uniquely eschatological shape. The unity of the narrative is found in the resurrection anticipated, described, and proclaimed. But the resurrection must also give narrative shape to subsequent human history; the single culminating event, God's kingship over the world, comes in a complex, twofold way: first, concretely in the death and resurrection of Jesus Christ, and finally and universally in the end of the world, the *Parousia*, the return of Christ. These two eschatological forms of the

---

a grand vision of salvation history as divine education. Jesus Christ is the typological fulfillment of the old Adam and the realization of the divine image promised in the kingdom, and so he is the focal center of all human history from creation to consummation. Within such a framework Irenaeus can imagine how the ignorance of the Gentiles who lived in the "childhood" of human history can be forgiven by and fulfilled in Christ, even though he affirms at the same time that the new age that dawns in Christ allows no rivals. For these themes see, e.g., Irenaeus *Against Heresies* 4.22ff., in *The Ante-Nicene Fathers*, ed. Alexander Roberts and James Donaldson, vol. 1 (Grand Rapids: William B. Eerdmans, 1979), pp. 493ff.

3. Frei, *The Identity of Jesus Christ: The Hermeneutical Bases of Dogmatic Theology* (Philadelphia: Fortress Press, 1975), esp. parts 4 and 5.

4. This well-worn word *eschatology* requires a definition. I use the term to refer, not only to the "last things" proper, but also to the way in which the impinging of these realities characterizes this final stage of human history.

one event draw borders around the life of the Christian and the continuing history of the world. All that the New Testament has to say about the life of the church is defined by this location in between.

To believe in the risen Christ rendered by this story is to understand the real world of time and space, the world of flesh-and-bone human beings, as a world belonging to, destined to be ruled by, Jesus Christ. One could equally well say that faith in the risen Christ makes a claim about the nature of human history, so long as it is clear that this claim is accessible only through the story itself, proclaimed, celebrated, and reflected upon in the community. In this essay I prefer the analogy to drama, for time and space are no longer neutral but are rendered as the time and space of the in-breaking end, the stage over which Christ presides and on which the church is called to act.

One must not understand such a position as *merely* perspectival, as if the scriptural story were just the church's own story, its own lens on the world, so as to be relevant only to the community's inner life. To be sure, the church must remember that there are other communities with other stories, but its entire story-shaped life amounts to a claim that *this* is truly how the world and history, time and space are to be understood. Here the work of Lesslie Newbigin is particularly helpful, since he has pioneered the conjunction of interest in narrative with reflection on the church's mission. He too can adopt the language of "perspective" or "lens," but he remains adamantly clear that the church offers this perspective in the public square with (to borrow a phrase from philosopher of science Michael Polanyi) "universal intent," for it is a claim to the truth — indeed, it is a claim about the eschatological truth, about how the world shall finally and clearly be.[5]

The epistemological status of the church's claim is consistent with the ineluctably eschatological character of its narrative. Its truth can only be a universal claim, for on the Lord's Day there can only be one truth for the whole world, but it is only on that last day that this claim will be clearly accessible for all. In the present time of the church this universal claim can only be made in the "scandalously" particular form of this weak and sinful community, proclaiming this story of this Jesus Christ. As a result the church must be especially clear to distinguish what it can and cannot know, what it must and must not claim. The church claims to know the world's destination in Jesus Christ, but how it is that all creatures will meet their end in the crucified, risen Lord

---

5. Newbigin, *The Gospel in a Pluralist Society* (Grand Rapids: William B. Eerdmans, 1989), chap. 3, "Knowing and Believing."

we cannot say. It is as if the Christian revelation shines the brightest light on the story of Christ, a light in turn projected onto the horizon of the end. Of this we must be confident. Wherever that story comes to be heard, the light also shines, illumining a corridor through history. A reverent, sober, hopeful agnosticism about how Christ's work will turn out in the still dim regions is required as well.

With this understanding of the scriptural narrative and of the nature of the church's claim in mind, I offer the main thesis of this essay. According to an abstract, "flattened" account of the Christian faith, mission might seem to be a secondary and practical matter. It might seem that one could first and separately understand the Christian claim, and then make a decision about mission, as if it were a kind of marketing or public relations decision. It would follow from such a view that mission is simply what each and every religion does (or doesn't do) to promote itself. By contrast I will argue that in a Christian theology of mission, the Christian mission has a distinctively eschatological reference.[6] So for a Christian, the meaning of this term is unique to the church. Now is not any time, but rather the time given by Christ for mission; mission cannot be defined apart from an understanding of the eschatological drama and so of the role for the church in this age. To discern who Christ is means to locate oneself between resurrection and consummation; and this location, in the New Testament accounts themselves, is defined by mission. It is to an exposition of this eschatologically dramatic understanding of mission in the Scriptures that I will turn in the next section.

Such an account of mission aims to put first things first (perhaps " 'last things' first" is better), and so to maintain the "three-dimensionality" of theology's account of God's "economy" or plan of salvation. Once this task has been accomplished, the questions that I discussed earlier in this introduction — concerning the possible salvation of unbelievers and the relation of the church to culture — find their rightful and secondary (though still important) place. They cease to be crises and become reflections on the working of Christ's one salvation in the varied dispensations and times of salvation history.

6. David Bosch rightly observes in the introduction to his *Transforming Mission: Paradigm Shifts in Theology of Mission* (Maryknoll, NY: Orbis Books, 1991) that the term *mission* was until a relatively late date used in theology solely as a term in trinitarian reflection. However, words related to the root for "sending" are prominent in the New Testament, and furthermore we are focusing here on the theme of evangelistic proclamation and outreach, which is frequently present in the Scriptures, though sometimes expressed by different terminology.

I will address these questions in the third and fourth sections of this essay. In my treatment of the possible salvation of unbelievers in the third section, I will rely on the distinction between what we can confidently affirm on the basis of the narrative and imaginative reflections tangential to the narrative about how Christ may be at work among those who have not heard the Word. These possible constructions retain an importance of their own, for they guard the church's more central affirmations as they help to ward off both unfounded confidence and despair.

In the fourth section, which deals with the more practical missiological question of the relation of the proclaiming church to diverse cultures and religious traditions, I will point out the elements of truth in proposals that have emphasized continuity and in those that have emphasized discontinuity. I will also stress the limited role theories can play here, for the focus must be on the actual encounters, what I will call "gracious collisions," with other religions and cultures, encounters impelled by the very missionary identity of the church. Such meetings do not lend themselves to systemization; instead, one must remain attentive to what actual resistances and affinities the meetings themselves present.

Before I commence the exposition itself, a word of explanation is required. I will use the term *Gentiles* in this essay in the biblical sense of "the peoples," all the nations of the earth other than Israel. In part this use is dictated by my dramatic argument, since it is only the Gentiles who were in the shadows of the Old Testament story, but, following the plot's decisive turn in the resurrection, have now come "center stage." I have deliberately left the question of the evangelization of the Jews in abeyance. In part this is a "division of labor" since the question is addressed by a colleague within this same volume. Excluding this question is also a matter of theological judgment. To be sure, the risen Jesus Christ is Lord of all, Jews and Gentiles; the children of Israel also need so to acknowledge him; they too cannot hear without a preacher. Still, the narrative warrants for such evangelism will move in a different direction, not to mention the eschatological complexity of Romans 11, which must be taken into account. So I will limit my attention to the twilight nations, the peoples whose moment has come: the Gentiles.

II. Mission as Eschatological Drama

> *Praise the* LORD, *all nations!*
> *Extol him, all peoples!*
>
> Psalm 117:1 (cf. Romans 15:11)

The understanding of Christian mission rooted in the New Testament is altogether and unreservedly eschatological.[7] According to the scriptural witness, to know Jesus Christ to be the risen and ascended Lord is to live in the midst of a specific eschatological scenario, to discern the time as that of the "mission to the Gentiles." This witness construes the entire expanse of the world, "to the ends of the earth" (as Isaiah or Luke would say), and the entire remaining expanse of time unleashed by the resurrection and brought to a close by the return of Christ as the stage or arena within which that mission is to take place. Under the sign of the cross, in the mode of weakness, by the word of folly, Christ calls his church to play its role.

Tension pervades the world stage on which the church proclaims the eschatological good news. The friction between "already" and "not yet" characterizes not only the Christian's life but the church's outreach to the Gentiles as well.[8] The kingdom present in Christ breaks in as Gentiles hear the gospel message. Together with this tension in the eschatological message is a second tension, found in the eschatological herald, the church. This peculiar people, called and formed uniquely by the biblical story, must press into all nations and proclaim the gospel universally. Yet the story itself is only truly comprehensible to those who live within the Christian community, where the habits and common life of worship, service, and suffering indispensably aid its interpretation. This ensures that the Christian truth will be often incomprehensible to the world and always discontinuous with its prevailing cultural assumptions. Inevitably the difficult task of communicating the gospel will succeed only by fits and starts.

7. I am reworking a sentence of Karl Barth's from *The Epistle to the Romans:* "If Christianity be not altogether and unreservedly eschatology, there remains in it no relationship whatever to Christ." It is cited in Jürgen Moltmann's *The Theology of Hope: On the Ground and the Implications of a Christian Eschatology* (New York: Harper & Row, 1967), p. 39.

8. For this now-classic contrast see Oscar Cullmann's *Christ and Time* (Philadelphia: Westminster Press, 1950), chap. 5, "The New Dimension of Time from the Central Point of the Redemptive History."

Because of this tension in both the content (the gospel) and the form (the church) of the good news, the Christian mission cannot eliminate its apocalyptic — that is, its discontinuous or in-breaking — dimension. Like the writers of Jewish apocalyptic literature, Christians too believe that God's reign cannot come by some simple fulfillment or synthesis but must rather crash in like a "thief in the night." But unlike those Jewish predecessors, Christians believe that God's gracious collision has happened definitively in Jesus Christ and so must and will happen again and again in the world of the Gentiles. In just such a disruptingly apocalyptic way came the message of Christ, and so came the rending events of cross and empty tomb. Christians look forward to such a consummation of the world. One should expect something equally discontinuous, equally collisional, from mission in the meantime.

One must keep the friction between "already" and "not yet," between church and world, in mind as one addresses every major question for a Christian theology of mission. An eschatological reading of the New Testament story, according to which the time of the church is the time for the Gentiles, makes mission imperative. The double tension defining the church's life makes mission unavoidably complex. Taken together, these pervasive characteristics of the Christian mission ensure its essentially conflictual, agonistic nature. The New Testament promises no separate peace for the church, nor smooth receptions for its good news; rather, the church must rush hopefully and headlong in search of collisions of scandal or equally cataclysmic conversion.

A major difference between Christian mission and all mere efforts at religious self-promotion is this *tension-laden location in an eschatological drama,* proceeding out of a persistently christocentric understanding of time and the world. But can one demonstrate such a view of mission in the Scriptures themselves? To be sure, the New Testament speaks of the mission to the Gentiles in a variety of ways. Still, the diverse images the canonical authors use share underlying assumptions about the predicament and promise for the Gentiles derived from the Old Testament. Furthermore, the claim made above serves as a common denominator for all the various New Testament ways of describing the church's mission. To defend my general claim, I need to review first the Old Testament background to the eschatological mission to the Gentiles, and then its most salient New Testament examples.

If the story of the election and redemption of God's people Israel occupies most of the Old Testament's attention, God's relationship to the nations is both a frame and a backdrop for the main action. In the story of the tower of Babel it is clear that the diversity of languages and peoples is inextricably tied to human rebellion and brokenness (Gen. 11:1-9). In the time of Israel the nations periodically rage and threaten God's people (Ps. 2); the full demonstration of God's Lordship, anticipated in the future and enacted in liturgy, would culminate in a triumphal procession of the now submissive nations. At the same time more positive prophetic dreams of a cosmic procession of obedient nations to Zion (Isa. 2; 66), of the worshipful praise of God's name throughout the world (Mal. 1:11), and the penitent acknowledgment of God's decisive act of redemption (Isa. 49) emerged with a growing emphasis on eschatological expectation. Passages that came to be interpreted messianically by the church stress the conversion or ingathering of the nations as well: the Son of man will be served by "all peoples, nations, and languages" (Dan. 7:14), and the Servant will make God's salvation "reach to the end of the earth" (Isa. 49:6). All New Testament views of mission share the obvious assumption that the extension of God's Lordship over the nations characterized his decisive, eschatological event, which for Christians commenced with Christ's resurrection and ascension.

For several of the New Testament authors, missionary activity is not only the appropriate response to the eschatological moment; it is also itself an important sign or harbinger of God's unfolding plan. Oscar Cullmann has argued convincingly that the first horseman of the apocalypse in Revelation 6:1-2 is in fact the proclamation of the gospel, for the same "white horse" appears in Revelation 19:11-13 as the "Faithful and True . . . Word of God."[9] It is worth noting, given the agonistic key in which I have set mission, that for John the church proclaims the "conquering" Word in the midst of "plagues," suffering, and mortal conflict. Likewise, in the "little apocalypse" of Mark 13, in the midst of the "Messianic woes" of persecution, desecration, and cosmic disaster (troubles associated in the writings of Jewish apocalyptic with the nearness of the end), one reads that "the gospel must first be preached to all nations" (v. 10). In both examples cited, mission is itself a necessary element in the preparation for the full revelation of God's kingdom.

Elsewhere the hearing of the Lord's command to proclaim is ingredient in the very recognition of the identity of the risen Lord

---

9. Cullmann, "Eschatology and Missions in the New Testament," in *The Theology of the Christian Mission*, ed. Gerald Anderson (New York: McGraw-Hill, 1961).

Christ. C. H. Dodd pointed out in a form-critical study of the resurrection that, along with the disciples' characteristic experience of fear and awe and the Lord's responding word of peace, the charge to go into all the world pervades all the varied accounts.[10] In the climactic words of Matthew 28:18-19, the risen Lord states, "All authority in heaven and on earth has been given to me. Go therefore and make disciples of all nations." To recognize Christ as risen, to acknowledge his proleptic (anticipatory) Lordship over all, is inseparable from a vigorous and expansive missionary self-understanding.

The mission to the Gentiles is constitutive of an understanding of the identity of the Lord Jesus as he is presented by the narrative of the New Testament, however variously. The point I have just made with respect to the resurrection could be equally well made concerning the ascension. When one turns to Luke/Acts, one must focus not on specific passages but rather on the larger architectural design of the work. Jesus Christ binds together a sweeping story that includes the time of promise for Israel, the center in Christ himself, and the time of the church. At the pivot of the two "books," the ascension of Christ and the sending of the Spirit lead immediately and irrepressibly to the missionary expansion of the church throughout the (known) world. The revelation of the divine identity and the unfolding of the divine plan, of which mission is a part, are inextricable: only the Father knows the times, but the disciples must witness to the Son in the power of the Spirit (Acts 1:7-8).

Playing on the idea of the captive nations as the booty of the newly enthroned king, St. Paul too implies an intimate connection between the ascension and the Gentile mission (in which he includes himself as the special apostle to the nations): "But thanks be to God, who in Christ always leads us in triumph, and through us spreads the fragrance of the knowledge of him everywhere" (2 Cor. 2:14). Throughout his writings the connection between the Lordship of Christ and the Gentile mission is in turn closely linked to his own special vocation within God's plan of salvation. An important passage in this regard is the reflection on his own ministry in Romans 15:17-21. Far from being a mere autobiographical aside, the passage sets the Gentile mission and Paul's central role in it at the heart of God's mysterious plan of salvation in Christ, now revealed. The time is that

10. See Dodd's "The Appearances of the Risen Christ: A Study in Form-Criticism of the Gospels," in *More New Testament Studies* (Grand Rapids: William B. Eerdmans, 1968), pp. 102-33.

of calling the Gentiles to praise God (vv. 9-12); the place for this ministry is the *oikoumene,* the whole world (vv. 19, 28). Paul employs the image of a cosmic liturgy, in which the Gentiles are the sacrifice, borne to the altar by Paul, made in honor of the Lord Jesus (v. 16). In the succeeding section Paul refers to his intention to bring a collection from the Gentiles to the suffering original church in Jerusalem. The collection would seem to symbolize the in-gathering of the Gentiles to Mount Zion in praise and gratitude foretold by the prophets (Micah, Isaiah). Here again the Gentile mission fulfills a stage of the unfolding eschatological drama.

A problem of course remains, for all that I have shown is that *for the writers of the New Testament* mission had this particularly eschatological meaning. But how should one appropriate this observation into contemporary theology? For many readers the eschatological dimension of the New Testament may seem hopelessly enmeshed in an archaic worldview and so best left behind. Such readers will learn to their surprise that the rediscovery of eschatology in this century has had a powerful tonic effect on systematic theology. Upon closer inspection one soon realizes that this theological locus has proved especially protean, open to a variety of conflicting construals. Eschatology would seem to have become a grab bag into which has been thrown existential decision, dedication to bringing about social change, the utter otherness of God, etc. Likewise, when mission hitches its fortunes to eschatology, it may be dragged where it does not wish to go.[11] The close connection between the two could degenerate into the notion that mission can *bring* the end (either in its conservative or in its radical forms), or into a rigid philosophy of history, or into a devotion to the indeterminacy of the future in and of itself.

Let us assume that the heart of the narrative is the rendering of Jesus Christ as risen, ascended Lord for the believer, and that the world of space and time must thereupon be construed as his domain. It then follows that the present must be seen as the time for the mission to the Gentiles, for this can be unfolded from the very meaning of resurrection and ascension at the heart of the narrative itself. No supposedly outmoded eschatological shell can be simply removed without removing the very purpose of the narrative. So a seam must be sewn to join such a rendition of Jesus Christ together with the understanding

11. The effect of eschatology on modern missiology is described in detail in Ludwig Wiedenmann's *Mission und Eschatologie* (Paderborn: Bonifacius-Druckerei, 1965).

of the world of space and time as the arena for such a mission. One would tear away the latter, the mission to the Gentiles, at the risk of serious damage to the former, the identity of the risen Christ.

The world, now understood as the risen Christ's domain, is no longer a neutral space but a stage defined by the story for the fulfillment of a specific missionary role by the church, over against which the nations are the other central dramatis personae.[12] In the same way, time is for the church no longer neutral, but rather is understood to be given by God for mission.[13] To be sure, the bounds of time and space have been seriously expanded since the time of Luke and Paul, but the theological relationship, the "seam," remains intact.

One must acknowledge that such a conclusion about mission requires the acceptance of the assumption about the nature and power of the narrative — namely, to render Christ and so to construe the world. I have argued in the opening section of this essay that such a view enables us best to appropriate the Christian tradition and to make the best sense of the Christian claim. Once we accept these premises, the recognition of the eschatological domain of Christ as the place for the mission to the Gentiles is entailed.

As a result, involvement in mission becomes a practice that is distinctive and characteristic of the Christian community. It both follows from a correct understanding of the narrative and helps the believer to read the narrative rightly. One may compare the relationship between the perception of the identity of Christ and the practice of mission to that which pertains between the virtue of humility and the recognition of Christ, who "did not count equality with God a thing to be grasped" (Phil. 2:6). Our humility both imitates the lowly Christ and helps us to grasp what the story means by "humility." Likewise, the recognition of the risen Lord impels the believer into mission, which in turn helps him or her to understand what it means to call Jesus Christ "Lord." In particular, this practice corrects self-absorbed or culturally constrained understandings of the life of the Christian community; it confronts the Christian again and again with the universality of Christ's claim on all humankind and the finality of his truth.

If the world between resurrection and *Parousia* (Christ's return) is the stage, if the coming of God's kingdom, already in-broken, is the

---

12. I am indebted to Hans Urs von Balthasar's *Theo-drama*, especially vols. I and II/I (San Francisco: Ignatius, 1988), for the image of the drama that I employ.

13. Karl Barth, *Church Dogmatics*, IV/I (Edinburgh: T. & T. Clark, 1956), chap. 14, par. 62.3, "The Time of the Community."

tension-filled plot, and if the church as herald and sacrament of that kingdom is the primary character, then the nations with their individuals, cultures, and religions emerge into the light acting the counterpart. Prior to the New Testament, the nations remained for the most part in the shadows, although they emerged occasionally to play the role of foil for God's elect people. In that half-light one sees at most glimpses of peoples, estranged from God, who rage and rebel. They appear from time to time as the unwitting agents of God's providence, as they bring punishment or protection to God's people. From time to time, in Job or Naaman or the people of Nineveh in the time of Jonah, we catch a glimpse of the Gentiles hoping for the God they cannot yet see and having to settle for intimations of him. Their role is an uncertain, ambiguous one, mixing obscure potentialities and resistances.

At the climax of the biblical story, however, the nations come center stage:

> But you are a chosen race, a royal priesthood, a holy nation, God's own people, that you may declare the wonderful deeds of him who called you out of darkness into his marvelous light. Once you were no people but now you are God's people; once you had not received mercy, but now you have received mercy. (1 Pet. 2:9-10)

And so the Gentiles may be understood to emerge, not out of the darkness of damnation, but rather out of the ambiguous, unlit periphery of the stage where humans can at best grope after God. At the preaching of the risen Christ, the light of God's consummation, his kingdom, the light that is God's own final glory *(doxa)*, shines back into the present; wherever they are so illumined, the nations attain a clear status before God and a certain share of his mercy.

The consuming action of the eschatological drama is that the light should stream into the world, should shine forth as it strikes Gentiles called into God's community and so anticipates the day when for all the nations "the Lord God will be their light" (Rev. 22:5). God's mercy for the Gentiles consists precisely in that he has called them out of futility into this role in his drama; this new role is a most positive one, though its blessing is found precisely as they look away from their own benefit and realize themselves to be the occasions for God's light to shine, as actors called into God's glorious drama. Still, we cannot shirk from admitting the possibility that in this new light the Gentiles may sometimes cast on the stage the silhouette of refusal as well.

The seismic change of the resurrection, the decisive act, impinges on the world again and again as Christ's church encounters the nations throughout the remaining expanse of history and pulls them into the drama. To reiterate, to be the place where the dramatic movement — the gracious impetus out of darkness and into that final and marvelous light — has occurred is for Gentiles the sum and substance of salvation. Thus mission, for the Christian, is doxology. The focus is always away from ourselves and toward the fact that the drama is *God's*. The Christian life becomes the opportunity for a Gentile to praise God for what he has done, for what he is, and for what he will do, a foretaste of the eternal thanksgiving banquet. If mission is doxology it ceases to make sense ever to wonder if a Gentile ought to be evangelized, if he or she ought to convert and join the church. One might as well ask if a few hymns should be sung to the Lord God, or if a polyphonous thunder of song ought to be poured out to him. Here we need to recall the idea, tied to the narrative of the ascension, of the Gentiles as the prizes and gifts laid at the feet of Christ. The plenitude of the nations, the full richness of tongues and customs, glorifies all the more fully the Lord in his triumphal procession.

Eschatological mission is thoroughly doxological in its motive. Lesslie Newbigin recently wrote, "mission is an overflow of gratitude and joy . . . the central theme is not 'how shall the world be saved?', but rather 'how shall the glorious and gracious God be glorified?' "[14] While preaching and conversion may also lead to spiritual advantages for the new Christians and perhaps to "betterment" for society, such reasons for the church's mission can never be primary.

Eschatological mission is thoroughly doxological in its performance, in its acts of preaching and hearing. Every Gentile individual, family, or tribe that responds to the proclaimed Word represents in itself the victory of God over the darkened world, an island of light reflecting back God's final glory. Just as the central action of the New Testament is the dramatic struggle and victory of Christ over the powers of this world found in the story of his cross and resurrection, so this drama is represented vividly and anew in each occasion of faith and conversion on the part of a Gentile. Each Gentile Christian is glorious proof, in spite of himself or herself, that the light has shined, and the darkness cannot overcome it.

Finally, eschatological mission is doxology because of the "end," the purpose of life, to which the Gentile convert is called within the

14. Newbigin, "A View of Mission in the 1990's," *International Bulletin of Missionary Research* 13, 3 (July 1989): 102.

church. He or she has indeed found the destination and goal of the whole human sojourn; each is able to do now in Jesus Christ what God created his human children to do: to praise him. This will be the eternal activity of all the nations in the new Jerusalem (Rev. 21). For Gentiles to live even here and now such a life of praise is itself totally gracious. But living such a doxological life cannot even be conceived outside the community formed by the narrative that makes the term meaningful. Doxology precedes conversion as the motive of the herald, it represents the ultimate significance of conversion itself, and it follows conversion as the goal of the new communal life.

As the great theologian of the proclaimed Word, Martin Luther, would surely remind us, the church must be careful when it develops a (in this case, missiological) "theology of glory." I should therefore hasten to emphasize that what is truly worthy of praise is that even we Gentiles, whose persistent sins, ignorance, and sleepfulness so resemble those of our brothers and sisters in the shadows, are called to be the place where God's name is extolled. Furthermore, the form of the church's witness *(martyria)* to God's glory will often be that of martyrdom. When the martyrs of Buganda walked to the fires singing the hymns that had so recently set them ablaze, when more recently Bishop Deqhani-Tafti of Iran, after the murder of his son, insisted that countrymen not be denied the "joy" of suffering for Jesus Christ, the ultimate meaning of "doxological mission" becomes clear.[15]

III. In "the Twilight of the Gods"

> *The times of ignorance God overlooked, but now he commands all [people] everywhere to repent, because he has fixed a day on which he will judge the world.*
>
> Acts 17:30-31

I have claimed that any theology that would understand Jesus Christ as risen, ascended Lord must understand time and space, history and the world as the drama of the gathering of the Gentiles in the last times. Having made this vision central, we can now address properly the nettlesome question, mentioned at the outset of this essay, of the salvation of unbelievers. What about those who remain at the periphery

---

15. Hassan Deqhani-Tafti, *The Hard Awakening* (New York: Seabury, 1981).

of the stage, who were never called from its penumbral background? Only now do we have the "three-dimensional" perspective native to the Christian understanding of history from which to answer this question without essential distortion of the Christian witness.

The place to begin is with the term *salvation* itself, which must also be understood in a thoroughly eschatological way. It refers to the acquittal and healing that God promises at the consummation of his kingdom to those who hear and by grace respond even now to the news of the end time. It implies a confidence that God will protect his people through the sufferings of the eschatological "time of trial" in order that they might reach that consummation. So St. Paul, for instance, is confident by hope that he and his fellow Christians will be saved, while the world is left inarticulately groaning for this salvation (Rom. 8). However, one should note here that fully meaningful talk of salvation presupposes hearing the eschatological news. The narrative not only explicates how God has acted decisively to save the world; it also provides the condition for the world to understand and hence to accept (or reject) God's grace. In other words, "salvation" can only be properly discussed where the end (which the term implies) has been proclaimed, where within the church the terms necessary for its comprehension are to be found.

As a result, one must understand the various, overlapping senses in which the Gentiles may be said to live "prior" to the advent of the gospel. Obviously the Gentiles of the Old Testament so lived, but one can also think of those Gentiles who even now have not heard the Word as living still "in the shadows." Indeed, even those who have never received an adequate presentation of the Word, who have never "heard" in the sense of comprehending, may also be thought to live lives anterior to the possibility of salvation. There is an essential correspondence between the role of the Gentiles within the narrative of the New Testament and the historical relationship of the Gentiles to the coming of the narrative itself into their lives. George Lindbeck suggests that Gentiles live in a world of discourse and thought not yet capable of salvation or damnation: "in terms of the basic New Testament eschatological pictures, non-Christians (i.e. Gentiles) would seem not yet to be confronted by the question of salvation; they are not headed either toward heaven or hell; they have no future, they are still trapped in the past, in the darkness of the old aeon."[16] In both narrative and

---

16. Lindbeck, *The Nature of Doctrine* (Philadelphia: Westminster Press, 1984), p. 58.

epistemological terms, the place of the Gentiles is in the shadows. Such a conclusion is thoroughly consistent with an eschatologically tensive understanding of the proclaiming church.

As I emphasized in my opening section on the narrative basis of Christian mission, we must maintain a careful distinction between what we know surely to be true for all human beings on the basis of the divine story and what we do not know about how God will work out his will for those who remain "in the shadows." So our approach will share the hopeful yet concerned silence on the question of salvation that has characterized much modern Protestant theology. Salvation is only in and by Christ, but we cannot constrain the mysterious possibilities of his mercy. Here the Baltimore Declaration strikes the right note: "While we do not presume to judge how the all-holy and all-merciful God will or will not bring to salvation those who do not hear and believe the preached Gospel, we do emphatically declare Jesus the rightful Lord and Savior of all humanity" (article 4).

What does such a distinction between what we know about salvation (in the light of the biblical narrative) and what we cannot know (in the twilight) allow and compel us to say about the salvation of unbelievers? Numerous modern commentators have correctly pointed out that the traditional axiom *"nulla salus extra ecclesiam"* ("no salvation outside the church") oversteps what it can know if the intent is to deny the possible salvation of an unbeliever. (In fact, the original context of the line claimed much less, namely that the apostate could expect no divine mercy.)[17] At the same time one can say with confidence *"ubi Christus, ibi salus"* ("wherever Christ is, there is salvation"); likewise, one can say that the very talk of salvation is only meaningful, as I have argued above, where the kingdom is already present in Christ (*ubi salus, ibi Christus* — "where salvation is, there is Christ"). Such statements follow as analytic judgments, since in narrative terms *Christ* and *salvation* are correlative and equally eschatological terms; the risen Christ anticipates that end time when salvation is to be found.

The careful discernment of the border between the light and the twilight does not, however, forbid theological reflection about how Gentiles living prior to the gospel might be saved. On the contrary, it mandates such considerations, so long as they are conducted consistently in the "subjunctive mood." The theologian should aim here

---

17. See, e.g., Gavin D'Costa's *"Extra Ecclesiam Nulla Salus* — Revisited," in *Pluralism and Unbelief: Studies Critical and Comparative,* ed. Ian Hammett (London: Routledge, 1990).

at a *docta ignorantia,* a learned unknowing, which first observes the border and then proceeds tentatively into the twilight with its attendant possibilities. Such acts of theological imagination serve to ward off misunderstandings of the narrative and its salvific claim, and so they fulfill a protective, corrective function. False claims that God *cannot* be at work in the twilight must be refuted, truncations of Christ's Lordship over all creatures must be avoided, and concern over the eventual fate of the twilight-people must be balanced with hope. Such acts of imagination, properly understood, do not overturn the claim of the narrative but rather hedge it in.

There have generally been two paths for such reflection in the Christian tradition. The major line of thought, represented classically by Thomas Aquinas and powerfully in recent times by Karl Rahner, has involved some notion of "implicit faith," an act of assent by one who does not know or acknowledge Jesus Christ, an assent that is, in spite of this fact, understood to be directed toward and empowered by Jesus. For Thomas himself such an act of implicit faith had a definite content — namely, acknowledgment that God "exists and that he rewards those who seek him" (Heb. 11:6). By contrast, for Rahner implicit faith does not require any particular content, but rather involves a certain aspect of human consciousness. Still, all proponents of implicit faith share the idea that Christ is the One acknowledged, "appearances notwithstanding."

Arguments for implicit faith may best be understood as exercises in imagining how God may be preparing unbelievers to be drawn into his kingdom. Such exercises ward off despair about the breadth of God's action and preserve humility, lest Christians claim to know who will come "from east and west, from north and south . . . [to] eat in the kingdom of God" (Luke 13:29, NRSV). By focusing on these limited objectives, the theologian can deal better with the standard criticism of implicit faith proposals — namely, that they disregard what non-Christians actually believe and do in a seemingly arbitrary way. Such proposals do not claim to describe accurately the actual beliefs of those in the twilight, but rather serve delimited and internal protective purposes "in the subjunctive mood."

Within the theological tradition, advocacy of prospective salvation has formed a "minority report." This solution asks believers to imagine that nonbelievers will have an opportunity to meet Christ and to acknowledge him at the last judgment. Such views clearly preserve the specificity of the Christian revelation and the centrality of Jesus Christ, which are so important to a narrative understanding of the Christian mission.

Critics have, however, pointed out that the scriptural warrants for prospective salvation are few and shaky; theories have often turned on interpretation of the obscure reference in 1 Peter 3:19-20 to Christ's descent among the dead "in prison," traditionally called the "harrowing of hell." The usefulness of prospective salvation as an act of imagination is enhanced, however, if we keep our attention fixed on the thoroughly eschatological nature of the New Testament. The tension of "already" and "not yet" that defines life in the present age requires us to imagine the most comprehensive destiny of the world to conform to the narratively focused story of the death and resurrection of Jesus Christ. In that act God has anticipated the cataclysmic redemption of the whole world; nonbelievers will all somehow confront the reign of God present in Christ quite simply because this is the destiny of all reality. Properly employed, concepts of prospective salvation help to maintain this larger eschatological orientation and so remind the believer of the universality of Christ's Lordship. Just as a theory of implicit faith can serve important purposes when it remains within the proper bounds, so also ideas of prospective salvation can protect and clarify the church's proclamation about the risen Christ.

When employed inappropriately, however, ideas such as implicit faith or prospective salvation can undercut the understanding of Christian mission they ought to subserve. As I indicated at the outset of this essay, when such theories usurp the primary theological place, questions become crises; when acts of imagination become hardened concepts, attack from the pluralist position is easier. If implicit faith or prospective salvation is no longer offered as one possibility but rather claims to describe actuality, theological balance and perspective are lost.

For example, in his theory of anonymous Christianity, Karl Rahner sought to avoid such dangers by stating that unknowing faith in Christ was only possible until the moment when the unbeliever truly heard the gospel.[18] But less temperate successors rushed to offer this salvific possibility as an actuality inherent in the other religions. One such follower, Heinz Schlette, argued that God normally brings salvation to the Gentiles through the religions, while he reserves eschatological salvation in Christ for Christians.[19] The real problem is that

18. Rahner, "Christianity and the Non-Christian Religions," in *Theological Investigations*, vol. 5 (London: Darton, Longman, & Todd), pp. 121ff.

19. Schlette, *Toward a Theology of Religions* (New York: Herder & Herder, 1966), esp. chap. 3, "The Religions in the History of Salvation."

distinctions in God's manner of working associated with what I have called "three-dimensionality," with the varied economy of salvation, are absolutized as separate spheres in which God saves in enduringly separate ways. The distance to pluralism — the God of which works separately, equally, obscurely — is a short one. Lost is the dramatic tension characteristic of the church's proper life, the gracious propulsion and collision of the Word into all nations that God now commands.

Likewise, if theories of prospective salvation slip out of the subjunctive mood, they can foster misunderstanding. St. Augustine objected, for instance, to wider interpretations of the "harrowing of hell" lest it become an actual disincentive to evangelism by encouraging Christians to leave pagans in their inculpable ignorance.[20] More generally, while the theory fixes appropriately on the diversity of the economy of salvation when it points out that many Gentiles may have lived "prior" to the arrival of the gospel, the dimension of eschatological drama, the pressure to proclaim the kingdom already dawning, must not be lost. Proponents of prospective salvation must be vigilant lest their theory lead to a salvation-historical compartmentalization (even though Christianity may be the central box) according to which the Gentiles are to be left for now "on hold." The tension of the eschatological drama, definitive of the church's life in the New Testament, must not be dissipated in this way.

Such distortions are in no way necessary for theories of implicit faith or prospective salvation; such theories can serve the protecting, encouraging role I described above. Their proper helpfulness can best be shown as I explicate representative versions of these theories, one classic and one contemporary, one supporting implicit faith and one supporting prospective salvation. An important criterion for the success of each theory will be its inclusion of appropriate limits to its claim.

I will begin with Thomas Aquinas, whose understanding of implicit faith coheres with the view I have advanced. Thomas sets his classic discussion of the idea (in *Summa Theologiae*, II/II.2.7) in the midst of an affirmation that all who are to be saved must have explicit faith in the mystery of Christ's incarnation. But Thomas also acknowledges that this must take into account the different dispensations, the unfolding nature of divine revelation. It is significant that Thomas has in mind first of all the people of God in the Old Testament, who had

---

20. See letter #164, "To Evodius," in *Letters*, vol. 2 (New York: Fathers of the Church, 1953).

faith without direct knowledge of Jesus Christ, and secondarily "holy pagans" such as Job, who seem to have had such faith as well. By the unfolding, teleological nature of God's revelation, vouched for in Scripture, one can be assured that their faith in the God who "exists and . . . rewards those who seek him" (Heb. 11:6) was faith in the One to come, in the one triune God incarnate in Jesus Christ.

When, however, Thomas departs the well-lit corridor of revelation for the penumbral realm of the status of Gentiles in general, when he engages in an act of "analogical imagination" as it were at a second remove, his conclusions become more tentative, somehow vague. "If, however, some were saved without receiving any revelation, they were not saved without faith in a mediator, for . . . they did, nevertheless, have implicit faith through believing in divine providence" (reply to objection 3). Thomas, curious about the possibility, will not foreclose the possibilities for God's granting the grace of faith, but neither will he come to any firm conclusions about where or how it occurs.

What was for Thomas a largely hypothetical question acquired urgency with the discovery of the Americas and the other expanses of lands as yet unevangelized. How strenuously later Catholic commentators, with the missionary situation in mind, sought to systematize Thomas's soundings![21] It soon became clear that the logic of implicit faith was a "slippery slope"; in the end one could not be sure that the most unreconstructed idolator didn't have some glimmer of faith in something beyond his stone god, a kind of implicit faith in providence, which in turn could be a kind of implicit faith in a mediator, and so forth. But by the same token one could never be sure. In the last analysis, the Christian theologian was left in an epistemological twilight of his or her own; implicit faith was everywhere possible, however remotely, but nowhere certain. In addition, however, one can stress, in contradistinction to Thomas's more liberal followers, that implicit faith could never rest solely on a faith in the comfortable gods of one's surroundings; it required a movement, however inchoate, outward toward the God who reveals and bestows. By the very dynamics of the argument, implicit faith is rendered both possible and problematic.

Matters become even more complex when one recalls that, for Thomas, only the infusion of all the theological virtues in tandem, faith, hope, and love, makes salvation possible (hence Thomas can

---

21. Louis Caperan, *Le Probleme du Salut des Infideles*, vol. 1 (Toulouse: Grand Seminaire, 1934), chap. 7.

speak of a "dead" faith, lacking charity, which is not salvific).[22] Now hope for Thomas requires a fiduciary element; one must know and trust the One in whom one hopes. But such hope is precisely what the unbeliever cannot have; he or she cannot say "it does not yet appear what we shall be, but we know that when he appears we shall be like him" (1 John 3:2). All of this leaves the reader of Thomas in a quandary, for Thomas erects a frame of speculation that he cannot possibly complete. But from the point of view of the argument I have set forth, this is exactly what the Christian can and must do; at the same time this is *all* that can be done. At the end of the day, implicit faith amounts to a useful exercise of the imagination, the applicability of which finds careful narrative bounds. At the most it guarantees a kind of expectant uncertainty. By the inner dynamics of the terms Thomas uses to reflect on the question, implicit faith thrusts one's attention forward to that comprehensive horizon where alone the mystery will be resolved.

We have seen how the concept of implicit faith can serve an important function, so long as it is conceived in such a way as to impose its own boundary and apply its own brakes. Under similar constraints, prospective salvation can serve a correspondingly useful role. In his recent book *The Diversity of Religions: A Christian Perspective,* Joseph DiNoia emphasizes a point highly congenial to my argument: one can only properly speak of "salvation" within the bounds of the particular Christian sphere of belief and practice formed by the biblical narrative. A major warrant for this claim is derived from the analytic philosophy of religion; DiNoia quotes approvingly from the philosopher William Christian that "there seems to be a deep-seated tendency in the major religious communities to develop a comprehensive pattern of life."[23] For DiNoia, such patterns, consisting of both beliefs and practices, coalesce around aims particular to the communities in question, but one must not assume that the central aim of one community can be readily compared with that of another. For Christians this unique aim is defined, in good Thomistic fashion, as the building up of the theological virtues of faith, hope, and love, bestowed by and enabling communion with the triune God, which Christians call "salvation."

With such an approach, DiNoia can defend vigorously the dis-

---

22. On the theological virtues, see *Summa Theologiae* I/II.a.62, and on "dead faith" see II/II.a.4 q.3-4.

23. DiNoia, *The Diversity of Reügions: A Christian Perspective* (Washington: Catholic University Press, 1992), p. 9. The passage DiNoia cites is from William A. Christian's *Doctrines of Religious Communities: A Philosophical Study* (New Haven: Yale University Press, 1987), p. 186.

tinctiveness of the Christian aim of life and the need to commend its truth in conversation with members of other religious communities. But his view also allows him elbowroom on the question of the possible salvation of nonbelievers in two ways. First, the aims of other religions may not be contradictory to that of Christianity, but rather irreducibly different. DiNoia suggests that skills required for other aims (e.g., Nirvana) might prove surprisingly helpful for the aim of fellowship with the blessed Trinity, just as "one might discover that one had unintentionally developed the potential to be a baseball pitcher by often throwing rocks while growing up."[24]

This possibility, which DiNoia calls the "providential diversity of religions," requires the second element, the idea of prospective salvation, given distinctly Roman Catholic expression in an extended interpretation of the purgatorial encounter with Christ. In this eschatological context the Christian aim of life may properly be said to supersede all others, though again the aims of other religions may prove to foster a felicitous meeting with the Lord. Both elements taken together allow DiNoia to affirm more strongly God's universal will to save humankind (cf. 1 Tim. 2:4) without compromising the specificity of the Christian claim.

DiNoia's argument, just summarized, can cohere with and lend logical and theological support to the approach of this essay. But this requires that we append several caveats or conditions. Such an argument must be understood as an act of imagination, the presentation of one possibility. One must grant logically that the diverse aims of the religions could equally well impede the eschatological encounter with Christ. DiNoia could justifiably argue that a "charitable reading" requires such an optimistic view of the potential of the other traditions, especially when one is engaged in interreligious dialogue. But the charitable imperative of evangelism is another matter, for it requires one to take into account all the possible effects of continued upbuilding in the dispositions of the other traditions. The point I am making does not contradict DiNoia's view but rather provides balance.

To be sure, DiNoia rejects any slackening of missionary zeal as a result of his ideas of providential diversity and prospective salvation. But he may open the door to such an unwanted result when he stresses that the Christian aim of life, alone toward salvation, supersedes all others with respect to class (by being *sui generis*), but not with respect to time.[25] By this he means to reject Karl Rahner's temporal emphasis on the

---

24. DiNoia, *The Diversity of Religions*, p. 64.
25. DiNoia, *The Diversity of Religions*, p. 77.

difference between the possibility of salvation for the unbeliever before and after "hearing" the gospel. We have seen in the preceding section of this essay how the factor of time is intimately connected to dramatic, tensive description of the Christian missionary imperative. Readers could draw the mistaken impression that, for now, lesser, preparatory aims can suffice for many of the Gentiles. Such an indifferent and demarcated view of the economy of salvation is the Achilles' heel of all prospective salvation schemes. The problem is hardly irremediable; one need merely add the proviso that providential diversity and prospective salvation are fruitful modes of reflection with respect to those Gentiles who live prior to the coming of the good news.

For the purposes of this essay, DiNoia's argument can be recast in the following way. Christians can and should dare to hope for the ubiquity of prospective salvation, though the real possibility of prospective rejection cannot be lost as well. The structure of the narrative suggests that, just as the "Messianic woes" — the suffering expected to come on the world in the last times — are anticipated on Calvary, so the consummation of the world can only be thought of in painfully discontinuous terms of crucifixion and resurrection. For those in the shadows the Last Day will be full of surprises, as it will be for Christians too; some will look weeping on the One whom they pierced, while others will wonder joyously when it was that they fed or visited or clothed Christ. Once we have this picture of the end in mind, a picture more mottled with light and dark, we can put to rest Augustine's worry that prospective encounter will prove a disincentive to mission. With this picture in mind Christians can validly imagine a saving encounter on the Last Day for the Gentile who has remained ever in the shadows.

IV. Denouement: Collisions of Judgment and Fulfillment

> . . . for [the LORD] comes,
> for he comes to judge the earth.
> He will judge the world with righteousness,
> and the peoples with his truth.
>
> Psalm 96:13

Clarity about the distinctively Christian meaning of mission orders theological reflection so that the question of the possibility of the salvation of unbelievers can enlarge rather than distort one's understanding of the gospel. Similarly, our narrative approach can lead to fruitful consideration of practical missiological questions. What should we say about the relationship between the gospel and the spectrum of religions and cultures of the Gentiles? The idea of eschatological drama requires that we emphasize actual encounters between the Christian message and the peoples in all their variety, rather than broader theoretical evaluations of "religion" or "culture." Until they come into the light of real meetings between Gentile and gospel, until the gracious collision takes place, the myriad of cultures and their component religions remains ambiguous. So in themselves "the religions" are not inherently sinful human "works" over against God; nor, on the other hand, are they any kind of "latent church" waiting to be uncovered.[26] In fact, they are not inherently or necessarily any one thing. I am reminded of the legendary baseball umpire Billy Klem who, when criticized for an apparent missed call, retorted, "They ain't nothin' 'till I calls 'em, then that's what they is." Likewise, other religions and cultures only come into relief as fulfillment or resistance in the actual encounters of the historical arena.

The missionary nature of the church, determined by its message of the risen Christ, the ever in-breaking presence of the kingdom, leads one to seek and expect just such gracious collisions. This Word of the risen Lord, racing back from God's future, makes contact with the Gentiles in the twilight. No one can predict or determine when the gospel will seem to be the long-awaited completion or when it will seem to carry the stench of death. One can reasonably (though hypothetically) expect both sorts of reactions. Still, one must pay less attention to abstract conjectures and more to the actual contacts that follow from the unavoidable, creative, painful struggle in the "time between the times." Carl Braaten deftly points to the heart of the matter:

> Consider . . . driving down the expressway at night. There are signs by the roadside . . . but we cannot read them until our headlights shine on them. . . . Only in the missionary encounters of the religions does this meaning come to light; otherwise, we are dealing with mere hypotheses from the science of religions which swim in a sea of relativity.[27]

26. An example of the former would be Karl Barth's *Church Dogmatics* I/II (Edinburgh: T. & T. Clark, 1956), part 3, par. 17.2, "Religion as Unbelief"; and an example of the latter would be Paul Tillich's *Systematic Theology* (Chicago: University of Chicago Press, 1963), vol. 3, part 4, II.B.4.b, "The Spiritual Community in Its Latent and in Its Manifest Stages."

27. Braaten, *No Other Gospel* (Minneapolis: Fortress Press, 1992), p. 71.

From the narratively focused, conflictual perspective I have traced, it is not possible to claim for any particular cultures or non-biblical religions, as entities in themselves, any sort of status with respect to revelation or salvation. Religions as wholes are oriented to aims other than the one to which God has now called the Gentiles. One must readily acknowledge that particular beliefs and practices of other religions, when thought of detached from the constellations of belief in which they naturally reside, may often be true and right, even when they do not correspond (and, of course, when they do not contradict) Christian beliefs and practices.[28] The church obedient to the Lord of all creation may justly hope and expect many such truths; when such valid insights are found, one may fairly speak of revelation in a general sense. Still, the ultimate test of truth will be the way in which these beliefs and practices supplement and enrich the understanding of the world of the risen Lord and so facilitate faith in him. This need in no way diminish the hope that at any particular point the religious and cultural "other" will be fraught with promising features, "other lights" that shine back in the actual encounter of the gospel.[29]

There is also at work here a "scandal of particularity," for the finality of the gospel can only be conveyed through the specificity of the scriptural narrative embedded in the practices and common life of the Christian community. Only by a complex process of translation, new in each of its encounters, can the gospel come to be heard and Gentiles drawn once more into the proleptic domain of the kingdom. But a process is always imprecise, and the "middle terms" opening up understanding cannot be predicted. Christians certainly can be confident that the Holy Spirit will make the Word heard, but that Spirit, blowing where it will, cannot be systematized or predicted.

So while the church is confident on theological grounds that the Word is in clarity breaking forth in the twilight of the Gentiles, it cannot in the practical reality of encounter lay claim to certain judgment about where that light has been refused and where it has not yet broken. The difference between denial and incomprehension remains veiled. The church must recognize this hidden and humble dimension of its witness. Here too, the life of the missionary church is in tension: it can neither dictate the terms of the collisions to which it is called nor judge definitively their results after the fact.

---

28. This paragraph assumes the discussion found in Christian, *Doctrines of Religious Communities*, chap. 7, "Doctrines and Alien Claims I."

29. Barth, *Church Dogmatics*, IV/III.1, par. 69.2, "The Light of Life," p. 97.

This does not mean that missiologists, when considering the gospel and culture, may no longer speak of fulfillment and adaptation on the one hand, or of dialectic and offense on the other. But it does cast doubt on the capacity for more general theorizing on the matter. Issues must be studied in a more ad hoc, descriptive, "decentralized" manner. Take, for instance, the conflicting evaluations of the Christian missionary encounter with Indian, primarily Hindu, culture. Some advocate a broad effort at adaptation to Hindu philosophical parlance, while others have pointed with repugnance to Hinduism's polytheism, to its monism, or to the religious foundation for the caste system. How should one conceive of the gospel's relationship to Hinduism?

If one starts with the historical encounter itself, one soon sees that no predetermined model can make sense of the apparent facts. For example, the strategies of philosophical adaptation employed by the great seventeenth-century Jesuit missionary Robert de Nobili may represent an angle from which an "other light" reflects back a ray of the gospel. At the same time the offense caused by the gospel's fundamental challenge to the caste system and the mass movements of conversion that resulted seem to reveal an angle from which Hinduism remained opaque to the in-breaking light. One can conjecture that aspects of Hinduism were judged and others fulfilled in these ways and in numerous other ways as well. The complex reality of encounter comprises the possibilities described by various theories.

In light of the perspective here advanced, one should understand the task of adaptation or indigenization to diverse cultures, which is so central to contemporary missiological discussion, as an ongoing pursuit of the real offense of the gospel. For when the gospel first arrives for a culture, the in-breaking of God's Word may be difficult to distinguish from the in-breaking of a mass of alien cultural influences. The study of indigenization ought to describe and counsel the effort to extricate the two, so that the scandalous challenge of the gospel, embedded in and represented by the local Christian community, takes on a unique form. Indigenization remains a valid subject of reflection, but never as a self-conscious accommodation or correlation to the culture encountered. Rather, the collision of the Word and its community with the Gentiles is ever accompanied by the community's own struggle against cultural compromise, a kind of replication of the missionary encounter itself.

The vision of the proclaiming church called to gracious collision also provides new insight into a second popular idea in missiology, the church as "universal sacrament of salvation." This metaphor has been popular since Vatican II, particularly but not only among Roman Catholics. It implies for Christianity a witness of presence among the religions in order to do its leavening, fermenting work; it emphasizes the church's role as intercessor and symbol of God's will to fulfill and lift the world into beatitude. One cannot deny the validity of such a witness and role. But it is primarily as a community of conversion — God's cataclysmic arrival — as a collective sign of contradiction, that the church symbolizes God's presence. It embodies the triumph of God in and for the world, in spite of the ignorance and sin of the community itself. In order to be missionary, the church must first understand *itself* as the enduring result of God's gracious collision.

If we look carefully, we discover that the sacraments themselves contain this collisional aspect as well, since the baptism of each new Christian is a drowning to the world of the old aeon and a participation in the death and resurrection of Jesus Christ. In this costly way each baptism celebrates God's in-breaking eschatological claim on the nations. Each is a promise that God's eschatological wave breaks even now on the world's shore. So, for instance, is baptism still understood by the courageous Christian members of a mainly Muslim community in east Africa (or elsewhere); a young person who hears the good news of Christ and decides, after much agonizing, to be baptized pays a heavy personal price. The sacramentality of baptism, its symbolizing of death and rebirth, cannot be separated from the suffering and upheaval that result from the decision to follow the Christian way.

My main argument, here concluded, is consistent with the affirmation of the Baltimore Declaration of the salvific exclusivity of Christ and the related need for evangelistic urgency. However, the order of these affirmations might be better reversed, in keeping with the distinctive meaning of "mission." The church is called into the twilight of the Gentiles, and it follows that wherever the eschatological message is understood and received, there indeed must be salvation. So the question of salvation can never be purged from the issue of missionary motive, but it ought not to define that motive. It is the inevitable corollary of mission as discerning the time. As the church embarks on that mission in the twilight, it can expect to find in its collisions, in a multitude of surprising ways, fulfillment and resistance as well.

*   *   *

Even a reader sympathetic to a narrative-theological vision of mission in God's drama might still validly ask: Are there any "nontheological" prospects that a similar vision of the church's mission will flourish in the church in general, and in the Episcopal Church in particular? Such a vision, with its accompanying discernment of the boundary between light and twilight, demands an attitude of humble assertiveness. By contrast, contemporary pluralists fail on both counts, for they lack the confidence to make the Christian claim while they advocate wholesale changes in all the religions. They feel compelled to undercut this claim because, disclaimers notwithstanding, they remain preoccupied with the West's position of cultural power. Their solution is a political one, motivated by the Enlightenment equation of particularity with fanaticism.

The church's situation today is a strange one, for the factors that drive some to pluralism could give others hope that a missionary attitude of humble assertiveness might make gains. The erosion of confidence in Enlightenment reason could lead the church to a new awareness of itself as a "fiduciary framework," a coherent and rational tradition of "faith seeking understanding," which can and must contend for its own truth.[30] The church's stance could come to resemble that of the first centuries, when missionary boldness was coupled with relative worldly powerlessness. The "younger" churches, living closer to the reality of conversion and often surrounded by non-Christian neighbors, often can more closely display this attitude, for they make the Christian claim boldly while they also fully expect to meet counterclaims. A more culturally peripheral position for the Western church could make the narrative, eschatological vision of mission more accessible, but nothing requires this more optimistic result.

Renewed attention to mission in this key would, I suspect, meet a mixed reception among Anglicans in the West of today. Gentiles are called into the Christian fellowship for the sake of praise, so that "from the rising of the sun to its setting" (Ps. 113:3) God's name might be exalted in the fullest variety of cultures and tongues. This doxological emphasis dovetails nicely with the Anglican strength in liturgy. But the accompanying stress on conversion as doxology, implying as it does confrontation with human cultures, would be harder for my own Episcopal church to hear.

Episcopalians live in communion with other Anglican churches, some of the most vigorous of whom would find this vision congenial. Sadly, in spite of enthusiasm for partnership with these younger

---

30. This is the main point of Lesslie Newbigin's *Foolishness to the Greeks: The Gospel and Western Culture* (Grand Rapids: William B. Eerdmans, 1986).

churches, the Episcopal Church often appreciates its companions in the Anglican Communion as reflections of its own preoccupations. Episcopalians are interested in the African church, for instance, more as a model of supposed cultural accommodation than as a model of conversion. Truly to hear the voices of one's African Anglican brother and sister, with their challenge to evangelism and the offense of the cross, is far more threatening, but potentially renewing as well.

This essay has included a reflection on the idea of implicit faith, which assumes that ignorance can imply inculpability. We contemporary Christians, as we look at the world of religions and cultures, are quick to seize on this notion. But we must bear in mind that Thomas Aquinas would have affirmed its inverse as well: those in whose hands the most has been committed bear the greatest responsibility. All of us depend solely on God's grace, and no one knows what God's final reckoning will be. Pastors and theologians are called to reflect boldly and freely on the mystery of God's economy of salvation. But finally, as the Baltimore Declaration reminds us, we are not at liberty to surrender Christ's sole agency for salvation. The biblical story, the backbone of the church's life, requires this. Nor are we at liberty to forget the call to witness given by the same risen Lord. On the last day, when he stands before all the nations, from us, the stewards blessed with this truth and this witness, he will require the most of all.

Two Millennia Later: Evangelizing Jews?

ELLEN T. CHARRY

ARTICLE 5 of the Baltimore Declaration reaffirms the condemnation of Christian anti-Semitism proclaimed by virtually all branches of Western Christianity since the Second World War. It then goes on to reaffirm the call to evangelize Jews, repudiating what has come to be called two-covenant theology. The latter is the theological arm of the Christian-Jewish dialogue movement of the twentieth century, which argues that from a Christian perspective there are not one but two ways to be related to God. Jews are related to God through the Mosaic covenant; Gentiles are related to God through Jesus Christ.[1] In the words of the Baltimore Declaration, two-covenant theology argues that "eternal salvation is already given to the chosen people of Israel through the covenant of Abraham and Moses, independently of the crucified Christ," and that therefore "the Gospel of Jesus the Messiah need not be proclaimed to them."

Article 5 follows the article on Christianity and world religions, which similarly argues for evangelization of all people. The idea that "salvation may be ultimately found apart from the atoning death and resurrection of Jesus Christ" (article 4) has grown throughout this century, stimulated by the writings of Rufus Jones early on and devel-

---

1. This movement is associated with the name of James Parks early in this century and more recently with the work of Roy and Alice Eckhardt, John Pawlikowski, Eugene Fisher, and especially Paul van Buren.

With thanks to Jouette Bassler and Ellen Davis for helpful suggestions in the writing of this essay.

oped recently by Paul Knitter, John Hick, John Cobb, and Houston Smith, among others. Lately, the recognition of the multiplicity of religious belief systems has emerged as an advocacy of "pluralism": each religious community's beliefs are to be embraced, not merely tolerated as an interim stage on the way to a higher truth. The Baltimore Declaration interprets pluralism as religious relativism, although some of the writers named above strive to protect the uniqueness of Christianity while recognizing the theological legitimacy of other faiths.

In response to the interfaith dialogue movement, whether between Christianity and all the world's religions or Judaism specifically, the Baltimore Declaration reminds Christians that Christ is the one and only savior of humankind, including Jews. Even though they be ignorant of that fact, even though they protest, even though they gave their bodies to be burned at the stake and in the ovens proclaiming their faith in the God of Israel revealed at Sinai, the origin and destiny of Israel lies with the triune God known through Jesus Christ.

Many issues are at stake in the two-millennia-old struggle between Jews and Christians: the doctrine of Scripture, the doctrine of God, the doctrine of election, Christology, pneumatology, ecclesiology, and eschatology. Rhetoric and politeness aside, on all of these issues Jews and Christians believe one another wrong. Let there be no doubt: the theological contempt is deep and mutual. The direct simplicity of article 5 shields an exceedingly complex and painful set of theological, historical, and pastoral problems. In trying to shed light (I hope not more heat) on this issue, it will be crucial to distinguish carefully between theological issues on the one hand and historical and pastoral issues on the other. While the former constitute the plumbline of the tradition, the latter are not to be taken lightly, particularly in this instance.

I.

In one sense the question of Jewish evangelism today is precisely what it was when St. Paul wrote to the church at Rome that "a hardening has come upon part of Israel, until the full number of the Gentiles come in" (Rom. 11:25). After two millennia we can safely say that most of Israel has failed to be persuaded that the gospel of Jesus Christ is a revelation of God that has to do with them. At the same time, the question of Jewish evangelism now is radically different from the situation in the first century. The New Testament writers all assumed the theological legitimacy of Judaism; it was the only way to be related to God. The question was whether Jesus had anything to do with God, if so what consequences this had for being a Jew, and finally what implications that had for God's relationship to Gentiles. The easiest way to grasp how serious the struggle was is to listen to New Testament witnesses. Two examples of how the earliest Christians justified their theological claims to other Jews are the accounts of the transfiguration (Mark 9:2-8 and parallels) and Peter's explanation of his decision to baptize Gentile believers (Acts 11:1-18).

The transfiguration accounts echo the revelation of God at Sinai recounted in Exodus 24 and 34. Exodus 24, as it has come down to us, is not clear as to who saw God. Seeing God was an awesome and frightening, indeed, a potentially fatal encounter attested to at numerous points in the Book of Exodus.[2] In 24:1-2, Moses, Aaron, Nadab, Abihu, and the seventy elders of Israel went up the mountain, but only Moses approached God. According to verses 9-11 the whole group saw God, who was transfigured before their eyes. The author is at a loss for words. In verse 10 he says, "Under his feet there was something like a pavement of sapphire stone, like the very heaven for clearness" (NRSV). The author is surprised that they survived the encounter, for he wrote, "God did not lay his hand on the chief men of the people of Israel; also they beheld God, and they ate and drank" (v. 11, NRSV). Verse 17 adds that from afar the glory of the Lord on the mountain looked like "a devouring fire." No wonder the Israelites thought Moses dead when he had not descended from the mountain after a month (Exod. 32:1).

In the account of the Sinai covenant in Exodus 34, the making of the second set of tablets, Moses is alone when talking to God. Verses 30-35 say that afterward his face glistened with the glory of the Lord, so that the Israelites "were afraid to come near him" (v. 30), presumably lest they be harmed by the fiery glory of God so palpable on Moses. After delivering the commandments of God to the people, Moses veiled his face, probably to protect the people from the power of the glory of God. Even God took similar precautions. He declined to accompany Israel into battle lest he destroy them en route (Exod. 33:3-5), and he protected Moses from seeing his face (Exod. 33:20-23).

The synoptic transfiguration accounts echo several elements of the Exodus story. Jesus, like Moses, takes the leaders of their fledgling

2. See Exod. 4:24; 30:20-21; 32:1; 33:3, 20-23.

movement up to a high mountain away from the rest, where he is transfigured. They, like the Israelites before them, were terrified, for this event classed Jesus with Moses and Elijah. Indeed, the transfiguration was reminiscent of the revelation of God himself in Exodus 24:10. The cloud representing the glory of God is also present (cf. Exod. 24:16), and the heavenly voice is similar to the standard rabbinic designation for the voice of prophecy, the *bat kol*.

The notion of erecting a third tent or shelter for Jesus along with those for Moses and Elijah also authorizes Jesus as their undisputed heir. Amos 9:11 promises the reestablishment of the Davidic dynasty. The Septuagint translates *succah* in Amos 9:11 as *skene*, the same word used by the synoptists for the temporary shelters to be built for the three leaders of Israel: Moses, Elijah, and Jesus. Clearly the transfiguration accounts condense many biblical allusions into one tersely focused revelation: Jesus is God's newly designated leader of Israel. But something radically new about God is disclosed in Jesus because he does not veil his face when with his followers. In Moses' time encountering God dealt death. But Luke implies that encountering God through Jesus brings resurrection and life. Nothing short of such drama could convince potentially sympathetic Jews of Jesus' legitimacy and authorize the mission of the disciples. Yet even this failed to persuade most Jews then or now.

Christians not only argued that Jesus equaled Moses, David, Jonah, Elijah, and others; they claimed that he eclipsed them all in the degree to which he revealed God. While this shift is taken for granted by Christians schooled by centuries of Christian teaching, the original premise, to say nothing of its subsequent strengthening, has never been granted by Jews. It is all a theological offense.

Acts 11 attacks the question of what this new action of God through Jesus means from a different quarter. By this time the apostles had been sent by the Holy Spirit to preach their conviction that Jesus was God's new way for Israel boldly. That Jesus was God's new way to lead Israel so radically transformed Judaism that most Jews were unable to grasp what God was doing. The parallels of Jesus in the New Testament not only to Moses and Elijah but to David, Jonah, and all the prophets indicate how passionately a few Jews sought to shake other Jews into awareness that God was again awake and alive in their midst.

Peter, however, took an even bolder step when, by authorizing the baptism of Gentiles, he suggested that this new awakening of divine activity was to spread the worship of God globally. The shock of this radical reformulation of the people of God has long since evaporated. But at the time it was so startling and unsettling that Peter had publicly to defend his decision even to the other apostles. And he did so with recourse to the same divine voice he had heard at the transfiguration of Jesus. God himself had ordained these dramatic departures from tradition! Most Jews rejected the authenticity of both the transfiguration and the outreach to Gentiles.

Today the situation between Christians and Jews is radically different. Now it is not an incredulous populace that needs to be convinced that the God of Israel is indeed revealed in Jesus; nor do Christians any longer doubt that Gentiles are grafted onto Israel through him. These foundations of Christianity, once so radical and subversive, are now the unexamined assumptions of a domesticated Christian world. Now the Christian consensus is the reverse: since Jesus is the final and definitive revelation of God, Israel without Jesus is Godless. From a Jewish point of view this idea was then and remains unintelligible.

Jewish defiance of the gospel angered Christians and led them to think contemptuously of Jewish beliefs, practices, and Scriptures. As the apostolic writings were canonized, what had been Scripture for the first Christians came to be considered inferior to explicitly Christian Scriptures. Marcion's suggestion that the Hebrew Scriptures be expunged from the Christian canon was wisely repudiated, but the aura of the inferiority of the Old to the New Testament lingers. Gradually, and perhaps under Neoplatonic influence, the understanding of Hebrew Scripture subtly changed. Instead of understanding Jesus as a further or revived testimony to the continuing involvement of God in Israel, as the New Testament authors had, in the patristic period the Old Testament came to be seen as the backdrop for the definitive revelation of God in Jesus, against which all prior work of God in history was but anticipation, mere shadows or inklings.

As Christendom strengthened, Jews came to be considered no better than godless pagans and were treated accordingly. In short, in the first century the burden of demonstrating theological legitimacy lay with Christians. Later Christians no longer assumed the authenticity of Judaism. They adopted a triumphalist stance, considering non-Christians blind and obstinate. In other words, the serious theological quarrel at the center of the Christian-Jewish argument was silenced by Christian success. Today Christian champions of two-covenant theology challenge the Christian claim that Christ died for Jews, too, by asserting the theological validity of Judaism.

The Baltimore Declaration does distinguish between the evangelization of Jews and that of all other non-Christians by recognizing that "God has gathered to himself the people of Israel to be his holy nation and royal priesthood, consecrated to his service in the redemption of the world" (article 5). But they do not note that thereby hangs a deep and momentous set of theological (as well as practical and pastoral) tangles that defy simple proclamations; indeed, by the mystery of God they may defy us still, sending Christians to prayer and penitence before planning missions to Jews.

One way of thinking about the current conflict between Christians who support and those who oppose missions to Jews is to ask whether the existence of Judaism poses a pastoral or a theological problem for Christians. One possibility is to suggest that, even if at Christianity's inception non-Christian Judaism constituted a theological threat to Christianity, today it no longer does. The issue is purely pastoral: how to preach the gospel to people who have been oppressed by the gospel for two millennia. The trick of evangelism is how to teach Jews to become their most feared enemies. For that is what it is for a Jew to become a Christian.

Sociologically and psychologically the Christianization of Jews is as traumatic an undertaking now as it was then, for it apparently involves the abandonment of God from a Jewish theological position, and — what may be worse in the eyes of many Jews — the betrayal and abandonment of the Jewish people. For a Jew to become a Christian is not analogous to a Methodist becoming a Roman Catholic. Jews understandably consider Christians their enemies. Under the banner of Christian love, Christians have oppressed and harassed Jews incessantly and in every conceivable circumstance. From a Jewish point of view, Christianity has little moral integrity. Ironically, the Christian caricature of the hypocritical Pharisees is precisely the image Jews have of Christians. Based on Jewish experience, it is not clear that Christians take the Beatitudes seriously.

And theologically speaking, Judaism finds Christian theological judgments about Jesus flat out wrong. Christians worship a different God, a triune God, a God who becomes human. The God of Israel is one, alone, and never incarnate. From a Jewish point of view, Jews alone (and Gentiles who convert according to Jewish law) constitute the true Israel, not Jews and Gentiles brought together in any other structure outside of Jewish law and tradition.

Even if one were to surmount these psychological and theological objections, one is then faced with a serious ecclesiological question exposed in the sacrament of baptism. What does it mean to baptize a Jew as opposed to baptizing a Gentile? To my knowledge this question has not been raised in the church. Baptism has assumed the form of an initiation rite. But in the case of Jews, things are not quite so straightforward. The baptismal service in the *Book of Common Prayer* greets the newly baptized with the words "we welcome you into the household of God." Now while for Gentiles — initially pagans — this formula is accurate, saying this about a Jew must stick in the throat. While it is true that Christians may welcome adventurous Jews into the body of Christ, it is simply not true that Christians can welcome Jews into the household of God, where they believe they have lived all their lives — unless, of course, God has abandoned non-Christian Jews since the incarnation.

Paul himself is somewhat ambiguous on this issue. In Romans 9:6-7 he says explicitly that "not all Israelites truly belong to Israel, and not all of Abraham's children are his true descendants" (NRSV). Yet in Romans 11:2 he says explicitly that "God has not rejected his people." Perhaps what Paul had in mind is the position that has dominated Christian thought. With the creation of the church, "Israel" has been redefined. God waits in hope that Abraham's descendants of the flesh will join with the children of the promise, comprising together with them a new Israel of God. God has not abandoned but rather has transformed Israel. Thus, what God has done in breaking down the wall between Jews and Gentiles in Jesus Christ is a very new thing that, while it may have been promised through the prophets (Rom. 1:2), or even "before the foundation of the world" (Eph. 1:4), never existed before. In this sociological sense Jews and Gentiles have had slightly different experiences. Jews must accustom themselves to thinking of Gentiles as the beloved of God rather than as the enemies of God, as had heretofore been assumed. Gentiles who enter this new community do so as neophytes related to God for the first time. Being aware of Jewish suspicion of their paganism, Gentile converts must overcome their sense of second-class citizenship now that they have been brought into the household of God on equal terms with the Jews. Paul, knowing that this new status might be wrongly interpreted, warns the Gentile converts against any pretensions to self-congratulation in Romans 11:17-22.

Theologically, the situation is somewhat different. Gentiles have been raised up to become children of God. They are no longer the people they have thought themselves to be. They are not free to select a god or a cult or a philosophy. They have been made Jews by God whether they like it or not! Jews who enter the body of Christ are still Israel, theologically speaking. But there are new tenants in the house, people whom they had heretofore considered socially uncivilized and beyond the reach of God. To them it must look like God has done a new thing, or, as Paul saw it, God has finally brought to fruition what had been intended all along: the destruction of sociological Israel for the creation of the new Israel, the body of Christ. In either case, the Jewish relationship to God is not changed; what has changed is the shape of Israel. From a Jewish perspective it is not a Jew's relationship with God that has changed — as is the case for Gentiles — but the form in which the people of God happens in the world. In short, from a biblical perspective it is theologically odd for Gentile Christians to welcome Jewish Christians into the household of God. As Acts 10–11 attests, historically the reality was the reverse. Now that the situation is so different, it is appropriate to welcome Jews into the body of Christ, which is continuous, theologically speaking, with the Jewish people.

To state it a bit differently, Jews coming into the body of Christ maintain their lifelong relationship with God. This is not to suggest that the incarnation has changed no more than the shape of the people of God. Not so, as I shall suggest below. The point here is that for Jews entrance into the body of Christ does not inaugurate a relationship with God, as it does for Gentiles. From this perspective, then, the body of Christ continues Israel's witness to God, now with Gentiles as equal partners. In terms of their relationship to God, nothing has essentially changed for Jews. In joining the body of Christ, Jews confess their understanding and support for God's gracious turn to the Gentiles.

While in a profound sense baptism signifies no change in a Jew's relationship with God, in another sense it represents a profound change. For the incarnation decisively changes not only how God is known in the world but also what we know of God. Gentiles, who know no other way of being related to God than through Jesus Christ, are transformed from pagans into Christians. For Jews it is different. For in the life, death, and resurrection of Jesus Christ, God's reconciling love is made known in a dramatically new way.

It is not the case that the reconciling love of God was ever hidden from Israel. Creation itself testifies to the love of God for creation. God's rescue of the human race through Noah speaks of God's compassion. The liberation of Israel from Egypt, God's guidance, care, and feeding of the people, even after the golden calf episode, speak of God's mercy. The return of Israel to its land, not only after the wilderness wandering, but again after the Babylonian exile, speaks of God's faithfulness to sinners. It could be that God's faithfulness to faithless Israel, the triumph of God's love over his justifiable wrath, recounted by the author of Psalm 78, stands as the ensign to all nations of God's graciousness. If God remains committed to this most ordinary of nations, is there not hope for all? The sheer survival of the Jewish people discloses the God who gives himself unreservedly to faithless humankind. Christians eager to make Jews into Christians, on the grounds that they do not know God, threaten the foundation upon which Christians themselves stand.

And yet, something of God is disclosed in Jesus Christ that we did not and could not know or see before. Perhaps this is because, before the incarnation, God could catch our attention for only a few moments. In times of suffering, to be sure, we know our need for rescue, but we lose sight of it at happier moments. And each time we experience shame and humiliation we are reminded that even the most skilled and educated among us is but partially and momentarily abled. We must continuously confess our sinfulness before God because our attention readily flags. All our knowledge, skill, insight, and best efforts fail to heal those who hurt, fail to succor the poor, fail to effect any solutions, fail to avert the tragedy we see all around us. When reminded of our sinfulness, we turn to God for forgiveness. Sometimes we are even able to hold onto our gratitude to God in moments of exultation at the graciousness of God in our own lives that supports and nourishes us. Yet at other moments we forget that God is the source of all our blessings.

Each time we reread an episode in God's salvage work with Israel, thereby coming to view ourselves and our own need for rescue more clearly, we reclaim our need for God. As we internalize the details of each vignette of the saga of Israel's history and God's faithfulness, our grasp of God's goodness deepens. Still, something is afoot in God's revelation in Jesus Christ that rivets our attention on God in a way that neither the history of Israel, nor the excellence of God's creation, nor the blessings and salvage work occurring in our own lives lays bare.

The story of God in Jesus is not the coming of God *to* us, for to this the history of Israel eloquently testifies; rather, in Jesus God comes *as* us, so precious are we to God. The gift of God in the cross is not the command of God to do his will that we might live, but the humiliation of God that we might know the depth and breadth of love freely given, even unto death on a cross. The power of God in the resurrection is not the controlling voice that inspires awe, but the invitation to hope in new life after hope has died.

Biblical Judaism and Judaism before A.D. 70 encompassed the

notion of atonement that was ritually reenacted annually. But in Jesus, reconciliation with God, undertaken by God rather than through expiatory sacrifice, assumes center stage. Adoption as children of God through forgiveness of sin rather than membership in an elect nation becomes the central bond between God and believers.

In short, while in one sense for a Jew to become a Christian changes nothing in his or her relationship with God, to confess Jesus as Lord is as new and startling as is the inauguration of a relationship with God for any Gentile. To become a disciple of Jesus, then, is the beginning of a new life for Jew and Gentile alike. To know death as a gift, to be formed and empowered through the cross, to understand leadership as servanthood, to be challenged by the strenuous ethical teachings of Jesus, to grasp hope of eternal life with God regardless of ethnicity, to be humbled as a loved sinner for whose sake God poured himself out and made himself one with us in humiliation and suffering — all this is new. It is not simply a clarification of something foretold in the history of Israel; it is a new disclosure of God. Advocates of a two-covenant theology who would deny that Jews need to know Jesus would deny them the deepest knowledge of God made known to humankind.

The foregoing discussion serves to warn all sides in the dispute against hastily lining up on either side of the debate on evangelizing Jews. There are profound historical and psychological reasons for respecting the Jewish right to privacy. The smell of the crematoria yet lingers in Jewish nostrils. At the same time, the love and humility of God made known in Jesus press to be spoken of, even to those who have been made to suffer at the hands of his self-proclaimed followers. Before moving on to assess strategies for action or inaction that are being proposed today, a further look at New Testament texts that grapple with the complexity of this issue will highlight both the continuity and the discontinuity that govern theological reflection on these matters and will alert participants in the discussion against facile recommendations.

II.

Respecting the complexity of the Jewish-Christian problem requires exegeting New Testament texts from the point of view of those involved in the crisis at its inception.[3] An understanding of that bloody war

---

3. The most helpful book I have come across in this regard is Richard Hays's *Echoes of Scripture in the Letters of Paul* (New Haven: Yale University Press, 1989).

would prepare Christians to speak with Jews more respectfully and less naively, whatever the practical outcomes of the conversation may be.

To aid this process I have selected New Testament passages from Paul, Luke, and Matthew. The goal of the exegesis will be to disclose the radicalism of Christian claims in the context of the first-century struggle among various factions of Christian and non-Christian Jews to define Judaism.[4]

The apostle Paul is one of the most influential voices in this conflict. His letters are permeated both with scriptural allusions and citations and with allusions or citations from rabbinic literature. Twice in his letters we find a repetition of phrases that have been interpreted as an early baptismal formula. Galatians 3:28 is the famous dictum, "There is neither Jew nor Greek, there is neither slave nor free, there is neither male nor female; for you are all one in Christ Jesus." In 1 Corinthians 12:13 the formula appears in connection with the discussion of the gifts of the Holy Spirit: "For by one Spirit we were all baptized into one body — Jews or Greeks, slaves or free — and all were made to drink of one Spirit." The order is the same, but the last phrase about gender is omitted. The omission of gender equality may be an indication of the delicacy of this issue, for in 1 Corinthians 11 Paul had spoken of the subordination of women to men at length.

While these passages may reflect an early baptismal confession, the formula is also found in rabbinic literature, although the order and wording vary from place to place. *Tanna debe Eliyahu* (an ethical compilation of midrashim usually dated to the second half of the tenth century) connects this formula to the presence of the Holy Spirit, as Paul did so long before: "I call heaven and earth to witness, that whether it be Gentile or Israelite, man or woman, slave or handmaid, according to the deeds which he does, so will the Holy Spirit rest on him."[5]

The formula also appears in a later midrashic compilation, the *Yalkut Shim'oni* or simply *Yalkut,* an anthology of more than fifty older midrashic works. The *Yalkut* was compiled in the first half of the thirteenth century. It renders the formula thus: "God said to Moses:

4. Jewish texts from the period and after have often been studied as critical sources for understanding Christian origins. But the reverse is also true. The New Testament is a set of voices of first-century Judaism, trying to define and organize the traditions in response to the momentous events that had overtaken them.

5. Cited in C. G. Montefiore and H. Loewe, *A Rabbinic Anthology* (New York: Schocken, 1974), p. 557.

Is there respect of persons with Me? Whether it be Israelite or Gentile, man or woman, slave or handmaid, whoso does a commandment shall find the reward at its side."[6]

In addition to these perhaps obscure citations (there may be others), both of which concur with the leveling effect the formula has in Paul's hands, the most striking occurrence of this motif is its liturgical use to the precise opposite end. Three blessings, one corresponding to each of the three phrases of the Pauline formula (in the Pauline rather than the midrashic order and wording), occur in the daily morning liturgy within a larger group of fifteen personal ablutions recited prior to public prayer. Each blessing praises God for *not* making the worshiper a Gentile, a slave, or a woman, the same order found in Galatians 3:28 and in shortened form in 1 Corinthians 12:13. It is noteworthy that only these three of the fifteen refer to issues of personal status. All of the others pertain to actions of awaking from sleep, stretching, getting out of bed, dressing, walking, washing, etc. Whether the inclusion of these three was a polemic against those rabbis (or Paul himself!) who took a more positive view of these categories of persons is not clear. Neither is it clear that the gratitude expressed in any way contradicts the theological equality that the midrashim and Paul both assume. It may be a pointed theological judgment against social class stratification.

While the dating of the insertion of these blessings into the daily liturgy may be uncertain, there is a further piece of evidence in the New Testament that may date it in the first century. The parable of the Pharisee and the tax collector in Luke 18:10-14 loosely paraphrases the blessings and excoriates the Pharisee for thanking God for his own piety. "The Pharisee stood and prayed thus with himself, 'God, I thank thee that I am not like other men, extortioners, unjust, adulterers, or even like this tax collector'" (v. 11). This paraphrase of the morning blessings focuses on moral conduct rather than personal status, including the work of the tax collector, who was viewed as an opportunist and traitor by the Jews, who were occupied by an oppressive foreign power. Thus, it is perhaps more revealing of common Jewish attitudes of the day than are the blessings in the prayerbook.

From the midrashic texts examined above it is clear that the equality of different classes before God freed everyone to be judged by the quality of their character rather than by their gender or social status. Judaism had to balance between its doctrine of election and this

6. Montefiore and Loewe, *A Rabbinic Anthology*, p. 559.

theology of deserts. The blessings, statements of gratitude, may have expressed a sentiment comparable to the phrase "there but for the grace of God go I," or "thank God I am not poor and that I had access to a good education," or something of this sort. Jews were citizens under Roman law, for which they were grateful. The rabbinic paraphrase may express gratitude for the benefits that accrued to them by virtue of this protected status. It is most unlikely that late antiquity would have viewed these advantages of privilege as implying prejudice against those who lacked them, as is common today. Being fortunate simply did not suggest to the ancient mind that this was achieved at the expense of others.

Even if the Lukan allusion is not to the ablutions and the blessings were redacted after Paul, the prevalence of the Pauline formula in rabbinic literature and liturgy suggests that Paul may have traded on an accepted theological rationale for the equality of all classes of persons before God and turned it into a central Christian rallying cry — perhaps even more abrasively, into a baptismal formula. And regardless of whether the Jewish liturgical unit predated or responded to the Pauline use, the territory charted by the argument between the two camps of Jews is clear.

Paul is saying that these gradations of earthly status are meaningless to those who are bound together by the Holy Spirit in Christ in this life. He was creating a new model of community that worked around (but did not abolish) distinctions of civil status. Paul, for example, did not focus concern on slavery or the subordination of women, precisely because these civil determinations, though socially binding, were theologically irrelevant.

The rabbis, for their part, recognized that their good fortune *was* related to issues of ethnicity, gender, and class. Even if these distinctions carried no ultimate soteriological freight, since God required moral conduct of all nations, still Jews perceived themselves as special in two ways. First, Judaism itself made high moral demands and protected Jews from living what they saw as the untoward life of pagans. And second, the election of Israel meant that Jews were more loved by God than others, even if that love involved suffering for God's sake. However, this should not be read as holding that Jews were saved and Gentiles lost, as the Christian doctrine of election later held concerning Christians and non-Christians. Rather, through election God honored and protected Israel on earth. The ambiguity and ambivalence of the rabbinic doctrine of election and the opinion of the salvation of Gentiles resulted from a weak or vague soteriology. Salvation, as Christians came to understand it, was simply not of primary import to rabbinic Jews.

Paul pushed the tangential rabbinic view that social status was soteriologically irrelevant into the foreground, making salvation a central plank in the Christian platform. This, of course, was jarring to rabbinic ears. But he went beyond this by preaching to pagans and bringing them into Judaism (that is, baptizing them into the body of Christ) in great masses. In the process, he disregarded the law of God (by not requiring circumcision) and the election of Israel by insisting that God transcended divisions of social class, gender, etc. And he also denied the need for social isolation that Jews felt was necessary in order to safeguard moral rectitude. This too was a bold assertion, and one that Paul himself may have struggled with at moments, perhaps in Corinth.

In other words, Paul's baptismal formula destroyed the sociological coherence of the Jewish people by capitalizing on a minor theological theme of equality before God regardless of status. And he attacked the theological coherence of Judaism by rejecting the election of Israel and the law of God in the name of trying to transform pagan society on theological grounds. Paul created a "Judaism" that destroyed the identity of the Jewish people, flouted divine law, and endangered Jewish morality. Is it any wonder that few other Jews then or now followed his lead?

Another example of the "no holds barred" struggle going on in the New Testament focuses on the interpretation of Scripture. Luke 4:16-30, the story of Jesus' commentary on his reading of Isaiah 61:1-2a in his home congregation in Nazareth, is a stunning example of Christian effrontery, and it is also related to Paul's concern about God's relation to pagans. The scene is a peaceful sabbath morn at the outset of Jesus' Galilean ministry. His reputation for healings had preceded him. The drama begins when Jesus says, "Today this scripture has been fulfilled in your hearing" (v. 21). Now the Scripture passage that had just been read was about proclaiming release to the captives, the recovering of sight to the blind, and freedom for the oppressed (Isa. 61:1). His audience craned forward expectantly, whispering to one another approvingly of his words, anticipating that he would speak to them, his kin and neighbors, of the release and healing he would bring to them as they chafed under Roman rule.

What he said, however, caught the pious Jews completely off guard. Rather than telling them of their release from Roman oppression or about the year of the Lord's favor that they awaited, he brought them two other Scriptures, 1 Kings 17 and 2 Kings 5, by means of which he authenticated his ministry.[7] The first of these Scripture passages is the story of Elijah, Jesus' prototype, who was sent by God first to curse King Ahab and the land of Israel with famine and then to a foreigner, a Sidonian widow, to provide her with food while Israel was parched with drought. There is no mention of the woman's piety or righteousness. Elijah not only provided her and her son with food throughout the famine; when her son fell ill and died, Elijah revived him. The upshot of the story is that the woman accepted Elijah as a true prophet of God and became a believer. And to make sure his neighbors got the point, Luke tells us, Jesus added a gratuitous jibe at his neighbors: "But in truth, I tell you, there were many widows in Israel in the days of Elijah . . . when there came a great famine over all the land; and Elijah was sent to none of them but only to Zarephath, in the land of Sidon, to a woman who was a widow" (Luke 4:25-26).

According to Luke, the other Scripture Jesus brought, 2 Kings 5, was a story of Elisha, Elijah's successor, another prototype for Jesus' own ministry. The story comes in the midst of a series of stories of Elisha's miracles of healing, like those the townspeople had probably been hearing about Jesus. These stories in 2 Kings taught that Elisha had separated water to allow passage over dry land and had purified undrinkable water (reminiscent of Moses), that he had greatly multiplied a jar of oil so that it reprieved a widow from debt, that he had raised a child who died suddenly, purified rotted food, and fed one hundred people from twenty pieces of bread, with some left over. The authenticity of Jesus' ministry is argued for on the basis of the integrity of God's love for Israel, demonstrated by prophets in the past extending back to Moses. Luke placed Jesus in the midst of the grand tradition.

In the segment of the narrative referred to by Jesus in Luke 4, Elisha healed the leprous commander of the Aramean army (Israel's enemy), Naaman, who had stolen a young Israelite woman for a concubine. The captive girl suggested that Naaman go to Elisha to be healed. This called for high-level diplomatic interchange between the two warring kings of Aram and Israel. After careful international protocols were observed, the diseased general traveled to Israel to be washed clean in the Jordan River. The upshot of this story is identical with that of the story of the Sidonian woman. Naaman became con-

7. Note well that the notion of typological use of Scripture is to authenticate the new events in terms of the only trustworthy source: Scripture. It would be utterly preposterous to think that for Luke the purpose, intent, or meaning of Scripture was to foreshadow Jesus.

verted to the God of Israel: "Behold, I know that there is no God in all the earth but in Israel" (2 Kings 5:16). And to add insult to injury, Jesus glossed the Kings narrative with another gratuitous insult, absent from the biblical text: "And there were many lepers in Israel in the time of the prophet Elisha; and none of them was cleansed, but only Naaman the Syrian" (Luke 4:27).

Jesus had led those who trusted him, pious Jews all, to believe that he was going to proclaim their release from suffering and heal them of their infirmities. Instead, in the middle of a worship service, he reminded them that the prophets of Israel in whose shoes he stood had brought food and healing to Gentiles who accepted God by dint of these miracles and healings, while Israelites starved, suffered, and died. There is no hint in the story that the Jews were being punished for some religious infraction or want of faith. It is small wonder, then, that Luke tells his own readers, perhaps potential Gentile converts themselves: "When they heard this, all in the synagogue were filled with wrath. And they rose up and put him out of the city, and led him to the brow of the hill on which their city was built, that they might throw him down headlong" (Luke 4:28-29). There can be no question of misunderstanding Jesus. They understood plainly. Jesus rubbed their noses in the fact that Elijah and Elisha — and perhaps he himself, by implication — were sent to claim pagans. He had come to them to taunt them in their sufferings while his real mission was to shower God's blessings on their enemies. Luke has Jesus announce to his kinfolk that he is betraying them under orders from God![8]

The last passage I will examine is the Matthean Beatitudes. The opening word of each beatitude, *makarios*, usually translated "blessed" or "happy," is a common word in the Psalms. In the Septuagint it is the exclusive translation of the Hebrew word *ashrey*, which appears twenty-four times in nineteen psalms, often at the beginning of a verse, as it does in the Matthean Beatitudes. Most psalmic beatitudes are short, pithy assertions or assurances of happiness for the pious and virtuous. They also convey a sense of privilege at being recipients of divine favor or simply of the joy that comes from piety and righteousness (e.g., Ps. 94:12; 106:3; 112:1; 119:1). Translating *makarios* as "privileged" would not be misleading and might be enlightening in the Matthean context. It is the opening word of five psalms (disregarding

8. An alternate and perhaps more popular interpretation of this text is that Jesus abandons his neighbors because they do not accept him. At face value, the text seems to argue the reverse, although the former is an arguable interpretation.

superscriptions) and, in fact, is the first word of the Psalter. In five psalms it appears twice, as the opening word of a couplet of two consecutive verses or in a parallelism within one verse (as in Ps. 144:15), in a form comparable to the Matthean Beatitudes. Jews familiar with the Greek translation of the Scriptures would immediately recognize the format of the Matthean Beatitudes.[9]

Of all the psalms, Psalm 37 is perhaps the most alluded to by the Sermon on the Mount, despite the fact that it does not use the beatitude format. The Matthean Beatitudes on meekness (Matt. 5:5), righteousness (v. 6), purity of heart (v. 8), peacemaking (v. 9), and persecution (v. 10) all echo Psalm 37 (vv. 11, 28-29, 18, 37, and 39-40, respectively). An additional three verses from Matthew 5 (vv. 16, 22, and 42) also echo Psalm 37 (vv. 6, 8, and 21-22, respectively), and Matthew 6:25 echoes Psalm 37:8 and 25.

The themes of Psalm 37 are quiet trust in God through adversity, perseverance in emotional self-control, imitation of the righteous in thought and action, the belief that God will rescue the faithful and reward them with blessing and eternal life, and the destruction of the wicked. With the exception of the retribution theme, the psalm anticipates central themes of the Sermon on the Mount and the Beatitudes.

In the first century the Jewish doctrine of election was understood to be based on membership in the Jewish people. The election of Israel was a central theme of the liturgy. In the central rabbinic prayer, the *Amidah*, already extant in the first century, God is referred to as the redeemer of Israel, the one who redeems the grandchildren of the patriarchs, the healer of sick Israelites, the liberator of the dispersed of Israel. The *Amidah* consistently refers to the Jews as "your people Israel" or "Israel your nation." The last blessing of the series prays for peace for Israel.

A *mishna* (Avot 3:14) attributed to Rabbi Akiva (a second-century teacher) probably reflects the tension in first-century Judaism between recognizing that all human beings are created in the image of God (Gen. 9:6), but asserting that only Israelites are called the children *(banim)* of God (Deut. 14:1). Examples from early rabbinic literature could easily be multiplied. As E. P. Sanders put it,

---

9. In fact, probably much later, a liturgical unit was constructed of three psalmic beatitudes from Ps. 84:4 and 144:15, which have to do with Israel's joy at being the people of God. These were prefixed to Ps. 145, and together they became the most often recited psalm text of the Psalter, prescribed three times a day in the Talmud (Berachot 4b).

The Rabbis maintained the biblical attitude of being especially chosen and set aside by God. . . . [They] were not more plagued by arrogance than any other people who have held a doctrine of election; indeed, the idea that suffering was entailed in the election . . . helps to give quite a non-arrogant tone to Rabbinic thought on election. The idea of being privileged as children of Abraham may have been abused, but abuses were criticized by the Rabbis themselves.[10]

The polemical power of the Beatitudes, and the Sermon on the Mount as a whole, takes shape against this scriptural and rabbinic background. Matthew took the side of Psalm 37 in constructing a view of the privileged of God that was grounded in virtuous character traits that could be consciously developed and honed. This theology loosened Judaism from a doctrine of election based on the unconditional and unaccounted for grace of God, as the election of Israel was. It sought to set Judaism on a path that valued righteousness above birth, moral striving above membership in the people of God. If one can assume that Matthew focused on an internal reformation of Judaism for Jews by birth (Matt. 28:19 notwithstanding), it appears that his moral emphasis would have looked like the creation of an elite among the elect. This is supported by the fact that several of the precepts of the Sermon on the Mount are radicalizations or intensifications of precepts of the Decalogue or biblical law (e.g., murder, adultery, and retaliation) or other rabbinic laws (divorce, ostentation in pious practices).

As evidenced by the discussion of Galatians 3:28 above, Jews were delicately poised between a doctrine of election that selected out the Jewish people as especially loved by God and a theology of deserts that honored righteousness above any birth-assigned status. The conflict in the first century between Jews who became Christians and those who did not was, in many ways, about resolving this tension. While Paul sought to define the Jewish people more broadly than the rabbis, Matthew defined it more narrowly. In either case the shock to Jewish sensibilities would have been great, unsettling Jewish self-understanding from several directions simultaneously.

The three texts that we have examined reveal some of the dimensions of the genuine theological conflict among first-century Jews, a conflict that was intensified by the destruction of the Temple by the

10. E. P. Sanders, *Paul and Palestinian Judaism* (Philadelphia: Fortress Press, 1977), p. 87.

Romans in A.D. 70. This must have sent Jews into serious reflection about their own election, and perhaps also about the goodness or the power of God. And it gave the fledgling Christian movement a strenuous shot in the arm, for it symbolized precisely the theology they advocated.

The legitimation of Christianity and eventual disenfranchisement of Judaism have silenced the bloody argument of the New Testament and rabbinic protagonists. Christians who are eager to evangelize Jews, even if they are cognizant of the disgraceful behavior of Christians before themselves, rarely stop to consider the theological underpinnings of the dispute. Still less do they consider the effrontery and slander heaped upon Jews and transmitted from generation to generation by the frozen snapshots taken in the midst of the battle that we know as the New Testament.

In short, God smashed Judaism open in Jesus Christ to bring all people together as one people of God and to reconcile all to himself. The problem is that neither Christians nor Jews have adjusted to this fact. Jews deny that it happened; Christians have forgotten what was broken open. The issues were never resolved, and it is nearly impossible for us to discern just how many parties there were in the fray. What we do know is that eventually two dominant parties emerged victorious and gathered smaller parties unto themselves. Matthew's ethically elite community was subsumed by Paul's broader vision, for example. And the Sadducees and Pharisees both gave way to the rabbinic sages, who painstakingly collated and preserved the sources that provided the backbone of Jewish law and custom that we know as normative Judaism.

III.

Keeping in mind these vignettes of how the ancient conversation went, we can now turn to the recent history of the conversation that has brought the Baltimore Declaration's position on evangelism to articulation within the Episcopal Church. Our church has vocal advocates on both sides of this issue.[11] Episcopal missions to Jews originated at the beginning of the nineteenth century with Joseph Frey, a Jewish

---

11. This brief discussion of missionary efforts with the Episcopal Church to evangelize Jews depends upon an unpublished paper by Rev. Philip Bottomley, Executive Director of the Church's Ministry among the Jews in the USA.

convert to Christianity. The London Jews Society, a splinter from the London Missionary Society, evangelized Jews in both England and the United States. Internal dissension and financial problems resulted in English control of the group, which changed its title after World War II to The Church's Ministry among the Jews, and more recently to A Christian Ministry among Jewish People, reflecting the growing unease with the idea of evangelism altogether. In the nineteenth century the group's work was carried forward by Jewish converts. As the Jewish community in the United States grew and organized in the second half of the nineteenth century, it objected to missionary efforts. Bishops in the Episcopal Church began to take positions on either side of the issue, especially in places like New York where there were large concentrations of Jews.

From 1816 to 1831 the Female Society of Boston and Vicinity for Promoting Christianity amongst the Jews, under the guidance of Miss Hannah Adams, represented a second strand of missionary effort. Like this Female Society, most other missions to Jews were small and of short duration, since they revolved around the energy and personality of one individual. Nevertheless, in 1841 the General Convention supported a plan to establish a chapel for Hebrew Christians in New York, run by converts when available.

Another avenue of evangelism was the opening of a school for Jewish children in New York in 1863, also run by a convert. The Jewish community set up a counter institution to rescue its children back the following year. A second school survived from 1866 to 1904, during which time seventy students were baptized.

A national ministry to Jews, the Church Society for Promoting Christianity amongst the Jews, existed in the Episcopal Church from 1878 to 1904, supported initially by thirty-two bishops. By 1897, as Jewish immigration swelled, the Bishop of New York withdrew support for the Society, supporting educational efforts among southern blacks instead. Although the national organization declined, local evangelism continued spottily during the 1910s and 1920s.

Contemporary efforts at Jewish evangelism by Episcopalians stem from the Anglican society that in 1815 was named The Church's Missions to the Jews (CMJ). The CMJ established an American branch in the late 1970s. It remains a tiny operation, located in Ambridge, Pennsylvania, headed by the Rev. Philip Bottomley, an Englishman. Its purpose is "to encourage Jewish people to recognize Jesus as their Messiah, and to educate Christians, especially Episcopalians, as to the Jewish origins of our Faith."

The other side of the story begins with the founding of the World Council of Churches (WCC) in 1948, which denounced anti-Semitism in the name of all its founding churches. Following the WCC's lead, local, national, and international church bodies have issued declarations and resolutions condemning anti-Semitism. In the mid-1960s, Vatican Council II issued a landmark proclamation known as *Nostra aetate,* releasing the Jewish people from the ancient charge of deicide. A similar resolution was adopted by the 1964 General Convention of the Episcopal Church.

In the 1970s an interreligious dialogue movement began in earnest. It was patterned on the ecumenical movement, with the important difference that, while the ecumenical movement aimed to reunite divided churches, the Jewish-Christian conversation did not. Instead, it aimed at cooperation on social issues and helping Christians come to a deeper understanding of the Jewish tradition and the emergence of the church universal from ancient Judaism. The Presiding Bishop established an Advisory Committee on Episcopal-Jewish Relations (PBACEJR), chaired by Bishop John Burt. The Committee drafted a programmatic statement on the issue for the national church. The 1979 General Convention, in a statement that reflected the dialogical tenor of the day, resolved to educate the church about ancient and modern Judaism. It commended the Committee to develop practical recommendations for implementation of the dialogue.

In the 1980s two new issues of primary concern to the Jewish community appeared on the agenda: Christian support for the State of Israel in the face of the protracted and increasingly ugly Middle East conflict and the rise of Palestinian nationalism, and opposition to intermarriage and proselytism. By 1987 the Episcopal Diocesan Ecumenical Officers adopted guidelines for carrying the national dialogue into individual dioceses and congregations, especially in communities with large Jewish populations. These guidelines included reading lists and recommendations to focus on the specific issues raised by the Jewish community.

In the same year the PBACEJR presented a much fuller set of Guidelines for Christian-Jewish Relations, which were adopted by the General Convention in 1988. These Guidelines are the immediate stimulus for article 5 of the Baltimore Declaration. The Guidelines repeated earlier condemnation of Christian persecution of Jews, counseled careful explanation of "New Testament texts which appear to place all Jews in an unfavorable light," stressed common concerns and beliefs, and elaborated principles of dialogue for local congregations.

They also raised the questions of Zionism and proselytism to new levels of visibility in the church. For the first time, and in response to the Jewish community's sensitivities, there was a section on "Authentic Christian Witness." It redefined Christian witness to Jews as dialogue: "a sharing of one's faith convictions without the intention of proselytizing," although it did not explicitly argue theologically for the validity of Judaism or propound a two-covenant theory.

The bottom line of the 1988 Guidelines is that preaching the gospel to Jews is now considered off-limits to Episcopalians. Perhaps the Declaration's authors believe that the church has capitulated to Jewish pressure and betrayed Jesus. In response to the Guidelines, the Declaration's authors "repudiate the false teaching that eternal salvation is already given to the chosen people of Israel through the covenant[s] of Abraham and Moses, independently of the crucified Christ, and the inference that the Gospel of Jesus the Messiah need not be proclaimed to them" (article 5).

IV.

Given the subtleties, subtexts, and suffering in all of the above, what is an appropriate Christian posture — dialogue or evangelism?

Theological dialogue is not feasible. For it is unlikely that either side would choose to reopen the theological debate on first-century terms. Jews have repeatedly been burned in theological debate and have largely lost interest in theology, partly as a result of experience and partly because they have been preoccupied with mere survival. And by now theological reflection is so identified with Christianity that it would feel like an alien exercise, undertaken as much to please the oppressor as to reflect on the community's faith.

Christians are unlikely to want to enter the lists because the very legitimacy of the faith would be open to question, and like Jews who do not want to see Judaism invalidated, even dialogically oriented Christians probably do not want to enter into a conversation that would question the legitimacy of their existence. This means that theological dialogue, of the sort undertaken among Christian churches to resolve issues resulting from the division of East and West or from the sixteenth-century Reformations, is inappropriate.

Even conversation aimed at "mutual understanding" may at times be frustrating. Jews are generally more hesitant than Christians to enter interfaith discussions precisely because they are attuned to the gravity of the divisions between the communities. Increased knowledge about and involvement with the other community, instead of leading to harmony, may only expose tensions normally checked by tact and/or ignorance. In general, neither Christians nor Jews have been at their best when dealing with one another.

Evangelism in any direct way is also ill-advised. If Christians want Jews to take them seriously, they must suffer being named as oppressors. And Jews may not be as forgiving as Christians might like them to be. The wounds of Europe — indeed, of two millennia of Christian power — are still raw. And Christians seeking to bring Jews to Christ may have the effect of keeping the wounds oozing. On the most practical level, Christians must listen first.

While no Christian has the right to withhold the gospel from anyone, it is paradoxical to discover that the gospel belongs fundamentally to Jews, and so of course it cannot be withheld from them, and yet to realize that they are offended by the gospel. This is all the more puzzling when one grasps the high degree to which Jews are secularized, alienated from their own theology yet offended by Christian theology — indeed, Christophobic. Judaism has been so successful at adapting to secular culture that it has forgotten its own knowledge of God.

Yet there is one thing that Christians might do, both in good conscience and in ways that Jews might recognize as helpful. Christians might intentionally encourage Jews to speak of God again. This avenue could prove helpful for both sides. For Jews raise the issue of theodicy in a way that Christians may need to hear. And Christians understand a theology of the cross that may comfort Jews who can no longer experience the grace of God because of the enormity of Jewish suffering. By a theology of the cross, in this case, I mean a theology that accepts suffering as part of the life of God for and with us. Christians know this only in the cross of Jesus Christ. But perhaps Jews first need to find their own language to express the love of God in the presence of burning babies,[12] before any talk of the cross of Christ.

In short, the most constructive approach to the question of Jewish evangelism is, I think, to help Jews turn to God in their own language, liturgy, and symbols. While we believe that full knowledge of God is only known through Jesus and that the full stature of humanness is

---

12. The allusion is to the following working principle of Irving Greenberg: "No statement, theological or otherwise, should be made that would not be credible in the presence of the burning children" ("Cloud of Smoke, Pillar of Fire: Judaism, Christianity, and Modernity after the Holocaust," in *Auschwitz: Beginning of a New Era? Reflections on the Holocaust,* ed. Eva Fleischner [New York: KTAV, 1974], p. 23).

only perfected as his disciples, we must also acknowledge that most of us Christians are the wild branches that have been grafted onto the cultivated olive tree. Our confession of faith in God's Son is only as strong as the testimony of Amos, Isaiah, Jonah, and Ruth to the faithfulness of the God of Israel.

Perhaps what we can learn from continued study of Scripture and history is that on this issue the way has not yet opened for us; therefore we are not permitted to proceed as if we were in control, for we are not in control. We should not withhold our own testimony from Jews interested in hearing it. But we do not know what God will do with that testimony in the life of that hearer of the gospel. It may send Jews back to or deeper into Judaism. Or it may arouse a curiosity to know Christ. That is not for us to say. But Paul's exhortation to the church at Corinth applies to us as well: "Give no offense to Jews or to Greeks or to the church of God, just as I try to please everyone in everything I do, not seeking my own advantage, but that of many, so that they may be saved. Be imitators of me, as I am of Christ" (1 Cor. 10:32–11:1, NRSV). Faithful Christian witness is genuinely pastoral.

All we can do is trust that God is in control and confess our willfulness in wanting more vision than we are granted. We must wait upon the mystery of God's goodness, which we cannot see clearly in this case. There will be Jews who are brought to Christ, but more through the grace of God than through the efforts of Christians eager to replenish sagging church rolls.[13] There will always be Jews who are offended by the name of Jesus. Evangelicals will have to reckon with the fact that in his infinite wisdom God can handle this. We would do well to listen to Paul, who was personally burdened by this issue more deeply than most of us: "Lest you be wise in your own conceits, I want you to understand this mystery, brethren: a hardening has come upon part of Israel, until the full number of the Gentiles come in, and so all Israel will be saved" (Rom. 11:25-26).

On the other hand, Jews will have to reckon with the fact that some Jews will find their way to God through Jesus and in ways unknown to Judaism. The betrayal that Jews feel when other Jews become Christians may understandably be experienced as an abandonment of the Jewish people. But what appears as an abandonment of the Jewish people is an embrace of God.

All of this is painfully unpleasant. Jesus still brings not peace on

13. There is no indication that the Baltimore Declaration has this intention in mind.

earth but division, a reality that makes Christians wince but that Jews assume. And it is understandable that most Jews and Christians work hard to avoid grappling with these divisions. But now is a time in history when the great sleeping issue for both the synagogue and the church has been raised — namely, each other. We disrespect it at our peril. May God grant both Jews and Christians the humility, patience, and courage to admit that God may still be out ahead of us this time.

III. Practicing Orthodoxy

Holy Preaching: Ethical Interpretation and the Practical Imagination

ELLEN F. DAVIS

> *He often tells them that sermons are dangerous things, that none goes out of church as he came in, but either better, or worse; that none is careless before his Judge, and that the word of God shall judge us. By these and other means the Parson procures attention; but the character of his sermon is holiness; he is not witty, or learned, or eloquent, but holy.*
>
> George Herbert, "The Parson Preaching"

> *Joan of Arc: "I hear voices telling me what to do. They come from God."*
> *Captain Robert de Baudricourt: "They come from your imagination."*
> *Joan: "Of course. That is how the messages of God come to us."*
>
> George Bernard Shaw, *St. Joan*

IN seventeenth-century England, preaching was the most popular form of public entertainment and sermons the most widely read literature. The great London preachers dazzled theologically sophisticated audiences, but they also drew the common people in crowds, for religious controversy was the daily news. And like all national celebrities, they had their less talented imitators in the provinces. When George Herbert asserted that the essential character of the country parson's sermon is holiness, he meant that pastors should stop trying to impress their people and instead move them to repentance and an all-involving commitment to the Christian life. The purpose of this essay is to urge a style of contemporary preaching that aims at such a commitment.

Specifically, I maintain that "holy preaching" is explicitly oriented toward the biblical text and characterized by a willingness to acquire new habits and categories of thought in order to read it with comprehension. Such a willingness to think in new ways is the disposition essential for ethical interpretation of the Scriptures; it is also the heart of the biblical concept of repentance. The two are in fact closely linked. I use the term *ethical interpretation* to designate an exploration motivated by curiosity about that which is unknown or different from ourselves, curiosity acute enough to open us to the possibility of personal change in response to what we learn. And profound personal change is what the Bible means by "repentance." The concept includes more than contrition for specific sins; it entails a radical reorientation of self (cf. Hebrew *shuv,* "turn"), a reordering of habits of thought (cf. Greek *metanoia,* "change of mind"). In this essay, I shall argue that the preacher's chief task is to establish and maintain within the worshiping community the conditions that make it possible to hear the Scriptures as the Word of God — that is, as an invitation and challenge to change.

Reading the Scriptures as the Word of God is the basic identifying activity of the Christian community. The essential form of the common life is in the broadest sense a conversation in which members of the community explore and debate their meaning and find ways to live together in accordance with what they have read. In what follows I stress the need for openness in conversation, so that many voices may be heard: the different voices within the biblical text, within the community, and also the voices of outsiders. Maintaining openness requires not only curiosity but also trust — trust among the members of the community and even more in the text that they have gathered to hear. This trust expresses itself in a conviction that, no matter how strange or unappealing a given passage may be, there is something in it for us, something to be gained from the work of painstaking, acute *listening,* which is the fundamental act of obedience (cf. Latin *ob-audire*). While the interpretive conversation is open-ended with respect to the form that a faithful response may take in the present situation, it is nonetheless rooted in a conviction of the necessity and finally the safety of listening to the text.

The body of this essay is concerned with setting forth the view of Scripture that I believe is most congruent with the work of repentance and with suggesting how that view has informed the tradition of

Anglican preaching and how it may continue to do so. But in order to clarify my discussion, it is necessary to state briefly what I consider to be the essential content of the Christian faith — that is, what constitutes the theological framework in which the interpretive discussion about Scripture takes place. For the trust, in both text and community, that is required to maintain openness must be based initially on certain common commitments. The faith commitments shared by all Christians are those made in baptism and nurtured through participation in the liturgy: profession of faith in a triune God, known by the name of Father, Son, and Holy Spirit; in the incarnation of God in Jesus Christ; in the redemptive value for all humankind of his suffering, death, and resurrection, in which we share through baptism; in the presence and power of the Holy Spirit animating the church. These basic commitments must obtain within the community of faith if its readings of Scripture are to be coherent — that is, if they are to be in basic continuity with the theological understandings of Christian communities in other places and times.

Yet continuity does not imply full agreement. Sometimes new historical or philological knowledge brings us into disagreement with formerly established interpretations. But much more significantly, we often and legitimately depart from the interpretations of our predecessors, or from our own earlier understandings, because Scripture addresses us as the living Word of God, and therefore it does not speak in identical fashion on every occasion. Freshened by the Holy Spirit, it is at each reading a new utterance, directed personally but not privately to each hearer and community.

I agree with the authors of the Baltimore Declaration that there are strong factors in the present cultural and theological climate that militate against a clear profession of the faith into which we are baptized. However, I believe that in its rhetorical strategy and on some substantive points the Declaration discourages or forecloses the possibility of the kind of conversation among Christians that might in fact help them to clarify their basic commitments as well as the range of disagreement that can be sustained without threatening the integrity of the gospel.

Specifically (to begin with a matter that is relatively minor), one could wish for greater sensitivity than is shown in the regular use of the male pronoun in reference to God, despite the denial of God's maleness (article 6). Although the offense to some readers may be slight, it could have been avoided entirely through some care in sentence construction, such as has become regular practice for many preachers who wish to reduce distractions from the central proclamation.

A related concern is raised by this statement: "We repudiate the false teaching . . . that we are free to ignore or suppress the revealed name of Father, Son, and Holy Spirit and worship the Deity with names and images created by our fallen imaginations or supplied by secular culture, unreformed by the Gospel and the biblical revelation" (article 1). What I have already said about adhering to the baptismal formulation of faith affirms the validity and necessity of naming God in worship as Father, Son, and Holy Spirit. But the Declaration's seeming repudiation of all other names and images as creations of "our fallen imaginations" is sadly limiting and would in fact eliminate much of the rich tradition of Christian devotional literature. Catherine of Siena, Bernard of Clairvaux, and John of the Cross experienced God as an infatuated or elusive Lover (as, arguably, did the poet of the Song of Songs). The Anglican preachers whom I will treat in the last section of this essay see no conflict between trinitarian orthodoxy and freedom of imagination. Lancelot Andrewes thinks of God as possessed of multiple wombs filled with the pity of many mothers; John Donne imagines God as a bird feathered with mercy, who gets caught in the bird-lime of our prayers.

That the authors of the Declaration themselves recognize to some degree at least the latitude that Scripture not only grants but encourages I gather from their statement, "The Father nurtures, protects, and cares for his children like a nursing mother" (article 6). But it is regrettable that they give no positive formulation to the work of the imagination informed by faith, or how the gospel and the biblical revelation might indeed reform images supplied by secular culture (cf. article 1). My essay attempts to develop the notion of the preacher's imaginative freedom, while also suggesting something of the discipline that is necessary for its proper exercise.

In my judgment, the repeated formula "We repudiate the false teaching that . . ." points to a problem with the Declaration's approach that reaches far beyond the matter of inclusive language and imagery. The identification of erroneous doctrine is, of course, part of what it means to love God with all our minds (cf. Matt. 22:37, et al.). But the emphatic repudiation implies a notion of falsity as the direct opposite of truth, whereas it is pedagogically more sound to recognize that we inevitably fall into errors major and minor on our way toward truth. Therefore in any intellectual endeavor, but above all in the journey of faith, advancement depends upon a process of continual disagreement, correction, and reorientation — a process that requires the kind of mutual trust of which I have spoken above. The polarization of truth and falsity that I believe is implicit in the Declaration's phraseology tends in fact to make correction more difficult, for it begs the important hermeneutical question of what makes for better or worse interpretations of the Scriptures. Thus it leads to entrenchment of positions by discouraging the kind of mutual exploration that may disclose aspects of truth previously unrecognized by any party to the discussion.[1]

In the first part of this essay, I shall argue that it is chiefly through the use of imaginative language that the Scriptures exercise what the Baltimore Declaration calls their "formative and evangelical authority" (preface), which is "primary and decisive . . . in matters of faith and morals" (article 7). For the chief faculty of moral discernment is a rich critical imagination; and the primary means by which it is to be nurtured and honed within the community of faith are the biblical stories, images, symbols, prayers, and exhortations. In the second section of the essay, I shall show that this is precisely how the Scriptures were regarded in the formative period of Anglicanism — namely, as addressed to an imagination disciplined by participation in the catholic tradition reaching from ancient times to the present. I shall consider the work of two gifted poet-preachers of the seventeenth century with a view to demonstrating how a contemporary homiletic might be informed by their insights and practices.

Uses of the Imagination

That there is little serious biblical preaching in mainline churches is most centrally a problem of a neglected and atrophied Christian imag-

---

1. A particular instance in which far more discussion is necessary than the Declaration allows is the question of the evangelization of the Jews (article 5). Among those who maintain, with the Declaration, that salvation may not "be *ultimately* found apart from the atoning death and resurrection of Jesus Christ" (article 4; italics mine), it is or should be a matter of careful consideration whether or how Christians should proclaim the gospel to the Jewish people. This question has been treated at length in another essay in this volume. In accordance with my own emphases, I will comment only that the issue is not whether proclamation is likely to succeed with the Jews. Rather, we must ask whether a focus on proclaiming the gospel to the Jews does not distract Christians from their own work of repentance. I would suggest that the first phase of that renewal of thought (and it should be a long one) should be contemplation of God's faithfulness in sustaining the Jews through more than two millennia of persecution, much of it carried out, shamefully, by the only other people who worship the God of Israel.

ination, to which the language of the Bible is largely unintelligible. I think it is safe to say that the Scriptures are less accessible to the average believer today than before the Reformation, even if most churchgoers own a personal copy in semi-idiomatic English. They are inaccessible, not because we lack historical information about the biblical world (indeed, we have more of it than any previous generation), but because we do not have the imaginative skills to probe the subject matter of the Bible: love and forgiveness, suffering and redemption, the persistence of evil and the birth of boundless hope. For the most part, secular education and the mass media have left us ill-equipped to deal with those nonmolecular facts of human existence that can be verified but not predicted — that can be proclaimed, probed, and understood both with reason and deep in the bones, but that are yet not fully explained in terms of logical concepts and a chronological succession of events.

The only language that is adequate to express and draw connections among such more-than-logical phenomena is the poetic language of symbol, including myth, metaphor, proverb, parable, and even the language of legal code (as Mary Douglas's brilliant work on Leviticus has demonstrated)[2] — language that (in Paul Ricoeur's terms) "redescribes" reality and thus "discloses a world" richer in meaning than the one we had previously inhabited. The language of Scripture, as many recent studies have shown (and the ancient commentators, both Jews and Christians, never doubted), is predominantly the language of symbol, and precisely that constitutes the gap between its epistemological presuppositions and our own. For modern technological culture, through an almost exclusive concentration on theory and conceptual analysis, is perhaps unparalleled among the "high cultures" of history for its ineptitude and impatience with the ambiguities of verbal symbolism.

With respect to the formulation of a style of "holy preaching," it is most interesting that the Bible itself in numerous instances evidences no opposition between imaginative proclamation and moral instruc-

2. Douglas, *Purity and Danger: An Analysis of the Concepts of Pollution and Taboo* (London: Routledge & Kegan Paul, 1966), pp. 41-57; see also her refinement of this original study in *Implicit Meanings* (London: Routledge & Kegan Paul, 1975), pp. 276-318. On the broader question of the function of symbolic language in Scripture, the work of Paul Ricoeur is seminal; see, e.g., *The Symbolism of Evil* (Boston: Beacon Press, 1967), and "Biblical Hermeneutics," *Semeia* 4 (1975): 27-148.

3. Cf. Garrett Green's treatment of this encounter, which he uses to illustrate the principle, "To save sinners, God seizes them by the imagination" (*Imagining God: Theology and the Religious Imagination* [San Francisco: Harper & Row, 1989], pp. 149-50).

tion, although the tone of the great biblical sermons is not "preachy." Nathan does not harangue David on violations of the sixth, seventh, and tenth commandments (2 Sam. 12); he uses a story, which the king may or may not have taken as fictional, that enables David to see the moral contours of the situation and render an accurate judgment on himself.[3] Isaiah sings a love song about a vineyard (Isa. 5:1-7); Lady Wisdom (in Prov. 1:20-33; 8:1–9:18) freely mixes prophetic summons, accusations, and promises with the reasonable appeal of a teacher and also womanly allure in order to win the ingenue to the right path. In every case, the preachers within the Bible appeal to the heart, which in biblical physiology is not distinct from the mind. Such an appeal would seem to be what Herbert intended when he commended "ravishing" rather than controversial texts to the country parson;[4] it is the heart ravished by just guilt and wholesome desire that is the best moral instructor.

These examples of biblical preaching all demonstrate a quality too little evident even in contemporary preaching that claims to take direct inspiration from the Bible — namely, preaching with an explicit social agenda that is sometimes termed "prophetic." The quality that marks the preaching of the genuine biblical prophets is irony. I believe that homiletician Charles Rice points to something fundamental in biblical preaching when he suggests that we need a more ironic and less heroic mode of discourse.[5] Ironic speaking implies a certain voluntary marginalization, a willingness to remain outside the power structure and to articulate a vision without a program attached, to speak fearlessly to the present situation and yet admit with all humility that the future remains obscure (cf. Jer. 28:5-11; contrast the "heroic" manner of the false prophet Hananiah). Much that goes by the name of "prophetic preaching" is in fact heroic, using the Scriptures to endorse our own programs rather than to call the premises of our programs into question. In Dietrich Bonhoeffer's terms, it is reading Scripture *for* ourselves rather than *over against* ourselves.[6]

---

4. In Herbert's words: "But [holiness] is gained first, by choosing texts of Devotion, not Controversy, moving and ravishing texts, whereof the Scriptures are full" ("The Parson Preaching," in *A Priest to the Temple, or, The Country Parson*, ed. John Wall [New York: Paulist Press, 1981], p. 63).

5. That is, oral communication.

6. Cf. the excellent discussion in "Living and Dying in the Word: Dietrich Bonhoeffer as Performer of Scripture," chap. 6 in Stephen E. Fowl and L. Gregory Jones, *Reading in Communion: Scripture and Ethics in Christian Life* (Grand Rapids: William B. Eerdmans, 1991), pp. 135-64.

I propose that the preacher's first and most important responsibility is to educate the imaginations of her hearers so that they have the linguistic skills to enter into the world that Scripture discloses and may thus make a genuine choice about whether to live there. The biblical preacher is a sort of elementary language teacher, not a translator, as is often considered to be the case. For whether or not preachers have read or remember Bultmann, they often engage in a program of demythologizing the Bible, translating it into the terms of modern rationalism. Thus, as I recently heard, John's version of the miracle of the loaves and fishes becomes a display of impressive generosity in a child who shared his lunch, moving others in the crowd to do likewise; and we also should emulate him in our own context.

The attraction of such an approach is obvious: it makes Scripture conformable to our accustomed categories of thought and supports socially valuable behavior. This combination of effects is what is usually meant by "making the Bible relevant." But the problem is that ready applicability has been purchased at the price of the story itself. While there might be some moral force to a story of public sharing of scant resources, the story the evangelist actually tells is quite different; he says that Jesus made more food on the spot. John invites us to contemplate a world where offering up all the little we have inexplicably yields more, in bewildering abundance. Responding to that invitation requires that we do something both more difficult and more ethically significant than sharing our lunch: namely, that we think in fundamentally new ways about the presence and power of God. As I have noted, the New Testament word for taking on new mental habits is *metanoia,* "a change of mind" — that is, "repentance," "transformation." The preacher who invites the congregation to contemplate the multiplication of the loaves and fishes or the parting of the Red Sea *without translating away the wonder* calls upon the congregation to repent.

It is evident that offering a conceptual translation is far easier for both preacher and hearer than sustaining imaginative attention to a text whose thought categories are so foreign to us. As anyone who has ever engaged in language study knows, success requires a dogged patience with the strange, which is perhaps the essence of intellectual generosity. The reward for learning to listen to the Bible on its own terms is that a more spacious world opens to us. There we see the terrible limitations that we previously accepted as givens of the human condition exposed and overcome in the faithfulness of God, kept in the face of Israel's faithlessness; in the suffering psalmists' utter trust in God, expressed equally in wild hope and bitter accusation; in the incarnation, death, and resurrection of Jesus Christ. The relevance of the Scriptures is that they take account of my genuine needs, my longing, and my despair, not that they conform to my thinking and life-style as they are presently constituted.

The miracle stories are parade examples of what is in fact the Bible's regular rhetorical strategy of using imaginative language to jostle us into radically new ways of looking at the world and at ourselves. But it is more customary for Christians to speak of the Scriptures as being "inspired" than as being "imaginative." While Anglicans have generally been reluctant to define too closely the nature of the Holy Spirit's inspiration, it seems valid to consider inspired utterance as a special category of imaginative speech, greatly exceeding even the author's own capacity for conceptualization. T. S. Eliot, speaking of secular as well as religious poetry, suggests that "if the word 'inspiration' is to have any meaning, it must mean just this, that the speaker or writer is uttering something which he does not wholly understand — or which he may even misinterpret when the inspiration has departed from him."[7] Certainly the images that Scripture itself uses to describe the Word of God suggest that it can be neither contained nor controlled: a hammer beating within a body until the blows resound in words, a fire raging inside, a baby insistent to be born.

A degree of indeterminacy is part of the character of inspired speech. Put more positively, inspired speech is an inexhaustible store of meaning, a treasure room out of which the scribe who has been trained for the kingdom of heaven brings what is new and what is old (Matt. 13:52). The reticence inherent in symbolic language is not separable from its richness; it begs and begets interpretation. This peculiar susceptibility to interpretation that characterizes imaginative speech, and that is developed to the highest degree in the Scriptures, would seem to be the quality that makes Scripture the source of continually renewed life in the church.

The imaginative character of the biblical witness bears directly on the task of ethical interpretation. The fundamental ethical question is whether we can reckon seriously with that which is different from ourselves.[8] Curiosity is a much underrated virtue, for it is the basis of

7. Eliot, *On Poetry and Poets* (1957; New York: Octagon Books, 1975), p. 137.
8. The implications of this view of ethics for the study of literature are explored by Wayne Booth in *The Company We Keep: An Ethics of Fiction* (Berkeley: University of California Press, 1988). The study is highly useful for preachers, who must reckon with a text (particularly the Old Testament) that is often ethically problematic.

the ethical stance: an interest in the character and perspective of the other, an initial willingness to grant them coherence. As I have suggested, the Scriptures are to us an "other";[9] they speak a language and express a view of reality vastly different from our own. There can be no ethical preaching that does not take respectful account of how deeply strange to us is this written witness to the word of God.

Imagination is the interpretive faculty by which we relate to that which is strange, not fully known, or not immediately present to us. And, of course, that is most of reality — past, present, and future. Hence, constant exercise of the imagination is a practical necessity for every healthy human being, and not only the science fiction writer or the religious mystic (if "mystic" is taken in the narrow sense of one with a special receptivity to visionary or auditory experience). We use it in composing a letter or a sermon (which is to be received sometime in the future in circumstances at which we can now only guess), in designing a garden or an investments portfolio, in figuring out why a teenager is sulking. A healthy, flexible imagination is the "coping mechanism" by which, moment by moment, we make the small extrapolations that give us a history and a world and that enable us to envision a future.

Although the imaginative capacity is universal and is employed in countless quotidian situations, it does indeed have a mystical dimension in the sense of involving us, to a greater or lesser extent, in an apprehension of the totality of life, which is essentially mysterious. As Richard Kroner has argued in a foundational study of imagination as an aspect of religious knowledge, "an image of ultimate truth is included in every practical situation, and . . . this image is truly religious, or, if not, then it is pseudo-religious and superstitious."[10]

For the spiritual life, the most important use of imagination is in coming to know God. The fact that we know God imaginatively is congruent with the way we know all other persons and also ourselves. We do not form a theory about our intimates; theorizing about persons, as a substitute for knowing them, is otherwise known as prejudice; and it is the basis of oppression and resentment, not intimacy. Rather, we form an image of those whom we would love based on the limited data of our own contacts and hearsay: a whole picture, although always to some degree incomplete, subject to

9. On the value of seeing Scripture as an outsider for the maintenance of interpretive humility, see Fowl and Jones, *Reading in Communion*, pp. 110-13.

10. Kroner, *The Primacy of Faith* (New York: Macmillan, 1943), p. 154.

change and refinement. Similarly, when we want to know about a stranger, we ask someone close to him for an approximation of his character: "What is he like? Tell me about him." We intuitively know not to ask for an objective measure of the person — who or what is she? — but for an impressionistic evaluation of what she is *like*. The qualifier "like" lends modesty to all assertions; it acknowledges the perspectival character of personal testimony.[11]

The biblical witness to the nature of God is likewise impressionistic and perspectival. Rigor in maintaining the modesty of our assertions would seem to be what underlies the prohibition against graven images. We must not try to show God directly; we can do no more than indicate what God is like. With respect to observing the proper limits on the witness of faith, there is an instructive contrast between idolatrous Israel proclaiming over the golden calf, "These are your gods, O Israel . . . !" (Exod. 32:4), and the prophet Ezekiel. The first chapter of the book of Ezekiel is the least dogmatical text imaginable. Ezekiel's report of his vision of God by the river Chebar is so full of qualifying particles that the Hebrew is almost untranslatable: "there was something like a throne, resembling sapphire; and up above the likeness of a throne was what resembled a human form. And above what resembled his loins I saw the like of gleaming amber, having the semblance of fire enclosing it all around, and below what resembled his loins I saw the semblance of fire, and there was flashing about him. The semblance of the bow in the midst of clouds on a rainy day — such was the appearance of the flashing all about. This was the appearance of the image of the glory of the LORD" (Ezek. 1:26-28a; my own translation). The prophet, who had a reputation as a great lyrical stylist (Ezek. 33:32), here willingly trips over his own tongue lest his description of God be taken as objective representation.

The work of interpretation is greatly complicated, and its interest is incalculably increased, by the diversity of perspectives with which the biblical witness presents us. There is an essential coherence, traditionally called "unity," to the Scriptures, which historical criticism has tended to obscure with its isolating emphasis on the (presumed) conditions and process of production lying behind a given text. The unity of the Scriptures derives from the fact that it is one God who is made known to us through Israel's varied witness. God is revealed as a

11. On the importance of the qualification, see Garrett Green, " 'The Bible as . . .': Fictional Narrative and Scriptural Truth," in *Scriptural Authority and Narrative Interpretation,* FS Hans Frei, ed. Green (Philadelphia: Fortress Press, 1987), pp. 79-96; see also Garrett Green, *Imagining God.*

coherent but not predictable character, not a stone idol of unchanging demeanor but a living God of whom certain basic traits are repeatedly affirmed: "merciful and gracious, slow to anger, and abounding in steadfast love" (Exod. 34:6; cf. Ps. 145:8; et al.). The extraordinary diversity of the Scriptures can be accounted for only by the partiality, volatility, and also gradual maturing of the relationship between God and Israel. The fact that the scriptural witness emerges out of personal relationship suggests that serious theological use of the Bible entails looking for constancy, not uniformity, in its delineation of God's character, and that demonstrating the normativity of Scripture entails discerning and articulating intelligible patterns in the revelation of God's nature and will for the world.[12]

The aim of all the Scriptures is to give us an inside view of committed relationship with the God of Israel, based upon the testimony of those most deeply experienced in it. But attempts to expound "the (single, immutable) meaning" of that testimony are inherently unethical, for they fail to respect the character of this "other" that is Scripture. The biblical witness is ineluctably personal, although not private; and the preacher who would be faithful to it must become personally involved in a process akin to the interpretation of poetry, a process to which intellect, emotion, memory, conscience, and will all contribute, and by which over a lifetime all are transformed. For "sermons are dangerous things"; no one comes out of the interpretive process as she went in, least of all the preacher. Wherever anyone succeeds in doing so, there the scriptural inspiration that animates the community of faith has been temporarily eclipsed.

The homiletical task is not to pronounce "the Truth," although a knowledge of truth will emerge when the partnership of mutual speaking and listening is faithfully maintained between pastor and people. Rather, the preacher is to articulate, over weeks and years, the text's multiple voices, so that those voices may form the background against which the voices within the community are heard and their differences adjudicated — and alongside them, the threats, accusations, and scepticism of outsiders, which are not wholly unjust. When the character of the sermon is holiness, listeners are invited into a wide-ranging but disciplined conversation, ongoing through the ages, and advanced with each generation of faith and unfaith into new areas of concern. That conver-

12. On the notion of pattern as the key to the unity and normativity of the Scriptures, see David H. Kelsey, *The Uses of Scripture in Recent Theology* (Philadelphia: Fortress Press, 1975), pp. 192-97; and Garrett Green, *Imagining God*, pp. 114-18.

sation enhances the coping skills of the participants, which is to say that it puts them in responsible relation to the whole of the created world. The responsibility is real, though it is assumed through an imaginative extension of themselves, guided by the Scriptures. In practical terms, for the ordinary North American Christian, that means being able to relate their present activity to a larger individual and family history, to the Apostles' Creed and the domestic and foreign policies of the current government administration, to the disobedience in the Garden and the fall of Jerusalem, the AIDS crisis and drug wars, the crucifixion on Golgotha and destruction of the rain forests.

Preaching that acknowledges the character of the Scriptures as a personal and imaginative witness to faith is genuinely inclusive, in two senses. First, it recognizes that in many or perhaps most cases, people may in good faith genuinely disagree about the correct interpretation of the facts and the right course of action. Through conversation we maintain the common life, which provides the only basis for serious and (relatively) safe exploration of a few options for faithful living. Second, such an acknowledgment facilitates conversation with outsiders and makes room for their voices to be heard within the community of faith, without disguising — indeed, while putting in the foreground — the personal commitment that obtains there. But respectful attention to others who do not share our own views and commitments should not be confused with the too-common error of liberalism in treating the Christian story (including Israel's history) as a matter of private and elective interest to believers. In a time when the dominant culture categorically denies the public relevance of the church and asserts that the search for truth is self-authenticating, the church is especially pressed within the context of its own shared life to test and criticize interpretations of the multifaceted truth to which the Scriptures attest.

Contrary to a misconception popular among seminary graduates (for it is too often fostered in the teaching of homiletics, theology, and also Bible), exegetical preaching is the surest way to maintain the breadth and openness of conversation within the community of faith. Thematic preaching tends to present and reinforce an established viewpoint. In Bonhoeffer's lectures on homiletics to the Confessing Church seminary at Finkenwalde, he warned: "Thematic preaching carries the danger that only the proposed problem and the suggested answer will be remembered; apologetic comes to the fore and the text is ignored."[13] The best

---

13. Bonhoeffer, *Worldly Preaching: Lectures on Homiletics* (New York: Crossroad, 1991), p. 129.

argument for exegetical preaching is that it allows the text to function as what it is: inspired speech, potent to introduce to the community of faith new directions for movement and also new problems, which are more fruitful than the ones advanced by our own agendas.

This inspiration becomes an operative force when not just the preacher but the whole community becomes concerned and competent to give close attention to the words and images of the Scriptures. Surprising metaphors challenge our ready categorizations: "Love is strong as death, passion fierce as the grave" (Song of Sol. 8:6, NRSV). This simile leads the preacher of a wedding sermon to consider that love may be more like death than it is death's polar opposite (as we generally think). Their likeness in strength and fierceness suggests that love is the only thing that consumes us as fully as does death; love teaches us to give ourselves wholly and freely, and thus it is the best preparation for death, to which the whole Christian life is directed. Consonant with the gospel and directly contrary to our cultural assumptions, death does not defeat what love has built but rather completes it.

Serious, on-going exegetical preaching, aimed at identifying patterns of faithful relationship with God and neighbor, exposes the inadequacy of narrowly issue-oriented resort to the text. In instituting a building program, it may be less effective for a congregation to study the account of Solomon's Temple construction than to consider the achievements and failures of the seven churches in the Revelation to John. Or again, the teaching about homosexuality in Leviticus should be studied in the context of the larger vision of holiness that that book sets forth, and further in light of Jesus' understandings of purity and community. There may not be a "right answer" to the questions that most deeply trouble us; but such an approach helpfully confounds the self-serving tendency to proof-texting on both sides and opens up the possibility of genuinely new insight.

To a very great extent, then, the church's life *is* its interpretive conversation. The Roman Catholic theologian Nicholas Lash has suggested that the proper business of the church is to be "an academy of word-care," a guild of (literally) philologists, most of them amateur, skilled lovers of the Word of God.[14] This business is carried on in worship and private prayer, in vestry meetings, hospitals, and classrooms, as well as in the pulpit. In those settings and countless others,

---

14. See Lash, "Ministry of the Word or Comedy and Philology," *New Blackfriars* 68 (1987): 472-83.

scriptural language is probed and its sense tested in light of all that we experience and know from other sources. At the same time, conversely (and crucial to the accuracy of our interpretation), our experience is scrutinized in light of the revealing images; the words of the Scriptures provide a measure against which the coherence of our thought and action is to be tested. Over the course of years, the disciplined care of words challenges the identity and commitments of every participant.

The opposite of what I have called ethical interpretation, which is fundamentally characterized by respectful curiosity about what is strange, is moralism — that is, insistence that one's own view is incontrovertible and stands in no need of reconsideration or supplementation. Throughout the history of the church, the Bible has often been wielded as a weapon in battles both internal and external, and what I have said about the imaginative nature of the Scriptures offers one way of understanding why such usage is unethical in its treatment not only of persons but of the text. For it mutes the call to new thinking, to repentance, which the Bible addresses continually to all its readers; in moralism, theoretical positions, not texts, are treated as canon.

At the beginning of this essay I expressed the concern that the language of the Baltimore Declaration tends to moralism in this sense — that is, to the exclusion from the interpretive conversation of certain positions or persons that might legitimately be heard. However, I believe that the current critical climate evidences even more strongly a different kind of moralizing, of which the authors of the Declaration are rightly wary (see especially article 7). Specifically, I mean a moralism that is directed *against* the Bible and that denies the authority of those portions that we take to represent moral insight inferior to our own. This was the first heresy identified by the church, in the form of Marcion's attempted exclusion of the entire Old Testament. It is not my intention to treat any particular instances of contemporary moralizing against the Bible; rather, I will point briefly to two safeguards of ethical interpretation of which the preacher should make regular use: first, historical criticism; and second, the church's tradition of scriptural interpretation, including especially the liturgy.

It should be emphasized that an imaginative approach to Scripture does not invalidate historical criticism; rather, it directs it toward the end of repentance, of mental transformation. It is not that the agenda of ethical interpretation mandates the investigation of only those texts or aspects of texts that are of obvious pastoral or spiritual relevance. I would suggest that the practical imagination is enriched

by any study, however technical, that draws us into deeper consideration of the words and form and images of the text — that is, study that
forces and enables us to read the text with care, rather than tempting
us to talk around or "get behind" the text in order to reconstruct social
settings or literary layers for which there is no direct evidence. Thus,
study that is practical for ministry includes advanced Hebrew syntax
and poetic structure as well as ancient Near Eastern agricultural and
funerary practices.

With respect to the problem of moralizing against the Bible, the
most important function of historical study is to keep us from imposing
our cultural assumptions upon a world we do not readily comprehend.
The work of Carol Meyers, for example, drawing on archaeology and
social anthropology, challenges the view that the social role of women
in early Israel was oppressively restricted, as she shows how economic
balance is maintained in a society where the home is the primary
production unit.[15] In so doing, she reminds us (obliquely) that the
consumer-oriented system in which virtually all North Americans, men
and women alike, participate is very far from the ideal for settlement
of the Promised Land. Again, study of ancient cultures could challenge
a sense of moral superiority to the vengeful composer of Psalm 137,
who longs to see Babylonian babies bashed against the rock. For the
decision-making elements in our society (which include the writer and
probably all readers of this essay) are more readily compared to the
Babylonian tormentors than to the defeated Israelites to whom we
would counsel mercy, and an educated imagination might well consider
who could legitimately wish that our empire would not last through
another generation.

The second counter to moralizing against the biblical text, the
tradition of premodern interpretation, seems to sort oddly with historical criticism. But it should be noted that "premodern" is not identical with "precritical" interpretation. The ancient and medieval commentators were not naive about the complexity of meaning, however
their hermeneutics might differ from our own; and the early Reformers reckoned seriously with the human and historical character
of the text, even though the Holy Spirit remained for them the real
author. But, unlike almost all modern biblical scholars, they were
essentially unconcerned about the problem of *historical* distance between the biblical world and their own. They saw (correctly, I believe)

15. Meyers, *Discovering Eve: Ancient Israelite Women in Context* (New York:
Oxford University Press, 1988).

that the real problem is the *moral* distance between the world that the text calls us to inhabit and the one in which we are too content to stay. Liturgical usage, including the daily lectionary, often provides valuable clues to traditional understandings that call into question the sophistication and adequacy of contemporary readings. For the preacher in the Anglican tradition, previously "unpreachable" texts may well be opened up by consideration of the moral purpose that this text is meant to serve at this particular time in the church year. Probably nowhere is this so true as with the Psalms.

For example, Psalm 149 seems at first to be especially ill-chosen for the Feast of All Saints, perpetuating the unhappy stereotype of the serious religious person as a ruthless fanatic:

> Let the high praises of God be in their throats
>   and two-edged swords in their hands,
> to execute vengeance on the nations
>   and punishment on the peoples,
> to bind their kings with fetters
>   and their nobles with chains of iron,
> to execute on them the judgment decreed.
>   This is glory for all his faithful ones.
> Praise the LORD!
>
> (vv. 6-9, NRSV)

This psalm might be dismissed as expressing "the spirit of the O.T., not of the N.T.";[16] yet many overtly irenic psalms were passed over in favor of this one to celebrate the glory of the saints. There must be something in the disconcerting conjunction between violence and praise that offers a key to the nature of sainthood. In fact, a regular pattern is discernible in the lives of the saints: contrition — that is, fighting the evil within — prepares the way for contending with evil in the world. Considered in this light, the psalm points, in the highly condensed and suggestive language of poetry, to the fact that the self-inflicted violence of penitence, turned against our own private empire-building, clears the way for God's praise.

It is a useful exegetical habit, when we find ourselves feeling morally superior to the biblical text, to consider whether we might be reading too literalistically — that is, whether we do not need to exercise our imagination to discover the perspective in which the passage may

---

16. A. F. Kirkpatrick (citing Delitzsch), *The Book of Psalms* (Cambridge: Cambridge University Press, 1902), p. 829.

speak to us as a genuinely new word of God, which calls on us to repent. The interpretation suggested here takes the two-edged sword as a metaphor for the word of God that "is able to judge the thoughts and intentions of the heart" (Heb. 4:12, NRSV; cf. Eph. 6:17; Rev. 1:16). There may be more modern utility than is first evident for Augustine's principle regarding figurative interpretation, "that what is read should be subjected to diligent scrutiny until an interpretation contributing to the reign of charity is produced. If this result appears literally in the text, the expression being considered is not figurative."[17]

The search for an interpretation that conduces to charity does not mean whitewashing the Scriptures to remove all signs of Israel's idolatry and vituperation. I do not believe it can be maintained that the writers of either Testament were at all times successful in upholding the mystery and radical grace of God's presence, while determining concrete ways in which to live with their fears and their enemies. But in this case and many others, a figurative interpretation is on several counts preferable to writing off the text as further evidence of the primitive warlike spirit of ancient Israel. First, it has the support of the explicit New Testament reading and amplification of the metaphor of the two-edged sword. Second, it respects the psalm as a witness to faith that can provide guidance for the Christian life, which is what the church has always affirmed by its use of the term "Old Testament." Our modern awareness of the historical character of the biblical witness makes impossible any simple repristination of allegorical interpretation; we cannot decode the Hebrew Scriptures as a timeless system of references to Christ. John Howard Yoder's suggestion that they are to be read "directionally," as a story of promise and fulfillment,[18] better accords with their historical character as well as their function in the moral formation of readers. Third, a figurative interpretation does not depend on a historical assumption for which there is no evidence — namely, that the Israelites were more primitive than ourselves in either humanitarian concern or literary usage.

The question that the preacher must continually ask is how to create an environment in which it is safe to be vulnerable to the Bible as God's Word. To call the Bible "the Word of the Lord" is to confess our vulnerability to this Word that is foreign to us, our willingness to think in radically new ways in order to receive it as gift and promise: "Thanks be to God." To refuse that effort is what the Bible calls

---

17. Augustine *On Christian Doctrine* 3.15.

18. Yoder, *The Priestly Kingdom: Social Ethics as Gospel* (Notre Dame: University of Notre Dame, 1984), p. 9.

"hardness of heart," which Paul treats as the antonym of "repentance" (Rom. 2:4-5; cf. Mark 6:52; Exod. 7:13, 22, etc.). Yet to accept it is difficult and painful, and so the assurance of safety is crucial if the congregation is to sustain the appropriate vulnerability that makes possible such new thought. The assurance the preacher must give is that listening to the text will never mean giving up one's own right to a questioning, critical voice in the interpretive conversation. The notion of "appropriate vulnerability" suggests a kind of responsiveness to the text that is somewhat different from that implied in Erich Auerbach's famous dictum that the Bible's claim to truth is "tyrannical" and its stories, in contrast to Homer's, "seek to subject us, and if we refuse to be subjected we are rebels."[19] While it is true that they far more often confound than flatter or enchant us, nonetheless the final aim of the Scriptures is not subjugation but rather "edification" (a word much used in seventeenth-century homiletics). They upbuild the community of faith by seizing and stretching its imagination to entertain new possibilities for human life.

Imaginative Preaching: The Seventeenth Century

"The new homiletic" is a phrase that appears frequently now in the literature about preaching.[20] It is widely agreed that the preaching task is presently being reformulated, perhaps more drastically than at any time since the Reformation. Reliance on deductive method and the language of the lecture hall is repeatedly targeted for criticism, as symptomatic of a scientific approach in which the preacher seeks to present a persuasive statement of the truth, using the Bible as a source-book of objective propositions. In this older model of preaching as the art of sacred rhetoric, the audience is addressed with a view to intellectual persuasion, although ideally they are dazzled in the process. The newer literature tends to speak less of persuasion than of imagination and of engaging the audience in a creative process. It reckons with scriptural forms, along with their contents, and often aims at a

---

19. Auerbach, "Odysseus' Scar," in *Mimesis: The Representation of Reality in Western Literature* (Princeton: Princeton University Press, 1953), pp. 14-15.

20. Richard Eslinger dates to the 1970s the serious development of alternatives to "the old homiletic," where audiences were left stranded in "the arid scrubland of topical preaching" (*A New Hearing: Living Options in Homiletic Method* [Nashville: Abingdon Press, 1987], p. 28; the collection of essays by several homileticians is a useful introduction to the current discussion).

sermon style that emulates the biblical writers in their use of story and metaphor. Thus Thomas Troeger summarizes the shift: "Homiletics, which began as the discipline of sacred rhetoric, is becoming the discipline of imaginative theology."[21]

As I noted at the beginning of this essay, in the formative period of Anglicanism, the view was common currency that scriptural language is addressed primarily to the heart (i.e., to an intellectual faculty that combines reason and affect; I believe that the term *imagination* as I have used it here parallels the usage of *heart* in traditional parlance),[22] and that the preacher is wise to follow the rhetorical practice of the Holy Ghost. In this section I turn to two early Anglican preachers who are distinguished for their fluency in the language of the Scriptures: Lancelot Andrewes, Bishop of Winchester, and John Donne, Dean of St. Paul's Cathedral.[23] Both were noted court preachers, the favorites of James I; Donne was also a popular preacher of wide reputation. The quality of their sermons gives them a permanent place in English letters; but more importantly for preachers, their understanding and use of the Scriptures can significantly inform our own. That this is true I know from having read their sermons with both seminarians and parish priests who had no prior disposition to antiquarianism. I would guess that the reason this is true is that, through a variety of influences, many modern preachers have come to a sensibility — an inkling, if not a fully articulated position — regarding the Scriptures and the preaching task that is akin and even remarkably close to that of the seventeenth century.

On at least two counts, early post-Reformation England may be compared to European and North American cultures of the late twentieth century. First, in both cases, one of the chief facts of life confronting the preacher is the erosion of public memory, a massive disruption in what Joseph Sittler calls the "mental, emotional, and image context of the past."[24] In the seventeenth century, churches

21. Troeger, "A New Look at Homiletics," *College of Preachers Newsletter* 37, 2 (Dec. 1991); cf. Troeger, *The Parable of Ten Preachers* (Nashville: Abingdon Press, 1992).

22. Cf. Green, *Imagining God*, pp. 109-10.

23. Space prevents my treating here one other important Anglican exegete: Joseph Hall, the Calvinist Bishop of Norwich. His brief "contemplations" on the biblical narratives are valuable especially for their study of motive and character and are an excellent point of entry to classical Anglican preaching. They will be treated in my forthcoming book *Disciplined Imagination: Old Testament Preaching in the Anglican Tradition* (Philadelphia: Trinity Press International).

24. Sittler, *The Ecology of Faith* (Philadelphia: Muhlenberg Press, 1961), p. 66.

were literally stripped of images and the familiar instruments of worship: windows and organs were smashed; crucifixes, vestments, hymnals, and prayer books were burned. People who had abandoned the Roman Catholic faith into which they were born agonized on their deathbeds over whether they had forfeited eternal life for temporal advancement or escape from persecution. In 1649, Oliver Cromwell arranged for the execution of His Majesty Charles Stuart, and a long deep groan went through the crowd when they saw his severed head (it is well to remember that people of the seventeenth century still retained the ancient sensibility of the monarch as a religious as well as a political figure). The remnants of medieval feudalism were rapidly being erased by the new mercantile economy and the attendant privatization of land, leading to widespread unemployment, inflation, vagrancy, and even the disappearance of villages. The new science and empirical philosophy began to figure importantly in the public mind, and in the latter half of the century, preachers who addressed educated audiences were contending with religious scepticism and a new phenomenon, atheism.

In a situation parallel to that in our own culture but fairly rare in history, within a couple of generations the entire mental environment changed drastically, yet without a major defeat in foreign war. What modern preachers may gain from these poet-preachers of early Anglicanism are resources to contend with the forces and consequences of our own rapid cultural erosion: loss of personal security on a massive scale, a technological society that does not provide intellectual and emotional nourishment or even prepare people to receive it, a future that threatens more than it invites.

A second point of similarity between seventeenth-century England and our own culture may well be related to the extensive religious, social, and intellectual change; and it is a point that bears especially upon the preaching task. There is within the contemporary church a heightened sensitivity to the richness, plasticity, and slipperiness of religious language, both biblical and liturgical. Modern biblical scholars and theologians have in this matter been greatly influenced by philosophers of language and by literary critics. But I would venture to say that with respect to a general awareness that bears upon the preaching environment, a far more significant influence is the variety of readily available Bible translations, concomitant with liturgical reforms that have given greater prominence to the Bible in worship. Ours is the greatest age of Bible translation since the sixteenth and seventeenth centuries. The fact that *The Atlantic Monthly* several years ago featured an article entitled "Translating the Bible"[25] suggests that even the well-educated secular public may be expected to take some "intellectual interest" in developments in this area, akin to the uninvolved fascination astrophysics might hold for them.

The prominence of translation activity in post-Reformation England is helpful in understanding the revolutionary style of evangelistic preaching that arose within the first decade of the seventeenth century. The court preaching of Lancelot Andrewes presented the first fully developed alternative to both the thematic oration of the Roman Church (modeled on medieval scholastic discourse) and the Puritan lecture, with its verse-by-verse exposition of the biblical text. Andrewes was the most accomplished linguist in England and a distinguished prose stylist; James I appointed him head of the translation team responsible for producing a new English version of Genesis through Kings. Andrewes's love of the words of the Scriptures is the outstanding mark of his preaching. He was a relentless exegete, never for more than a moment turning away from the language of the text, digging into it with a determination and playfulness that confounds our modern sensibilities. Each word of the text is "chewed" (in the phrase of the medieval monastic commentators whom he resembles) until it releases its full sweetness; the images are turned over and over as every aspect is explored.

His Lenten sermon on the text "Remember Lot's wife" (Luke 17:32) is essentially a meditation on the single word "remember," repeated some sixty times in Latin and English. With Andrewes's regular concern for practical instruction, the theme of memory is directed toward using the biblical narratives for our moral benefit: "So to read stories past, as we make not ourselves matter for story to come."[26] Andrewes understands the biblical stories and images primarily as a stimulus to memory, and this is the key to his exegetical style. Modern preachers often use biblical stories illustratively, on their way to the point they really wish to make; the phrase "This story reminds me of . . ." is a clear sign that no serious encounter with the text will follow. But Andrewes fixes on "the words of the wise" as goads (Eccles. 12:11, NIV) that remind us of ourselves, and that, as his

25. Barry Hoberman, "Translating the Bible," *The Atlantic Monthly*, Feb. 1985.

26. The sermon, preached before Elizabeth I on March 6, 1594, appears in *Ninety-six Sermons by the Right Honorable and Reverend Father in God, Lancelot Andrewes* (Oxford and London: James Parker, 1878; repr. New York: AMS Press, 1967), vol. 2, pp. 61-77. The sermon will also appear, along with an essay on Andrewes, in my forthcoming study (see n. 23).

younger contemporary Donne observed, is the hardest thing to remember.[27]

Focus on the words gives a remarkable concreteness, almost a
sacramental quality, to Andrewes's preaching. "Nominals be reals";
Andrewes subscribes to the ancient hermeneutical principle that every
word and even the morphology and syntax of Scripture are designed
to give specific insight into the divine life and enable us to share more
fully in it. And indeed the sacrament of the eucharist is his constant
point of reference, especially in the sermons on the Nativity and the
Passion of Christ. His Christmas sermon on Micah 5:2 ("And thou
Bethlehem Ephratah . . .") makes the city of Christ's birth an unfor-
gettable symbol of divine humility: "great out of little, Christ out of
Bethlehem"; and further, that "house of bread" becomes a nearly
visible sign of the spiritual benefit we gain from the birth.[28] Andrewes's
vibrant pictorial imagination is most stimulated by narrative texts, and
always he works toward the end of heightening wonder at what God
has done for us in Christ. His homely description of the Christ Child
in the manger is typical of his evocative style, which makes heavy use
of antithesis in order to express the central paradox, the incarnation
of grace in nature:

> There lieth He, the Lord of glory without all glory. Instead of a
> palace, a poor stable; of a cradle of state, a beast's cratch; no pillow
> but a lock of hay; no hangings but dust and cobwebs; no attendants,
> but *in medio animalium* [in the midst of beasts], as the Fathers read
> in the third of Habakkuk [Hab. 3:2]. For if the inn were full, the
> stable was not empty we may be sure.[29]

Attending to the words of the text is how Andrewes respects its
mystery, while at the same time presenting it as a moral and spiritual
guide. The relation between mystery and manifestation is crucial to
his view of the nature of revelation and the life of the church. He charts
"a way of peace" among Christians with the principle that became the
platform for Anglican exegesis and ecclesiology: "Those [points of
religion] that are necessary [God] hath made plain; those that [are] not
plain [are] not necessary."[30] The Scriptures are "a plain mystery,"

27. *The Sermons of John Donne*, ed. G. R. Potter and E. M. Simpson (Berkeley:
University of California Press, 1953-62), vol. 2, p. 73.
28. *Ninety-Six Sermons*, 1:153-74 (preached Christmas Day, 1615).
29. *Ninety-Six Sermons*, 1:204 (preached Christmas Day, 1618).
30. *Ninety-Six Sermons*, 1:35.

inexhaustible yet open to all who sincerely wish to become partners in the mystery of godliness. Confining himself to disciplined, premeditated reflection on the words (contrary to the custom of the time, Andrewes prepared a full manuscript before preaching), he shuns obscurantism while leaving a place for silence. Above all, the rigor of his method excludes empty enthusiasm, which Andrewes saw as the great danger in the preaching of his day, and throws into relief the real demand of the text: "The only true praise of a sermon is, some evil left, or some good done upon the hearing of it."[31]

Despite Andrewes's practice of "following [a text] hard" (as he describes the exegetical style of Gregory the Great), he never isolates it from the rest of Scripture. He was chiefly an occasional preacher; the majority of his extant sermons are for the great feasts and fast-days: Christmas, Ash Wednesday, Lent, Good Friday, Easter, Pentecost. Yet Andrewes always keeps the whole Christian story in view while expounding his text for the present occasion. Incarnation and crucifixion are held firmly together as the foremost demonstrations of what is for him the central theme of the gospel: God's astonishing humility in seeking our salvation. His adherence to the full gospel as the context for treating any text or occasion leads to surprising effects: the justly famed Nativity sermons refer to Christ's death as often as to his birth. But this is a practice of real ethical significance and is perhaps the aspect of Andrewes's preaching that is most worthy of consideration by modern preachers. Bonhoeffer aptly warns against the distortion of the Christian life that arises from absolutization of any one part of the gospel: "A Christian ethic constructed solely on the basis of the incarnation would lead directly to the compromise solution. An ethic which was based solely on the cross or the resurrection of Jesus would fall victim to radicalism and enthusiasm. Only in the unity is the conflict resolved."[32]

John Donne would be surprised and almost certainly disappointed to be famed chiefly as a poet; it was his prose, and especially his sermons, for which he expected to be remembered. And indeed, the same intense personalism that animates the erotic poems, and through the Holy Sonnets admits us to his religious experience, in the sermons is bent upon proclamation of the gospel. But even more than

31. *Ninety-Six Sermons*, 1:430.
32. Bonhoeffer, *Ethics* (London: SCM; New York: Macmillan, 1965), p. 131, cited in Fowl and Jones, *Reading in Communion*, p. 154. I have not been able to confirm this reference in the editions available to me.

from personal experience, the energy of the sermons derives from the language of the Scriptures, which Donne read, used, and emulated with a poet's awe at the power of words.

Donne, like Andrewes, accepts Augustine's judgment that the best model of eloquence is the Scriptures themselves: "whatsoever hath justly delighted any man in any man's writings, is exceeded in the Scriptures."[33] And the aspect of the Holy Spirit's art of discourse that most impresses Donne is the use of metaphor:

> My God, my God, thou art a direct God, may I not say, a literal God, a God that wouldest be understood literally, and according to the plain sense of all that thou saiest? But thou art also (Lord, I intend it to thy glory . . .) a figurative, a metaphorical God, too: a God in whose words there is such a height of figures, such voyages, such peregrinations to fetch remote and precious metaphors, such extensions, such spreadings, such curtains of allegories, such third heavens of hyperboles, so harmonious elocutions . . . as all profane authors seem of the seed of the serpent, that creeps; thou art the dove, that flies.[34]

The bold use of metaphor is the most constant and memorable feature of Donne's rhetoric. As both poet and theologian steeped in catholic tradition, he knew well what modern scholars have recently rediscovered: that the real function of metaphor is not decorative, nor is it (as some of Donne's Puritan contemporaries contended) an annoying dilution of logical argumentation. Rather, metaphorical language is in many if not most cases irreducible to nonfigurative speech, for metaphor is the most precise vehicle for representing some phenomena, including almost all aspects of the spiritual life.[35] Moreover, metaphor is often the best means of applying God's word directly to the human heart. And this application is for Donne the aim of all devotion and preaching: "but this is *exquisita scrutatio*, the true searching of the Scriptures, to find all the histories to be examples to me, all the prophecies to induce a Savior for me, all the Gospel to apply Christ Jesus to me."[36]

---

33. *Sermons of John Donne*, 2:171.

34. Donne, "Expostulation 19," in *Devotions upon Emergent Occasions*, ed. Anthony Raspa (Montreal and London: McGill-Queen's University Press, 1975), p. 99.

35. See Janet Martin Soskice, *Metaphor and Religious Language* (Oxford: Clarendon Press, 1985), and Frank Burch Brown, *Transfiguration: Poetic Metaphor and the Languages of Religious Belief* (Chapel Hill: University of North Carolina Press, 1983).

36. *Sermons of John Donne*, 3:367.

Donne follows the Reformers in upholding the literal sense of the text, which he defines as "that which the Holy Ghost doth in that place principally intend."[37] But that definition makes it impossible to draw any absolute distinction between the literal and figurative senses; for the Holy Ghost is a poet, and therefore in many cases the primary sense is figurative. It is possible to be "too literal" with a book that is meant to make us long for heavenly things (the Revelation), just as it is possible to be "too allegorical" with one that teaches us about earthly matters (Genesis); and such a narrow literalism "will take from us the consolation of many spiritual happinesses, and bury us in the carnal things of this world."[38]

Seeking always to wean his hearers from a suffocating love of this world, Donne holds up the figures of the Scriptures. His own propensity for extravagant imagery makes him the greatest English-speaking preacher of the Psalms: the shadow of God's wings[39] and the arrows of temptation and affliction[40] become palpable emblems of spiritual realities. Further, he amplifies the biblical metaphors by his own inventions, with the daring ease of one fully at home in the imaginative world into which they open. Most striking are the figures for the Godhead, which repeatedly sacrifice divine dignity in order to make explicit and memorable the dynamics of redemption. To the soul "sunk even into the jaws of desperation," he offers the Johannine image of the seed of God abiding within (1 John 3:9) and draws this homely inference: "The Holy Ghost hath sat upon that seed, and hatched a new creature in thee, a modest but yet infallible assurance of the mercy of thy God."[41] The Holy Ghost is a hen; Christ is "the Sewer of all the corruption, of all the sins of this world";[42] the three Persons of the Trinity are "so many handles by which we may take hold of God, so many breasts, by which we may suck such a knowledge of God, as that we may grow up into him."[43]

The scriptural metaphors do not limit Donne's imaginative speaking about God but instead provide the warrant for it. This is instructive

37. *Essays in Divinity,* ed. Evelyn Simpson (Oxford: Clarendon Press, 1952), p. 40.

38. *Sermons of John Donne,* 6:62.

39. Sermon on Psalm 63:7 (preached at St. Paul's, January 29, 1625), *Sermons of John Donne,* 7:51-71.

40. Sermon on Psalm 38:2 (preached at Lincoln's Inn, 1618), *Sermons of John Donne,* 2:49-71.

41. *Sermons of John Donne,* 4:185.

42. *Sermons of John Donne,* 7:55.

43. *Sermons of John Donne,* 3:263.

with respect to the current debate about inclusive language and imagery and their place in worship, noted at the beginning of this essay. The pulpit should be a place of dramatic freedom in speaking about God, adventurous imagining about what God is *like*. But freedom is useless without guidance. It means nothing that I am free to speak Russian if I lack adequate instructional tools to do so or refuse to listen to others who already have that skill. As I have said, coherent thinking and speaking about God requires something like the discipline of language study, for which the Bible *in its entirety* is our primer. Truth cannot be secured by censuring the Scriptures when they do not speak as we would choose, as though they must be the last word on God or the Christian faith, rather than its first and best witness. On the contrary, it is by listening well to the Scriptures, taking seriously their perspectival character and metaphorical reticence, that we may discover in the large area of silence that surrounds them the freedom to articulate our own witness of faith.

Indeed, the very fact that the church claims an ancient canon that is diverse yet nonetheless limited in scope implies the sense in which Scripture "contains all things necessary to salvation." What is authoritative for Christian life is the groundwork of our theology and worship as it is set forth in Scripture, not the current state of our theological understanding. Preachers may find grace in that, if they will accept it. For it means that the sermon need not be a neat summary of correct theological positions; rather, it can be a starting point for thought, prayer, discussion, argument, and action — that is, all the work that leads to true knowledge of God. Indeed, the work of "theologizing" cannot be done adequately in the pulpit, if that is the only place where it is done; nor can deft adjustments at the lectern render the Scriptures an acceptable Word of God with the power to transform us. The preacher's task is less to solve problems in our understanding of Scripture than to identify those problems that are most fruitful for the congregation's life, those with which they must contend if they are to grow toward God. Holy preaching provides a serious introduction to the problems that should be held up for reconsideration again and again in a ceaseless educational process that embraces every aspect of the congregation's common work.

What Andrewes and Donne offer is a way to get involved with the problems that Scripture presents. They do it by teaching us how to "speak Scripture," the language not only of the biblical writers but also of the ancient and medieval commentators and theologians, as well as those who throughout the centuries composed the great poem of the liturgy. Their sermons initiate the reader into a long and deep conversation about what God is like. At a time when European Christians were slaughtering each other for their religious opinions, Andrewes and Donne made a step toward peace with their appeal to authorities from every age, Roman Catholic and Jewish as well as Protestant, and their acknowledgment of disagreements and areas of uncertainty. The diversity of the tradition stands as a reminder of the limitations of any historical vantage point and a caution against pronouncements on all but the few essential matters of faith. Donne commends those authorities who evidence the wisdom of reserved judgment: "Calvin will say, *Videtur,* It seems to be thus; Melancthon, It can be no otherwise but thus. But the best men are but problematical; only the Holy Ghost is dogmatical. Only he subscribes this surely, and only he seals with infallibility."[44]

Participation in that conversation is not an exercise in archaism; rather, it guides us in reaching new and crucial knowledge of ourselves. "The art of salvation is but the art of memory";[45] regaining fluency in the language of the Scriptures and the long tradition of their interpretation can enrich the depleted memory of the church. For that language of story and symbol is the key to a store of memories that stretch all the way back to our creation in God's image, memories of ourselves as God's people, which have the power to draw us beyond the fearful and unimaginative absorption in the present that is such a strong element in the spiritual malaise of our time.

Simone Weil asked the question that weighs even more heavily now, fifty years after her death: "Where will a renewal come to us, to us who have spoiled and devastated the whole earthly globe?"; she answered, "Only from the past, if we love it."[46] Because words always come freighted with history, it is in large part the work of the poet, the true philologist, to teach us to love the past, and in that love to find curiosity and even confidence about the future. Andrewes and Donne can help modern preachers recognize their own poetic obligation: not to be versifiers, but to dwell on words and thus to mediate between past and future. The preacher who loves the words of the text is a true evangelical, out of memory bringing forth the promises that enable them to move forward responsibly and with hope.

44. *Sermons of John Donne,* 6:301.
45. *Sermons of John Donne,* 2:73.
46. Weil, quoted by Czeslaw Milosz, *The Witness of Poetry* (Cambridge: Harvard University Press, 1983), p. 114.

Is Christianity Good for Us?

ELLEN T. CHARRY

I.

THE Baltimore Declaration calls orthodox believers to reclaim the tradition from "heresies and theological errors infiltrating the Church . . . [i]n the name of inclusivity and pluralism" (preface). As a manifesto it is able to identify, but not respond to, criticisms of the church. A defense of the tradition must be mounted with reasoned arguments, lest defenders of the faith think that loudly affirming and repudiating positions is all that the church's faith requires or critics conclude that the defenders of the faith are deaf to serious moral concerns.

Article 1 of the Declaration objects to the loss of trinitarian language within the church. Support for some feminist objections to traditional trinitarian language threatens to replace worship of the Father, Son, and Holy Spirit with the worship of the Creator, Redeemer, and Sustainer or other abstractions. These feminists seek to release the contemporary world from what they see as morally destructive side effects of patriarchal doctrines and language on women.

Defenders of the tradition should respond to the criticisms being leveled at the tradition in terms that the critics would need to take account of; a proper apology must respond to the concerns raised. It must assume that we do *still* need to be brought to God, and that the body of Christ is *still* able to accomplish this. But it must also take the criticisms seriously.

With thanks to Margaret O'Gara for many helpful suggestions on both of my essays in this volume.

This essay argues that if traditional trinitarianism has had negative side effects on women, it is not because it has been taken too seriously but rather because it has not been taken seriously enough by men. We need to move more deeply into rather than abandon the biblical teaching that the intimacy between God the Father and God the Son has to do with our salvation. The feminist suggestion that feminine imagery and language in prayer will enhance our grasp of the love and self-giving of God is sure to be genuinely helpful. Talking about divine love without access to the image of the love of a mother for her children is indeed an impoverished form of human expression. This, however, should be a question of attaining a proper balance to the limited means of expression at our disposal. It is not simply a matter of replacing deleterious masculine language with beneficial feminine language.

Before proceeding to the argument at hand, two caveats need to be registered. First, a scripturally normed defense of the tradition should not be misconstrued as implying that there is not a shadow side to Christian history. The church has made, does make, and will continue to make serious errors. The positions that the Baltimore Declaration repudiates all developed out of moral concerns. Scripture tells us plainly that the disciples were slow-witted bumblers; they, remember, are now us. Despite our limitations, the body of Christ is called to proclaim the gospel. Because we are Christians, we must do so clearly, yet with deep pastoral concern, not with a naive optimism that ignores the dangerous possibilities that inhere in any way of life humans put their hands to.

The second warning to be noted has to do with the functions of doctrine. Doctrine states tersely what Christians teach and confess about God and God's gracious, saving work on our behalf. In addition to being the means of our knowledge of salvation, doctrine may also turn out, upon inspection, to have moral dimensions. While our moral formation is not our salvation, which we celebrate and reenact in praise and thanksgiving, it is probably not too much to say that God is not displeased if, when grasping God's work of salvation, we are morally aroused. Kenneth Scott Latourette put this position well when he wrote of Calvin's theology, "We are not saved by character, but salvation issues in character. We never become perfect in this life, but we are always to strive to advance 'in the way of the Lord.'"[1] It is well to attend to

---

1. Latourette, *A History of Christianity*, vol. 2 (San Francisco: Harper & Row, 1975), p. 755.

the moral payoff of doctrinal language for those who repeat the creed and the doxology in their prayers. This does not suggest that the primary function of doctrine is moral engineering; the primary function of doctrine is to impart to believers knowledge of God's grace: salvation by the forgiveness of their sins. This essay limits itself to a defense of the moral, not the soteriological, integrity of the doctrine of the Trinity. It assumes that God undertook a particular course of action to effect our salvation (as testified in Scripture) for cogent, not cavalier, reasons. One of our tasks as disciples, but only one, is to attend to the rationale behind God's actions, which we assume to be for the eternal health of our souls, and perhaps for our edification in this life as well.

In short, this essay is a modest effort to assist the church in self-examination using one moral issue alluded to by the Declaration: the objection to trinitarian language.[2]

At its best, the Christian tradition has maintained both that Christianity is good for us because it is true (i.e., from God) and that it is true because it is good for us. God would not make himself known to us in ways that harm us. As Karl Barth noted, "Brutal grace is not the grace of the true and living God." In the thought world of ancient Greece that was inherited by the church fathers, truth and goodness coincided. For both Clement of Alexandria and Origen, the good that Christianity brought in its wake testified to its truth. For St. Augustine, to increase in the knowledge of God is to increase in goodness and virtue; both of these were embodied in Christian salvation. Amendment of life accompanied knowledge of God, even if it was not the goal of such knowledge. With these two qualifications on the table, I will turn to an assessment of the tension between the tradition and the current psychologically attuned climate that underlies the disagreement between defenders and some feminist critics of the church.

Today the mainline Protestant denominations, including the Episcopal Church, are dominated by a therapeutic climate aimed at physical, emotional, and social well-being. In this climate the burden of proof is on Christian doctrine to demonstrate its benefits. The therapeutic climate defines what is salutary as that which supports and fosters personal growth and individual or group self-expression and advancement. And to the extent that the tradition has inhibited the growth and well-being of women, Jews, and others, both within and

---

2. This discussion focuses on trinitarian language. It is not an argument about all-male language for God.

beyond the church, it is judged to be wanting by members of those groups and their advocates. Ironically, the contemporary therapeutic dimension of religious belief is structurally, although not materially, related to the assumption of the patristic age (inherited from classical Greece) that truth and the pedagogy that educes it ought to model and aim for *paideia:* morally formative education. Both believe that true religious belief is helpful, not harmful. The difference between them lies in what they consider beneficial and what they consider harmful.

The theological psychology (usually termed "theological anthropology") of the patristic age assumed that Christianization is morally formative because God knows that we really need moral formation. God's grace leads us to truth, which is an instrument of human betterment. All this is to say that while God is concerned both that we know him as the source and destiny of our salvation and that we glorify him accordingly, theologians have assumed that God is also concerned about the kind of people Christians become from knowing him.

One of the most graphic expressions of the classical theological psychology stretching back to Augustine comes from John Calvin's adoption of the image of the human personality as a cross between a horse who needs to be reined in and a mule who needs to be goaded into action. The image is from Psalm 32:9:

> Do not be like a horse or a mule, without understanding,
>   whose temper must be curbed with bit and bridle,
>   else it will not stay near you.
>
>   (NRSV)

The Christian life bridles the bucking horse in us and goads the stubborn mule in us to curb our natural inclination to indulge the animal side of ourselves and to develop the spiritual side of ourselves by drawing us to God. The church fathers believed that it *is* possible for one to grow into one's best self (not a perfect self), but only with the assistance of divine grace within the context of a church-guided life. Societal institutions, both sacred and secular, were assumed to be authoritative. Responsibility for one's deportment lay with the individual.

Modern pedagogical psychology, under the influence of Jean-Jacques Rousseau's educational psychology in *Emile,* has a radically different point of departure. Instead of treating the human person as being in need of taming by family, church, and the public and private sectors, modern pedagogy shifts responsibility to the institutions, considering them to be corrupting and deforming. The true function of education is to release undeveloped potentialities of the personality or to repair damage within the personality. Instead of seeing social institutions and the discipline they teach as necessary sources of guidance and formation, the therapeutic culture, relying on pathological models, tends to see social institutions and structures as instruments of personality distortion.[3] Responsibility for deportment lies not with the individual but with society at large. Social entitlement programs are predicated upon these assumptions. The church has not been exempt from this social criticism.

The attack on Christian doctrine is partly the result of classical theological psychology's clash with the modern therapeutic mind-set. The difference may be seen in terms of divergent understandings of need and who determines it. Christianity classically assumed that God knows what we need; salvation also makes us into our best selves. What is good for us presses against what we want; what benefits us may not be appealing at first sight. What we need may look like bad-tasting medicine, but that misperception is from a sinful and misguided desire for self-gratification. Life with God is good for us in the long run but hard to swallow. St. Augustine's *Confessions* are the *locus classicus* for this view.

Modern psychology has tended to see need as closer to desire and us as the proper judges of both. Psychotherapies encourage clients to assess their emotional needs for intimacy, validation, and emotional nurturance and to plan a strategy for getting these needs met. On this view getting what we need is gratifying, not onerous.

In a static world where providence controlled events, questions about the justice of God's judgments were untoward. Social arrangements and personal circumstances, reflected in the "orders of creation" or the orders of the church, expressed the will of God. In a fluid world, however, everything might be otherwise. The tradition and modernity agree that character *is* shaped by social institutions. But the church has viewed piety as an active vehicle of human excellence, while modern psychology has, at times, viewed it as repressive and unhealthful.

3. It is popular for new-class and executive-class persons to see the family as the root of their problems, which are remediable by insight-oriented psychotherapy. Working-class persons, poor persons, and racial minorities tend to hold larger social institutions (business, education, the state) or pervasive abstract attitudes (e.g., racism, sexism, anti-Semitism) responsible for their problems and tend to seek governmental redress, either legislative or judicial. In both models one starts out whole and is progressively damaged by social institutions.

The church believes God to be a better judge of what is good for us than we ourselves.

In the modern period the social order was seen as a human creation and not the result of divine providence. Social institutions were recognized as powerful shapers of human character. Modern psychology has categorized personality types as emotionally healthy or unhealthy and has tagged social institutions as partly responsible for mental health. Some critics have held parents accountable for psychological dysfunctions in their children. Critics of Christianity have tended to hold the church responsible for language and beliefs that teach repressive behavior, attitudes, and policies. Blame for social and emotional problems has shifted from the individual to society (or the institutional church) at large.

The Christian tradition assumes a fallen humanity, regardless of individual gifts, talents, and acts of righteousness, on the model of congenital illness. The church supplies the therapeutic environment in which symptoms can be alleviated even though the condition cannot be eradicated. Modernity, on the other hand, assumes a healthy infant reared in a dysfunctional environment. People are not naturally misogynist, imperialistic, rapacious, intolerant, or materialistic; they become so through social conditioning. Dysfunctional families and discriminatory legal statutes, as well as Scripture, liturgy, hymns, ecclesiastical policies, etc., contribute to the marginalization of specific groups of persons. The words of the Rodgers and Hammerstein song ring clearly here: "You've got to be taught to hate and fear. It's got to be drummed in your dear little ear. You've got to be carefully taught." Later in life individual psychotherapy, social change, or judicial redress are required to effect an attitudinal cure to unlearn what was mistakenly taught by the institution, family, or church.

The tradition and the temper of our day both agree that we all start out on an equal footing, but they disagree on what that footing is. Defenders of the tradition cling to the view that we are all *incurvatus in se* (self-absorbed) regardless of the environment we are raised in, while critics argue that fallen institutions are responsible for social and emotional problems. Both the Christian and the modernist parties agree that what is wrong can be righted, but they disagree on how it is to be corrected. Traditionalists tend to rely upon Christian piety to control (not eradicate) sin; critics seek to amend the language of prayer, sacred texts, and doctrines — in short, the tools of the tradition — in order to correct the product of that piety.

While these two options do characterize different outlooks of premodern and modern thinking, they are not polar opposites. The Baltimore Declaration itself does not deny that Christians have erred egregiously in the course of Christian history. The authors disagree with their opponents, however, about the *degree* to which the tradition should be held accountable now that these ill effects have been revealed. Were they able to hear one another, both parties to the dispute might see that their disagreements turn on different considered judgments. As it is, they may see one another as stock caricatures. The line between heresy and orthodoxy has always been this thin.

II.

Without rehearsing the details, it is not hyperbolic to say that the church, just like communism and capitalism spawned by modern liberalism, is vulnerable to social injustices and the manipulation of power and wealth for the benefit of the few. Christians are on target when they speak of human sinfulness as inescapable. Even if the Augustinian vision of sin as a sexually transmitted disease does not sit quite so well now as it once did, human sinfulness as the striving after pleasure rather than goodness is enduringly encountered. If Christians are correct that life with God benefits us, imbuing one another with the story of God's condescension and self-giving on our behalf in the church ought to help us. Arguing for this position would respond to contemporary critics.

Recognizing that Christianity has a shadow side should not lead one to judge the tradition as inevitably bad for us either in whole or in part. Rather, from our own vantage point, we see that benefit and detriment often overlap or play themselves out differently on persons occupying various social locations and historical periods. Purely good or evil social systems are imaginary.

Liberals may argue that the Christian tradition (especially in the hands of a Thomas à Kempis or a Calvin) has portrayed humans as incorrigibly sinful and powerless to reform on their own. On this view, practiced self-loathing and self-denial through utter humility and obedience to superiors in a hierarchically ordered universe may reflect obedience to God. This type of the Christian penitent has been played out with special ferocity upon women, who found themselves at the bottom of a hierarchically ordered social structure.

The resulting social arrangements fostered distorted self-images for both women and men. Women were viewed as little more than incitement to men to act out their sexual impulses (and thereby their power); women were rendered socially powerless, outside exclusively female institutions, as punishment. The social virtues of obedience and humility rendered women obsequious to men (often fathers and husbands) in authority.

Renunciation of women and family became the norm of Christian manhood that only the most stouthearted could achieve. Until Luther married Katharina, avoidance of women became a test of strength of character, perhaps rendering women all the more to be shunned and feared.[4] As late as the seventeenth century, Calvinist John Bunyan's hero, Christian, in *The Pilgrim's Progress* abandons his wife and children to make his pilgrimage to heaven. Men who fell short of this religious ideal assumed the role of master and authority over their wives and children, modeling themselves partly on biblical imagery of God as lord, master, and king, and partly on Greco-Roman social structures.

The Christian model of God as all-powerful and good, and of the human person as powerless and sinful, thus (seemingly) benefited men while harming women. Now a response to this history that meets the criticism on its moral terms will not seek to ignore the historical accuracy of this dynamic. For as I have argued above, Christianity on the far side of these criticisms must acknowledge the shadow side of the tradition. But at the same time, neither would a genuine response judge the tradition necessarily deleterious. The approach to be pursued here suggests that the bearers of the tradition may have worked with a selective (perhaps even a self-serving) slant on the tradition itself and therefore reinforced images of womanhood and manhood that run counter to central Christian doctrines. To the extent that Christian tradition has fostered distorted ideals of both womanhood and manhood, it has had to distort the biblical message that Jesus Christ came into the world, taught among us, suffered and died, and rose from the dead to reconcile us to God. To support this thesis I will examine several prevalent feminist objections to traditional theological language and specific doctrines.

4. In the opinion of this writer, this classical view, while perhaps an extreme caricature that may seem quaint to some, contains a grain of truth that contemporary feminists may disregard at their peril. Physiological sexual differences between women and men, and a failure by both women and men to take these differences seriously, may underlie the current controversy about rape and date or acquaintance rape. Modesty of women's dress, a norm of Christian deportment now widely neglected, may reflect a genuine need for women to protect themselves from men lacking in self-control.

Some feminists object that trinitarian and hierarchical language are deleterious. While these two features of the tradition have often coincided, they are really distinct issues. I will consider each separately. Some feminists claim that trinitarian language has enabled men to identify with God while denying this possibility to women. To repair the error some would proscribe biblical talk of God the Father and of his Son. Others propose goddess worship. The assumptions underlying both suggestions are (*a*) that religion is to be designed to express the felt needs of its practitioners, (*b*) that identification with God is appropriate, and (*c*) that gender is a necessary component in such identification.

Regarding the first assumption, while certainly bearers of the tradition have relied on their own knowledge and experience in framing theological issues, Christianity is not a religion designed by its adherents. It is a tradition that stands on the disclosure of God. While it is necessary to articulate the faith in understandable language in every age, Christians are not free to redesign the faith to align it with the tenor of the times.

On the second point, the tradition has generally qualified the craving to "become" God that is evident in the church fathers — for example, Irenaeus and Athanasius. On the one hand, we are not God; if anything, we are the opposite of God, as the polarity "divine-human" suggests. Cultivation of a self-image as sinful and powerless before God reinforces that self-contempt. An image of maleness as self-dependent, self-directed, beholden to or requiring guidance from no one is not an image of the Christian disciple. Jesus' disciples are barely able to envision the future that awaits them. The modern secular model of manhood is the opposite of that of the disciple of Jesus of Nazareth.

At the same time, the patristic writers, and not only the Greek fathers, viewed *theosis,* divinization, as the goal of Christian life and faith. The goal of the Christian life is, however, not to think of ourselves as comparable to God in nature but to approximate God's graciousness in his condescension to us by a practiced abandonment of physical pleasure and by cultivation of spiritual pleasures through ascetic disciplines. The goal of Christian discipleship is to humble the human spirit before the glory and goodness of God, while at the same time imitating the love of God for us made known in the cross — that is, in the act of Jesus Christ, who put his body between God's judgment and our failing.

Followers of Jesus are women and men who relinquish pursuit of honor, power, and pleasure and submit themselves to the rule of God made known in the life and death of Jesus. I will develop this more fully in the discussion of the notion of the hierarchical arrangement of the universe that consistently accompanied classical Christian theology. The point here is that if men have identified manliness with an understanding of divine fatherhood and sonship that reinforces their own proclivities to control, subjugate, or wreak violence upon others to bolster their own feelings of power, they have gerrymandered the Christian doctrine of the Trinity, the reason for the incarnation, the power of the cross, and the hope of resurrection.

The growing popularity of eliminating traditional trinitarian language obscures the Christian teaching that God's love for us is made known through the Persons of the Trinity. Banning talk of the Father and the Son because of the fact that historically men have subordinated women not only renders God a series of abstractions; it also renders the incarnation (and with it the entire tradition) utterly incoherent and disqualifies the Bible as Scripture. And in so doing we are deprived not only of the knowledge of the means of our salvation but also of the primary models of compassionate human personhood — caring fatherhood (cf. Hos. 11; Luke 11:11-13) and filial devotion (cf. Phil. 2:5-8) — which have guided Western civilization (if bumpily) for two millennia.

Christian theology teaches that God craves our salvation. Submission to him is the means of our release from the self-destructiveness of sin. Men who have latched onto those elements of the tradition that reinforce their own understanding of manhood have had to suppress the fact that Christian faith turns on the gentleness, compassion, and empathy as well as the judgment of God made known through the work of the Father, Son, and Holy Spirit.

The dominant picture of manhood in Western culture, including the church, unites hierarchically ordered social arrangements derived from a tradition exemplified by Cicero (upon whom Augustine relied) with an authorization of violence for political or theological ends. Support for violence as a disciplinary measure to "correct" those in their charge comes from both the Old Testament and ancient Greece.[5] Today this image, applied specifically to fatherhood and more broadly to manhood, is reinforced by the advertising, sports, and entertainment industries and the corporate world they promote.

In a corrupted popular form, some men today feel justified in resorting to violence against others, be they women, children, or other

---

5. St. Anselm's biographer, Eadmer, cites several incidents in which the saint strongly opposed punishment as a form of discipline.

men, in the face of frustration and anger born of failing to have their way, or simply from a lust for power. Men guided by this ideal see others either as impediments to be got rid of, as instruments in the procurement of self-gratification, or as opportunities for increased wealth, power, status, and pleasure. The salient question is whether this view of manhood truly derives from biblical and patristic doctrine or whether it is an unbalanced — indeed, an unchristian — portrait.

The ideal of manhood as an authoritarian and slightly sadistic controlling repository of power, exploiting weaker or subordinate charges, even for the sake of justice, is at best a partial, and, I submit, skewed view of the fatherhood and sonship of the Holy Trinity. If the tradition has taught a distorted and harmful vision of womanhood, it is no less true that it has taught a distorted and harmful view of manhood.

Jesus' teachings on love and compassion, especially love of enemies, are more central to Christian discipleship than are Greco-Roman teachings on justice. Jesus' manliness contrasts sharply with an image of manhood and power as violent conquest and subjugation or even destruction of others. Perhaps women who birth and nurture children (and endure untoward behavior from some men) are more intimate with the Christian virtues of self-control, loving compassion, and self-giving taught by Jesus and his passion. In Christian terms, this points to women's integrity, not their weakness. It is true that there are biblical images of God as a man of war and that the Old Testament at times countenances violence against foreigners and enemies. But at the same time, the prophets stand in judgment of violence in the name of God, especially against children and women — be it sexual, physical, or economic. And God's taking flesh in Jesus Christ, the definitive expression of God's grace, makes normative a decidedly different understanding of power and strength than was known to the ancient Israelites, the Greeks, or the Romans. In the Gospels Jesus defines power by healing the sick; he gives meaning to the word *strength* by enduring suffering so that others, including his shallow disciples, might be saved from the wrath of pernicious power holders in spite of themselves. He explicates the word *courage* by his submission to death.

The Pauline tradition highlights the soteriological power of the cross to reconcile us to God. In the New Testament God puts his own body on the line to rescue people in an act of love. Perhaps the urgency now is not to point out that the Christian tradition has failed women but to show that it has more seriously abandoned *men* by failing to note that, in addition to saving us through the death of his Son, God has revealed the standard of true manliness in Jesus Christ.

Another frequently heard feminist concern is that the language of God as father offends incest victims and women who have experienced violence from their fathers. At the present moment, images of manhood and fatherhood in our culture are widely criticized. The movement to unmask dysfunctional families may leave the impression that most fathering — and a substantial amount of mothering — is of poor quality and sometimes nonexistent or even destructive, and this for reasons too complex to concern us here. While there can be no doubt that there are, and always have been, poor husbands and fathers among every race and class, it is also true that, while every family has problems and stresses, not everyone is seriously damaged by their family of origin. And critics should consider whether pedagogically it is advisable to promote purely negative images of manhood as a means of promoting familial responsibility and positive interactions between men and their wives and children.

Strategic considerations aside, many, though perhaps not most, women and children are abused by men. Indeed, this essay argues that trinitarian language is needed for their sake. Again, a commonly proposed feminist remedy is to eliminate the language of God as father out of respect for such persons. But while this may be the treatment closest at hand, is it clear that God has not already provided us a better way if only we can make use of it? Is the hope of female victims of violence solely to denounce or is it more seriously to correct twisted and irresponsible views of fatherhood that enable men to abandon or abuse their children? Is the treatment for abuse simply to remove oneself from the source of pain and avoid men for the rest of one's life? Or is healing accomplished through accumulating positive interactions with men so that slowly, gently an alternative repository of experience builds up until abused women are capable (even if for the first time) of healthy relationships with loving men? Is that not the point of a commercial film like *Sleeping with the Enemy*? To settle for less would be to surrender to sickness and suffering. Jesus came that we might have life abundantly.

At the same time, if God the Father suggests a loving and gentle rather than abusive and violent father, should not a serious (and careful) encounter with God the Father be part of an abusive man's therapy? St. Paul's understanding of the fatherhood of God in Galatians 3 and 4 allowed that Gentiles, who had been excluded from the household of God prior to Christ, are now made children of God, raised up by the sacrifice of Christ and liberated as heirs who are loved and have faith in Christ. And St. Athanasius brings us the vision of a father yearning to rescue his children from the folly that leads to their own undoing and the ruin of the whole creation. Athanasius, who did not always practice what he preached, noted that knowledge of God in Christ was transforming pagan society without recourse to violence (*On the Incarnation* 51-52).

What, by the same token, would be the effect of eliminating trinitarian language on those men who are given to violence against women and children? Without the norm of God the Father, who models the responsibilities and skills of adulthood, and God the Son, who gives his life to rescue others from death, images of manhood would be restricted to those found in popular culture. Scripture presents God as the Father who created, protects, and lovingly chastises his children and aches watching a languishing creation. Without a corrective of the stature of God, what is to prevent abusive men from feeling justified in their actions? Why should men who abandon or abuse children take seriously the secular law that halfheartedly requires child support, if God the Holy Trinity does not also stand in stark judgment of their irresponsibility?

In short, the Christian belief in the sinfulness of humankind has been exaggeratedly leveled at women; the doctrine of the Trinity, which teaches self-sacrifice for the sake of one's children, must now be brought to bear against men, who need to know God the Holy Trinity who is the norm of manhood. Men with weak impulse control who readily resort to violence in the face of frustration of their desires need to form themselves after the Son of God who died for them and for those they abuse. God the Father and God the Son condemn the belief that one's wife and children are one's property to be dealt with to meet one's own needs. Together the Father and the Son inverted contempt for family responsibilities. God sent his Son to become flesh, to suffer as one of us, and to die among us, not to meet God's own needs to display power or to impose an absolute and commanding will, but to rivet our attention on love and compassion by example.

Indeed, one might go further. Modern medicine now recognizes that male sexuality is much more labile and volatile than female sexuality. It is men who commit rape. The caricature of women as satanic temptresses, and therefore the fount of sin, results from men's fear of the violent proclivities of their own sexuality, which they have projected onto women. While no doubt both men and women experience lust, there can be no doubt that male lust more readily results in violence against women than the reverse. In such circumstances the traditional idea that women are inherently more sinful than men because they are "lascivious" or "emotional" is absurd. Male violence growing out of uncontrolled sexuality or lust for power is sinful. When the Christian tradition reckons seriously with this reality, it will begin to apprehend its own teaching on the relationship between sin and sexuality. In the meantime, other issues still trouble those concerned with the practical implications of Christian belief.

Another doctrine critics charge with encouraging male violence is the atonement. Why would a merciful and loving God resort to or permit his own Son to be slaughtered in order to rescue his earthly children? If God were capable of some other strategy why select this one? St. Anselm, among others, tried his hand at answering this troubling question of the rationale behind the cross, and modern readers are often disappointed at the result, reading his famous treatise on the atonement, *Cur Deus Homo?* as being obsessed with the honor of God and the requirements of absolute justice.[6] But most critics fail to note that Anselm argued that we cannot damage God's honor. He took pains to argue that the self-sacrifice of the Son to redeem us was not undertaken solely out of obedience to the commanding will of the Father or to fulfill the requirement of justice; rather, it was done voluntarily, out of both the Son's own commitment to justice *and* his love for humankind (2.17, 18). Even for Anselm, wrongly deemed the bloodless commender of the forensic theory of the atonement, learning obedience is never separated from loving justice and pursuing mercy concomitantly.

Anselm labored mightily with the tension between God's justice and mercy, an enduring theological problem that each age may resolve differently. The fact that Christians have had to reexamine this question time and again is precisely because so much is at stake if we release either pole of the tension. In the context of this discussion, the relationship between justice and mercy impacts directly on the operative models of manhood that are at work in the popular culture and that Christian theology seeks to counter. To put it directly, the transforming power of God's love poured out in Jesus Christ speaks against the popular and unfortunate habit of associating manliness with the imposition of justice and femininity with the bestowal of mercy and compassion.

This is not to deny, however, that violent men do not require

6. My own assessment of Anselm's result will appear in my forthcoming book *Educating the Soul*. A précis of my position appears in "The Moral Function of Christian Doctrine," *Theology Today*, April 1992.

further instruction in the proper use of justice from God. The Christian doctrine of the atonement can be viewed from the perspective of either justice or mercy, both of which speak to the needs of violent men. From one perspective the innocent Son of God who dies in our place speaks of the need to submit to the requirements of justice — a powerful social lesson upon which ordered societies all rest. Men who take justice into their own hands or who transgress the law or the canons of public or personal decency to settle disputes or to satisfy their desires flout the requirements of justice incumbent upon every member of society.

At the same time, and perhaps more pointedly, the self-giving of Christ on the cross proclaims the mercy of God. But what does the story of Abraham, told by God to sacrifice his son, and the Christian teaching that God sent his own Son to die for others say to human fathers and sons looking to God for guidance and models of mercy? And what can such theology offer to a society that needs rebuke and a model to counter violent proclivities in men? The Christian doctrine of the atonement teaches that true manhood lies in rescuing, not in violating others; God the Father ached to rescue humankind from itself; Christ sacrificed himself to accomplish this. Christian doctrine teaches that these two Persons of the Trinity cooperate in the salvation of the human race. It is a far more potent demonstration of teamwork, and most assuredly to a higher end, than the most delicately choreographed football play to which many men attend.

The Christian teaching on the atonement challenges the tendency of some to seek self-esteem, respect, or revenge disguised as a quest for justice in which others are harmed or intimidated. Christ did not die to warn us of the fate that awaits us if we do not obey his Father's commands. Men who see violence as a way to gain "respect" (we now have an entire subculture of inner-city youths who commit criminal acts to gain and maintain the "respect" of their peers) desperately need help to see that the incarnation, cross, and resurrection of Christ teach that genuine respect and self-respect come from rescuing, protecting, and enhancing the lives of others, even when self-sacrifice and humiliation are required. Christian men do not need to derive their self-respect from the cowardly need to intimidate others; their self-respect comes from the path charted for them by Christ. As noted above, Christ's incarnation, ministry, and death define the power, strength, and courage so central to masculinity. For Christian men — and women — the goal of discipleship is "Christoformity," not formation on the models of war heroes, economic gladiators, or professional athletes.

Now, unless adults are confident that in the face of competition from the sports, entertainment, and advertising industries we can, on our own, teach this Christian model of manhood — indeed, of personhood — to our children using only ourselves as models, is it wise to banish the interaction between the Father and the Son in the rescue mission of humanity for the more antiseptic and abstract images of creator, redeemer, and sustainer that only the college-educated understand?

The other object of feminist criticism, noted at the outset of this section, is the strictly hierarchical structure of society in which women sat toward the bottom of the social ladder (with only slaves and children below them). In response to this hierarchical and controlling construal of power, some feminists object to designating God as lord or king. Here the recommendation is not to replace the offending language with a female counterpart — *lady* and *queen* are equally out of favor currently. The ban on hierarchical language carries with it a principled rejection of authority in almost any form because of the intimate link between authority and power that exploits rather than protecting and empowering those who occupy subordinate positions.

Yet this confuses proper exercise of power with abusive uses of authority. Knowledge, training, and experience do outfit some persons to hold positions of power in certain fields and others to submit themselves to their care. Pharmacists, physicians, fire fighters, and police officers hold positions of authority not only by virtue of their skills, knowledge, and office but also because we trust in their integrity to use their authority to serve and not harm the rest of us. The feminist concern is not so much with the idea of specialized areas of expertise and authority derived from that expertise as it is with the use of gender as the precondition for access to that expertise and authority. The feminist rejection of hierarchy should not be confused with a rejection of authorized structures of power and authority generally. The issue is not authority and power in themselves, but the ends toward which and the means by which authority and power are employed — for the welfare and benefit of others or simply for enhancing self-interest, whether that be economic, political, or social.

The Christian life counsels humility and obedience before God and imitation of Christ in our common life. It is not subordination of itself that feminists should find objectionable, but rather the automatic subordination of women to men to build up men's self-esteem. The secular worldview no longer assumes a hierarchically structured universe and corresponding social order. Degrees of authority and responsibility vary with social roles and the skills, training, and experience necessary to execute those roles. And the multiplicity of social roles played by any one individual provides continuous realignment of expressions of authority and power as opposed to submission and guidance in a single life as well as in corporate life.

The feminist worldview, perhaps out of an understandable distrust of power, proposes equality and mutuality as an alternative to traditional hierarchical social structures. Moderns feel more comfortable with the teaching on the mutuality of marriage that St. Paul admonished in 1 Corinthians 7:1-11, for example, as a model of relationships between women and men than with the more hierarchical teaching of Ephesians 5:22-24. But perhaps we have chosen the weaker path. Perhaps the Christian teaching of humility and obedience before God should model not only our relationship with God but our marriages as well. To put it bluntly, perhaps the Christian fault lies not in counseling wives to be submissive to their husbands but in failing to extend the biblical counsel to husbands to do likewise. Seen in this light, a doctrine of mutuality is not opposed to a doctrine of authority and submission so much as it encompasses the dynamic flow of power and submission both within the structure of any interpersonal relationship and within the variegated social roles embodied in any one life.

The tradition itself is not oblivious to the nuances and shifting dynamics of relationships of power and authority in social relationships. Augustine states clearly that domestic authority and obedience are based on an ethic of care presented as an ethic of justice: "In the household of the just man . . . even those who give orders are the servants of those whom they appear to command. For they do not give orders because of a lust for domination but from a dutiful concern for the interests of others, not with pride in taking precedence over others, but with compassion in taking care of others" (*City of God* 19.14).

If it is true that women and children civilize men, what is to become of men if the Trinity is effectively eliminated? Will it help men to become better husbands and fathers, or will they be abandoned to false and harmful fantasies of machismo arising from their own sinfulness? Is it not shortsighted to want to undermine the family because it does not always function perfectly? If the goal of some feminists is to create separate men's and women's religions, or even spiritualities, with their respective gods, communication between the sexes will become even more strained than it already is. If the negative experiences of some women with some men are not countered by the model of the Son of God who loves unconditionally, is unstintingly merciful, and goes around compulsively healing those who hurt, even to the point of his own demise, what will help men to see that they have been betrayed by exploitative economic interests?

Creating separate spiritualities for men and women is deleterious because it abandons men. This, in the long run, is bad for the women upon whom men who are unformed by Jesus prey. Feminists are correct; Scripture and tradition have been used to oppress and denigrate women. But some feminists have been slower to see that men, too, have been abused by a church that has difficulty Christianizing them.

As stated at the outset, the point of this discussion is not to deny that images of God that extend beyond those of monarchy and feudalism, some of them biblical, may be genuinely helpful in freeing our thinking about God from constraints that were imposed upon the tradition by prevailing social structures at the time doctrinal and liturgical language took shape. It is rather to suggest that dismantling traditional doctrines — aside from eviscerating the faith — may not be the hoped-for panacea. Banning the word *Lord* is an example. More is at stake than the discomfort of having to adjust to new phrasing after a lifetime of liturgical numbness. Neither is the issue one simply of updating medieval social arrangements to suit the modern democratic mind-set. At issue is the point that in Jesus Christ God leads us to a life we can neither envision nor enact alone. To ban the language of submission — whether that means use of the word *lord* or some other term — would mislead us back into the false security of an exaggerated self-confidence that denies our dependency and need for guidance, a self-confidence that many men could do without.

Some feminists attack the traditional Christian virtues of humility and obedience because these are thought to encourage passivity, dependency, and selflessness to the point of irresponsibility. Although these character traits have had devastating effects on women, many modern men seem to have escaped their tutelage unscathed. Have men fared better without them? Is the point of replacing humility with assertiveness and obedience with self-direction for women, rather than encouraging recognition of talents and skills as gifts of the Holy Spirit, not liable to encourage in women precisely those traits that they disapprove of in men? If men view sexual and economic power (let us say) as means for personal gratification, rather than as volatile but nevertheless genuine gifts of God to be protected and employed prudently for the upbuilding of society, what check is there on the abuse of these gifts? Christian faith instills a divine standard of judgment within the heart and conscience of believers. It appears to me that, with the maxim "challenge authority" and with the goal of life as self-fulfillment, late twentieth-century society may sacrifice both humility and obedience.

A Christian view of self-development, by contrast, has two aspects. First, it provides a stark divine standard for moral self-assessment. The believer who trusts that God is the standard for human behavior constantly scrutinizes her or his behavior in this light. Second, a Christian view of self-fulfillment is communal rather than individualistic. It sets all human gifts in the broader context of God's love for creation, leveling and binding us together. Christians know themselves to be graced and mutually responsible to employ God's gifts to the ends for which they were given: adoration of God and protection and repair of God's creation.

The soteriological work of the atonement concretizes and models the cooperation of Father and Son for the rescue of the helpless. In the Augustinian tradition, the Holy Spirit is the love that binds the Father and Son together in their salvific mission for us. In coming to understand the Trinity, we come to participate in the life of God and are absorbed into the mission of the trinitarian Persons (2 Cor. 5). Trinitarian doctrine teaches that both power and obedience are tools for creation and redemption, undertaken freely and lovingly. What is to become of us if we abandon the Trinity or create a women's religion that abandons men to their own visions of manliness?

One might respond that, if the practical influence of doctrine is seriously considered in light of the poor track record of male God-talk, we should feminize God-talk in hopes that it might attract at least heterosexual men, much as male language traditionally reached heterosexual women. Maybe instead of a male god for men and a goddess for women, we ought to try separate heterosexual models on the psychological judgment that heterosexual relationships are more likely to shape the majority of us. But this option falls into the same trap as does the same gender god theory. Both assume that biology rather than the life, death, and resurrection of Jesus Christ rescues us and then shapes and guides us once God has our attention. Since St. Paul, the Christian story has been understood to lift us beyond the bounds of gender, race, and class by binding those far off from God into the very life of God through baptism into the death of Christ. The point is to see that clinging to nationality, gender, and class, as if these were the primary realities that shape our destiny, capitulates to or elevates the finite and obscures the graciousness of God, who became flesh to lift us into a new realm of the divine life made known to us in and through his Son. Focusing on gender as if it determined our relationship with God perverts Christianity into a self-fulfillment support group. It obscures the point of the incarnation, cross, and resurrection — to call us from self-absorption to life with God revealed in Jesus Christ.

If God-talk comes to mirror our gender and sexual preferences we might move toward separate religions for heterosexual women, lesbians, heterosexual men, and gay men. This is already beginning to happen with the creation of a separate denomination for gays and lesbians, for example. The creation of denominations around biology rather than issues of faith, while perhaps understandable politically, is an affront to the gospel theologically speaking. The gospel calls believers to set issues of biology in the broader context of one's confession of Jesus as Lord. What is born out of justice issues may become a fashion. Now seminaries have separate worship services accommodating themselves to the various cultural and ethnic tastes and gender differences of the students. Are we creating new religions that celebrate ethnicity, language, culture, and sexuality instead of God's grace in Jesus Christ? Little could make the New Testament authors and the church fathers turn over in their graves faster than dividing up the church into linguistic, cultural, and biological fiefdoms. They would see such a new sectarianism as the defeat of Christ. For Christ came, not to reinforce our cultural comforts and social divisions, but to lead us away from celebrating ourselves to life with God, thereby bringing these divisions down.

Those whose imaginations are unable to reach beyond their own gender or pain, or whose sexuality is too overweening to permit them to raise their eyes from their sexual desires, are precisely those whom Christ came to liberate. Christian discipleship is not found in celebrating one's own gender, sexuality, ethnicity, class, language, or nationality, nor is it found in celebrating the gender, sexuality, ethnicity, class, language, and nationality of Jesus. It emerges from being pressed by Jesus to risk seeing these aspects of one's identity as penultimate and, when necessary, subordinated to the service of God.

True, the Christian case rests on God's revelation in a Jewish man who lived and taught in Palestine during the Roman occupation and was put to death in an act of political expediency. True, the Christian faith is not a set of moral principles or metaphysical postulates; it is a call to discipleship of Jesus, the one whom Christians confess reveals and carries us to life with God. Either to elevate Jesus' historical circumstances as ends in themselves or to dehistoricize the Christian story in the name of inclusivity by treating Jesus as a cipher and projection of our own historical circumstance obscures God's work in the incarnation. God has come to us in the concreteness of a single human life to show us that we are loved and reconciled to God in the concreteness of our own lives. Jesus was not Chinese or Indian, nor did he speak German or English; he was not a woman, nor was he a Christian.

At the same time, perhaps Christian discipleship arrests our attention because it is a morally cogent, indeed a demanding way of life. It leads one beyond the historical accidents of Jesus' life (and one's own), without leaving these behind for a wispy world of nice feelings and good intentions. Christian faith sees more at work in the life and death of Jesus of Nazareth than a timely renewal of the prophetic call of Elijah, Jonah, and Isaiah to a pure and faithful life. The Christian faith claims that in Jesus Christ God was revealed in a way unparalleled before or since; in becoming bound into the body of Christ through baptism into his death, one is marked as Christ's own forever. This new identity as a member of Christ's body places the components of one's earthly identity into a larger story of the very life of God, like strands of a vast tapestry. Each Christian's life is endowed with holiness and sacred responsibility by God's decisive action in Christ, which is repeated for each Christian in the action of the Holy Spirit in baptism. One's life is no longer one's own but belongs to God and the whole body of Christ. This does not guarantee that one will avoid hardships and suffering during one's life. But it does promise that one is not alone when these come.

The ability of each Christian to absorb this new identity depends upon the cogency of how this reconciliation took place. One must experience oneself as bound together with other Christians who are similarly lifted beyond their biological identities and taken up into the divine life. On this basis believers act in the world together as ambassadors for Christ. In other words, the Christian story must retain clarity and stability of presentation in order for the church to execute its calling. This does not mean that additional metaphors are inappropriate. They may well be advisable or even necessary for the well-being of the church. But serious changes in the presentation of the Christian faith must be undertaken prudently and judiciously and only after a long period of testing.

In conclusion, I have argued that the belief that the Trinity is deleterious may be historically understandable, but it is not necessarily accurate. Feminist recommendations that we either ban talk about the divine Persons or feminize God-talk have negative side effects for men that should give one pause. I have argued that the oppressive consequences of trinitarian language arise from an abuse of Father-Son language — indeed, from abuse of the Christian teaching on the Trinity altogether — rather than from the maleness of trinitarian language per se. And I have tried to suggest that hierarchical language, which is alien to moderns in a way that was simply never the case before in history, may not itself be deleterious if it is used to encourage submission to the will of God and responsible behavior by those entrusted with power and authority in various spheres of endeavor.

This essay has focused on the limited goal of defending the moral function of doctrine against critics who claim that it produces morally questionable attitudes and values about women. This apologetic work must be undertaken if the church is to respond seriously to critics' valid moral concerns. Whether this particular attempt to defend Christian language is adequate is another matter. The general point is to remind ourselves that serious moral concerns deserve serious consideration and response. Simply insisting on the tradition and repeating its language will not do. The criticisms of feminists and others are important. Let us reflect on these matters prayerfully and with gratitude to those who give voice to issues that have slept in the church for centuries.[7]

7. This essay is dedicated to Anna and Helen who have suffered at the hands of their violent father, to Suzanne who was sexually abused by her husband, and to the blessed memory of Anita who perished by the hand of her foster son.

Memory and Communion:
Ecumenical Theology and the
Search for a Generous Orthodoxy

DAVID S. YEAGO

I. The Plight of Ecumenism
and the Future of Orthodoxy

THE situation addressed by the Baltimore Declaration is by no means unique to the Episcopal Church; it is perhaps the central dilemma confronting the Western churches in our time. It is a situation in which the very idea of "orthodoxy," the very expression of a concern for the distinctively Christian identity of an ecclesial fellowship, is greeted with suspicion and hostility by an influential body of opinion within nearly every such fellowship. Such concern, it is assumed, must always mask a grab for power, a self-serving ploy to exclude inconvenient voices and unpalatable claims.

In such a climate of suspicion, tensions escalate: advocates of communal identity are tempted to become ever more narrow in their definitions of orthodoxy and ever more shrill in its defense. The outcome is the polarization of the public life of the churches between the partisans of what might be called "inclusivism" and "integralism." By "inclusivism" I mean the habit of mind for which sheer diversity is itself somehow redemptive, and the very suggestion that Christian identity and understanding have a distinctive shape and character of their own is already an act of tyranny; on the other hand, "integralism" refers to the disposition to regard Christianity as a timeless and immobile system of doctrinal propositions and institutions (whose immutability is required by such propositions) and to invest all of these propositions and institutions with equal sanctity and importance.

Ironically, one of the chief victims of this climate is the ecumenical

247

enterprise, an "inclusive" undertaking, one would have thought, if ever there was one. The rocky fortunes among Lutherans of the proposed Concordat of Agreement[1] between the Episcopal Church and the Evangelical Lutheran Church in America (ELCA) are, sadly, a clear case in point. Many Lutherans troubled by the theological disorientation of the ELCA, and therefore tempted to integralism, have seen in the Concordat only a typical move on the part of the elite, "New Class" enemies of Lutheran identity, yet another blow to the confessional heritage. The well-publicized escapades of certain revisionist Episcopal bishops have of course contributed to this suspicion.

At the same time, however, Lutherans on the other side of the fence have regarded with deep distrust the Concordat's proposal to incorporate Lutheran bishops into the historic episcopate. Anglican concern for historic continuity is seen as a threat to the redemptive inclusivity of the post-orthodox church: Bishop Browning, it is suspected, is only a stalking-horse for Cardinal Ratzinger. Despite the manifest facts of life in the Anglican Communion, the claim is often passionately if confusedly advanced among Lutherans that Episcopalians cannot *really* support both the historic episcopate and the ordination of women.

Thus ecumenism falls between two stools: it is too traditional for the inclusivists and too venturesome for the integralists. But just for this reason, I would like to suggest, ecumenical theology may be of crucial relevance to the contemporary impasse in the Western churches. The peculiar refractoriness of ecumenism in the present context, its resistance to neat classification along conventional lines of intra-church warfare, may be a hopeful sign that revisionist inclusivism and integralist conservatism do not exhaust the possibilities for reflection and action, that new departures and more promising ways of stating the issues are imaginable. It might indeed be the case that ecumenical theology has as much to contribute toward healing the fractures *within* Christian communities as it does toward reconciling them with one another.

---

1. Cf. William A. Norgren and William G. Rusch, *"Toward Full Communion" and "Concordat of Agreement": Lutheran-Episcopal Dialogue, Series III* (Augsburg: Forward Movement, 1991; cited as *LED III*). The Concordat calls for recognition by each church of the existing doctrine and ministries of the other and the gradual development of a unified ministry through the joint consecration of all bishops in either church by bishops of both churches. At the end of the process, the Episcopal Church and the ELCA would "share one ordained ministry in two churches that are in full communion, still autonomous in structure yet interdependent in doctrine, mission, and ministry" (*LED III*, p. 104).

To anticipate the claim I shall be making more directly, the ecumenical enterprise, by its deepest internal logic, calls for the transcendence of the unsatisfactory alternatives presently competing for the minds of our churches. As a search for genuine *unity,* a unity of heart, mind, and common life grounded in unity of faith, ecumenism is essentially incompatible with the sort of inclusivism that celebrates pluralism as somehow redemptive in itself. For such inclusivism has in reality given up the ecumenical dream of *communion,* the reconciliation in the one Christ of a human family disintegrated by sin and schism. It cannot be said too often that we have not been *reconciled* simply because we have been *included* under a pluralist umbrella.

On the other hand, however, ecumenical commitment is equally born of a dissatisfaction with, a refusal to accept as final, the unities and the identities we already possess in our condition of division, precisely because they must be, as such, insufficiently *Christian,* insufficiently *orthodox,* an inadequate reception of the fullness of Christ. The option of withdrawal into a rigidly structured theological shell, which understandably becomes attractive as familiar identities decompose, is likewise death to the ecumenical dream, for such integralism bestows a tragic finality on the truncated and malformed identities we have acquired through schism and separation.

Thus the ecumenical vision does indeed confront our churches with a "new challenge of orthodoxy" — with the challenge, that is, of orthodoxy newly conceived as an instrument of communion rather than division. That "orthodoxy" is necessary *for the sake of reconciliation and communion* is precisely what neither of the warring parties among us can imagine. The one side equates orthodoxy with divisiveness and concludes that we must therefore abandon orthodoxy, but in so doing it surrenders the hope of genuine reconciliation. The other side likewise assumes the divisiveness of orthodoxy, concluding that we must embrace division and exclusion for orthodoxy's sake, yet in the process it separates itself from the authentic Christian tradition and immures itself in sectarian peculiarity. The ecumenical enterprise challenges us to conceive orthodoxy anew, to develop a convincing account of what I will call a *generous* orthodoxy, an orthodoxy in the service of communion.[2]

2. The phrase "a generous orthodoxy" comes from my late Yale teacher, Hans Frei; cf. his "Response to 'Narrative Theology: An Evangelical Appraisal,'" *Trinity Journal* 8 (1987): 21, cited by George Hunsinger, "Hans Frei as Theologian: The Quest for a Generous Orthodoxy," *Modern Theology* 8 (1992): 103-28. Frei was an Episcopal priest, though (he never let you forget it) a *Reformed* theologian. I

In this essay, I can do little more than indicate one path of theological reflection toward such an orthodoxy of communion. I want to propose that the ecumenical conversation has generated promising new categories and ways of thinking related to just this issue; in a time when it has become almost fashionable to speak of ecumenical dialogue as a colossal failure, I will suggest, the real challenge is for the churches to take much more seriously the remarkable conceptual resources it has accumulated.

At the same time, I shall be making, more or less obliquely, a suggestion about the way in which the Baltimore Declaration might most helpfully be received and interpreted. Little will be gained if the Declaration is simply co-opted into the sterile theological standoff between inclusivism and integralism. That is why it is so important that the ongoing discussion of the Baltimore Declaration be accompanied by reflection on the mystery of the church and the proper *character* of her orthodoxy; everything depends on what such notions as "confessing the faith" and "taking a stand for the orthodoxy of the church" are taken to *mean*. I believe that one important strand of contemporary ecumenical theology offers a way of interpreting these notions that transcends the standard assumptions underlying our internal divisions.

In what follows, I have two sorts of conversation partners especially in mind. On the one hand, there are many people in the churches who are troubled by the corrosive effects of inclusivism but who are likewise congenitally suspicious of assertive, "confessional" pronouncements like the Baltimore Declaration. Anglicans in particular have a deeply rooted aversion to the sort of confessionalist polemics that have played such a destructive role in the post-Reformation Western churches, for reasons that I believe are at least in part quite well founded. I hope that this essay might suggest to them that there could be a way of taking seriously the Declaration's protest and affirmation without falling into the clutches of integralism. On the other hand, these same reflections might also be taken as a friendly admonition to the partisans of the Baltimore Declaration, among whom I count myself: nothing could be more futile than to run down the blind alley of integralism to escape the dead end of inclusivism. We must, I believe, persist as obstinately as we can in refusing those alternatives, and it is this persistence that I most hope to encourage in these reflections on memory, communion, and the search for a generous orthodoxy.

---

have no idea what he would have made of this essay, but I hope that it shows some trace of his spirit.

II. Imagining Christianity:
The Theology of Communion[3]

At the heart of much recent ecumenical convergence has been the notion of communion, *koinonia*. Indeed, there seems to be emerging in the ecumenical discussion something like a consensus that the notion of communion is the most fruitful and adequate starting point for theological reflection on the *being* of the church, on the church's *nature*.[4] Thus, for example, as the summary statement in the introduction to the Anglican–Roman Catholic International Commission (ARCIC) I *Final Report* puts it:

> Union with God in Jesus Christ through the Spirit is the heart of Christian *koinonia*. Among the various ways in which the term *koinonia* is used in different New Testament contexts, we concentrate on that which signifies a relation between persons resulting from their participation in one and the same reality (cf. 1 John 1:3). The Son of God has taken to himself our human nature, and he has sent upon us his Spirit, who makes us so truly members of the body of Christ that we too are able to call God "Abba, Father" (Rom. 8:15; Gal. 4:6). Moreover, sharing in the same Holy Spirit, whereby we become members of the same body of Christ and adopted children of the same Father, we are also bound to one another in a completely new relationship. *Koinonia* with one another is entailed by our *koinonia* with God in Christ. This is the mystery of the Church.[5]

Ecumenical commissions and their reports very properly limit the scope of their claims to what is essential in responding to a given situation, and, as noted, the immediate context in which the concept

---

3. I shall draw primarily on the work of the Anglican–Roman Catholic International Commission (ARCIC), both the ARCIC I *Final Report* (cited from Harding Meyer and Lukas Vischer, eds., *Growth in Agreement: Reports and Agreed Statements of Ecumenical Conversations on a World Level* [New York: Paulist Press, 1984], pp. 62-118; cited as *Final Report*), and the ARCIC II Agreed Statement "Church as Communion" (*One in Christ* 28 [1991]: 77-97). The latter document is a significant attempt to explicate the theological horizon within which the ARCIC process is operating. I shall also draw extensively on the work of Fr. J. M. R. Tillard, a Roman Catholic member of both ARCICs and a moving spirit in each.

4. Cf., e.g., J. M. R. Tillard's splendid essay "What Is the Church of God?" *One in Christ* 20 (1984): 226-42.

5. *Final Report*, p. 65. Cf. also the Faith and Order text adopted by the World Council of Churches (WCC) at Canberra, "The Unity of the Church as Koinonia: Gift and Calling," *One in Christ* 27 (1991): 376-78.

of communion has most often been elaborated is ecclesiology — especially, as in the *Final Report,* difficult issues of ministry and order. Nevertheless, it is difficult to avoid the impression that the way in which the concept is used has potentially much wider implications. Some of the documents indicate this at least obliquely, for example "Church as Communion":

> There are advantages in adopting the theme of communion in an exploration of the nature of the Church. Communion implies that the Church is a dynamic reality moving towards its fulfillment. Communion embraces both the visible gathering of God's people and its divine life-giving source. We are thus directed to the life of God, Father, Son, and Holy Spirit, the life God wills to share with all people. There is held before us the vision of God's reign over the whole of creation, and of the Church as the firstfruits of humankind which is drawn into that divine life through acceptance of the redemption given in Jesus Christ.[6]

Although this text announces that the communion theme will be employed in "an exploration of the nature of the Church," what follows goes beyond any narrowly ecclesiological focus to sketch a vision of the whole divine-human story, beginning with the inner life of the triune God and culminating in the eschatological kingdom. The notion of communion here begins to function as something more than a limited, topical proposal for untangling the problems of one controversial locus of doctrine. It is rather on the way to serving as the focal point for a construal of the logic of the Christian mystery as a whole, and as such, as a perspective on what might be called the *christianum,* the "Christian thing."

In his influential study *The Uses of Scripture in Recent Theology,* David Kelsey suggests that any theological position that intends to play a critical and constructive role in the life of the Christian community rests finally on "an imaginative construal of the mode of God's presence *pro nobis* ["for us"] that tries to catch up all its complexity and utter singularity in a single metaphorical judgement."[7] Such a construal then shapes decisions about the way in which theological issues are related to one another and the terms in which they are considered. The emerging ecumenical ecclesiology of communion seems to contain

6. "Church as Communion," p. 79.
7. David Kelsey, *The Uses of Scripture in Recent Theology* (Philadelphia: Fortress Press, 1975), p. 161.

within it just such an imaginative construal, a way of grasping the mode of God's saving presence with consequences for the ordering of questions and the terms in which they are discussed.

It is not, therefore, that the notion of communion could or should be taken as a first principle from which a theological system might be derived, a uniform ecumenical dogmatics or even a "universal catechism." Rather, as the ecumenical conversation unfolds, "communion" seems more and more to be functioning as a sort of organizing perspective, a way of grasping the complex totality of the *christianum,* the mystery of God's presence *pro nobis.*[8] The coherence of an ecclesiology of communion is open textured rather than reductive, a context for conversation and discovery rather than a systematic straightjacket. It serves less as an exclusive alternative to other ecclesiologies and more as a common language, a shared perspective, within which very different Christians can press their distinctive agendas and concerns without simply ceasing to communicate. Thus the function of the notion of communion is essentially *heuristic,* suggesting, for example, ways of understanding the plot of the biblical story[9] or the unity of the purposes of God.[10] It does not provide solutions to theological problems deductively, but rather indicates the way in which questions are to be framed and the lines along which answers might be sought.

In the perspective of communion, God's saving presence is construed as operative in the mode of *earthly-historical trinitarian communion,* in the *koinonia* of those whom the Spirit has gathered into oneness with Jesus Christ to the glory of God the Father. Such communion is both historical and eschatological, concretely social and divine mystery, the firstfruits in space and time of that reconciliation of human beings with one another and with God in bonds of mutual self-giving that is the goal of all God's ways.

The trinitarian shape of this construal is of its essence: it is the salvation of the *God of Israel,* inextricably bound up with the person of *Jesus of Nazareth* and his singular career, which the Christian *koinonia* experiences in the power of the *Holy Spirit.* That which the community

---

8. The preface to the *Final Report* (p. 63) refers to *koinonia* as the "governing concept of what follows here."

9. Cf. "Church as Communion," p. 80: "The relationship between God and his creation is the fundamental theme of Holy Scripture. The drama of human existence, as expounded in Scripture, consists in the formation, breakdown and renewal of this relationship."

10. Cf. "Church as Communion," p. 83: "God's purpose is to bring all people into communion with himself in a transformed creation."

shares *in common* can only be accounted for in terms of this "primary trinitarianism," which is logically (and historically) prior to the development of trinitarian doctrines and theologies. Paul's reference to "the grace of the Lord Jesus Christ, the love of God, and the *[koinonia]* of the Holy Spirit" (2 Cor. 13:13, NRSV) marks out precisely the irreducible contours of the shared reality that constitutes the church.

Equally essential is the interpenetration of earthly-historical common life and eschatological mystery in the being of the church. God's presence is neither a function of human sociality as such — as the depth dimension of our diverse cultures and communities — nor is it related to history in a sheerly dialectical or transcendental way.[11] Rather, God is eschatologically present "in, with, and under" (if a Lutheran may be permitted the phrase) the concrete practices of common life in a particular community that confesses Jesus Christ as Lord. The earthly-historical coming together and living together of the Christian *koinonia* is the *sacrament* of God's eschatological presence, a sign that participates in what it signifies.[12]

Such imaginative construals of the mode of God's presence for us are, as Kelsey points out, subject to assessment in a variety of ways: they must, for example, be (*a*) capable of consistent formulation and reasoned elaboration, (*b*) suggestive of real possibilities for the living out of Christian identity in the contemporary world, and (*c*) consonant with the fundamental structures of the historic Christian tradition.[13] The imaginative construal of the mode of God's presence implicit in the ecclesiology of communion can thus be regarded as a sort of hypothesis whose value and adequacy must be tested by the ongoing ecumenical conversation itself. At the very least, however, one can

11. The ecclesiology of communion seems to be compatible with a variety of accounts of the ways in which God may *also* be said to be present outside the church in human culture and society; it only stipulates that his eschatological presence *pro nobis* in the ecclesial *koinonia* is importantly different from these. But it does seem to be incompatible with views (e.g., Bultmann's) of God's eschatological presence as sheerly dialectical, without extension in space and time. Cf. my essay "Lutherans and the Historic Episcopate: The Theological Impasse and the Ecclesial Future," *Lutheran Forum* (Reformation, 1992) for a description of one such account.

12. On the notion of the church as sacrament, cf. Walter Kasper, "The Church as a Universal Sacrament of Salvation," *Theology and Church* (New York: Crossroad, 1989), pp. 111-28, and Gunther Gassmann, "The Church as Sacrament, Sign and Instrument: The Reception of this Ecclesiological Understanding in Ecumenical Debate," in *Kingdom, Church, World: The Church as Mystery and Prophetic Sign*, ed. Gennadios Lemouris (Geneva: WCC, 1986), pp. 1-17.

13. Cf. Kelsey, *The Uses of Scripture in Recent Theology*, pp. 170-75. Kelsey puts the last point differently.

already say that few theological proposals have emerged from a more wide-ranging conversation or have exposed themselves to questioning by a more diverse constituency.

Our present discussion may be viewed as part of that testing process. If the perspective of communion proves to be helpful in the quest for a generous orthodoxy — an orthodoxy in the service of reconciliation, transcending the destructive impasse between relativist inclusivism and repristinating confessionalism — that will itself be a strong point in its favor.

III. Communion and Memory

It should be clear that for the ecclesiology of communion, the *koinonia* of the church is not just any kind of human togetherness, self-justifying and self-sufficient, constituted merely in the fellow feeling and commitment of its members. As ARCIC II puts it, in the New Testament the noun *koinonia* "usually signifies a relationship based on participation in a shared reality (e.g. 1 Cor. 10:16)."[14] J. M. R. Tillard spells this out more fully:

> Obviously, this notion of *koinonia* implies that of unity. But it is not a question of any kind of unity. It is the unity resulting from the participation in the same unique good, like that of children born of the same couple, heirs of the same fortune, members of the same body. These are not simply joined one to the other like two pedestrians walking side by side or two persons in the same crowd. They are united because they are bearers of the same value, associated in the same reality. In this situation the reality they have in *common* accounts for the depth of their unity.[15]

Thus the *koinonia* of the church is the mutual participation of her members in a *koinon*, a shared good. And this shared good, as we have already seen, is irreducibly trinitarian in character: the saving gift of God the Father, inseparable from the person and story of his Son, Jesus Christ, made known to the church by the Holy Spirit. This constitutive *referentiality* of the church's communal existence, the impossibility of accounting for her being and unity without making reference to the

14. "Church as Communion," p. 81.
15. Tillard, "What Is the Church of God?" pp. 232-33. Cf. also his "Koinonia — Sacrament," *One in Christ* 22 (1986): 104-44, esp. 111-12.

concrete gift in which her members all share, and in sharing which they are reconciled to one another, is the starting point for a recon-ception of orthodoxy in the perspective of communion.

How this is so can be seen more clearly with the help of one further notion, itself complex, which is coming to play an important role in ecumenical reflection on *koinonia:* the concept of *memory* or *anamnesis*. This notion describes more concretely the church's neces-sary communal self-reference to the person and history of Jesus of Nazareth: the communion of the church is her participation in the salvation that he concretely embodies, and so she can only live in perpetual mindfulness and remembrance of him. But the concept of ecclesial memory cannot be reduced to categories of individual or social psychology;[16] rather, as constitutive of the church's communion, it shares in the *trinitarian structure* of that communion.

Thus the church's *anamnesis*, directed toward Jesus Christ, is always at the same time an appeal to the Spirit *(epiklesis)*, in whose power the community's remembrance of Christ is filled with reality, not a mere groping after one who is absent but a transforming encounter with one who is present.[17] Just so the church's *anamnesis* of Christ and *epiklesis* of the Spirit are inseparable from *thanksgiving* to the Father, from whose generosity we receive both Christ and the Spirit. This trinitarian complex of remembrance of Christ, appeal to the Spirit, and thanksgiving to the Father is not simply one aspect of the church's life; rather, it is the very act of the church's life, the act in which the church's being as *koinonia* is realized. The church is that community whose common life *is* a lively remembrance of Jesus Christ, in the power of the Spirit, to the glory of God the Father. And it is in this way that the communion of the church in history becomes a living sign of the eschatological reconciliation of the world with God.

Concretely, of course, this means that the church is the commu-

16. Such categories may of course be helpful in theological reflection on *anamnesis;* cf. Anthony Thiselton, "Knowledge, Myth, and Corporate Memory," in *Believing in the Church: The Corporate Nature of Faith* (Wilton, CT: Morehouse, 1982), pp. 45-78.

17. This sentence summarizes a great deal of twentieth-century biblical study of *anamnesis*. Cf. Alan Richardson, *An Introduction to the Theology of the New Testament* (London: SCM, 1958), pp. 366-71; Nils A. Dahl, "Anamnesis: Memory and Com-memoration in Early Christianity," in *Jesus in the Memory of the Early Church* (Mil-waukee: Augsburg, 1976), pp. 11-29; and Max Thurian, "The Eucharistic Memorial, Sacrifice of Praise and Supplication," in *Ecumenical Perspectives on Baptism, Eucharist, and Ministry* (Geneva: WCC, 1983), pp. 90-103.

nity that celebrates the eucharist.[18] The eucharist is by ecumenical consensus the corporate act in which "the community of God's people is fully manifested,"[19] and it is of crucial importance that the central identity-defining rite of the Christian community is precisely a rite of *remembrance,* an act in which the many are united in a common turning in the Spirit to *one in particular,* to the Palestinian Jew Jesus, through whose life and in whose person the salvation of the God of Israel is confessed to have been conclusively bestowed on humankind. With the eucharist at its heart, it is not too much to say that the whole common life of the Christian *koinonia* has an anamnetic texture: it is a life lived in constant mindfulness of *another,* of Jesus of Nazareth, crucified and risen. "And whatever you do, in word or deed, do everything in the name of the Lord Jesus, giving thanks to God the Father through him" (Col. 3:17).[20]

This verse from Colossians deserves closer attention, for it contains within itself the whole tension of the church's life in history. Its reference to "whatever you do, in word or deed" turns toward the indefinite variety of situations within which Christian communities and their members must speak and act, in the midst of the diversity of human cultures and the chances and changes of human history. Yet all this diversity, all this variety, is to be referred, in the life and practice of the church, to *one* name, the name of a particular person, a Jew of Nazareth crucified under Pontius Pilate.

The warrants for so improbable an undertaking are compressed into the one word *Lord:* this Jesus is the one in whom all fullness dwells, to whom every power in history is subject, in whom the community also participates in eschatological fullness (Col. 2:9-10). Precisely because Jesus is Lord, his community has confidence that every historical situation and every cultural location is an appropriate context for his remembrance, that every such situation and location can be addressed redemptively, in word and deed, in his name.

This distinctive Christian ascription of universal saving significance to one particular name generates a peculiar interplay of diversity and unity in the life of the church. Precisely because Jesus is Lord in every situation, the church must, as the Nairobi Assembly of the World Council of Churches put it, "affirm the necessity of confessing Christ as specifi-

18. Cf. the now classic account of the meaning of the eucharist in *Baptism, Eucharist, and Ministry* (Geneva: WCC, 1982), pp. 10-15.
19. *Baptism, Eucharist, and Ministry,* p. 14.
20. Subsequent biblical citations in this essay are from the New Revised Standard Version, unless otherwise noted.

cally as possible with regard to our own cultural settings."[21] Yet it is equally necessary to take care that it is indeed Jesus of Nazareth whom we are remembering and confessing, in his particularity and singular identity in which all fullness dwells, otherwise our engagement of history becomes merely the expression of our own "desires and interests."[22]

Thus it is necessary that "the word of Christ, in all its richness, find a home" (Col. 3:16, NJB) in the church's memory. This is the matter of the *apostolicity* of the church, which involves something more than theological correctness or legitimate ministerial succession. Apostolicity is rather the continuity of the church's common life with the *form of life* of the apostolic communities, the first to receive Christ and to confess him.[23] In the life of those churches, comprising "the apostles' teaching" but also *koinonia,* "the breaking of bread and the prayers" (Acts 2:42), the Spirit has, so to speak, uttered the basic, primary "word of Christ" through which alone we have access to him. If we want to remember Christ, *what* we remember must be concretely the "word of Christ" embodied in the life of the apostolic churches. "To keep alive the memory of Christ means to remain faithful to all that we know of him through the apostolic community."[24]

Holy Scripture is, of course, preeminent among the means by which this apostolic word of Christ is made available for the church's *anamnesis,* but in the perspective of communion Scripture is, as Nicholas Lash has suggested, as much a script for communal practice as a textbook of doctrines.[25] As the traditional hermeneutic of the church has always insisted, it witnesses to the life of the "whole Christ," to the communion of the head with the members of his body. Scripture's center of gravity is not so much doctrine to be transmitted from mind to mind as it is life in *koinonia* to be passed from community to community — a life at whose heart is the singular figure of the one

21. "Confessing Christ Today," Nairobi 1975, in *Apostolic Faith Today: A Handbook for Study,* ed. Hans-Georg Link (Geneva: WCC, 1985), p. 125.

22. "Confessing Christ Today," p. 131.

23. "The *paradosis* is not primarily transmission of a collection of truths, but *continuity* in the same life, of which the mother-cell is, in the Spirit, the community of Easter night (John 20:20) or of the upper room (Acts 1:13), welded by the memory of Jesus" (Tillard, "Ministry and Apostolic Tradition," *One in Christ* 27 [1991]: 17).

24. "Church as Communion," p. 86.

25. Cf. Nicholas Lash, "Performing the Scriptures," in *Theology on the Way to Emmaus* (London: SCM, 1986), pp. 37-46. See also Stephen E. Fowl and L. Gregory Jones, *Reading in Communion: Scripture and Ethics in Christian Life* (Grand Rapids: William B. Eerdmans, 1991).

Lord in whom all are reconciled. To change the metaphor, the Scriptures provide us with a verbal icon of *koinonia,* an intricately complex, densely imagined, richly suggestive representation of the communion of God with his people, received from the memory of Israel and the apostolic communities to nourish the memory of the church in every generation.

> This memory, realised and freshly expressed in every age and culture, constitutes the apostolic tradition of the Church. In recognizing the canon of Scripture as the normative record of the revelation of God, the Church sealed as authoritative its acceptance of the transmitted memory of the apostolic community. This is summarised and embodied in the creeds. The Holy Spirit makes this tradition a living reality which is perpetually celebrated and proclaimed by word and sacrament, pre-eminently in the eucharistic memorial of the once-for-all sacrifice of Christ, in which the Scriptures have always been read. Thus the apostolic tradition is fundamental to the Church's communion which spans time and space, linking the present to past and future generations of Christians.[26]

This citation brings us back to the link between memory and communion. The church's vocation to be the sacrament of universal reconciliation, her audacious prophecy that "all the richness of human diversity"[27] will in God's mercy become the occasion for love and mutual exchange rather than division and murder, depend utterly on her living memory of Jesus of Nazareth, in whose crucified and risen body there has been concretely realized the eschatological peace of God into which all may be gathered in one communion of life.

IV. Orthodoxy and Communion

From its very beginnings, Christianity has been an uncommonly *assertive* religion; the impetus toward such things as canon, creed, and standards of orthodoxy seems to have been present in it from the start, despite the indisputable diversity of the early Christian communities.[28]

---

26. "Church as Communion," pp. 87-88.
27. "Church as Communion," p. 88.
28. On this, see Rowan Williams's suggestive essay "Does It Make Sense to Speak of Pre-Nicene Orthodoxy?" in *The Making of Orthodoxy: Essays in Honour of Henry Chadwick,* ed. Rowan Williams (Cambridge: Cambridge University Press, 1989), pp. 1-23.

There is a widespread awareness today of the dangers inherent in this assertive, "confessional" dynamic, and we need not deny that "orthodoxy" has often enough in the history of the church been the occasion or pretext for destructive anger, neurotic narrow-mindedness, and the exercise of unjust domination in the community. But in the context we have just considered, the context of memory and communion, we may also see the *necessity* of "orthodoxy" within the logic of the *christianum*, as well as the *possibility* of imagining a generous orthodoxy, an orthodoxy of communion, in the church today.

As J. M. R. Tillard has written, "At the root of the need for 'confession' is buried the experience of a poverty."[29] And he goes on to speak eloquently of the basis for this interrelation of orthodoxy and poverty in the deep structures of biblical faith:

> Judaism and Christianity are, so to speak, haunted by an awareness of God's transcendence, that is, of his grandeur, which is so great that the human mind can never succeed in grasping its features, of even having an intuition of its nature. . . . The human mind has always had a veil of poverty cast over its eyes when it looks towards God. So, once God himself deigns in his goodness to lift up some corner of his mystery, all this "data" becomes a treasure to be kept and preserved not simply from forgetfulness, but from everything that would mean its contamination by the obscure forces of religion, of myth trying to make them fit its own measure. The creed is such a piece of gold preserved in the casket of Tradition. If it should be lost, if it should be weakened by speculations of religious traditions too much on "the human scale," it would be all the riches of what God himself has made known of himself that would disappear. And we would find ourselves groping our way once more towards the living God.[30]

The confessional impulse in Christianity, therefore, its apparently innate tendency to formulate ideals and standards of orthodoxy, is something more than a persistent neurosis; it originates rather in an awareness of poverty, a sense of the utter dependence of the Christian *koinonia* on its "living memory" of God's singular act of generosity in Jesus his Son. If that memory is lost or attenuated, the church loses more than mere abstract correctness; she loses her *peace*, she loses the bond of her communion, and so her life becomes only another of the

---

29. Tillard, "We Believe," *One In Christ* 27 (1991): 3.
30. Tillard, "We Believe," p. 3.

world's battlegrounds rather than the sacrament of the world's redemption. This deep connection between memory and communion, grounded in the knowledge of our poverty before God and one another, is what needs to be shouted from the housetops in the present disorientation of our churches.

Thus, for example, the book of Deuteronomy can be read as one long sermon on remembering and forgetting, according to which, to cite Tillard one more time, Israel's salvation depends on "a covenant of 'memories.'"[31] Israel's hope is in the mercy of the Lord God who "will not forget the covenant with your ancestors that he swore to them" (Deut. 4:31); indeed, her own history of unfaithfulness is an essential dimension of what she "remembers."[32] But for Israel to live in the covenant and enjoy the mercy, it is also necessary that she in turn "remember" the Lord through all generations:

> But take care and watch yourselves closely, so as neither to forget the things that your eyes have seen nor to let them slip from your mind all the days of your life; make them known to your children and your children's children. (4:9)

This is, moreover, much more than the retention of doctrinal propositions *about* the Lord God; what is to be remembered is the whole form of life founded on the Lord's self-commitment to Israel:

> Take care that you do not forget the LORD your God, by failing to keep his commandments, his ordinances, and his statutes, which I am commanding you today. (8:11)

Israel's whole life together as an elect family, therefore, her *communion*, is at stake in her remembering of the Lord and his commandments. Thus it is preeminently in the solemn communal *anamnesis* of the great festivals, such as Passover and the Feast of Weeks, that the communion of the whole people together in the Lord is manifested:

> Rejoice before the LORD your God — you and your sons and your daughters, your male and female slaves, the Levites resident in your towns, as well as the strangers, the orphans, and the widows who

---

31. Tillard, "Ministry and Apostolic Tradition," *One in Christ* 25 (1989): 15.

32. Just as the church's eucharistic remembrance of Jesus includes the memory of his betrayal from within the circle of his disciples. On this, see Rowan Williams, *Resurrection: Interpreting the Easter Gospel* (New York: Pilgrim Press, 1982), pp. 65-66.

are among you — at the place that the LORD your God will choose as a dwelling for his name. Remember that you were a slave in Egypt, and diligently observe these statutes. (16:11-12)

Moreover, the responsibility of the prosperous to "remember" the poor, the enslaved, the socially marginal widow, orphan, and resident alien, and to acknowledge very practical bonds of communion with them, is grounded in this communal remembering of the Lord: "Remember that you were a slave in Egypt and the LORD your God redeemed you from there; therefore I command you to do this" (24:18; cf. 24:22; 5:15; 15:15). Deuteronomy insists on the "orthodox" Yahwism of the *Shema* ("Hear, O Israel . . . ," 6:4-9) and the careful *paradosis* ("tradition") of the community's identifying narrative (6:20-25) because the children of Israel cannot *live* together in covenant unless they can *rejoice* together before the one Lord in remembrance of the mercies that have knit them together as a people.

Paul's admonition in 1 Corinthians 11:17-34 has precisely the same logic. The Corinthians have forgotten the crucified generosity of the founder of their feast: "When you come together, it is not really to eat the Lord's supper" (v. 20). And this has immediate consequences for their life together: they "show contempt for the church of God and humiliate those who have nothing" (v. 22). The ecclesial form of life that binds rich and poor together in *koinonia* begins to disintegrate. Therefore Paul must *remind* them of the one in *remembrance* of whom they are to gather, recalling them to the apostolic *paradosis:* "On the night when he was betrayed . . ." (v. 23).

Here again orthodoxy and communion are inseparable. The disorder in the Corinthian community is simultaneously "doctrinal" and "moral," a defection from apostolicity and a corruption of common life. Moreover, the two can only be remedied together. The damaged Corinthian *koinonia* can only be restored by their joint *anamnesis* of the *koinon*, the common good that can bind them together, the love of the Lord Jesus who gave his body and shed his blood for all. As this remembrance, made possible by the apostolic tradition, becomes a "living memory" in the power of the Spirit, the Corinthians will have to reckon with what it would mean for their communal eating and drinking to "proclaim" *this* death, the *Lord's* death, what it would mean for their *koinonia* to make present in the world a love that yields its life to establish covenant and communion.

Thus Paul's admonition to "discern the body" exhorts at one and the same time to a right ("apostolic") judgment about Christ, a right use of the eucharistic feast for his *anamnesis,* and a right apprehension of the church's common life as the sacramental embodiment of his love. As Lionel Thornton has written,

> to discern the Body is to perceive the glory of Christ's sacrifice. It is to recognize that his life which we receive is sacrificial, and that in receiving it we also become sacrificial. It is to recognize the joy of self-giving to others in the One body, even as Christ gave himself up for us and to us. To be partakers in Christ's sacrificial action in the Holy Eucharist is a joyful solemnity whose counterpart is equally joyful, namely, to be ourselves the organs of that sacrificial action towards the brethren in Christ. These two are, so to speak, the concave and the convex of the same figure, the inward and the outward aspects of the same sacrificial life.[33]

Adapting Thornton's language only a little, we can say that orthodoxy and communion, apostolic memory and newness of life, are the concave and the convex of the one reality of the church's *koinonia,* inseparably interrelated dimensions of her sacramental representation of God's reconciliation of all things in Christ. The quest for orthodoxy arises out of an awareness of our poverty in the face of that vocation: we who by ourselves are divided and divisive can only be knit together in *koinonia* by the lively remembrance of the *koinon,* the shared good of the crucified love of Jesus, in a common reception of the apostolic tradition.

V. Beyond Integralism: A Generous Orthodoxy

It is no accident, then, that when community is played off against orthodoxy in the name of "inclusivity," the life of the church is regularly reduced to a zero-sum game among rival interest groups whose only bond is their joint competition for influence and resources. And we may indeed suspect that much of what passes for "inclusivity" in the church today is in fact a sort of sentimental nihilism, at whose heart is a denial of the very possibility of reconciliation and communion among human beings. Our only alternatives, it seems to be assumed, are either the oppressive domination of some by others or else an uneasy coexistence in atomistic pluralism. Such an assumption, when it appears in

33. Thornton, *The Common Life in the Body of Christ* (London: Dacre, 1942), p. 343.

the church, is a denial of the *gospel,* for it assumes that even the apostolic memory of Jesus can only be one more instrument by which humans seek to dominate and oppress one another, rather than the instrument by which men and women are liberated to communion with God and among themselves.

But granted that the ecumenical theology of communion gives us good reasons to suspect the futility of "inclusivity" won at the expense of orthodoxy, does it also help us to escape the other horn of the contemporary dilemma, the temptation to withdraw into a sort of confessionalist integralism, drawing the circle of orthodoxy ever tighter, and in effect embracing orthodoxy at the expense of communion?[34] Here we may recall some wise words of the late Albert Outler, which in their own way summarize all that we have said so far:

> At bottom, heresy is contempt for the Christian community and its particular center of faith and life and its peculiar role in the transmission of the Gospel. . . . Thus, heresy disrupts the continuity of the Christian community and "breeds off the line." Its end-product is a *different kind of community,* with a different center of authority and a different bond of fellowship. Orthodoxy, in its best and proper sense, is care for the Christian community. It is the understanding of what brought the community into being, what holds it in being, what thrusts it forward through history.[35]

This points us in the right direction: orthodoxy construed in the perspective of communion will avoid the temptation of integralism precisely because of its *integral* care for the life of the Christian *koinonia.* Its passion will be directed, not to doctrinal "correctness" viewed as an absolute, abstracted from all context, but to those things that make the communion of the church possible and sustain its health: its "source of authority" and its "bond of fellowship," the apostolic tradition and the communal *anamnesis* of Christ. Its focus, that is to say, will be the complex, irreducible *totality* of the church's sacramental anticipation of eschatological reconciliation, within which the point even of apostolic teaching can be grasped only in its function of forming a common life.

Such an orthodoxy would be quite different from the confessional sectarianism dominant in the Western churches since the Reformation,

34. One thinks here of the sad paradox of dissident Anglican groups forming separatist sects in the name of catholicity.

35. Outler, *The Christian Tradition and the Unity We Seek* (New York: Oxford University Press, 1957), p. 79.

whose disastrous effects account for much present-day disaffection with the very idea of orthodoxy. This is not simply a difference in tone, as though an orthodoxy of communion were only a more temperate version of integralism; rather, it is a difference in principle, for confessional sectarianism and the orthodoxy of communion proceed from two very different construals of the nature of God's eschatological presence *pro nobis*.

Understandings of orthodoxy since the sixteenth-century schism have regularly assumed that the teaching and learning of theological propositions is the *prius* of Christian community, the locus of divine presence in which the church originates. The immediate effect of the death and resurrection of Jesus is thus the appearance in the world of a *doctrine,* a teaching, and it is through the acceptance of this doctrine that men and women are brought into the eschatological presence of God and so into theologically authentic community with one another.

In such a version of orthodoxy, doctrinal correctness is indeed disengaged from communal context, because it is seen as the presupposition of any authentic Christian community. It is easy to see why such orthodoxies have tended both to define the necessary doctrinal uniformity as maximally as possible and to breed internecine sectarian conflict. If the teaching and learning of true theological propositions is the locus of divine presence on which the being of the community is founded, then theological diversity within the community is a crack in its foundations, calling into question the integrity of the common life, the very *right* of its members to live together in communion. And when members of the community are perceived to affirm deviant doctrines, they are just thereby placed outside the bonds of *koinonia,* outside the divine presence that establishes communion. If it is acceptance of theological propositions that binds the community together, then those with whom we differ theologically are simply people with whom we have nothing important in common.

As the theology of communion construes the mode of God's eschatological presence, however, lived community is the *prius* of doctrine and theology, and not vice versa.

Before the Church performs acts of teaching, she exists and lives. Her existence and her life are the work of the triune God who calls her into being and sustains her as his people, the Body of Christ, the fellowship of the faithful in the Spirit. The authority of the

Church has its ground in this *datum* of her being. The whole Church teaches by what she is, when she is living according to the Gospel.[36]

To enter the eschatological presence of God, on this construal, is to be initiated into a particular community's life of worship and witness and mutual care, to share in its distinctive practices and patterns of social interaction. The proximate result of the salvation event in Christ is thus not the emergence of a *doctrine*, around which there then forms a community; rather, it is the formation of a new *community*, which subsequently formulates doctrines and elaborates theologies as an important and necessary way of accounting for and safeguarding its own distinctive mission and life.

That life is distinctive, to borrow Outler's terms, by virtue of its distinctive "center of authority," the apostolic *paradosis*, and its distinctive "bond of fellowship," the corporate *anamnesis* of Jesus Christ. But this reference to *paradosis* and *anamnesis* is not a way of sneaking in doctrinal integralism again by the back door. The apostolic tradition is more and other than a system of doctrine; it is a concrete tradition of corporate *life*, centered in the eucharistic feast, transmitted through a network of specific communal practice. Even Holy Scripture transmits the apostolic tradition, not as a bare text, but in its entanglement in a complex web of communal *uses* of Scripture, in worship, preaching, prayer, and catechesis. It makes equal sense to say that the central instrument of the apostolic tradition is the Bible in its manifold liturgical employment or to say that it is the liturgy in its perpetual actualization of the Scriptures; these are not alternatives but symbiotic aspects of the single complex *paradosis* of the apostolic memory of Christ in the church.[37]

If this is so, then the apostolic tradition can never be exhaustively captured in theological paraphrase; its complex biblical-liturgical concreteness has a kind of communicative *density* that cannot be replaced by any system of sentences. Text and rite together nourish the church's memory of Jesus in "ways that are inseparable from their sheer givenness and quality as things in our shared world."[38] This does not mean

---

36. "Towards Common Ways of Teaching and Decision-making," Faith and Order Committee Report, in *Sharing in One Hope: Documents and Reports from the Meeting of the Faith and Order Commission, Bangalore 1978* (Geneva: WCC, 1978), p. 258. Cf. Outler, *The Christian Tradition*, chap. 3.

37. On Scripture and liturgy, cf. Alexander Schmemann, *The Eucharist* (Crestwood: St. Vladimir's, 1988), pp. 65-80.

38. The passage reads in full: "every communication occurs as a use of *objects:*

that we can live *without* communal reflection, teaching, and argument; the struggle for the truthful articulation of the deep logic of the apostolic tradition, in a faithful confession of Jesus Christ as the one who is universal Lord precisely in his singularity, is itself an indispensable practice of the church's life. Yet the apostolic memory of Christ by which our reflection, teaching, and argument must be informed is most centrally communicated in the more-than-propositional particularities of the tradition:[39] the unfolding of the canonical narrative, the shape of the rites, the concrete textures of biblical discourse, the nonconceptual specificity of proper names.[40] Of such a tradition one can say that its adequate commentary must *finally* be found in the "givenness and quality" of human lives formed by immersion in it; the core theology of the church is thus the "connatural" knowledge of the saints, and the true theologian, as the church fathers teach us, is the person who knows how to pray.[41]

Thus an orthodoxy of communion has good reasons not only to tolerate theological diversity but to insist on its necessity, for no single theological exposition can capture the dense plenitude of significance with which the apostolic tradition testifies to Jesus Christ, nor can any

---

we make or find sounds, statues, marks, gestures, or whatever, and set them between us, thereby to share a world. These may be objects used to make sentences; but they also function in our communicating in more-than-verbal ways, ways that are inseparable from their sheer givenness and quality as things in our shared world" (Robert W. Jenson, *Visible Words: The Interpretation and Practice of Christian Sacraments* [Philadelphia: Fortress Press, 1978], p. 10; cf. also pp. 12-17).

39. I am suggesting in effect that communion in the apostolic tradition is to the practices of reflection, teaching, and argument as character is to moral choice in a virtue-ethic. We must make choices, but the substance of the moral life is nonetheless not located in choice making, for it depends on character whether we will even notice that our situation calls for choice. Likewise, there must be reflection, teaching, and argument in the church, but the substance of ecclesial life is not located in those activities. Our capacity to reflect, teach, and argue relevantly and truthfully depends on our formation by the "more-than-propositional particularities of the tradition" in the *koinonia* of the church. Doctrinal confusion in the church is a sign of inadequate *formation in communion* and must be addressed at that level; doctrinal argument without a common formation in the apostolic tradition inevitably becomes a mere battle of words.

40. For the relevance of this point to the controversy over the trinitarian name, see Robert W. Jenson, " 'The Father, He . . . ,' " in *Speaking the Christian God: The Holy Trinity and the Challenge of Feminism*, ed. Alvin J. Kimel, Jr. (Grand Rapids: William B. Eerdmans, 1992), pp. 95-109.

41. On the "theology of the saints" see Hans Urs von Balthasar, "Theology and Sanctity," in *Explorations in Theology I: The Word Made Flesh* (San Francisco: Ignatius, 1989), pp. 181-209.

one exposition anticipate the discoveries the church will make as she renews her articulate celebration of his lordship in new cultural settings and new historical situations. Moreover, within the perspective of communion, a wide range of reactions is also possible toward what is rightly perceived as error; even serious theological mistakes need not destroy continuity with the apostolic *paradosis,* or disrupt the sharing of life in remembrance of Jesus.[42]

One might, with Vatican II, account for this generosity of the orthodoxy of communion toward diversity and even error in terms of a "hierarchy of truths," according to which certain doctrines become more urgent as they approach more closely "the foundation of the Christian faith."[43] Or one might, with George Lindbeck, speak of doctrines in the strictest sense as communal rules of discourse that regulate not so much what theological propositions are affirmed as the categorical scheme within which they are formulated; on these terms, it would be possible for irreducibly diverse theologies, even erroneous ones, to be framed within the church's "apostolic" universe of discourse in such a way that they neither forbid her common *anamnesis* of Jesus nor fracture her continuity with the apostolic tradition.[44]

This can be explained in different ways within the horizon of communion.[45] What is important for our purposes is that the "generosity" of an orthodoxy of communion is not incidental, for on this construal, God's eschatological presence is located *in* the dense anamnetic texture of the church's concrete *koinonia,* a common life that theology cannot fully comprehend and that error need not automatically dissolve. Thus, in contrast to sectarian integralism, an orthodoxy of communion will be "generous," not as a compromise, but *for or-*

---

42. Since the issue is the character of the common life, judgments of the consequences of error must always be contextual: what are the implications of *this* error (or inadequacy or one-sidedness), which is being put forth in *this* way in *this* situation? Thus, for example, we know that the early church survived a good deal of subordinationism; one could argue that it was only when Arius and his followers developed subordinationism in specific ways, so that particular questions became inescapable, especially in worship, that subordinationism became impossible to contain within the *koinonia.*

43. "Decree on Ecumenism," chap. 2, par. 11, in *Vatican Council II: The Conciliar and Post Conciliar Documents,* ed. Austin Flannery, revised edition (Northport: Costello, 1988), p. 462.

44. Cf. George A. Lindbeck, *The Nature of Doctrine: Religion and Theology in a Postliberal Age* (Philadelphia: Westminster Press, 1984).

45. My own judgment is that Lindbeck's proposals have a conceptual subtlety and adequacy that are lacking in the "hierarchy of truths" approach, but I need not press the point here.

thodoxy's sake, out of respect for the unparaphrasable concreteness of the apostolic tradition.

It should be clear also where an orthodoxy of communion will locate the *limits* of diversity. Those limits will have to be specified, not by an immediately propositional criterion ("You must say X and Y"), but rather in terms of the practice of common life. What Michael Root has written of consensus between divided churches we may apply to communion within each church and the whole church:

> The visible communion that is sought between the churches is not an exclusively or even primarily intellectual or even conceptual unity. It is oneness in the body of Christ, in the reality of a life lived in the Spirit. This life has forms, activities, in which its identity is realized: prayer, proclamation, sacraments, discipline, reflection. It is unity in this life that is decisive for the unity of the church. . . . Our doctrinal agreement is sufficient when we can live this life together without violating our convictions on the essential identity of that life.[46]

In the perspective of communion, we can say that the limits of diversity are reached when we can no longer live together in a lively common remembrance of Jesus Christ, in continuity with the apostolic tradition. It is when the "source of authority" for the community threatens to become located elsewhere than in the apostolic *paradosis* or when its "bond of fellowship" threatens to become something other than the *anamnesis* of Jesus of Nazareth that the *koinonia* of the church is in danger, for that is the point at which it is ceasing to be Christian *koinonia* at all, but is becoming, in Outler's words, "a different kind of community" altogether.

This can, of course, happen in more than one way.[47] A community may become alienated in various ways from the apostolic tradition, so that the figure of Jesus Christ becomes distorted or even unrecognizable in its memory; this is what was perceived to be at stake in the trinitarian and christological controversies of the ancient church, as well as in the Reformers' complaint that the Christ of Western Christen-

46. Root, "Identity and Difference: The Ecumenical Problem," in *Theology and Dialogue: Essays in Conversation with George Lindbeck,* ed. Bruce D. Marshall (Notre Dame: University of Notre Dame Press, 1990), p. 183.

47. In this essay, I have ignored divisive issues of ministry and order that arise in connection with the notion of continuity with the apostolic tradition, since our present concern is with intra-church problems; here I can do no more than register awareness of their existence. For a careful Roman Catholic statement of the problem, cf. Tillard, "Ministry and Apostolic Tradition."

dom had become a "new Moses" rather than a Savior. Or a community may grow forgetful of its vocation of reconciliation, so that its common life loses its distinctiveness and becomes a mere extension of the surrounding culture; it comes to be held together by secular interests and passions, following the world's patterns of exclusion or inclusion, rather than by the corporate *anamnesis* of Jesus Christ. It may be that this was the perception that alarmed both the evangelical and the Oxford movements in the Church of England. There is no neutral testing mechanism that can gauge the orthodoxy of our churches and tell us when their *koinonia* is truly endangered; one can only attempt to test the spirits, practice careful discernment, and exercise that "care for the Christian community" which is at once the heart of true orthodoxy and the baptismal vocation of the whole people of God.

In any event, genuine disintegration of orthodoxy always announces itself concretely in the common life. Christians begin to find it difficult to pray together and to bear witness together to the one Lord before the world; they fragment into parties that can scarcely comprehend one another's deep concerns or talk to one another in a common language. As common engagement of the concrete apostolic tradition ceases to inform their reflection, teaching, and argument, these become idiosyncratic and antagonistic. The community as a whole may become more "exclusive" or more "inclusive," but it ceases to be a communion in which men and women are reconciled to the triune God and so to one another. Thus renewal must be sought precisely on the way of reconciliation; the restoration of *orthodoxy* can only be a restoration of *communion*, a mutual recovery of the apostolic memory of Jesus Christ, with prayer for the Spirit, to the glory of God the Father. A struggle for orthodoxy in the perspective of communion will be governed throughout by the *ut omnes unum sint* ("that they may all be one," John 17:21) of the Johannine Jesus.

The Baltimore Declaration is well constructed to serve as an instrument for such an orthodoxy of communion.[48] I refer especially

---

48. I must, however, register some dissatisfaction with the *wording* (though not, I think, the *intention*) of article 5 of the Declaration, especially the paragraph of "repudiation." It is, I believe, unhelpful to pose the question of the church's relation to Israel in terms of the possession of salvation rather than in terms of the universal lordship of Jesus. Moreover, it would have been well to have acknowledged that there could be theological and moral grounds for serious reservations about "missions to the Jews" as we have known them in the last century or so, quite apart from relativistic views of the saving significance of Jesus.

to its focus on the church's common life, her identity and mission to the world, which bespeaks an implicit understanding of orthodoxy as "care for the Christian community." One notices, for example, how the first article, instructed by St. Basil, carefully indicates the diverse and irreducible ways in which the trinitarian name is woven into the central, distinctive *practices* of the church's life, beginning with baptism. In general, moreover, its focus on the trinitarian and christological faith of the Niceno-Constantinopolitan Creed aligns it with a growing ecumenical consensus that discerns in that creed the authentic "summing up" *(symbolon)* of the whole church's aspiration to orthodoxy.[49]

Thus the question that the Baltimore Declaration puts to the Episcopal Church (and by implication to others) is neither sectarian nor narrow; it is simply the question of *what kind of community* the Episcopal Church, in all its welcome diversity, desires to be. Will it continue to be a community reconciled in a lively trinitarian *anamnesis* of Jesus Christ, or will the disintegration of its communion continue until it reaches that state of institutionalized internal schism toward which American denominations generally seem to be headed?[50] Read thus, the Declaration is not calling the Episcopal Church to integralist uniformity but rather to a renewing engagement with the biblical-liturgical substance of the apostolic tradition, through which the Spirit gathers the scattered children of God into a reconciled communion in Christ.

But a proposal of reform is always only the beginning of an arduous process of reception, the outcome of which will depend largely on the terms in which the proposal is related to the life and identity of the church. It is profoundly important, not only for Episcopalians, that the Baltimore Declaration be received in the Episcopal Church with as much clarity and as few distractions as possible. That can only happen if its reception is accompanied by serious reflection on the mystery of the church and the character of her orthodoxy, a task to which this essay is no more than an invitation.

49. Those who would dismiss the Baltimore Declaration as reactionary and "exclusive" must take into account its surprising congruity with the Faith and Order Study Program, "Towards the Common Expression of the Apostolic Faith Today," certainly the most wide-ranging and "inclusive" consultation on the essentials of the faith in modern times. Cf. the documents assembled in Link, *Apostolic Faith Today*, as well as the final document, *Confessing the One Faith: An Ecumenical Explication of the Apostolic Faith* (Geneva: WCC, 1990).

50. It should be noted that prominent Lutherans express similar concerns about the ELCA. For a vigorous summary of these concerns, see Carl E. Braaten, "The Gospel or What?" *Lutheran Forum* (Reformation, 1992).

A Confessing Faith:
The Baltimore Declaration

ALVIN F. KIMEL, JR.

WHATEVER else it may be, the Baltimore Declaration is an anomaly. Not only does it originate from within a denomination of mainline liberal Protestantism — that constellation of religious communities which, until recently, has been the bearer of American civil religion and piety — but it specifically originates from within an ecclesial tradition that self-consciously identifies itself as being nonconfessional. Presbyterians and Lutherans might issue confessions of doctrinal belief, but such confessions are virtually unknown within the Episcopal Church and worldwide Anglicanism. Yet the times are anomalous, and strange things are happening.

In May of 1991 I and five other Episcopal priests in the Diocese of Maryland decided that it was time to break clearly and decisively with the prevailing ideology of American liberal Protestantism. This ideology is known by a variety of names, but perhaps the most common one today is "inclusivity." The church is envisioned as a community that welcomes absolutely everyone, without distinction, demanding nothing of anyone except that they too embody this same spirit of openness. "There will be no outcasts!" is the clarion call within my own denomination.

In the following statement, the Reverend Alvin Kimel, a co-author of the Baltimore Declaration, describes the circumstances and intentions of the original authors. Readers of the present volume have doubtless observed ways in which the contributors evaluate the Declaration's specifics differently. Likewise the contributors may or may not agree with the opinions that follow. — EDS.

After a particularly discouraging diocesan convention earlier that month, my colleagues and I became convinced that the prevailing ideology of inclusivity is encouraging — indeed, demanding — a virtually infinite tolerance within the church of all sorts of heretical teachings and pagan spiritualities. Beliefs and practices that in an earlier generation would have been quickly dismissed as hostile to the gospel and contrary to evangelical faith are increasingly advocated by clergy and laity alike. Orthodoxy is rapidly becoming simply one option among many. It was time, we decided, for explicit and unequivocal confession of the gospel of Jesus Christ, time to call the church to repentance and conversion.

We took as our model the Barmen Declaration of 1934, issued by the Confessing Church in response to the liberal syncretism of the German Christians. Its threefold structure of Scripture, affirmation, and repudiation provided us with a suitable framework for a clear, unambiguous, and provocative statement of the catholic faith in rejoinder to contemporary false teachings.

It is perhaps not insignificant that the authors of the Baltimore Declaration are parish pastors rather than seminary theologians. Academic theology is no longer sure of its purpose nor of its subject matter. Divorced from the life and witness of the worshiping community and fatally invested in the concerns, projects, and politics of institutional academia, professional Ph.D. theologians are particularly vulnerable to the latest ideological and intellectual movements. Within the current culture of seminary and university, the temptation to subject the gospel to the canons of rational and political correctness is perhaps irresistible. Thus we in the church find ourselves in an odd and intolerable situation — a situation in which it is our theologians who are themselves the primary engineers of disbelief and apostasy within the church.

Christian theology, properly understood, exists only to serve the proclamation of the gospel. It has no existence independent of that community which celebrates the faith of Jesus Christ in Word and Sacrament. It is therefore the parish pastor who is most directly concerned with the integrity of preaching and teaching, for it is the parish pastor who is most directly involved in the formation of authentically *Christian* community. The church cannot be church apart from a clear grasp of the faith that defines who we are as church. It is this burning pastoral concern for the identity of the church — and thus for the spiritual life and well-being of the people we serve — that generated the Baltimore Declaration.

It is ironic but encouraging that a group of academicians should

choose to write a volume of essays responding to a confessional statement of an obscure group of parochial theologians. Hopefully this is
a sign of a dialogue, collaboration, and mutual accountability that will
now begin in earnest. The mission of the gospel in American society
requires the union of seminary and pastorate, theology and worship,
intellectual rigor and evangelical conversion.

What is our hope for the Baltimore Declaration? It is very hard
to say. We wrote it not because of expectations of effecting change
within the institution but because we felt we had to make a stand for
the sake of the ministry to which we were called. Personally, my hope
is that it will stimulate a confessional movement both within my own
denomination and throughout all of mainline American Protestantism
for the clear and vital proclamation of the gospel. Reform will only
occur if the laity and clergy stand up and announce that apostolic faith
given to us in our baptism and insist that teachings manifestly contrary
to this faith have no place within the community of the church.

Needless to say, such a posture immediately places one in a
position of conflict with the church establishment and the supporters
of the "inclusive" status quo. Numerous individuals have commented,
"I agree with your affirmations; it's the repudiations that trouble me."
These comments have confirmed our belief in the necessity of the
repudiations: it is the repudiations that give clarity and punch to the
affirmations.

The example of the Council of Nicaea (A.D. 325) is helpful here.
The large majority of gathered bishops knew that Arius's teaching of
the creaturehood of Jesus was unacceptable. The challenge was how
to formulate this conviction in a way that excluded the heresy. This
was not as easy as it might first appear: the Arians surprised everyone
by assenting to the Council's early attempts at credal definition; they
found refuge in the ambiguity of the language. Only when the bishops
declared that Jesus was "begotten not made, of one being with the
Father" did the supporters of Arius balk.

The lesson is this: *when Christians state what we believe, it is also
necessary to state what we disbelieve.* It is precisely this clarity that drives
away the fog of ambiguity and confronts us with the decision of truth.
On Mount Carmel Elijah had to make clear to Israel that she could
not evade the choice between Yahweh and Baal. The God of the
Scriptures is a jealous God and does not tolerate equivocacy of faith
or the worship of false gods. We are called to decision, to conversion
and discipleship, to confession of belief.

But is not such a confession of faith divisive and destructive of the church's unity? Perhaps the only proper answer to this serious question is, Yes, we hope so. Nothing is more injurious to the church's spiritual life and evangelical ministry, as well as just personally stifling, than this demand to be inclusive of heretical teachings. As Stanley Hauerwas once commented, "The church is being destroyed by tolerance." Such inclusivity is a coercive suppression of theological conviction and renders the church impotent to protect itself against beliefs and practices hostile to its fellowship and mission. Unity in the faith of Jesus Christ by the Holy Spirit must not be understood in terms of mutual acceptance. A unity that must ignore the claims of truth and catholic doctrine reduces itself to the level of institution, settling for the absence of conflict and division as a sufficient substitute. True Christian unity is personal and dynamic, grounded in the personal unity of the Father and the Son in the communion of the Holy Spirit.

The political intent of the inclusivity dogma must also be noted. Today the call to inclusivity functions as a powerful tool for the maintenance of the institutional and bureaucratic status quo. Serious challenges to the wielders of power are routinely dismissed as being exclusive, absolutist, and uncharitable. Orthodox believers are thus pushed to the periphery of their respective denominations. It is not surprising, therefore, that virtually all of the liberal Protestant bureaucracies have embraced the new "gospel."

The reform of the church requires a profound repentance. We must repent of our tolerance and return to the catholic faith of the one and true God: Father, Son, and Holy Spirit. It is this faith, and only this faith, that is the one true hope for a lost and unbelieving world. Only thus will we discover our true unity in Christ. The authors of the Baltimore Declaration are not Elijahs. We are just parish priests. But we believe that the Holy Spirit has moved us to present this confession of faith, with all of its flaws, before the church.

The Baltimore Declaration

Throughout the history of the Christian Church, there have been times when the integrity and substance of the Gospel have come under powerful cultural, philosophical, and religious attack. At such times, it has been necessary for Christian believers, and especially for pastors and preachers, to confess clearly, unequivocally, and publicly "the faith which was once for all delivered to the saints" (Jude 3), and to define this faith over against the heresies and theological errors infiltrating the Church. Thus the Church is led into a deeper comprehension of the Gospel of Jesus Christ and the communal identity of the Church is strengthened in its mission to the world.

We, the undersigned, who are baptized members of the Episcopal Church of the United States, believe that such a time has now come upon the Church which we serve. We are now witnessing a thorough-going revision of the faith inconsistent with the evangelical, apostolic and catholic witness, a revision increasingly embraced by ecclesiastical leaders, both ordained and lay. In the name of inclusivity and plural-ism, we are presented with a new theological paradigm which rejects, explicitly or implicitly, the doctrinal norms of the historic creeds and ecumenical councils, and which seeks to relativize, if not abolish, the formative and evangelical authority of the Holy Scriptures. This par-adigm introduces into the Church a new story, a new language, a new grammar. The "revelations" of modernity, infinitely self-generating and never-ending, supplant and critique that historic revelation which God the Holy Trinity has communicated by word and deed in the life, death, and resurrection of Jesus the Israelite.

Fully aware of our own sinfulness, as well as the spiritual dangers inherent in issuing such a call, we humbly and prayerfully summon the Church to return to and remain steadfast in that Gospel entrusted to it by the Apostles of Jesus Christ. We also summon the clergy of the Church to stand up boldly and declare that Trinitarian faith which they have sworn at their ordinations to uphold and preach. We are well aware of the possible personal and professional costs of such a confession in the present situation; but we are convinced that the integrity and substance of the Gospel, that Gospel which is the only hope and salvation of the world, are at stake. The Lord is calling us to fidelity to him — and to him alone.

We offer, therefore, the following Declaration of Faith. This is not a comprehensive confession. It addresses those critical theological issues which we believe to be at the heart of the present crisis.

I

"All authority in heaven and on earth has been given to me. Go therefore and make disciples of all nations, baptizing them in the name of the Father and of the Son and of the Holy Spirit, and teaching them to obey everything that I have commanded you." (Matt. 28:18-20)

By the command and mandate of her risen Lord, the Church of Jesus Christ is commissioned to baptize disciples into the revealed name of God: Father, Son, and Holy Spirit. This proper name faithfully identifies the Savior and Lord of the Holy Scriptures. While human linguistic formulae cannot exhaust the mystery of the ineffable Deity, the threefold appellation — given to us in the resurrection of Jesus — truly names and designates the three Persons of the Holy Trinity as disclosed in the biblical narrative, and summarizes the apostolic experience of God in Christ. To reject, disregard, or marginalize the Trinitarian naming is to cut ourselves off from that story which shapes and defines the identity of the Church; ultimately, it is to cut ourselves off from the God of Israel himself. The confession of the triune name is required in the celebration of Christian baptism, and it properly structures the liturgy and prayer of the Christian community: We rightly pray to the Father, through the Son, in the Holy Spirit. As St. Basil the Great declared: "For we are bound to be baptized in the terms we have received and to profess belief in the terms in which we are baptized, and as we have professed belief in, so to give glory to Father, Son, and Holy Spirit."

We repudiate the false teaching that God has not definitively and uniquely named himself in Jesus Christ, that we are free to ignore or suppress the revealed name of Father, Son, and Holy Spirit and worship the Deity with names and images created by our fallen imaginations or supplied by secular culture, unreformed by the Gospel and the biblical revelation.

II

"In the beginning when God created the heavens and the earth, the earth was a formless void and darkness covered the face of the deep, while a wind from God swept over the face of the waters. Then God said . . ." (Gen. 1:1-3)

"Long ago you laid the foundation of the earth, and the heavens are the work of your hands. They will perish, but you endure; they will all wear out like a garment. You change them like clothing, and they pass away; but you are the same, and your years have no end." (Ps. 102:25-27)

The triune God is the holy creator who freely speaks the universe into contingent existence out of nothing *(creatio ex nihilo)*. He is the sovereign Lord, utterly transcending his creation, yet actively immanent within it, guiding and directing it to its eschatological fulfillment in the Kingdom. As creator, God is free to act within his universe, both providentially and miraculously, to accomplish his purposes and ends.

We repudiate the false teaching of monism, which indissolubly unites deity and cosmos into an interdependent whole, the world being construed as God's body, born of the substance of deity, and thus divine. On the other hand, we repudiate the false teaching of deism, which distances the creator from active involvement in the preservation, redemption, and consummation of his creation.

III

"In the beginning was the Word, and the Word was with God, and the Word was God. He was in the beginning with God. All things came into being through him, and without him not one thing came into being. What has come into being in him was life, and the life was the light of all people. . . . And the Word became flesh and lived among us, and we have seen his glory, the glory of the Father's only Son, full of grace and truth. . . . From his fullness we have all received, grace upon grace. The law indeed was given through Moses; grace and truth came through Jesus Christ. No one has ever seen God. It is God the only Son, who is close to the Father's heart, who has made him known." (John 1:1-4, 14, 16-18)

"All things have been handed over to me by my Father; and no one knows the Son except the Father, and no one knows the Father except the Son and anyone to whom the Son chooses to reveal him." (Matt. 11:27)

Jesus of Nazareth is God. He is the Word made flesh, the incarnation and embodiment of the divine Son, truly God and truly human, "of one being" *(homoousios)* with the Father and the Spirit. In this wondrous union of deity and humanity, the triune God is perfectly and definitively revealed. In Christ, and in him alone, we are freely given true apprehension of God in his immanent reality, freely given to share in the Son's knowledge of the Father in the Holy Spirit. The crucified and risen Lord, in all of his historical particularity, is thus the source and foundation of our knowledge of the living God. We rejoice in the triune God's gift of himself in Jesus Christ, and declare Jesus as the eternal Word who judges all preachings, teachings, theologies, actions, prayers and rituals. We acknowledge that God is free to communicate himself in many and diverse ways to the peoples of the world; but we confess that saving and authentic knowledge of the Deity in his inner Trinitarian life is possible only in and through the incarnate Son, Jesus Christ, the God-man.

We repudiate the false teaching that Jesus Christ is only one revelation or manifestation of God, that there are other revelations and other experiences (political, ideological, cultural, or religious) to which we may look or must look to gain knowledge of the true God.

IV

"I am the way, and the truth, and the life. No one comes to the Father except through me." (John 14:6)

"This Jesus is 'the stone that was rejected by you, the builders; it has become the cornerstone.' There is salvation in no one else, for there is no other name under heaven given among mortals by which we must be saved." (Acts 4:11-12)

By his incarnation in Jesus the Israelite, the eternal Son of God has assumed to himself our human nature, cleansing and healing it by the power of the Spirit, redeeming it from sin and death by the cross of Calvary, raising it to everlasting life in his resurrection, and incorporating it into the triune life of the Godhead by his ascension to the right hand of the Father. Thus this Jesus, who is called the Christ, is the Savior of the world, the one mediator between God and humanity, in whom, by faith, repentance and baptism, we find forgiveness, rebirth in the Spirit, and eternal life in the Kingdom. While we do not presume to judge how the all-holy and all-merciful God will or will not bring to salvation those who do not hear and believe the preached Gospel, we do emphatically declare Jesus the rightful Lord and Savior of all humanity, and we embrace the Great Commission of our Lord to proclaim with evangelical fervor his Good News to the world. To deny this historic conviction in the absolute lordship of Christ Jesus and his exclusive mediation of salvation is to eviscerate the heart and vitality of the Church's evangelistic mission.

We repudiate the false teaching that the salvation of humanity by the sovereign action and grace of God is unnecessary or that salvation may be ultimately found apart from the atoning death and resurrection of Jesus Christ. We repudiate the false teaching that Jesus is merely one savior among many — the savior of Christians but not of humankind.

V

"The hour is coming when you will worship the Father neither on this mountain nor in Jerusalem. You worship what you do not know; we worship what we know, for salvation is from the Jews. But the hour is coming, and is now here, when the true worshipers will worship the Father in spirit and truth, for the Father seeks such as these to worship him." (John 4:21-23)

"So that you may not claim to be wiser than you are, brothers and sisters, I want you to understand this mystery: a hardening has come upon part of Israel, until the full number of the Gentiles has come in. And so all Israel will be saved; . . . As regards the gospel they are enemies of God for your sake; but as regards election they are beloved, for the sake of their ancestors; for the gifts and the calling of God are irrevocable. Just as you were once disobedient to God but have now received mercy because of their disobedience, so they have now been disobedient in order that, by the mercy shown to you, they too may now receive mercy. For God has imprisoned all in disobedience so that he may be merciful to all." (Rom. 11:25-26, 28-32)

By the call of Abraham and the covenant of Moses enacted on Mount Sinai, the triune God has gathered to himself the people of Israel to be his holy nation and royal priesthood, consecrated to his service in the redemption of the world. To them he has entrusted his Torah, Wisdom, and prophetic Word. From this people God has brought forth his Messiah, born in Bethlehem of the Virgin Mary, Jesus the Jew, the son of David, who is the fulfillment of the promises of God to Israel and the Savior of humanity and of all creation. For these majestic reasons, the Jews are to be regarded by Christians as a reverend and blessed people. Following the teaching of the New Testament, we eagerly look forward to that time when Gentile and Jew will be fully reconciled and made one people in eternal communion with the crucified and risen Messiah in the New Jerusalem.

We repudiate the false teaching that the Jews may be persecuted by Christians and we especially repudiate the repugnant and fallacious charge of "Christ-killers," which has been used by Christians down the centuries as an excuse for hatred, bigotry, and violence against the Jews. All anti-semitism in thought, word, or deed is vicious and is to be decried and condemned by Christians. But we also repudiate the false teaching that eternal salvation is already given to the chosen people of Israel through the covenant of Abraham and Moses, independently of the crucified Christ, and the inference that the Gospel of Jesus the Messiah need not be proclaimed to them.

VI

"But now, apart from the law, the righteousness of God has been disclosed and is attested by the law and the prophets, the righteousness of God through faith in Jesus Christ for all who believe. For there is no distinction, since all have sinned and fall short of the glory of God; they are now justified by his grace as a gift, through the redemption that is in Christ Jesus, whom God put forward as a sacrifice of atonement by his blood, effective through faith." (Rom. 3:21-25)

"For by grace you have been saved through faith, and this is not your own doing; it is the gift of God — not the result of works, so that no one may boast." (Eph. 2:8-9)

The Gospel is the proclamation of the unconditional love, grace, mercy, and forgiveness of God the Father, mediated through Christ crucified in the power of the Spirit. The Father nurtures, protects, and cares for his children like a nursing mother; he strengthens, directs, and disciplines them like a steadfast father. His love embraces all humankind equally, female and male, and is communicated to us in the preaching of the Word and the celebration of the sacraments, received by the faith granted us in the gift of the Gospel. This love cannot be earned nor bought: We are freely justified by the grace given to us through Christ in his sacrificial death and victorious resurrection, not by our religious, political, psychological, or moral works.

We repudiate the false teaching that God is male (except in the incarnate Christ) and that men are consequently superior to women, or that God has institutionalized in family, society, or the Church the authoritarian and sexist domination of women by men. We repudiate the false teaching that God the Father is the oppressor and subjugator of women, or that the divine Fatherhood is rightly construed as the psychological projection upon the Deity of the experience of human fatherhood. We therefore repudiate the false teaching that the Father of Jesus Christ is inaccessible or unavailable to contemporary women.

VII

"Do not think that I have come to abolish the law or the prophets; I have come not to abolish but to fulfill. For truly I tell you, until heaven and earth pass away, not one letter, not one stroke of a letter will pass from the law until all is accomplished." (Matt. 5:17-18)

"All scripture is inspired by God and is useful for teaching, for reproof, for correction, and for training in righteousness, so that everyone who belongs to God may be proficient, equipped for every good work." (2 Tim. 3:16-17)

We confess the Holy Scriptures of the Old and New Testaments to be the Word of God, and to contain all things necessary to salvation. The Holy Spirit, the ultimate author of God's Word written, was active both in the inspiration of the sinful human writers, redactors, and editors and in the process of canonization. Interpreted within the tradition and community of the Christian Church, with the use of responsible biblical criticism — always under the guidance and lordship of the Spirit — the Scriptures, in their entirety, are the reliable, trustworthy, and canonical witness to God's self-revelation in Jesus Christ, and are our primary and decisive authority in matters of faith and morals. Through the Holy Scriptures the Church hears anew every day that Word who frees us from the tyranny of the fashionable, that divine Word who renews and inspires, teaches and corrects, judges and saves.

We repudiate the false teaching that the plain testimony of the Holy Scriptures may, in whole or part, be supplanted by the images, views, philosophies, and values of secular culture. We repudiate the false teaching that only those sayings of the preresurrection Jesus which can be demonstrated to be certain or probable by historical criticism are authoritative for the life and mission of the Church. We repudiate the false teaching that the Old Testament is not to be interpreted in light of its messianic fulfillment in the person of Jesus Christ as witnessed in the New Testament, or that the Old and New Testaments stand hermeneutically, materially, and formally independent of each other.

Pray for the Church.

The Feast of the Holy Trinity
26 May 1991

The Rev. Ronald S. Fisher
The Rev. Alvin F. Kimel, Jr.
The Rev. R. Gary Mathewes-Green
The Rev. William N. McKeachie
The Rev. Frederick J. Ramsay
The Rev. Philip Burwell Roulette

We invite all who find themselves in agreement with the above to formally subscribe to this Declaration of Faith. Please write to: The Baltimore Declaration, St. John's Church, 3738 Butler Road, Glyndon, Maryland 21071.

Synopsis

Preface: The Preface states the felt need to make such a Declaration beyond the specific event which precipitated its writing. It states that a revision of our faith inconsistent with Holy Scripture and the Creeds has been gaining ascendancy in our Church, and that a bold stand against such teachings must be taken.

Article I: This article affirms the Church's belief in the Trinity as Father, Son, and Holy Spirit according to the Baptismal command of our Risen Lord in Matthew 28. It repudiates the false teaching that we can substitute other names and images from our own imaginations or experience.

Article II: This article affirms that God is the Creator who, by his Word and Spirit, has brought the universe into existence out of nothing and is still active within it. It repudiates the false teachings of either monism (we are made of the same substance with God) or deism (God created the world with natural law and then set it off with no further involvement).

Article III: This article affirms that Jesus is God incarnate, at the same time truly God and truly human. It repudiates the false teaching that Jesus Christ is merely one revelation or manifestation of God among many.

Article IV: This article affirms that Jesus is the Way, the Truth, and the Life and that no one comes to the Father except through him. It repudiates the false teaching that salvation can be ultimately found apart from his atoning death and resurrection.

Article V: This article affirms that the Jewish people are a chosen and blessed people through whom God has worked to bring salvation to the world. It repudiates both persecution of the Jewish people in the name of Christ and the false teaching that the Gospel of God's reconciling work through Jesus the Jew need not be proclaimed to them.

284

Article VI: This article affirms that salvation is solely by grace through faith and is available to all humanity equally. It repudiates the false teachings that God is male or is the subjugator of women. It also repudiates the false teaching that the Fatherhood of God is to be regarded as merely the psychological projection of the human experience of fatherhood upon the Deity.

Article VII: This article affirms that God the Holy Spirit is the ultimate author of Holy Scripture. It affirms that God was active both in the original writing and in the process by which the Bible was put together. It repudiates the false teaching that only the words of the earthly Jesus as decided by scholars are authoritative. It also repudiates the false teaching that the Old Testament is not to be interpreted in light of its messianic fulfillment in Jesus Christ.

Things Yet to Come: An Afterword

PHILIP TURNER

AN afterword can serve many purposes. This one has the single aim of pointing to "things yet to come" — to the issues raised but not fully resolved by these essays. The future, of course, is not determined, but there are critical moments that refract its possibilities. More than the confession made by the authors of the Baltimore Declaration itself, the publication of these reflective responses to its content and purpose comprises such a moment.

The moment belongs to those in all the "mainline" denominations who, as Russell Reno has said, "raise objections to the substantive *form* of confession, even as they genuflect in some vague way to the content." Reno suggests that many of these people are "faint-hearted and apathetic" (Reno, p. 106 above). He is no doubt correct. Most of us, however, are simply troubled and confused. We are troubled both by the pluralist ideology of the left and by the reactionary stance of the right. We are troubled by revisions of Christian doctrine that are no longer recognizable as Christian doctrine. We are equally troubled by confessional statements like the Baltimore Declaration that can be read as an attempt to bring closure to debates that are far from settled.

These troubled and troubling thoughts are followed by confusion. What ought those who are caught between left and right to do? No answer appears obvious and for this reason we denizens of the middle tend to muddle about, trying on the one hand to avoid the seriousness of the issues under dispute and on the other to urge the contending parties to avoid extremes, to practice charity, and to seek a synthetic compromise of their opposing positions.

If I read them correctly, the people whose responses to the Baltimore Declaration are here collected wanted nothing to do with the present strategies of the ecclesiastical middle. None of them counsels either avoidance or synthetic compromise. Without exception, they urge fresh and constructive theological effort.

Because they respond in this way, their essays act as a prism that refracts certain possibilities for the future of the Episcopal Church and I believe for other "mainline now sideline" denominations. If the great middle in all these churches takes these essays with the seriousness they deserve and, in response, chooses to engage the issues they raise in a rigorous and constructive way, we can anticipate a prolonged church struggle that has at least the possibility of producing a communion of belief and life that is both faithful and vital. If, on the other hand, the middle continues on its present course of avoidance, denial, and compromise, one can almost certainly predict that the "mainline churches" will become less and less credible as their "middle" becomes increasingly vacuous and their extremities increasingly virulent.

The project of theological construction advocated by these essayists reminds me in certain ways of the one Richard Hooker set for himself. Contrary to common opinion, in charting a middle way between the Puritan left and the Roman Catholic right, he essayed no synthesis of the positions of his two major adversaries. His project was rather a fresh account of Christian belief that was faithful to the tradition and responded to the most profound religious, social, and political issues of the age.

By invoking this historical analogy, I intend to make a fundamental claim about these essays. As I read them, their authors suggest that it would be a mistake to enter the theological lists with either the protective agenda of the right or the iconoclastic agenda of the left. Their proposal is to espouse a "generous orthodoxy" that eschews both programs. Such orthodoxy has a distinctly positive purpose. It originates in neither fear nor repugnance but "in an awareness of poverty, a sense of the utter dependence of the Christian *koinonia* on its 'living memory' of God's singular act of generosity in Jesus his Son" (Yeago, p. 260 above).

Their program assumes, in short, that unless God both reveals his nature and acts to reconcile and redeem a lost and ignorant human race, we can do no more than invent God. Such is the inevitable result of the theological programs based upon either an attempt to "fix" doctrine in timeless propositions or to create it *de novo* from the three assumptions of contemporary consciousness — namely, ambiguity, relevance, and inclusivity (Reno, p. 111 above).

What, then, are the contours of the positive, rather than protective or iconoclastic, theological work these men and women urge upon us? What are "the things yet to come"? The authors whose essays are collected here are not of one mind, but there are, nonetheless, similarities in the issues they say need to be addressed. The first similarity pertains to the reclamation of the Bible as Holy Scripture — as the basis for all aspects of the life of the churches. Apart from such a reclamation, God's self-revelation in Christ Jesus recedes beyond reach, and apart from access to God's self-revelation, the mind is left, as W. H. Auden once said, "to promiscuous fornication with its own images."

The reclamation of the Bible as Holy Scripture is no simple task, however. As Christopher Seitz points out, neither its propositional use in support of doctrine nor its dissection by critical method yields anything like holy writings that can and ought to provide the basis for the worship, prayer, doctrine, life, and witness of the churches. Seitz's observation is correct, but the question of how the Bible is to be reclaimed as Holy Scripture remains.

Will Childs's canonical criticism do the trick? Will Ellen Davis's plea for the use of an instructed imagination render the Bible once more as Holy Scripture? Is there a "plain sense of Scripture" that presents a "narrative" that can be used as a basis for theological reconstruction? And what response can and ought to be made to the feminist criticisms that Ellen Charry tracks?

The answer to these and other critical questions is far from obvious. Because of their difficulty, the reclamation of the Bible as Holy Scripture is not a project that will be completed overnight. If it is undertaken, however, other theological tasks will present themselves soon enough. The most important of these will be to undertake generously orthodox renditions of the biblical narrative that display God's nature and purposes in ways that both topple our idols and address the particular illnesses of our life and times. David Yeago's case for the organizing notion of "communion" provides, for me at least, a convincing and ecumenically inviting way into such a project.

The articulation of a comprehensive theological vision will, however, place its advocates immediately in the sort of struggle Ephraim Radner has identified. It is no doubt the conflictual character of theological work that in part explains the timidity that we guardians of the middle so frequently manifest. Theology as struggle has not been a part of the irenic formation that shapes our moderate and moderating intentions and reactions. We wish to be faithful to what Bob Prichard, following C. S. Lewis, has called "mere Christianity," but we do not wish to appear in any way closed-minded or condemnatory. It is precisely the eschewal of the sort of theological combat that Radner says is inescapably a part of the history of the church that has left the middle of the Episcopal Church and the rest of mainline Protestantism so vacuous.

Though it grates upon the sensibilities of the prudent middle to say so, it is, nonetheless, more than likely that attempts to reclaim the Bible as Holy Scripture and to articulate a generous orthodoxy based upon its reading will issue not only in clarifying debate but also in painful and sometimes bitter struggle. The "things yet to come" will certainly contain both if the churches in any way rise to the theological task that lies before them.

My belief is that if the required debate and struggle occur, they will be set off by the issues discussed in this volume by George Sumner and Ellen Charry. Do Christians have anything to say of life-and-death significance about who God is and what God is up to? This is a theological question that leads inevitably to a discussion of the nature and mission of the church. Theology will not be the source of the ecclesiological debate, however. It has arisen and will continue to arise because of the often noted "pluralism" of the age and because of the accompanying change in the social place of "mainline" Protestantism within American society.

The point I wish to make, however, is not about the sociological origins of a debate. It is about the relation of this discussion to the issues I have already raised. The main point is that, as the discussion of the nature and mission of the church heats up, more fundamental theological commitments will come into play. If we want to talk about the life and mission of the churches, we will at some point have to defend what we say by giving an account of who we think God is and what God is up to.

Thus, for Episcopalians, the "decade of evangelism" called for by the Lambeth Conference of Bishops and the General Convention of the Episcopal Church may signal, not a great new expansion of the church, but the beginning of an internal debate and struggle about what Christians ought to believe and what they ought not to believe. Indeed, it is my belief that a renewed impetus to "bear witness to the gospel of God" cannot and will not take place apart from rather serious theological debate and struggle.

This observation brings me to the last point I would like to make about the "things yet to come." The theological work that these essays suggest lies ahead is simply beyond the capabilities of any and perhaps all of the Protestant denominations. All but one of these essays have been written by Episcopalians. Each in his or her own way writes out of a concern for the faithfulness of their church. Nevertheless, the fact that their collection ends with an article on ecumenical theology written by a Lutheran may indicate that they share my conviction about the theological inadequacy of our present denominational arrangements. If the theological debate required is undertaken and the church struggle subsequently enjoined, a new form of ecumenism is likely to emerge. This new ecumenism will not eliminate the search for institutional unity that heretofore has characterized the ecumenical movement. It will, however, assume more significance than the old ecumenism for the simple reason that its practitioners will be forced to focus more discretely on "the Christian thing" itself. The new form of ecumenism will therefore track lines that cross denominational boundaries but leave them intact. The lines will be ones that link people who have, within the confines of their particular denominations, committed themselves to the theological work these essays call for. Their common allegiance and work will in a new way bind them together in the communion of saints. Their most fundamental allegiance, as Yeago suggests, will be the *koinon*, the common good of Christians, and their work will be a generous orthodoxy based upon a reading of the Bible as Holy Scripture.

Contributors

Ellen T. Charry is professor of theology at the Perkins School of Theology, Dallas, Texas.

Ellen F. Davis is professor of Old Testament at Yale Divinity School.

George A. Lindbeck is Pitkin Professor of Historical Theology at Yale University.

Robert W. Prichard is professor of church history at the Protestant Episcopal Theological Seminary in Virginia.

Ephraim Radner is an Episcopal priest living in Stamford, Connecticut, and is presently a doctoral candidate in theology at Yale University.

Russell Reno is professor of moral theology at Creighton University.

Christopher R. Seitz is professor of Old Testament at Yale Divinity School.

George R. Sumner has served the Episcopal Church as a missionary in Tanzania and Navajoland and is presently a doctoral candidate at Yale University.

Philip Turner is Dean of the Berkeley Divinity School at Yale and Associate Dean of Yale Divinity School.

David S. Yeago is professor of theology at Southern Lutheran Theological Seminary.

Index of Names

Adams, Hannah, 188
Andrewes, Lancelot, 200, 216, 218-20, 223-24
Andrews, Charles Wesley, 25
Anselm, St., 234n.5, 238
Aquinas, Thomas, 9, 13, 156, 158-60, 168
Arius, 268n.42, 274
Athanasius, St., 46, 62, 233, 236-37
Auerbach, Erich, 215
Augustine, St., 139, 158, 162, 214, 221, 227-29, 234, 241

Barr, James, 95
Barton, John, 95
Basil, St., 271
Bernard of Clairvaux, 200
Bonhoeffer, Dietrich, 36, 40, 107-8n.2, 115-16n.8, 203, 209, 220
Booth, Wayne, 205n.8
Booty, John, 42-43, 88n.4
Borsch, Frederick, 88n.4, 95
Bosch, David, 143n.6
Bottomley, Philip, 188
Braaten, Carl, 163
Bradford, Samuel, 22

Bray, Thomas, 18
Brooks, Phillips, 31-33
Brown, William Montgomery, 33, 34
Browning, Edmond Lee, 42
Brunner, Emil, 36, 117n.10
Bucer, Martin, 17
Bullinger, Heinrich, 74, 75
Bunyan, John, 232
Burgon, John, 89n.6
Burnet, Gilbert, 77
Burt, John, 189
Butler, Joseph, 77

Calvin, John, 96, 120n.11, 122n.13, 228, 231
Catherine of Siena, 200
Cave, William, 64
Chadwick, Owen, 64
Childs, Brevard, 7-8, 99-100
Cicero, 234
Clement of Alexandria, 227
Cobb, John, 170
Cranmer, Thomas, 17, 73, 74, 97, 98
Cullmann, Oscar, 147
Cuthbertson, Philip, 89n.6, 95, 100

292

Index of Scripture References

Genesis

9:6	185
11:1-9	147

Exodus

3:14	117
7:13	215
7:22	215
24	171
24:1-2	171
24:10	171, 172
24:11	171
24:17	171
32:1	171
32:4	207
33:3-5	171
33:20-25	171
34:6	208
34:30	171

Deuteronomy

4:9	261
4:31	261
5:15	262
6:4-9	262
6:20-25	262
8:11	261

14:1	185
15:15	232
16:11-12	261-62
24:18	262
24:22	262

2 Samuel

12	203

1 Kings

17	182

2 Kings

5	182, 183
5:16	184

Psalms

2	147
22	49
32:9	228
37	185, 186
37:6	185
37:8	185
37:11	185
37:18	185
37:21-22	185
37:25	185